CHINA'S OPEN DOOR POLICY

University of British Columbia Press
Asian Studies Monographs

China's Open Door Policy is the fifth volume in a continuing series of studies in Asian history and society published by the University of British Columbia Press.

Other volumes in the series are:
1. *China's Intellectual Dilemma: Politics and University Enrolment, 1949-1978*, by Robert Taylor.
2. *Agrarian Class Conflict: The Political Mobilization of Agricultural Labourers in Kuttanad, South India*, by Joseph Tharamangalam.
3. *The Political Economy of Productivity: Thai Agricultural Development, 1880-1975*, by David H. Feeny.
4. *Arming the Chinese: The Western Armaments Trade in Warlord China, 1920-1928*, by Anthony B. Chan.

China's Open Door Policy
The Quest for Foreign Technology and Capital

A Study of China's Special Trade

Samuel P. S. Ho
and
Ralph W. Huenemann

University of British Columbia Press
Vancouver
1984

CHINA'S OPEN DOOR POLICY:
THE QUEST FOR FOREIGN TECHNOLOGY AND CAPITAL
A Study of China's Special Trade

This book has been published with help of a grant
from The Canada Council.

Canadian Cataloguing in Publication Data.
Ho, Sam P.S.
China's open door policy
Includes index.
Bibliography: p.
ISBN 0-7748-0197-2
1. China — Economic policy — 1976-
2. Technology transfer — China. 3. Investments,
Foreign — China. I. Huenemann, Ralph W., 1939-
II. Title.
C427.92.H6 1984   338′.951   C84-091113-0

This book is printed on acid-free paper.

ISBN 0–7748–0197–2

Printed in Canada

Contents

Tables

Preface

The open door policy that has evolved in China over the past several years is one of the most significant policy changes that has occurred since 1949. The political ramifications of this new policy, both internationally and domestically, form a complex and fascinating topic of inquiry in their own right. The focus of this monograph, however, is on the economic facets of the Open Door. Whenever possible, we have tried to offer quantitative measures of the changes that have occurred, but it must be noted at the outset that the qualitative changes that have taken place (in attitudes and in institutions) are at least equally important.

The essence of the Open Door is a quest for accelerated economic development through the adaptation and diffusion of foreign technology. A strategy of importing technology — even capitalist technology — is not new in China, however. What distinguishes the Open Door from the earlier waves of technology import since 1949 is the recent willingness to use foreign capital as well as foreign technology. This explains why the open door policy is also referred to as "special trade" — thereby distinguishing it from the arm's-length transactions that characterized earlier dealings with the West. Even in the period of the Open Door, a substantial amount of technology transfer has occurred by means of these more traditional arm's-length mechanisms, and the importance of these transactions should not be underestimated, but the discussion in this monograph focuses on the innovations that collectively are called "special trade."

Generally speaking, our discussion takes account of developments up to October 1983. The discussion of equity joint ventures in Chapter 4 analyses the environment that existed from 1 July 1979 to 30 June 1983. In August and September 1983, the Chinese changed this environment in some minor ways; these changes are described in Chapter 7. Thus, Chapter 7 should be read in conjunction with Chapter 4.

In part, this monograph is based on a variety of published sources, as indicated in the footnotes and bibliography. More importantly, however, this monograph derives from an extensive series of interviews, most of which were conducted in China during May-July 1982. We recognize all too well the dangers of generalizing from a small number of examples, but we hope that our readers will find these case studies as interesting and illuminating as we did. During our trip we were the guests of the Chinese Academy of Social Sciences (CASS), and we benefited greatly from the generous assistance provided by that institution, but it must be emphasized that the views expressed in this book (unless otherwise attributed) are solely those of the authors.

Apart from our very great debt to CASS, we would also like to acknowledge and thank all of those people, in China and outside, who so willingly and patiently answered our barrage of questions. The Canada-China Trade Council assisted with the arrangements of our research visit to China. In addition, we would like to express our gratitude to both the Max Bell Foundation and the Donner Canadian Foundation for their generous financial assistance, as well as to the Institute of Asian Research and the Institute of International Relations at the University of British Columbia for their logistical support and general encouragement. We would also like to express our appreciation for the constructive criticisms offered by two anonymous readers. Last, but certainly not least, we would like to thank our families for their affectionate support and understanding.

For the most part, we have romanized Chinese names and phrases according to the pinyin system. The only conscious exceptions are the names of Hong Kong and Macao, which we thought would be more familiar to Western readers in their traditional form.

In closing, we would note that, all too often, assessments of China's economic performance generally, and of the prospects for Western trade with China more particularly, succumb either to euphoria or to despair. In our judgment, however, neither of these extreme reactions is warranted. Rather, we believe that healthy economic relations between China and the capitalist world cannot be sustained unless both sides have a realistic appreciation of both the difficulties and the opportunities inherent in economic interdependence. To this end, each side must learn more about the other, and it is our hope that this monograph will make some modest contribution to this process.

1

China's Development Strategy and the Open Door

Since the death of Mao Zedong and the purge of the Gang of Four in 1976, the phrase *kaifang zhengce* (which has been variously translated as "an open door policy" or "a more open economic policy" or "a policy of opening to the outside world") has appeared with increasing frequency in Chinese commentaries and policy pronouncements. Not surprisingly, this new policy has caused considerable controversy. Foreign businessmen have generally asked, "*Will* China really open the door and keep it open?" But Chinese discussions have naturally tended to ask, "*Should* China pursue a more open policy? And if so, on what terms?"

The broad outlines of this new policy began to emerge during 1977 and 1978, closely paralleling the second political rehabilitation of Deng Xiaoping. In March 1977 a high-level Japanese economic delegation held discussions with Li Qiang and reached an agreement for increased coal and oil exports to Japan. In April, *Renmin Ribao* (People's Daily) editorialized that, while China should remain self-reliant, this did not exclude the possibility of importing certain essential new techniques and equipment from abroad. In July, in a speech to a national conference of foreign trade, Yu Qiuli repeated the message that self-reliance was not to be confused with a closed door policy. In August President Tito of Yugoslavia – the country with the most open economy in Eastern Europe – visited Beijing and was warmly welcomed.

Early in 1978, with the establishment of the Chinese Academy of Social Sciences (CASS), the discussions of the open door policy found an organizational home.[1] In July Hu Qiaomu, then the president of CASS, gave a lengthy lecture on economic policy to the State Council, in which he argued bluntly that "the

People's Republic will soon be 30 years old; we must no longer use lack of experience as a pretext to explain away our mistakes."[2] Hu Qiaomu went on to say that

> we must of course guard against and correct the tendency to think highly of everything foreign, the tendency to think that China can bring about the four modernizations only by relying on foreign countries, and not on itself. But this tendency is not the main danger at the moment; the main danger at the moment is . . . indulgence in self-exaltation and complacency, conservatism which is content with staying where one is and overweening conceit, as well as the harmful influence of the "gang of four" who set self-reliance against learning what is advanced in other countries.

As the Chinese themselves put it, the "historic turning point" for the open door policy came in December 1978, at the Third Plenary Session of the 11th Central Committee of the Party.[3] The communique of the Third Plenum announced that China would be "actively expanding economic co-operation on terms of equality and mutual benefit with other countries" and would be "striving to adopt the world's advanced technologies and equipment." Within a few days of the Third Plenum, Li Xiannian told a group of foreign visitors that, provided China's sovereignty was not impaired, his country was prepared to accept not just technology, but investment as well, from the developed countries of the capitalist world. On 8 July 1979, China promulgated its new "Law of the People's Republic of China on Joint Ventures Using Chinese and Foreign Investment," thereby taking a major symbolic step toward confirming and implementing the open door policy.

Only five short years have passed since the Third Plenum, but much has happened in that time. The intent of this monograph is to trace the developments of this period — not merely to describe the genesis of the open door policy, but to offer some evaluation of the experience to date, to point out some problem areas, and to provide some educated guesses about what the future may bring. We begin in Chapter 1 with a discussion of the recent Chinese debates over economic policy and performance and of the role that the open door policy is expected to play in China's current development strategy. Chapter 2 describes the new institutional setting that has evolved around the open door policy. Chapter 3 offers a brief summary of the results to date. Chapter 4 discusses the equity joint venture, which — because it so closely resembles foreign direct investment as that term is understood in the West — can perhaps be said to be the most radical of the new institutions that have developed since the Third Plenum. Chapter 5 describes some of the more flexible institutional alternatives that have evolved alongside the equity joint venture. Chapter 6 discusses the special opportunities and problems of the energy sector. Finally, in Chapter 7 we offer our own evaluation of the open door policy and its prospects.

CHINA'S DEVELOPMENT STRATEGY AND ECONOMIC PROGRAM

The open door policy is an integral part of China's new development strategy, and indeed is only one of the many policy shifts that have occurred in China since 1976. Its implications are therefore best understood in the context of that strategy and of the problems that led the Chinese to believe the recent policy shifts were necessary. A thorough examination of recent policy changes would require a comprehensive review of the history of the People's Republic of China, a task that is beyond the scope of this study. The brief discussion that follows focuses on only a few strands of that history, those that have especially influenced China's economic policy and development strategy.

It is useful to think of the policy shifts in China since 1976 as the most recent development in a continuing debate that dates back to at least the mid-1950s. The debate centers on three fundamental questions:[4] 1) Should China give first priority to the development of productive forces (that is, economic construction) or to the transformation of productive relations (that is, the development of socialism)?[5] 2) What development strategy will give China the most rapid economic growth? 3) What sort of economic management system is most appropriate for China?

How Marxists answer the first question depends critically on their analysis of conditions in China. Those who believe that China's main problem is the lack of means of production would argue for assigning first priority to the development of productive forces. However, those who believe that the development of productive forces is hindered by existing production relations in China would want to give first priority to the building of socialism, in the belief that once production relations are fully transformed a rapid development of productive forces will follow.

The question regarding development strategy refers to a debate between those who favor an unbalanced growth strategy (high investment rates, the construction of new plant and facilities on a large scale, and the priority allocation of investment to the capital goods sector) and those who favor a balanced growth strategy. Those who support unbalanced growth do so generally because they subscribe to the following views: 1) The rate of economic growth is determined by the size of the capital goods sector. Since heavy industry in China is small and underdeveloped, increased economic growth can be attained only by rapidly expanding the capital goods sector. 2) Economic sectors tend to be competitive so that the capital goods sector can be expanded only at the sacrifice of the consumer goods sector (agriculture and light industry). If the consumer goods sector is to expand, it must do so in such a way that it does not compete with heavy industry for scarce resources. 3) It is possible to expand production through political mobilization. Therefore the "storming" of ambitious targets is an important method to be used in attaining rapid economic growth. Needless to say, supporters of unbalanced growth include the powerful central ministries responsible for China's heavy industry, since they have a clear vested interest in the continued rapid expansion of the capital goods sector.

Advocates of balanced growth take the position that unbalanced growth leads to a wasteful use of scarce resources and to strong inflationary pressures. When the country undertakes too many capital construction projects, they argue, the average construction and gestation period of such projects is prolonged, thus wasting resources and lowering the rate of return on investment. A high level of investment in the capital goods sector, because it increases urban disposable income, also creates additional demand for consumer goods (food and manufactured products) that cannot be satisfied because agriculture and light industry have neither the means nor the incentive to produce more. The advocates of balanced growth are not opposed to the development of heavy industry. Rather they take the view that, because sectors in the economy are interrelated, stressing heavy industry alone is not necessarily the most effective way to achieve either rapid growth or a large capital goods sector. More specifically, they argue that a certain minimum amount of investment must be allocated to the consumer goods sector to provide the necessary incentive and stability without which sustained economic growth is not possible.

Economic management refers both to the planning and regulation of the economy at the macro-level and to enterprise management at the micro-level. The debate over economic management centers on two related issues:[6] 1) the extent to which market mechanisms or economic levers (for example, prices, taxes, and subsidies) should be used to regulate a socialist economy, and 2) the degree of autonomy that should be granted to enterprises. On the one side are those who favor the use of directive or administrative methods to plan and manage the economy. In this system, enterprises follow orders and therefore do not, and indeed should not, have much autonomy. Among those who support directive planning are some who would decentralize planning in order to increase local initiative and enthusiasm. However, decentralization in this context means only the transfer of the power to issue directives from the central level to the local governments. Enterprise autonomy would remain extremely limited.

On the other side are those who favor a greater reliance on market mechanisms to regulate the economy and those who would like to see enterprises permitted a greater degree of autonomy. Some who support this view do so because they believe that directive planning cannot be effectively implemented in an economy like China's, where there still exists a large and important collective sector and where individual proprietorship still has a role to play. In other words, directive planning needs to be supplemented by market regulation because socialism is not as yet fully developed in China. Others support this view because they believe that market socialism is the type of socialist economy that should be created in China. In either case, supporters of this view still see a role for planning done at the central level, although there is decentralization in the sense that enterprises are permitted to develop market relations with one another according to guidelines and regulations established by central authority.

The political faction that was in ascendancy in China for most of the period between 1966 and 1976 generally favored continued struggle to develop socialism, unbalanced growth, and directive planning. Thus the economic policy pursued in this period stressed the closing of gaps and differences (between peasants and workers, cities and the countryside, and manual and mental labor), the use of political exhortation and mass mobilization instead of economic incentives to motivate the population, the "glorification" of capital construction, and directive planning (done partly at the central level and partly at the local level). A key component of this economic strategy was "self-reliance" (*zili gengsheng*). Since self-reliance is sometimes interpreted as the antithesis of the open door policy, it may be useful to review briefly the convoluted history of this expression.

The phrase itself gained currency during the difficult days of the 1930s and the 1940s, when the Chinese Communist Party had no choice but to make do with the limited resources and backward technology of the guerrilla base areas. Thus the expression *zili gengsheng*, viewed in its historical context, carries a connotation of economic self-sufficiency, even though the literal meaning of the phrase is less extreme. In the 1960s and the 1970s, the phrase acquired two different interpretations. When used at the local level, self-reliance meant that localities should strive for self-sufficiency in agriculture ("taking grain as the key link") and in industry. It was a policy that encouraged the dispersion of industrial activities in the countryside, stressed the maximum mobilization of local resources for development (so that rural industrialization would not compete with heavy industry for scarce resources), and promoted a more integrated local economy. When used at the national level, the slogan "self-reliance" was a reminder that China must depend mainly on its own resources in economic development and a caution against becoming too dependent on foreign trade and foreign financing.

The current interpretation of recent history is that the Gang of Four romanticized the experience of the guerrilla war period and therefore distorted the concept *zili gengsheng* to justify a policy of economic isolationism. In fairness to the historical record, however, it must be said that the published versions of the ultra-Left point of view do not entirely support this interpretation. It is true, of course, that spokesmen for the Gang of Four criticized Deng Xiaoping's policies in the most vitriolic terms imaginable. For example, an article in *Hong Qi (Red Flag)* in the summer of 1976 described Deng's policies as "selling off China's natural resources and sovereignty" and "opening the door to imperialist plunder of our people's sweat and blood."[7] The authors went so far as to say that Deng was willing to "grovel behind the foreigners' buttocks." Yet this same article argued that a closed door policy would be a mistake and that the proper interpretation of the slogan *zili gengsheng* was merely that China should rely primarily on its own efforts and resources and keep foreign assistance in a supplemental role. Indeed, the authors explicitly insisted that the importing of some foreign technology and machinery was "absolutely essential" to China's economic modernization.

Furthermore, in evaluating the ultra-Left point of view, we must remember that Mao Zedong himself, at least in his writings of the 1940s and 1950s, clearly rejected the notion that *zili gengsheng* meant economic isolationism. On one occasion, Mao wrote that the economic autarky of the guerrilla base areas had been "a special product of the special conditions" of that era, which would be "unreasonable and incomprehensible in other historical conditions.[8] A few years later, Mao reaffirmed his opposition to a policy of self-sufficiency:

> We have put forward the slogan of learning from other countries. I think we have been right . . . . We must firmly reject and criticize all the decadent bourgeois systems, ideologies and ways of life of foreign countries. But this should in no way prevent us from learning the advanced science and technology of capitalist countries and whatever is scientific in the management of their enterprises.[9]

In short, both the earlier writings of Mao and the later writings of Mao's ultra-Left allies seem to reject a policy of economic isolationism. However, the gap between words and actions can be a wide one. What the ultra-Left leaders stood for in theory and what they created in practice may have been two quite different things. The chaos and xenophobia of the Cultural Revolution were hardly conducive to international economic co-operation. Similarly, while some of the words used in *Hong Qi* in the summer of 1976 seemed to hold the door open for economic dealings with the capitalist world, the strident tone of the rhetoric effectively slammed the door shut. After all, if a lifelong Communist with the prestige and status of a Liu Shaoqi or a Deng Xiaoping could be attacked to toadying to the capitalists, what sensible middle-level official would show any enthusiasm for business dealings with the West? For that matter, how many Western business representatives, after being berated for their selfish motives and depraved lifestyle, would be inclined to participate in such negotiations? Seen from this perspective, the current view that the ultra-Left policy was essentially a closed door policy becomes more plausible.

After the purge of the Gang of Four, the strongest advocates of continued socialist revolution, Chinese policy shifted from a stress on the building of socialism to an emphasis on economic construction. At every opportunity, Chinese leaders referred to the new national objective of modernizing agriculture, industry, defense, and science and technology (the Four Modernizations) by the year 2000.[10] Indeed the Four Modernizations were formally included in both the Constitution of the Chinese Communist Party (CCP) adopted by the 11th Party Congress in August 1977 and in China's National Constitution adopted by the First Session of the Fifth National People's Congress (NPC) in early 1978.[11] The core of the Four Modernizations was the Ten-Year Plan (1976–85) approved by the Fifth NPC at its first session. In his report to the Fifth NPC, Hua Guofeng revealed some of the plan's objectives. It called for total agricultural output to rise at an annual rate of 4 to 5 percent and for industrial production to rise annually by about 10 percent, both higher than past performance.[12] To achieve these ambitious goals, huge investment programs were announced. In total, the capital funds budgeted for 1978–85 were to equal the total for the previous twenty-eight years. There was nothing new in China's desire to modernize. What was new was the announcement that China would turn to the Western developed economies for advanced technology and assistance to achieve its objectives. Self-reliance was still held up as one of China's cherished principles, but international economic co-operation and the use of foreign funds were now seen as important means towards the achievement of this goal. Thus the Four Modernizations and Hua's Ten-Year Plan signalled on the one hand a continuation of the unbalanced growth strategy and, on the other, a strong repudiation of the relatively isolationist policy of the previous ten years. But as it turned out, the days of unbalanced growth were also numbered.

At the Third Plenum in December 1978, eleven months after Hua's report to the Fifth NPC, the Ten-Year Plan was discarded and with it the unbalanced growth strategy. A new long-term plan was not introduced to replace the Ten-Year Plan. Instead, the government announced that while the Four Modernizations are still China's ultimate goal and that while it still adheres to the open door policy, the economy would temporarily be "put on hold" to undergo a program of "readjustment, restructuring, consolidation, and improvement" (hereafter, readjustment and reform). The new policy not only marked the beginning of a new development strategy for China, but it also had important implications for the conduct of the open door policy — as Western businessmen soon discovered, when contracts they had signed with various Chinese foreign trade corporations at the end of 1978 and the beginning of 1979 were suddenly postponed or cancelled.[13] It is therefore useful to examine why the Chinese leaders now feel that readjustment and reform are necessary.

Readjustment is needed, according to Chinese, to correct the serious imbalances that exist in the economy, the legacy of past unbalanced growth. A detailed and authoritative analysis of these problems can be found in the report that Premier Zhao Ziyang presented to the Fourth Session of the Fifth NPC in late 1981, in which he spoke of the principles of economic development in terms of ten guidelines.[14] The fundamental premise of Zhao's report, and of many other recent Chinese statements on the subject, is that the "extensive" (*waiyan*) growth strategy of earlier years is no longer adequate and must now be supplemented or even replaced by "intensive" (*neihan*) growth. In other words, although *quantitative* change (simply producing more machines and building more factories) may be a reasonably effective growth strategy during the early stages of industrialization, *qualitative* change (technological innovation, better management, and so on) is essential to sustained economic growth at a more sophisticated stage of development. As Zhao said in discussing his fourth guideline; "In the past, we carried on expanded reproduction chiefly by building new factories . . . . Now we will have to rely chiefly on the technical transformation of existing enterprises and on their initiative for expanded reproduction in the future." This idea that simple capital formation by itself is an inadequate source of economic growth is, as the Chinese are well aware, a point of view that Russian and East European economists have been espousing for many years.[15] It is also one of the main conclusions that emerges from the research of Western economists on the sources of growth.[16] However, it seems likely that China's present strategy has been influenced primarily by the lessons drawn from China's own experience, rather than by the ideas of foreign economists.

Closely related to the view that brute capital formation is not an efficient engine of growth is the idea that in the past China has tended to overemphasize investment at the expense of consumption, with severely harmful consequences for morale and motivation. As Zhao Ziyang said in discussing his tenth guideline, "For a rather long period in the past, we one-sidedly stressed capital construction to the neglect of improvements in the people's standard of living." Zhao's views on this issue are also supported by the research of such economists as Dong Fureng at CASS. On the basis of the findings summarized in Table 1.1, Dong has argued that "too high a rate of accumulation tends to affect the national economy adversely . . . . It is no exaggeration to say that the imbalance between consumption and accumulation has been the primary cause of economic setbacks in China since 1958."[17] In 1978 the share of accumulation in national income surged to 36.5 percent, but by 1981 it had been pared back to about 30 percent, and some Chinese commentators have suggested that a share of about 25 percent would be even more appropriate.[18]

In addition, it should be noted that, when per capita income is low, increased consumption results in increased output, in that better nutrition, health, and housing increase labor productivity. In other words, the distinction between investment and consumption becomes blurred at low per capita incomes, because consumption often amounts to investment in human capital.

The intense struggles that accompanied these readjustments came into the open at the 12th Party Congress in September 1982, when the 1978 slogan "organize a new Great Leap Forward" was denounced, and "the principal leading comrade in the Central Committee at the time" (Hua Guofeng) was criticized for continuing to make "Left" mistakes.[19] In 1980 Deng Xiaoping suggested that China's per capita GNP would quadruple by the end of the century, from about US$250 to about US$1,000.[20] In 1981 Zhao Ziyang announced a somewhat more conservative variation on the same theme — quadrupling the gross annual value of industrial and agricultural production by the year 2000.[21] Neither of these targets is unambitious, but the emphasis in both cases is on avoiding "Great Leaps" and maintaining steady, feasible growth over an extended period.

Table 1.1   THE RELATIONSHIP BETWEEN ACCUMULATION AND ECONOMIC GROWTH

Years	Accumulation as a % of National Income	Annual Growth Rate of National Income	Increase in National Income per 100 Yuan of Accumulation
1953–57	24.2%	8.9%	35 yuan
1958–62	30.8	−3.1	1
1963–65	22.7	14.5	57
1966–70	26.3	8.4	26
1971–75	33.0	5.6	16

Source: Dong Fureng, "The Relationship between Accumulation and Consumption in China's Economic Development," in George C. Wang, ed. and transl., *Economic Reform in the PRC* (Boulder, CO: Westview Press, 1982), p. 60. It should be noted that the definitions of accumulation and national income used by Chinese economists are somewhat different from those used in Western economics.

The struggle over the share of national income to be allocated to consumption has been closely linked to a parallel criticism of the past practice of allocating too much investment to heavy industry and "productive capital" (plant and equipment) and too little to light industry and "unproductive capital" (housing and infrastructure). Within heavy industry, investment has also been unbalanced, with insufficient funds allocated to the energy sector. Speaking to a national science awards conference in October 1982, Zhao Ziyang emphasized the importance of the energy bottleneck in the following terms:

By the end of this century, we can probably double our supply of energy. With doubled energy output, will we quadruple the gross output value? The answer is — it's possible we will and it's possible we won't. However, if we continue to use present-day technology and maintain the present ratio between the gross output value and energy, then we will only be able to double the gross output value . . . . Equipment that uses fuel inefficiently must be replaced in every trade and profession. Furthermore, each field should make a series of major technical transformations, change technological processes and the mix of products. Only thus can we substantially reduce unnecessary energy consumption.[22]

Outside observers have reached similar conclusions about China's energy sector. The World Bank, for example, has suggested that "slow-growing energy supplies will be the most serious constraint on China's growth rate in the 1980s."[23]

To correct these imbalances and to return the economy to a balanced growth path, the government, in 1979, began to curb and tighten its control over capital construction, to emphasize the urgency of energy conservation and exploration and the development of transportation, to reallocate resources from the capital goods sector to the consumer goods sector,[24] to improve the economic environment facing Chinese farmers and workers,[25] and to increase the effort to up-grade and renovate existing industrial enterprises. In November 1982, the long awaited Sixth Five-Year Plan (1981–85) was announced, and it reaffirms the leadership's commitment to readjustment, reform, and the balanced development of the economy. In his report on the Sixth Five-Year Plan, Zhao Ziyang revealed that the plan calls for the gross value of industrial and agricultural production to rise by 4 percent per year during 1981–85 and that the planned level of capital construction for 1981–85 will be about the same as that for the previous five years but that far fewer large and medium projects will be undertaken.[26] Energy and transportation, the two high-priority sectors, will receive 38.5 percent of the total investment in capital construction during 1981–85. Total fixed investment planned for the five years will amount to RMB ¥360 billion, of which 38 percent is earmarked for improving existing enterprises.[27] Education, science, culture, and public health will receive 68 percent more funds for development in 1981–85 than in the previous five years. Most importantly, the Sixth Five-Year Plan commits the government to increase per capita consumption by 4.1 percent per annum, a substantially higher growth rate than that achieved in the previous twenty-eight years.

To date the attention of the Chinese leadership has been focused primarily on the problem of readjustment. Now that the imbalances in the economy are being corrected, the policy-makers are turning to the issue of reform — that is, how best to restructure China's economic system to improve productivity and economic efficiency. Judging by what they have said about reform, the Chinese are primarily concerned about correcting the following practices: 1) the tendency towards "absolute egalitarianism," 2) the overdependence on directive planning and administrative control, and 3) the lack of enterprise autonomy.

The two aspects of "absolute egalitarianism" that concern the Chinese are the practice of "eating from the big pot" and the "iron rice bowl". At issue is the incentive and reward system for individuals and enterprises that developed in China during the 1960s and 1970s. "Eating from the big pot" describes the practice whereby workers who work hard and get good results receive the same pay as those who work less hard and achieve inferior results.[28] It also refers to the fact that, since enterprises receive everything from the state and return everything to the state, there is no incentive to lower cost or to improve management. In other words, well-managed enterprises are not rewarded, and poorly managed enterprises are not penalized. The "iron rice bowl" refers to the practice of permanent employment in industrial enterprises and the tradition that government cadres may be promoted but never demoted. "Eating from the big pot" is now criticized because it "dampens labor enthusiasm," discourages good enterprise management, and is contrary to the socialist principle of "to each according to his labor." The "iron rice bowl" is under criticism because it encourages lax discipline and indolence among workers and perpetuates incompetence in China's bureaucracy.

The importance that the government attaches to breaking the practices of eating from the big pot and of giving everyone an iron rice bowl can be seen from Zhao Ziyang's recent remark that the current struggle to enforce the principle of "more pay for more work, less pay for less work and no pay for no work" is "no less significant than the socialist transformation of private industry and commerce" in the 1950s.[29] This policy is embodied in what is called the "responsibility system," which ties an individual's reward to his work effort. The responsibility system was first introduced in agriculture, where it has apparently succeeded beyond all expectations, and it is now being implemented in industry and commerce as well.[30]

Where enterprises are concerned, the current official assessment of China's economic management system is that decision-making power is "overconcentrated" and that the system has failed "to separate the functions of the government from those of enterprises in matters of management."[31] For example, until a few years ago, Shougang (Capital Steel Company), one of China's ten largest steel plants (with fixed assets of RMB ¥1.05 billion and a labor force of 72,000 workers), had so little autonomy that its director did not have the power to authorize any expenditure over RMB ¥800, and nearly all the decisions affecting Shougang were made by higher government departments.[32]

Reforms designed to give enterprises greater flexibility, autonomy, and responsibility were first introduced on an experimental basis in six enterprises in Sichuan Province in October 1978; not coincidentally, Zhao Ziyang was First Secretary of the Party in Sichuan at the time.[33] Within two years the reforms had been extended to about 6,600 key enterprises throughout the country. Although by number these 6,600 enterprises comprise only 16 percent of all state-owned industrial enterprises, they account for about 60 percent of the total value of output for the same group, so it is clear that the reforms have begun with the largest, most productive factories.[34] In essence, the recent reforms give enterprises some incentives to improve product quality and to cut costs and at the same time give them some of the managerial autonomy and financial resources needed to achieve such goals.

Under the reforms, an enterprise enjoys several new rights:[35] the right to produce outside the plan (once the plan quota has been fulfilled), the right to market — at home or abroad — any product not taken up by the state marketing agency, the right to retain a percentage of after-tax profits and to use these retained earnings according to stipulated guidelines for workers' welfare, workers' bonuses, or enterprise development, the right to develop its own bonus scheme (provided the aggregate bonuses annually total no more than twice the factory's monthly payroll), and the right to discipline or even dismiss unsatisfactory employees. A parallel reform, introduced on a trial basis in August 1979 and expanded gradually since then, is to allocate new investment funds as interest-bearing bank loans, rather than as free grants from the state budget.[36] Yet another aspect of the reforms is that enterprises which, because of small scale, backward technology, and so forth are hopelessly uneconomic are now being pressured to "close down, suspend, merge, or shift to other work" (*guan, ting, bing, zhuan*) — that is, to face the catharsis of receivership and bankruptcy.[37]

Predictably, the relatively backward enterprises and regions have resisted these reforms.[38] Furthermore, even staunch advocates of the reforms recognize that because of differences in resource endowments and past investment and the distorting effects of an irrational price structure, equally well-managed and hard-working enterprises may receive unequal benefits under the reforms.[39] In principle these differences can be compensated for by using different profit-sharing schemes or by adjusting tax rates, prices, and other economic levers, but this is not so easy to implement in practice. Greater enterprise autonomy, given the existing irrational price structure, has also produced results that are unexpected and undesirable from the viewpoint of the national interest. Furthermore, as long as remittances from industrial enterprises (taxes and profits) remain at the center of the revenue structure, any reform that increases the earnings retained by enterprises is a direct threat to the state's fiscal position. The inherent contradiction is clearly visible in Hu Yaobang's recent remarks that

> funds at the disposal of local authorities and enterprises have grown greatly and have been used for many projects which may seem badly needed from a local point of view; but this inevitably makes it difficult to adequately meet the national needs . . . . While continuing to enforce the present financial system and ensure the decision-making power of enterprises, we must appropriately readjust . . . the distribution of national and local revenues and the proportion of profits retained by enterprises . . . .[40]

Not surprisingly, in November 1982 Zhao Ziyang reported that the State Council, in order to raise sufficient funds to finance key projects in the national plan, had decided that, with some exceptions, "all localities, departments, and units are to turn over a certain proportion of their receipts not covered in the state budget to the state" and that all large urban collectives are to turn over to the state a share of their after-tax profits.[41]

While the government has accepted the view that both directive planning and market regulation are necessary to manage the economy properly and that enterprise autonomy needs to be expanded, it has moved cautiously in introducing the necessary reforms. Indeed, government efforts in the past few years have concentrated more on rebuilding the planning system and on tightening central control lost or eroded during the 1960s and the early 1970s than on reforming the existing economic management system. The current official view is that the three years that remain in the current Five-Year Plan should be used to draw up an overall plan to reform the economic system and to work out concrete measures for its implementation and that comprehensive reform of the economic system will take place gradually during the Seventh Five-Year Plan period (1986–90).[42] Specifically, the long overdue price reform, without which many of the other reforms cannot be effectively implemented, has been postponed to 1986 at the earliest.

Although the reforms are still in the planning stage, the type of economic system that the current leadership wants has become fairly clear.[43] In the new system, directive planning will continue to play the leading role in economic management, but it will be supplemented by market regulation. The central government will have strict control over major economic matters (for example, the overall investment rate, investment allocation among sectors, key capital construction projects, aggregate consumption, and interprovincial transfers), but localities and enterprises will be allowed greater autonomy over such routine matters as the day-to-day operation and management of enterprises, the purchase and sale of goods, and employment. Enterprises will be divided into several categories. The key enterprises and those producing commodities vital to the economy or to consumer welfare will be subjected to mandatory planning, and presumably they will operate much as they do today. Those enterprises producing a diversity of products, or products less important to the economy, will be subjected to guidance planning, under which presumably they will have at least limited decision-making power over such matters as product-mix and will be partly regulated by market forces. Finally, small enterprises will organize their production totally on the basis of market conditions. Once prices have been realigned, the remittance of enterprise profits will be replaced by a progressive enterprise income tax. Prices will become generally more flexible, and some will be allowed to fluctuate according to changes in market conditions. Furthermore, collectives and individual proprietorship will be permitted a larger role in the economy. In short, China appears to be moving towards a mixed economy where planning and the market will co-exist, with the bulk of the state enterprises and the more important industrial sectors managed by planning and with the remaining parts of the economy regulated by the market.

THE LESSONS OF THE FOUR WAVES

The open door policy does not represent China's first attempt to transfer technology from abroad. But the recent commentaries on the Open Door have stressed that China's earlier experience with borrowing foreign technology since 1949 — an experience commonly described in terms of four waves or cycles — was not entirely satisfactory.[44] Presumably the purpose of these commentaries is not only to condemn the relatively isolationist policy of the Gang of Four but also to shed light on how to transfer technology more effectively in the future.

The general pattern of the four waves can be seen in Table 1.2, which shows China's annual imports of machinery and equipment — that is, the imports in SITC category 7 — from 1952 to 1982. When examining the data in Table 1.2, it is well to remember that not all of the subcategories in SITC category 7 represent a transfer of technology, while conversely some subcategories outside category 7 (such as 861, "scientific, optical, measuring and controlling instruments," and 892, "printed matter") may be quite important as channels of technology transfer. Also, it should be remembered that Table 1.2 measures actual shipments and therefore displays a pattern that lags a year or two behind the policy-making process.

Table 1.2   CHINA'S IMPORTS OF MACHINERY AND EQUIPMENT
(US$ million)

Year	Imports	Year	Imports
1952	193	1967	335
1953	276	1968	235
1954	381	1969	214
1955	411	1970	398
1956	545	1971	481
1957	566	1972	524
1958	715	1973	797
1959	933	1974	1,605
1960	840	1975	2,013
1961	272	1976	1,716
1962	102	1977	1,171
1963	100	1978	2,033
1964	162	1979	3,832
1965	302	1980	5,352
1966	443	1981	4,661
		1982	3,401

Notes and Sources: Figures for 1952–74 are from U.S. Government sources, quoted in A. Doak Barnett, *China's Economy in Global Perspective* (Washington, D.C.: The Brookings Institution, 1981), p. 190. Figures for 1975–1982 are from C.I.A., *China: International Trade Annual Statistical Supplement*, February 1982, p. 53. and *China: International Trade, Fourth Quarter, 1982*, June 1983, p. 11.

As Table 1.2 shows, the first wave of technology transfer occurred in the 1950s, when 256 complete plant projects from the Soviet Union and a similar number of turnkey projects from East European sources provided the technological core of China's First Five-Year Plan. One Western analyst has called this "the most comprehensive technology transfer in modern industrial history."[45] During our discussions in Beijing, a senior researcher at CASS offered an equally positive assessment of this first wave, emphasizing that the Soviet aid had involved much more than the construction of turnkey plants. She told us that 50 to 70 percent of the Soviet equipment came with full blueprints and specifications, thereby making it relatively easy to do repairs, to produce spare parts, and even to duplicate the equipment for other factories. Furthermore, from the beginning the Chinese machine-building industry was encouraged, with the help of Russian documentation and advisers, to produce some of the machinery for the 256 plants domestically, thereby facilitating learning-by-doing and creating an indigenous technological capability. (During the 1950s, some 10,000 Soviet technicians worked in China, and at least 15,000 Chinese technicians and workers were sent to Russia for training.[46]) It came as a great shock when, in 1960, the Soviet Union "tore up contracts, withdrew its experts, and discontinued the supply of equipment." Fortunately for China, most of the Russian projects were already completed at that point. Furthermore, the East European countries only partially followed the Russian lead, which also cushioned the blow to some extent.

With Russian supplies of machinery and equipment cut off, China turned to alternative sources. Negotiations with Japan for the construction of two synthetic textile factories, begun in September 1962, marked the start of China's second wave of technology import.[47] From small beginnings, this wave grew rapidly for about three years, during which China purchased a variety of complete industrial plants (variously reported as forty-six, "fifty or more," or "over eighty" in number) from Japan and West Europe.[48] But the outbreak of the Cultural Revolution halted the second wave before it had developed very far. Foreign businessmen and technicians were harassed by the Red Guards, and the absorption of foreign technology was severely disrupted. For example, the imported truck factory at Wuhan, begun in 1964, did not manage to produce its first vehicle until 1977.[49]

The third wave of plant and machinery imports developed in the early 1970's, as the disruption and xenophobia of the Cultural Revolution were receding. The China National Technical Import Corporation (usually called TECHIMPORT for short) was revived in 1972,[50] and in 1973 the State Council approved a plan to spend US$4.3 billion on imported equipment over a four-year period. Taking its name from the planned level of expenditure, this third wave of imports came to be known as the "Four Three Programme" (though the contracts actually signed by the end of 1977 totaled only about US$3.5 billion).[51] Of the various commentaries on the "Four Three Programme" that have appeared in the Chinese press, one of the most detailed, and certainly one of the most astringent, is an article by Chen Huiqin that appeared in the CASS journal *Jingji Guanli (Economic Management)* in 1981. Chen's criticisms were focused on three problem areas, as indicated in the following excerpts from her article:

1) *Failure to meet construction schedules*: Of the complete plants built under the "Four Three Programme," not a single one was debugged and brought on stream according to the deadline specified in the contract. Of the 24 projects originally set to be turned over to China by the end of 1979, there were more than eleven that were more than a year late, and some of these — such as the vinylon factory at Changshou — will be delayed by more than three years.

2) *Operating at less than full capacity*: In 1979, the ethylene project at the

Yanshan Petrochemicals Company in Beijing was able to achieve a utilization rate of only 76 percent, because the scheduling of capital construction was not synchronized. The vinyl chloride project at the No. 2 Beijing Chemical Factory attained a utilization rate of only 65 percent because, although there was an adequate supply of PVC resin, there was an insufficient supply of certain auxiliary chemicals. Six other projects (namely, the 1.7-metre steel rolling mill at Wuhan, the electrical generating plant at Yuanbaoshan in Inner Mongolia, and the four large-scale synthetic ammonia fertilizer plants at Chishui, Guangzhou, Nanjing, and Anqing) achieved utilization rates of less than 50 percent. Furthermore, there is a group of machinery projects, producing gas turbines, turbine compressors, bearings, etc., which have absorbed investment of about RMB ¥2 billion but which still face severe problems because there is no steady work for them to do.

3) *Poor return on investment*: A project which can recapture its investment in three or four years can be considered to have relatively good economic effectiveness (*jingji xiaoguo*). But three-fourths or more of the projects in the "Four Three Programme" exhibited rather serious shortcomings in this regard. For example, the 1.7-metre steel rolling mill at Wuhan, which required about 16 percent of the total investment [by implication, about US$560 million of foreign exchange, plus any complementary investment in RMB], was adversely affected after it was completed in December 1978 because the supply of electricity was inadequate. Only after the two provinces of Hubei and Henan integrated their power grids in May 1979 was it possible to alleviate this shortage of electricity. However, at the present time the utilization rate at the rolling mill has still only been raised to about 20 or 30 percent, because of endemic internal problems: inadequate supplies of ore and pig iron, deficiencies in smelting operations, delays in completing the processing facility for silicon steel, heavy reliance on imports for spare parts, etc. Even in a good year profits have been only a few tens of millions of RMB.[52]

Chen Huiqin has not been the only one to criticize the 1.7-metre rolling mill at Wuhan. Meng Xiancheng, who participated in the construction of the mill, wrote in 1980 that

viewing the project as it is now, the result is not satisfactory. . . . Output is too low and costs are too high, so that its products cannot compete on the international market and do not sell well at home, although the equipment is first class and the quality of the products first rate.

In order to turn out the most urgently needed products ourselves, train technical personnel and develop technology, it is necessary to buy advanced technology and equipment. But their cost must be carefully considered.

Usually the most advanced technology and equipment are very expensive. They are difficult to operate, to look after and to maintain. Therefore we must do our best within our own limitations.[53]

These criticisms of the 1.7-metre rolling mill at Wuhan have not gone unnoticed or unchallenged. For example, Xu Zhiying, an assistant chief engineer at the Wuhan mill, has recently published an article in which he argues that the project was definitely worthwhile, despite its shortcomings.[54] Xu admits that the shortage of electricity has been "a headache" for several years, but he says that this problem is now being resolved by drawing electricity from the new hydropower station at Gezhouba. Xu also admits that the shortages of iron ore and smelting capacity are urgent problems, and he confirms that the rolling mill is operating far below its designed output level of three million tons per year and will be forced to continue doing so until the plant can either increase its ore production and renovate its smelting furnaces or "get ore and raw steel from mines and plants in other parts of China." (Although Xu does not say so, it is reasonably clear that both of these alternatives would require substantial additional investment, either in the facilities at Wuhan or in the extra railroad capacity needed to bring ore and steel from other places.)

Having conceded this much, however, Xu Zhiying then vigorously disputes the critics' view that the Wuhan project has shown a poor return on investment and that the German and Japanese technology is inappropriate for China. Xu notes that the foreign exchange cost of the rolling mill was about US$600 million, thereby confirming Chen Huiqin's implicit figure, and he adds that these foreign exchange expenditures were only 54 percent of the total costs, which came to RMB ¥4 billion altogether. In 1981 the Wuhan Iron and Steel Works turned over to the state a total of RMB ¥523.66 million in profits and taxes, and according to Xu these earnings came primarily from the new rolling mill. Thus, Xu concludes, even though production is well below capacity, "simple arithmetic indicates that the economic benefits far outweigh the initial costs." Furthermore, he argues, the benefits to China cannot be measured solely in terms of profitability. Precisely because the mill uses sophisticated technology, it has forced the Chinese, "who had been separated from developments in the outside world for a long time," to upgrade their technical and managerial skills. In fact, Xu notes, it might be argued that the technology at Wuhan is not as advanced as it should be, for the equipment "was only at the advanced level of the 1970s, and industry worldwide has moved on."

As can be seen even from these short excerpts, both the critics and the defenders of the "Four Three Programme" agree that China's third wave of technology transfer had problems and shortcomings. However, says Chen Huiqin, "not only did we not earnestly study the lessons of this period, but we immediately launched another big wave. Within the single year of 1978, foreign contracts worth US$6.4

billion were signed."[55] In the eyes of the critics, this unprecedented surge of technology imports was a classic case of "more haste, less speed." In an article published in *Jingji Guanli* in 1981, Lin Senmu, one of these critics, has suggested that there are four lessons to be learned from the mistakes of 1978.[56] First, if a factory is to be imported, careful provision must be made for the complementary domestic inputs: fuel, utilities, transport, housing, etc. As an example, Lin points out that the twenty-two key projects in the fourth wave, once completed, would require over ten million tons of petroleum and twenty million tons of coal annually, "which is simply unmanageable in our country's present energy situation." Second, it is important to be sure that a project encourages self-reliance. (Lin judges self-reliance by asking two questions: Does the project use domestic components whenever possible? And is it free from the "push-button mentality"? — that is, does it avoid excessive automation?) Third, no project should be approved until its technical and economic feasibility has been carefully checked, for as Lin says, "Blind enthusiasm leads to fatal economic illness." And fourth, China must become much better informed about the ways of the Western business world. Quoting Lenin, Lin argues that "when one runs with wolves, one must learn to howl like a wolf."

When the discussion of the fourth wave gets down to cases, the critics most often zero in on the giant Baoshan General Iron and Steel Works near Shanghai. The Baoshan project, for which construction began in December 1978, has the distinction of being both the largest and the most controversial plant that China has ever imported. As originally designed, Baoshan was to have two immense blast furnaces, each capable of producing about 3 million tons of pig iron annually. The two blast furnaces together would then feed a 2.05-metre hot-rolling mill with a capacity of 4 million tons a year, a 2.03-metre cold-rolling mill with a capacity of 2.1 million tons, and a seamless tube mill with a capacity of 500,000 tons.[57] However, it is not clear when Baoshan will reach these planned output levels. The target date for bringing the first blast furnace into operation was originally October 1981; it was pushed back to the summer of 1982 and then to late 1983. When we visited the Baoshan site in June 1982, we were told that one blast furnace and the seamless tube mill would be operational by 1985. When we asked about the other blast furnace and the two rolling mills, we were told that these facilities will definitely still be built but that "the timing has not yet been decided." In March 1983 it was announced that the State Council has definitely decided to go ahead with the second phase of the Baoshan project (the second blast furnace and the two rolling mills), but no precise timetable was indicated.[58]

The problems at Baoshan are not surprising, since the project was, as the Chinese say, "outside the plan." In the rush to get Baoshan started, decisions were made and contracts were signed before feasibility studies were even done. The site chosen turned out to be too swampy to support heavy industrial installations, and tens of thousands of piles had to be driven into the spongy ground before stable foundations could be poured.[59] Because domestic iron ore is unsuitable for the Baoshan equipment and the Yangzi River is too shallow for bulk carriers, an expensive new port had to be built at Beilun to handle ore imports from Australia.[60] When an investigative group from the State Council visited Shanghai in 1980, it noted that China's largest city was already suffering from serious bottlenecks in transportation and communications and from shortages of fuel and electricity and concluded that the Baoshan project could only exacerbate an already difficult situation.[61] As Lin Senmu has put it, "Our experience proves that the idea of insulating these foreign projects from the domestic economy is untenable."[62] Writing in *Renmin Ribao* (*People's Daily*) in March 1980, an official of the Ministry of Metallurgy criticized Baoshan for its excessive automation and its environmental pollution, among other problems.[63] During our visit to the site, we were told that the Japanese have kept certain aspects of the engineering secret, which does not augur well for assimilation of the technology. Furthermore, we were told that research and development (R&D) for Baoshan will be done by a unit in Beijing, which makes it seem unlikely that innovative modifications of the technology will be developed.

This list of Baoshan criticisms is a lengthy one, but the most fundamental problem of all has not yet been mentioned. Even if construction were on schedule, even if supplies of all inputs were assured, even if domestic equipment were used whenever possible, and so on, the basic question would still remain: Why build Baoshan at all? Are there not other projects, especially in light industry, that are more urgent?

When we posed this question at Baoshan, the engineer who was our guide gave us a two-part answer. First, he said, Baoshan will have lower unit costs than can be achieved with older, smaller-scale factories. (From his discussion, it was clear that he had a partial definition of unit costs in mind: fewer units of raw material, especially coal, used per ton of steel produced. Whether total costs per ton, including capital costs, would be lower at Baoshan remained a moot point.) Second, he continued, China produces only about thirty-five million tons of steel per year and more is needed for modernization. When asked about the rate of return on the Baoshan investment, he replied that the payback period would be "between one and two decades" (*shiji nian*). But, we persisted, is this not a rather low rate of return compared to other sectors? "China is a socialist country," he replied, "and we must have both light and heavy industry."

The critics have been quick to challenge such an argument. As an editorial in *Renmin Ribao* in February 1979 put the issue:

A big country like ours naturally needs more steel, and the slogan of "taking steel as the key link" reflects this need. But the slogan of "taking steel as the key link" is certainly not an objective economic law, immutable for all time. . . . To increase the output of steel inevitably means that investment in agriculture and light industry must be reduced. But agriculture and light industry exhibit quick returns on modest investments, and they are essential to the people's livelihood.[64]

Other commentators have added that over the long period from 1952 to 1979, state investment in light industry was only one-tenth of that allocated to heavy industry, and thus while "the iron and steel industry and other industries which directly serve it . . . grew bigger and bigger, the textile and other industrial departments which produce daily necessities for the people had to make the best of whatever equipment they had."[65]

These lively discussions of the lessons to be learned from China's four waves of technology import are strikingly different in quality from the sterile policy debates of a few years ago. Fervent reiteration of the slogan *zili gengsheng* was never a satisfactory substitute for careful analysis of complex policy choices. Accusations of "groveling behind the foreigners' buttocks" were equally unconstructive. But the tone now is quite different. Examples are cited. Data are provided, at least selectively. There seems to be a general recognition that the question "Should China pursue an open door policy?", like the question "Should China be self-reliant?", is too vague to be particularly helpful. Instead, attention is shifting to questions that are much more specific: Which will contribute more to China's economic development, an ethylene plant in Beijing or a chemical fertilizer plant at Chishui? If Guangdong Province increases its electricity supply, should it do so with thermal, hydro, or nuclear generation? Is it wise or unwise to invest in coal mines in Guizhou Province in the hope of selling coal to Japan? Furthermore, China's scientists and technicians are now insisting quite vocally that such questions cannot be answered adequately without careful investigation, scientific evidence, and "the collective wisdom of experts."[66]

KEY ELEMENTS OF THE OPEN DOOR POLICY

Superficially, the phrase "open door" might appear to mean simply trade liberalization, but this is a misinterpretation. True, China's foreign trade has grown to unprecedented levels since the Third Plenum in 1978. This can be seen from the trade data presented in Table 1.3, even after some mental adjustment is made to the data to correct for price inflation. However, this increase in trade does not mean that the Open Door is just a synonym for Free Trade in the conventional textbook sense. China is not about to permit an unfettered flow of commodities, much less of capital, across its borders. This is evident from the frequency with which Open Door advocates insist that "we should not import things which can be made at home"[67] — an argument which, interpreted literally, could almost eliminate trade altogether. These same protectionist sentiments are also evident in the campaign against consumer goods imports that appeared in the Chinese press in the early months of 1982.[68] As the Chinese explain it: "The State Council's decision to restrict imports . . . is a protectionist measure normal to every sovereign country. It is not an act of backing away from the open door policy, but one that aims to keep China's growing foreign trade and economic co-operation with other nations on the right track."[69] Indeed, the indiscriminate import of foreign goods, in the view of the Chinese leadership, may impair the development of China's national economy and thus diminish its ability to be self-reliant.[70]

Thus, the logic of the Open Door is not the logic of trade liberalization, although some of the consequences are the same. Rather, the essence of the Open Door is to be found in the Third Plenum's call to "strive to adopt the world's advanced technologies and equipment." As Deng Xiaoping and Zhao Ziyang have both stressed, the door is being opened because the Four Modernizations require it.[71] Perhaps a more accurate description of the Open Door is that it is an outward-looking policy that stresses not only increased technological exchanges with other countries but also the speedy "entry of Chinese products into the world market" and the vigorous expansion of foreign trade. In supporting this view of the Open Door, Zhao Ziyang argues that

Expansion of exchange is a basic feature of large-scale socialized production, and it has extended from internal trade in China to trade with the world at large. By linking our country with the world market, expanding foreign trade, importing advanced technology, utilizing capital and entering into different forms of international economic and technological co-operation, we can use our strong points to make up for our weak points. . . . Far from impairing our capacity for self-reliant action, this will only serve to enhance it.[72]

Yet, although technology transfer is once again the central concern, the Open Door is not just a replay of the four earlier waves. Because of the recent changes in development strategy and because of the lessons learned from earlier mistakes and difficulties, more attention is now being paid to how technology is acquired and to the conditions that influence the effectiveness of such transfer. For example, a new attitude is evident in China's willingness, as indicated by the 1979 Law on Joint Ventures, to facilitate technology transfer by accepting long-term capitalist participation in some projects and even to grant the foreigners day-to-day managerial authority. (Joint ventures with long-term foreign participation are not a new idea in China, since they were also a feature of the first wave in the 1950s, but the partners then were not capitalists. The implicit judgment seems to be that the profit motive, though less exalted than feelings of socialist fraternity, is more reliable as a basis for long-term economic co-operation.)

The change from an extensive to an intensive growth strategy and previous difficulties in absorbing advanced technology have caused the Chinese to define

Table 1.3   CHINA'S FOREIGN TRADE 1950–1982

	U.S. Estimates			Chinese Estimates			
	Imports		Exports	Imports		Exports	
Year	c.i.f. US$ (billion)	f.o.b. US$ (billion)	f.o.b. US$ (billion)	RMB¥ (billion)	US$ (billion)	RMB¥ (billion)	US$ (billion)
1950s (average)	1.4	n.a.	1.3	4.8	1.4	4.5	1.3
1960s (average)	1.7	n.a.	1.9	4.9	1.7	5.7	1.9
1970	2.2	2.0	2.2	5.6	2.3	5.7	2.3
1971	2.3	2.1	2.5	5.2	2.2	6.9	2.6
1972	2.8	2.6	3.2	6.4	2.9	8.3	3.4
1973	4.9	4.6	5.1	10.4	5.2	11.7	5.8
1974	7.3	6.7	6.8	15.3	7.6	13.9	6.9
1975	7.4	6.8	7.1	14.7	7.5	14.3	7.3
1976	6.0	5.6	7.3	12.9	6.6	13.5	6.9
1977	7.1	6.6	8.2	13.3	7.2	14.0	7.6
1978	11.2	10.3	10.2	18.7	10.9	16.8	9.8
1979	15.6	14.4	13.5	24.3	15.7	21.2	13.7
1980	20.8	19.3	18.9	29.1	19.6	27.2	18.3
1981	19.3	17.9	21.6	36.8	22.0	36.8	22.0
1982	17.3	16.1	22.4	35.8	17.0	41.4	21.6

Notes and Sources: For U.S. estimates: 1950–1969 from C.I.A., *China: Major Economic Indicators*, Feb. 1, 1980; 1970 and 1971 from C.I.A., *China: International Trade First Quarter, 1981*, August 1981; 1972–1982 from C.I.A., *China: International Trade, Fourth Quarter, 1982*, June 1983. The U.S. estimates are derived from trade partner statistics. For a description of the procedures used, see C.I.A., *China: International Trade Quarterly Review First Quarter, 1979*, September 1979, pp. 9–12. For Chinese estimates: 1950–1980 from PRC, State Statistical Bureau, *Statistical Yearbook of China, 1981* (Hong Kong: Economic Information & Agency, 1982); 1981 from *Beijing Review*, March 14, 1983, p. 18; 1982 from State Statistical Bureau, "Communique on Fulfillment of China's 1982 National Economic Plan," April 29, 1983, and *Beijing Review*, February 7, 1983, p. 14. The US$ figures were derived from the RMB¥ figures by using the foreign exchange rates issued by either the People's Bank of China (1950–1978) or the Bank of China (after 1978). The Chinese statistics strongly suggest that import statistics are on a c.i.f. basis and export statistics are on a f.o.b. basis.

technology more broadly, interpreting it to encompass management and marketing skills and know-how rather than just engineering in a narrow sense.[73] The economists at CASS would have no trouble agreeing with the General Motors executive who suggested that

> the secret of industrial development and of technology assimilation is not in the import of expensive turnkey plants from abroad but in the orchestration of the myriad details into a harmonious whole . . . . [T]here are good reasons why countries are willing to pay hundreds of millions of dollars to Western manufacturers to come in and license them. These manufacturers are not licensing the design; they are licensing the *system* and the *processing*. What they need is not the prototype to copy but the drawings with the material specifications and the tolerances, the routing sheets, and the basic understanding and expertise to orchestrate everything so that millions of things can come together to make a truck.[74]

It now appears that the Chinese are interested in acquiring not only technology that is embodied in machinery and equipment and technology that is codified (that is, documented in blueprints, drawings, and engineering specifications), but also disembodied and undocumented technology (that is, information, skills, and know-how stored in the minds of individuals).

Because of the current emphasis on improving the productivity of existing enterprises and the increased awareness of the importance of assimilating and absorbing new technology, China is now more careful about what technology it imports as well as what mechanism is used to transfer the technology. In particular, the Chinese are anxious for foreign participation in the technical transformation of China's older enterprises. This will undoubtedly involve the import of some new equipment, but it will also require engineering and management assistance. Because of these concerns, Chinese leaders, in recent years, have said repeatedly that

> From now on, China should mainly import technology and single machines or key equipment which cannot be produced domestically. We should not import complete sets of equipment every time and must avoid duplicating imports. We should not import equipment without know-how or fail to assimilate the imported technology and to popularize what we have learnt from it.[75]

Another reason why the Open Door is closely linked to the intensive growth strategy, apart from the concern for effective assimilation of technology and the interest in other means of transferring technology than the purchase of complete sets of equipment, arises from the recognition that a policy of squeezing consumption too hard is actually inimical to economic growth because it undermines morale and motivation. As Mao Zedong himself said at an earlier date, it is foolish to drain the pond to catch the fish. Hence the recent reduction of the share of accumulation in national income to below 30 percent. But of course the increase in consumption's share reduces both the resources available for domestic capital formation and the resources available for export to pay for imported investment goods, thereby exacerbating both the savings constraint and the balance of payments constraint on growth. This squeeze on investment certainly helps to explain the recent intense interest in the methodological issues surrounding the evaluation of economic effectiveness, as exemplified in Li Qiang's remark that China must distinguish between "what is in urgent need and what can wait."

The reality of scarcity and the squeeze on investment also explains China's unprecedented willingness to welcome long-term foreign financing, both equity and debt, from capitalist sources. In 1974, Li Qiang insisted that China did not intend to utilize foreign capital or engage in joint ventures; only five years later, Li argued that

> from a Marxist-Leninist point of view, the methods we are adopting for utilizing foreign capital in joint ventures to develop China's resources are correct in principle. . . . We are paying for some major imported items with deferred payments, bank credits or loans. These are beneficial to expediting the Four Modernizations and solving the problem of payments within a specified period of time.[76]

The current policy towards foreign capital is that "to speed up our economic construction, it is definitely necessary to utilize as much foreign capital as possible. . . . The amount of foreign capital we can utilize is not determined by our subjective desires but by what we can do at home, that is, mainly by our ability to repay, to provide the necessary accessories and to assimilate advanced technology."[77]

To dilute the rigidity of debt with an admixture of equity, China is utilizing such innovations as joint ventures and the joint development of energy resources on a compensation trade basis. These projects are all, in one fashion or another, profit-sharing in nature and therefore will not be saddled with inflexible foreign payments if they fall on hard times. Furthermore, the Chinese have imposed the requirement that, generally speaking, these ventures must have adequate export potential to cover their own foreign exchange needs.[78] Because these equity arrangements shift more of the risk onto the foreign participants, they are likely to be acceptable to the foreigners only if they are allowed a substantial voice in management. Since, from the point of view of encouraging an effective transfer of technology, this kind of long-term foreign participation in management is an advantage, not a disadvantage, equity financing is doubly attractive to the advocates of the Open Door. Yet of course foreign financing, for all of its attractions, is no economic panacea and may be politically explosive as well. Equity financing entails all of the frictions, compromises, and complexities of genuine partnership, while debt, if not managed judiciously, can lead to the kinds of repayment problems that now confront Poland and Mexico.

To help finance the import of technology and the other foreign exchange requirements of the Four Modernizations, China is now boosting its exports more aggressively than ever before. It takes the view that "greater exports are the key to the expansion of foreign trade. We should boldly enter the world market and strive to maintain a rate of increase of exports higher than the rate of growth of the Chinese economy."[79] Most significantly, China has softened its past stance against the "selling off of natural resources" and is now willing to expand its export of oil, coal, and some rare metals in a planned way. Indeed China now welcomes "foreign investment in developing its energy resources," specifically its coal and offshore oil deposits. That slow growth in energy supply is the most serious constraint on China's economic growth undoubtedly also contributes to its willingness to accept foreign participation in the development of its energy output. The promotion of exports is also related to the intensive growth strategy. As Zhao Ziyang explains it: "Putting China's products to the test of competition in the world market will spur us to improve management, increase variety, raise quality, lower production costs and achieve better economic results."[80]

Another important aspect of the Open Door is that a special role and considerable autonomy have been given to the coastal regions. Zhao Ziyang, speaking for the leadership, has emphasized that "to expand economic and technological exchanges with foreign countries, we must make full use of the coastal areas, and especially the coastal cities. Shanghai, Tianjin, Guangzhou, Dalian, Qingdao Fuzhou and Xiamen, among other cities, should make a bigger contribution in this regard."[81] The special regional orientation of the Open Door is understandable since the urban coastal areas are among China's most developed regions and therefore have greater capacity to absorb foreign technology and investment. The coastal cities mentioned by Zhao have all had a rich history of interactions with foreign countries. In addition, some of them have strong ties with Overseas Chinese communities, a source of capital and expertise that China is now anxious to tap. Furthermore, China may be hoping that the development of economic linkages between its coastal regions and the Overseas Chinese communities will smooth the way for the eventual return of Hong Kong, Macao, and Taiwan to Chinese administration.

Of course, the regional approach is also related to the policy of readjustment and intensive growth. This is quite natural, since the Open Door and the policy of "readjusting" (tiaozheng) the economy both had their policy origins at the time of the Third Plenum and have been developed simultaneously. One of the key features of readjustment, as already noted, has been the shift of emphasis away from heavy industry toward agriculture and light industry and from investing in new construction to the upgrading of existing enterprises. Unlike the mega-projects that typify heavy industry, many projects in light industry and the renovation of existing plants are small in scale and lend themselves well to decentralized control. Projects under local control are also attractive because they can adjust more effectively to local conditions, they can appeal to the regional identities and loyalties of Overseas Chinese communities, and so on. Coincidentally, much of China's light industry and many of its older enterprises are located in the urban coastal areas.

The interconnection between regional autonomy and small-scale projects in light industry has been particularly evident in the lists of proposed projects that various local authorities have begun to circulate to potential foreign investors. So far, we have encountered seven of these lists: 24 proposals for Liaoning Province, 27 proposals for Hubei Province, 116 proposals for Fujian Province, 33 proposals for Anhui Province, 64 proposals for the city of Shanghai, 46 proposals for the city of Tianjin, and finally the 130 proposals (from twenty-two different provinces) put forward at the China Investment Promotion Meeting held in Guangzhou in June 1982.[82] Almost without exception, the proposals on these lists are for the renovation of existing enterprises, and the great majority are in various sectors of light industry: food processing, textiles, basic building materials, housewares, simple electronics, and so forth. As can be seen from Table 1.4, the median value of the 130 proposals discussed at Guangzhou was about US$5 million, of which about US$2.7 million would come from the foreign investor.[83] The proposals on the other lists are similar in scale and character.

Because the policy of readjustment is expected to have achieved its objectives by 1985,[84] while the Open Door is described in more permanent terms, the current emphasis on light industry may in the future be a less noticeable feature of the Open Door. But, since China is committed to an intensive growth strategy, renovation projects, large and small, will probably continue to be an important aspect of the Open Door. For both economic and geographic reasons, the regional orientation of the Open Door will probably also persist.

In summary, it might be said that at present the Open Door has five key features. Three of these — namely, the concern for an effective transfer of technology, the desire to expand exports, and the willingness to utilize foreign financing — are essential elements of the Open Door itself and therefore, by definition, will endure as long as the door remains open. The other two — namely, the special attention to the energy sector and the emphasis on the coastal region — are not so essential to the meaning of the Open Door perhaps, but they serve important purposes in their own right and are therefore unlikely to disappear while the door is open.

Table 1.4   130 PROJECTS PROPOSED AT GUANGZHOU: SIZE DISTRIBUTION BY TOTAL INVESTMENT SOUGHT

	Number of projects
Less than US$1 million	4
US$1-3 million	31
US$3-5 million	19
US$5-7 million	14
US$7-9 million	9
US$9-15 million	18
US$15-20 million	14
US$20-50 million	17
US$50-100 million	3
Over US$100 million	1

Source: Economic Reporter, April 1982, p. 11.

2

The Institutional Setting

With the adoption of the open door policy, institutional changes were introduced that were designed to strengthen the contribution that foreign technology and capital could make to the Chinese domestic economy. Most obvious was the development of new mechanisms for foreign economic relations and trade, including a general decentralization of the organizational arrangements. The purpose of this chapter is to examine these changes and to provide the necessary institutional background for the more detailed discussion of the key components of the open door policy appears in subsequent chapters.

NEW MECHANISMS FOR FOREIGN ECONOMIC RELATIONS AND TRADE

For nearly three decades, from 1949 to 1977, China's commercial relations with non-socialist countries were relatively inflexible and largely limited to arm's-length trade. The Chinese resisted foreign buyers' specifications, designs, packaging, trade marks, raw materials, and machinery in producing goods for export and acquired foreign technology primarily through the import of complete plants. Credits were used only sparingly. In the 1960s China accepted only short-term trade credits, largely to finance its grain imports, and in the 1970s it used progress payments and deferred payments to finance its import of plant and equipment.[1]

One practical consequence of the open door policy is that the Chinese have adopted a more flexible approach to foreign economic relations and trade.[2] Anxious to expand its exports, China is now more sensitive to the needs and demands of foreign buyers, including their need for export credit. Increasingly,

China is using licensing arrangements to acquire advanced technology.[3] But the most interesting development is the use of what may be described as "special trade" arrangements (to distinguish them from "normal" or arm's-length trade) to acquire foreign technology and to absorb foreign capital. Because foreign funds are used to finance special trade, the Chinese also refer to the foreign participation in these schemes as "foreign investment," which of course is not consistent with the usage of this term outside of China. What follows is a brief discussion of what these special trade arrangements are and why China finds them attractive. The Chinese identify five main types of special trade as follows:[4]

Processing/Assembling (lailiao jiagong/laijian zhuangbei). In these arrangements, the foreign participant supplies the raw material or the components and parts, either in total or in part, which the Chinese enterprise then processes or assembles according to the foreigner's specifications and design for a fee. Frequently the foreign participant also supplies the Chinese with machinery or equipment, in which case the cost of the equipment is deducted from the fee installments.

Compensation trade (buchang maoyi). Under this arrangement, the foreign firm supplies China with machinery or equipment and receives product in installments as compensation. The Chinese distinguish two types of compensation trade: i) direct compensation, with products produced by the machinery supplied, and ii) indirect compensation, with products not produced by the machinery supplied. In all compensation trade arrangements, title to the equipment passes to the Chinese once it arrives in China.

Joint venture (hezi jingying). This arrangement, which is sometimes also translated as an equity joint venture, refers only to those enterprises established according to the "Law of the People's Republic of China on Joint Ventures Using Chinese and Foreign Investment." Under this law, the joint venture must be a limited liability company with a board of directors composed of representatives selected by the participants. Usually, the foreign contribution is in the form of foreign exchange and technology, while the Chinese contribution is in the form of buildings, equipment, site, and Renminbi. The company is managed jointly, and profits and losses are distributed in proportion to the participants' equity shares in the venture.

Co-operative venture (hezuo jingying).[5] This category covers joint projects or activities involving Chinese and foreign partners where the arrangement is not strictly according to China's joint venture law. The arrangement may involve the creation of a new economic entity or it may not. The liabilities, rights, and obligations of both parties (including how output, earnings, or profits are to be shared) are stipulated in the contract. In other words, the arrangement may take any form as long as it is agreeable to both sides. Usually, the Chinese participant contributes land, natural resources, labor, plant, and some equipment, while the foreign participant supplies capital, technology (including specialized machinery and equipment), and material. At the end of the contract period, the Chinese participant retains the equipment supplied by the foreign partner.[6] Thus, the contribution of the foreign participant is considered a loan and is repaid in installments from the enterprise's depreciation fund.

Co-operative development (hezuo kaifa). This category refers to the exploration and development of China's natural resources, particularly its offshore oil. Foreign participants carry out the exploration at their own expense and risk. In the development stage, however, both China and the foreign participants invest in the project. Once production begins, the output, after deduction for production cost, is divided between China and the foreign participants according to prearranged proportions.

Processing and compensation trade are considered by China as ways to absorb foreign funds because the foreign parties to these arrangements are in effect providing their Chinese counterparts with loans. In the case of a compensation trade contract, the principal amount of the loan is the value assigned to the machinery and technology supplied by the foreign participant, and since interest is paid on the loan, the value of the product payback will exceed the value of the imported equipment. The value assigned to the imported equipment and the price of the product used as repayment are, of course, matters of negotiation between the Chinese and the foreign party.[7] In most cases, the Chinese participants to these agreements expect to pay off their loans in two or three years. But the payback period may be as short as three to six months for processing agreements involving a small amount of imported equipment or as long as five or more years for large compensation trade deals.[8]

The Chinese are attracted to processing and compensation trade for a number of reasons: 1) Chinese enterprises, through these arrangements, can acquire the foreign machinery they need to up-grade their manufacturing capabilities[9] or import the raw material they require to produce the higher quality products demanded by the export market without spending any of China's own scarce foreign exchange. 2) Since the foreign party takes the full responsibility for marketing the finished products, it is an easy way for Chinese enterprises to gain access to foreign markets for the products. This is particularly important since most Chinese enterprises have had little experience in the marketing aspect of international business. 3) Since the foreign parties to these agreements may provide the Chinese with advice and know-how concerning design, packaging, and quality control, these arrangements may serve to convey a limited amount of disembodied technology and business know-how to Chinese enterprises. 4) Because of the self-liquidating nature of these arrangements, they are more compatible with the Chinese planned economy than import arrangements that do not generate their own foreign exchange earnings.

Foreign enterprises that engage in processing and compensation trade do so usually for one or both of the following reasons. China's lower production costs, particularly its lower labor cost, makes it a potentially attractive alternative source of supply for labor-intensive intermediate goods, components, and finished manufactured products. The use of compensation trade arrangements may also be the only way some foreign companies can sell machinery and equipment to China, in view of its shortage of hard currency.

Co-operative ventures, joint ventures, and joint developments of natural resources are also arrangements through which foreign funds are made available to China. However, the expectation is that foreign participants involved in these three types of arrangements will interact more actively with their Chinese counterparts than would be the case in processing and compensation trade. Thus, China hopes that these arrangements will provide it not only with funds to import technology embodied in machinery and equipment but also with a good deal of disembodied technology and general business and managerial know-how.

Because co-operative ventures need not be arranged according to the Chinese joint venture law, they involve fewer formalities and usually define a somewhat less permanent relationship between the Chinese and the foreign party than is the case for equity joint ventures. For example, since co-operative ventures need not distribute earnings and profits according to equity shares, there is no need to assess the value of each party's contribution to the project. Some co-operative ventures are engaged in property development and some are in services, and these in general do not transfer much technology other than general business and marketing know-how.[10] Most co-operative ventures are in manufacturing, and they may take many forms: co-production (where each side agrees to produce specific parts of an end-product which are then exchanged for final assembly in China or abroad), joint production (this differs from co-production in that there is usually a greater degree of technical co-operation and technology transfer and that the foreign participant takes a greater responsibility for the training of Chinese workers and the supervision of production at the Chinese end), and subcontracting. All these arrangements have considerable potential for the transfer of highly specialized technology as well as general manufacturing skills from foreign to Chinese enterprises.[11]

The attraction of the co-operative venture is its flexibility — everything about the arrangement is negotiable. But it also has a greater degree of ambiguity. For example, the Chinese have said that in a co-operative venture, "both sides co-operate in operations and management in line with the contract, but without forming a unified organ of authority."[12] Thus, it is unclear what real authority, if any, the foreign participant will have under this arrangement. Apparently, unlike joint ventures, co-operative ventures are not normally included in the state plan. One implication of this is that co-operative ventures may be assigned a relatively low priority for receiving centrally allocated supplies. Because of these ambiguities, one suspects that when the amount of capital involved in a proposed manufacturing project is large or when considerable technology transfer is involved, the foreign participant may prefer the better defined and more permanent joint venture arrangement.

The only special trade arrangement involving foreign investment, as the term is understood outside of China, is the equity joint venture. In this arrangement, the Chinese and foreign parties pool their assets and form a new legal entity. Profits and risks are shared in proportion to each participant's equity contribution, and the enterprise is jointly managed through a board of directors. Normally, there is a continuous flow of technology from the foreign participant to the joint venture during the life of the agreement.

For two reasons, the joint venture is generally considered to be one of the most effective means of technology transfer. First, because the foreign participant has a vested interest in the success of such a venture, it is likely to be more involved in its operation and in all aspects of the technology transfer from plant design and equipment selection to the training of local personnel. Such active involvement, of course, tends to improve the chance that the transfer will be successful.

The second reason is related to the fact that technology is an important corporate asset; indeed, frequently it is proprietary technology that gives a firm the edge it needs to improve or maintain its position in an industry. Thus, the willingness of a firm to transfer its technology to others depends, on the one hand, on how important the technology is to the firm and, on the other, on the extent to which it can control the use of the technology once it is transferred.[13] The latter factor, in turn, is determined to a large extent by the mechanism used to effect the transfer. The mechanism that gives the most complete control to the foreign supplier of technology is the wholly owned foreign subsidiary, a form of organization not normally permitted in China.[14] Among the mechanisms currently employed, the one that gives the foreign participant the most control over its technology is probably the joint venture. Because foreign investment and the potential control it gives to the foreign investors are still matters of controversy in China, one should not be surprised if attempts are made to limit the degree of control foreign participants can actually exert on a joint venture. Of course, any effort to limit control will also reduce the willingness of foreign firms to transfer technology through the joint venture mechanism.

The joint development arrangement contains elements of both compensation trade and the joint venture. As in compensation trade, foreign companies supply technology and equipment to China in exchange for the resultant output. As in a joint venture, joint development involves risk sharing and close interaction between foreign engineers, technicians, and workers and their Chinese counterparts. Obviously, the development of natural resources can be done through either compensation trade or a joint venture. That a special form of co-operation is used is partly because of the very large investment and risk that are involved and partly because of the reluctance of the Chinese to permit direct foreign investment in resource development.

We conclude this general discussion of special trade arrangements with two observations. First, it is important to note that we have followed the Chinese practice of discussing the special trade arrangements as if they always exist in their pure forms. Actually it is not difficult to find mixed arrangements that combine features from several categories. Thus, in practice, the special trade arrangements tend to shade into one another, so that sometimes it is difficult to state unequivocally that an arrangement is of a specific type.

Secondly, whether a technology can be successfully transferred to China through a particular institutional arrangement depends on the industry, the nature of the technology, and the technological level and absorptive capacity of the Chinese party to the arrangement. For example, if the Chinese enterprise lacks only a specialized foreign-made machine, then obviously compensation trade would be an adequate mechanism to achieve the transfer. But if the technology is for an industry where the Chinese technological level is very backward, then a successful transfer of technology would probably require a more active mechanism — one in which the foreign participant is directly and intensively involved in the transfer process, such as a co-operative venture or joint venture. The nature of the technology may also be important. For example, the transfer of firm-specific technology (knowledge and skills accumulated by a firm over time as the result of its own activities) usually involves the transfer of company personnel and requires a sustained relationship between the two sides, and this is likely to be extensive only under certain types of institutional arrangements, such as the joint venture. That China is now willing to use a wide variety of special trade arrangements is confirmation that it too recognizes that multiple mechanisms are needed if a wide range of technology (including general business and managerial know-how) is to be successfully acquired from abroad.

DECENTRALIZING FOREIGN ECONOMIC RELATIONS AND TRADE

A second consequence of the open door policy has been the introduction of changes in the organization of China's foreign economic relations and trade. To better understand the rationale behind these changes and to put the reorganization in perspective, it is helpful to review briefly the system that existed before 1979.

The Old Arrangement

From 1952 to 1979 the Ministry of Foreign Trade (MFT) was the leading body responsible for China's international commerce. It had the primary responsibility for formulating and implementing the annual trade plan. Under its direct supervision, state-owned foreign trade corporations (FTCs) handled all of China's imports (including technology) and exports. The FTCs were organized along product lines (for example, foodstuffs, textiles, machinery and complete plants, chemicals, metals and minerals) with head offices in Beijing and branch offices in selected provinces and cities.[15] Foreign trade bureaus (FTBs) also existed at the provincial level as well as in most cities and counties. The branch offices of FTCs and the provincial and local FTBs were under the dual leadership of the MFT and the local authorities concerned. However, on business matters, they reported directly to the Ministry or the head office of one of its FTCs. In other words, the MFT was at the head of the two interconnected networks, the one (FTCs) organized according to related commodity groups and the other (FTBs) according to administrative divisions.

In many ways, the FTC operated like an import-export broker. It imported goods on request from end-users for a service fee as well as goods for the domestic commercial channels which were settled at predetermined prices. It also purchased domestic goods at prices set by the state for export at world market prices. Since domestic prices were isolated from world market conditions and since the RMB ¥ was overvalued, FTCs generally exported at a loss and imported at a profit. As a rule, only the head offices of FTCs had the authority to sign contracts, and branch offices were limited to the export of selected commodities according to guidelines set by their head offices.[16] Market information was also gathered centrally by the MFT and its related agencies (such as the China Council for the Promotion of International Trade) and then distributed to the relevant industrial ministries and their enterprises.

For Chinese enterprises, the process of foreign trade under this system was tortuous. For example, when an enterprise required a foreign product, it first had to report its need to its immediate supervisory unit (depending on whether it was a central or a local enterprise, the supervisory unit would be either a department or corporation under an industrial ministry or a local industrial bureau) and apply for a foreign exchange allocation. If the supervisory unit approved the request for foreign exchange, it then forwarded the application upwards (through the local government or the industrial ministry) to the State Planning Commission (SPC) for its review and approval. Only after the application had the approval of the SPC could the industrial ministry (or the planning commission of the local government) request the MFT to contact foreign suppliers on behalf of the enterprise. The negotiation with foreign suppliers was done exclusively by the appropriate FTC. Of course, under this system, the FTCs constituted the only window opened to foreign firms interested in trade with China.

From China's viewpoint, this highly centralized trade system, despite its cumbersomeness, had certain advantages. For one thing, it helped to isolate the Chinese economy from the vicissitudes of the outside market economies. For another, it enabled the country to allocate its scarce foreign exchange according to its planners' priorities. But if the system was adequate to China's trade requirements before 1979, it was very much less suited to China's needs once it turned outward and adopted the open door policy.

The fundamental problem with the Chinese trade system was that it inhibited rather than promoted international economic relations and trade. Indeed, most foreign traders found the layers of bureaucracy that separated them from the Chinese producers and end-users a nearly insurmountable obstacle to trade. Frequently the FTCs were more of a bottleneck than a channel for the flow of information between foreign companies and Chinese enterprises. The system was also unable to respond quickly and flexibly to the ever-changing needs of the international market. But even more serious was the fact that the system discouraged localities and individual enterprises from taking initiatives and becoming directly involved in international trade. Another major deficiency of the system was that it reduced the effectiveness of international trade as a vehicle for technology transfer. The transfer of technology requires close interaction between the transferor and the recipient; the more contact, the quicker and more successful the transfer is likely to be. This is particularly true when the technology is not embodied in machinery nor codified but exists in disembodied and undocumented form as knowledge stored in the minds of individuals. But under the Chinese trade system, contacts between foreign businessmen and engineers and their Chinese counterparts were kept to a minimum since most of the transactions between the two sides were conducted through an intermediary, the FTC. In view of these deficiencies, it is not difficult to understand why, once the Chinese decided on the open door policy, with its emphasis on technology transfer and the expansion of foreign trade, they felt it necessary to modify the existing system.

The Emerging New Trade Structure

Although some changes were introduced in 1978, the modification of the foreign trade system did not begin in earnest until 1979, and the process continues to this date. The changes introduced were of three general types: 1) incentives to stimulate foreign trade in general but to promote export in particular, 2) institutions to set policy for and to administer the new special trade, and 3) a decentralization of the existing foreign trade structure to make it more flexible and responsive and to bring Chinese producers and end-users into closer contact with their foreign trading partners.

To induce localities and enterprises to look outwards for economic opportunities and technical assistance, the government modified the existing incentive structure governing foreign economic relations and trade and made it somewhat more attractive. Specifically, the more important measures adopted were as follows: 1) Export earnings are to be settled at the more realistic internal rate of US$1 = RMB ¥2.8 instead of the official rate of approximately

US$1 = RMB ¥1.8 − 2.0. 2) Localities and ministries are permitted to retain a share of the foreign exchange earnings generated by enterprises under their control. 3) Goods and components imported for processing or assembling are exempt from import duties. In addition, on a case-by-case basis, the Chinese Maritime Customs is now willing to consider applications from enterprises for the reduction or exemption of duties on imported goods used in the manufacturing of export products. 4) Enterprises involved in special trade arrangements are given priority claims on a share of the foreign exchange they earn. This does not mean that these enterprises have discretionary control over the foreign exchange in question. When they need to import, they must still apply for foreign exchange allocations, but their requests are likely to be approved, and the process is quicker. Given the scarcity of foreign exchange in China, even a modest advantage such as this is valuable to an enterprise. Joint venture enterprises, however, retain control over their entire foreign exchange earnings. To make Chinese goods more attractive internationally, China is also experimenting with various export credit schemes for buyers. Supplier's credit and deferred payment schemes are available to foreign buyers of complete sets of machinery and transport equipment, and more recently the Bank of China has become involved in the supply of long-term (eight-year) export credits.[17]

In addition to these specific measures, there were others associated with the economic reform and readjustment policies that have implications for foreign economic relations and trade. New economic policies have been adopted that permit many enterprises to retain a share of their profits and that exert considerable pressure on enterprises to increase product variety, to enhance product quality, to lower production cost, and generally to improve efficiency. Because frequently the most effective and quickest way for Chinese enterprises to acquire the technology and the managerial know-how that would enable them to achieve some of these objectives is through economic co-operation with foreign firms, many have become unusually anxious to expand their contacts with foreign companies.

Several new central agencies directly responsible to the State Council were established in 1979 to implement and administer the open door policy. They include the State General Administration of Exchange Control (SGAEC), the Foreign Investment Administration Commission (FIAC), the Import-Export Administration Commission (IEAC), and the China International Trust and Investment Corporation (CITIC). (It should be noted that China's English-language publications refer to these organizations by various names. For example, the FIAC is also called the Foreign Investment Control Commission (FICC) and the Foreign Investment Commission (FIC).) SGAEC was given the responsibility to plan and manage China's foreign exchange receipts and expenditures. FIAC was given the authority to set policy and guidelines for joint ventures, to review and approve joint venture agreements and contracts, and generally to administer foreign investment in China.[18] IEAC, which shares staff with FIAC, was given authority over special trade not involving direct foreign investment. It also shares with the SPC and MFT the responsibility for China's overall foreign trade plan, although the latter two organizations continue to take primary responsibility for normal trade. CITIC was empowered to promote foreign investment, to help foreign investors to find business opportunities and partners, to raise funds abroad for investment in China, and to engage in joint ventures and to invest in projects in China on its own account.[19] In addition to these new organizations, the Bank of China (BOC), which handles all of China's foreign exchange transactions, became officially a state-owned enterprise responsible directly to the State Council and also revised its Articles of Association to include among its function the raising of foreign funds through the issuing of bonds and securities (in addition to borrowing).[20]

The decision to give industrial ministries and localities an enlarged and more direct role in foreign trade and in the import of technology was probably made in 1978. However, this aspect of the decentralization process did not gather momentum until early 1979 when industrial ministries, provinces, and municipalities, in increasing numbers and with increasing boldness, began to take the initiative in searching for and negotiating normal as well as special trade deals (including the import of technology). Some local authorities were given the authority to approve small and medium-size special trade agreements.[21] Another feature of the decentralization process was the appearance of FTCs that are more specialized. An example is the China National Silk Corporation (formerly a part of the China National Textiles Import and Export Corporation). Branch offices of FTCs under the MFT were given greater authority to conduct foreign trade and also became more responsive to the local authorities. To carry out the policies of the various central departments involved in foreign economic relations and trade and to direct the work of the local FTB, the branch offices of FTCs, and other local agencies involved in foreign trade and investment work, a local counterpart to the IEAC-FIAC was created. The new organization reported to the IEAC-FIAC but also to the local authorities concerned. On the whole, these changes increased the authority of localities and of industrial ministries over trade matters — at the expense of the MFT.

As was to be expected, the changes just described led to considerable confusion among foreign traders, who were used to dealing with a monolithic foreign trade system through the head offices of FTCs in Beijing. There were also complaints from overseas agents, particularly those in Hong Kong, who saw their position as the "exclusive" distributor of Chinese goods threatened as foreign buyers and Chinese producers began to contact one another directly.[22]

From the Chinese viewpoint, a more serious development than these minor adjustment problems was that the provinces began to compete with one another for a larger share of the export market by undercutting each other's prices.[23] It was also not unknown for provincial branches of the same FTC to compete fiercely with one another. Such competition was clearly not in China's interest, and came under heavy criticism. *Hong Qi (Red Flag)* noted that such a lack of co-ordination between exporting regions can "let the foreigners drain all of the fertilizer and water onto their own fields."[24] Furthermore, since international economic co-operation frequently takes on some of the features of both normal and special trade, the authority of the various central organizations was bound to overlap, which created the potential for interdepartmental disputes and the resulting delays.

In early 1981, the central government stepped in, reasserted its authority, and returned some semblance of order to the foreign trade system.[25] More specific guidelines concerning trade matters were worked out, local authority over trade matters in some provinces was apparently curtailed, and tighter controls were placed on important exports. Then, in early 1982, as a part of the first stage of a general reorganization of the central government, the Ministry of Economic Relations with Foreign Countries, MFT, FIAC, and IEAC were all combined into one new entity, the Ministry of Foreign Economic Relations and Trade (MFERT).

THE FOREIGN TRADE AND INVESTMENT SYSTEM IN 1982[26]

While some minor changes, particularly at the local level, may still be forth-coming, it now appears that the Chinese are not contemplating further major revisions of the foreign trade and investment system. Given that the present system is likely to continue more or less unaltered, it is useful to consider it more closely. As of mid-1982, the foreign investment and trade system was more complicated than the one in existence before 1979. For one thing, there are many more players. For another, the relationships among the players and between the players and the central authorities are different than before. And, finally, several regions, most notably the provinces of Guangdong and Fujian, have special privileges and flexibility in the conduct of foreign economic relations and trade.

The Players

A wide assortment of trade organizations now have the authority to negotiate and conclude trade and economic co-operation agreements directly with foreign companies. Below they are roughly grouped into eight categories according to their functions and characteristics.

1) There are the traditional FTCs that used to be under MFT and are now under MFERT, with head offices in Beijing and branches in the provinces and munic-ipalities.[27] These national foreign trade corporations (NFTCs) are involved mostly

in normal trade but some, such as the China National Technical Import Corporation, are also actively engaged in arranging special trade deals.

2) Most industrial ministries and a small number of other central agencies under the State Council (for example, the Chinese Academy of Sciences) are now operating their own FTCs.[28] Typically, a ministerial FTC (MFTC) is permitted to export the products produced by enterprises under the authority of the ministry and to handle the imports (including technology) of the ministry and its subordinate units. MFTCs conduct both normal and special trade.

3) A small number of provincial or municipal FTCs (PFTCs) also exist. They are primarily responsible for importing on behalf of local departments but also do some exporting of local products, usually in small quantities. While the PFTCs are in principle under the dual leadership of MFERT and the local authorities, "leadership rests mainly with the local authorities."[29] As more localities become involved in foreign trade, the number of PFTCs is likely to increase.[30]

4) In addition to CITIC, fourteen provinces and municipalities have formed provincial or municipal trust and investment corporations (PTICs) to help negotiate and handle special trade arrangements on behalf of local enterprises as well as foreign companies.[31] There is no direct link between CITIC and the PTICs, although some of CITIC's directors also serve on the boards of directors of some PTICs. CITIC does provide the PTICs with advice and, sometimes, also financial assistance. They also refer business to one another.

5) In mid-1982, a small number of so-called "integrated export corporations" (IECs) were authorized to export specific lines of products on behalf of groups of industrial enterprises.[32] They function very much like export associations and are permitted to handle both normal and special trade. Apparently, the IECs are not under the direct jurisdiction of any government unit, but of course their member enterprises are.

6) NFTCs and "key industrial enterprises" have occasionally co-operated to form joint ventures to handle the foreign trade and economic co-operation projects (including the import of technology) of the industrial enterprise. An example is the China Yanshan United Foreign Trade Corporation, which is jointly run by the Beijing Yanshan General Petrochemical Corporation, the China National Chemicals Import and Export Corporation, the China National Technical Import Corporation, and the Beijing Foreign Trade Corporation.[33]

7) There is also a small group of specialized state corporations that operate under the State Council and are permitted to conduct their own normal and special trade. These corporations are usually engaged in large projects that involve several provinces and ministries. Examples include the Southwest China Joint Energy Development Corporation and the China National Offshore Oil Corporation.

8) Finally, in mid-1982, about twenty centrally controlled industrial enterprises

and a small but unknown number of locally controlled enterprises (mainly in Fujian and Guangdong) had permission to export their products directly.

Administration and Control

Table 2.1 summarizes the current foreign investment and trade structure in diagrammatic form.[34] The system operates according to what the Chinese describe as "the principle of centralized leadership and decentralized control." The leading body in the area of foreign investment and trade is MFERT. It gives unified leadership to and has the primary responsibility for the planning (in co-operation with the SPC and the SEC) and the administration of foreign trade and foreign economic co-operation — that is, both normal and special trade. Its main functions include[35] "the implementation of the state foreign economic and trade policy . . . development of foreign trade, co-operation with Third World countries in economic and technical aid, absorption and utilization of foreign capital, importation of advanced technology, etc." The responsibility for the planning and administration of normal and special trade are shared by four departments or bureaus within MFERT.[36] The Foreign Trade Administration Bureau (FTAB) is "in charge of the administration of foreign trade" while the Import-Export Bureau (IEB) is "in charge of import and export business" and the operation of the NFTCs.[37] In other words, FTAB is the planning unit and IEB is the operational unit. The Foreign Investment Administration Bureau (FIAB) oversees special trade projects and those projects financed by foreign loans (government and commercial). Finally, the Technical Import and Export Department (TIED) is in charge of the import and export of technology and of complete sets of equipment. Presumably this department is responsible for assessing and controlling the technology that China purchases through its regular imports, licensing, and special trade arrangements.

At the provincial or municipal[38] level, the body responsible for the planning and the administration of foreign economic relations and trade is the provincial import-export commission (PIEC).[39] This PIEC is under the dual leadership of the provincial government and MFERT, its counterpart at the central level. Under the present decentralized system, the provincial government plays the primary leadership and supervisory role while MFERT provides guidance on policy matters. The planning of provincial foreign trade is done under the supervision of PIEC[40] and in co-operation with the provincial planning commission (PPC) and the provincial economic commission (PEC). We were told that all the provincial commissions shown on Table 2.1 have within them a section that is responsible for foreign economic work and that this section acts as the liaison with PIEC on foreign trade and investment matters. Once completed, the provincial trade plan is submitted to the central government for inclusion in the national plan. PIEC is also responsible for devising concrete rules and regulations to implement the state's policy on foreign economic relations and trade in the province and for promoting and developing economic relations with foreign companies.

Following the pattern at the central level, PIEC also divides the responsibility for administering normal trade and special trade among its various departments. Normal trade is handled by the provincial foreign trade bureau (PFTB) and its alter ego, the provincial foreign trade corporation (PFTC). The Chinese describe PFTB and PFTC as "the same unit but with different labels." PFTC handles the imports for provincial departments and supervises the provincial branch offices of NFTCs and of production or trading units that have permission to export directly. Special trade is handled by the provincial trust and investment corporation. PIEC also works closely with and supervises the branch offices of a number of central organs, such as the Bank of China, the General Administration of Customs, and the Commodity Inspection and Testing Bureau. Some provinces have labor service companies that contract out workers for construction and other types of projects abroad. These labor service companies are under the supervision of the provincial labor bureau, but they receive guidance from PIEC on its foreign economic work. Finally, it should be noted that foreign economic commissions or sections exist below the province at the district or city level and sometimes also at the *xian* (county) level. At the discretion of PIEC, it may delegate some of its authority over normal and special trade to these lower units.

In China, nothing may be exported or imported without a license, and all special trade arrangements require government approval. In this respect the system in 1982 is no different than what existed before 1979. What has changed is that under decentralization there is now a division of control over foreign trade and investment among central authorities and between the central government (MFERT) and the local authorities. We have already taken note of the fact that MFTCs are now authorized to export products produced by enterprises under the industrial ministries and to handle the imports of the industrial ministries and their subordinate units. The industrial ministries are also permitted to retain a share of the foreign exchange earned by their subordinate enterprises and have the power to decide how the retained foreign exchange is allocated among competing needs within the ministry. Thus, in effect, the authority to issue export and import licenses to subordinate units of selected industrial ministries has been transferred from MFT (now MFERT) to the industrial ministries.

China's exports are classified into three categories, depending on their importance to the economy and as earners of foreign exchange. The division of control over these exports between the central authorities and the localities is as follows: 1) The head offices of NFTCs have exclusive control over the export of a small number of category I commodities[41], and the export prices of these goods are determined centrally. But, at the discretion of the head office, it may delegate the actual export transaction to branch offices. 2) Under central guidance, local authorities may handle the export of some 100 and more category II commodities. The export

Table 2.1 CHINA'S FOREIGN INVESTMENT AND TRADE SYSTEM, 1982

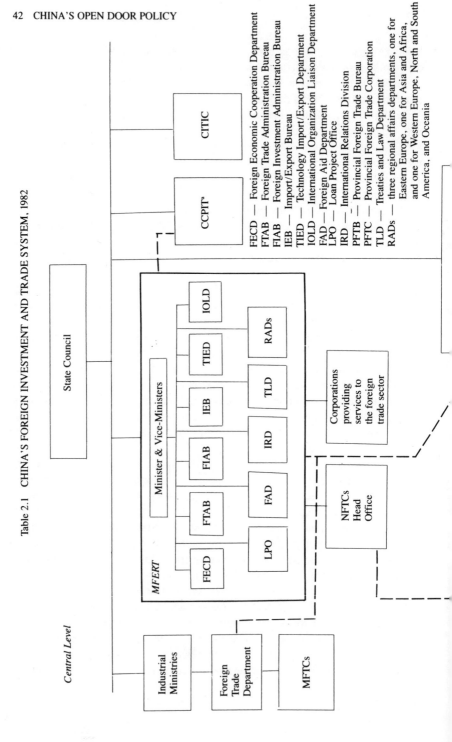

FECD — Foreign Economic Cooperation Department
FTAB — Foreign Trade Administration Bureau
FIAB — Foreign Investment Administration Bureau
IEB — Import/Export Bureau
TIED — Technology Import/Export Department
IOLD — International Organization Liaison Department
FAD — Foreign Aid Department
LPO — Loan Project Office
IRD — International Relations Division
PFTB — Provincial Foreign Trade Bureau
PFTC — Provincial Foreign Trade Corporation
TLD — Treaties and Law Department
RADs — three regional affairs departments, one for
        Eastern Europe, one for Asia and Africa,
        and one for Western Europe, North and South
        America, and Oceania

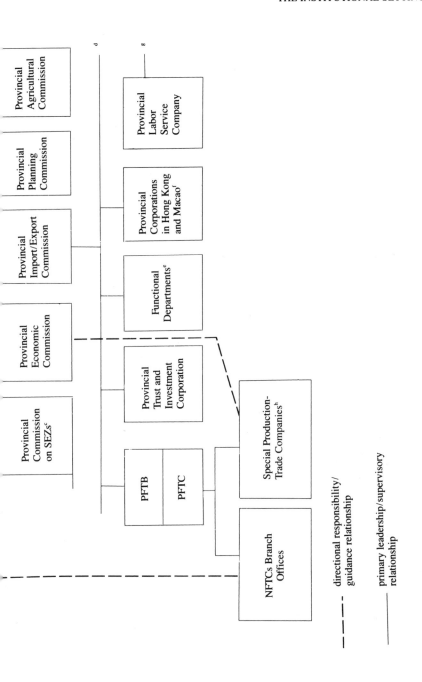

Provincial Agricultural Commission

Provincial Planning Commission

Provincial Import/Export Commission

Provincial Economic Commission

Provincial Commission on SEZs[c]

Provincial Labor Service Company

Provincial Corporations in Hong Kong and Macao[f]

Functional Departments[e]

Provincial Trust and Investment Corporation

PFTB

PFTC

Special Production-Trade Companies[h]

NFTCs Branch Offices

- - - directional responsibility/ guidance relationship

——— primary leadership/supervisory relationship

Notes to Table 2.1:

a. The China Council for the Promotion of International Trade is officially a non-governmental organization involved in promoting China's foreign trade and in liaison work between Chinese trade organizations and foreign companies. But, in fact, it is an integral part of China's foreign trade system and is under the guidance of MFERT.
b. The foreign investment and trade structure at the provincial level varies a great deal. The organizational structure shown here is based primarily on information gathered in Shanghai, Tianjin, Guangdong, and Fujian. They are, of course, among the most commercialized regions in China. The foreign trade organization of the inland provinces is probably much simpler.
c. Only in Guangdong and Fujian. Guangdong has three Special Economic Zones (SEZs), at Shenzhen, Zhuhai, and Shantou. In Fujian there is one SEZ at Xiamen. The Administrative Commission of the Xiamen SEZ is at the same level as the other provincial commissions.
d. PIECs are usually delegated the authority to supervise the work of the provincial branch offices of central organs involved in foreign trade, such as the branch offices of the Bank of China, the General Administration of Customs, and the Commodity Inspection and Testing Bureau.
e. These departments do promotional and liaison work, devise rules and regulations to implement government policies in the area of foreign investment and trade, and co-operate with other agencies in the planning of foreign investment and trade.
f. Only a few selected provinces are permitted to have trade offices or trade corporations in Hong Kong and Macao. The most prominent of these are Guangdong and Fujian.
g. The Labor Service Company is under the supervision of the Provincial Labor Bureau.
h. Either integrated export corporations or provincial enterprises that are permitted to export directly. We were told that fifteen to sixteen such companies exist in Guangdong, about eighteen in Fujian, and two in Shanghai. There may be more in other regions.

prices of these goods are set locally, but they must be within the ranges established by the central authority. Sometimes, the central authority also designates the export markets. The export of category II goods is handled largely by the branch offices of the NFTCs under the supervision of the local authority. 3) All other goods are in category III and may be exported at the discretion of local authorities. The export prices of category III goods are determined locally and, in principle, are uniform within each locality. The export licenses for the planned export of category I and category II goods are issued routinely to the enterprises concerned by the head offices of NFTCs and by PFTB (or PFTC) respectively. However, if an enterprise wants to exceed its planned export, then depending on whether the good is in category I or category II, it must apply to the planning authority at the central or the provincial level for approval. If the request to exceed planned export is approved, then another export license for the additional amount is issued by the appropriate FTC. Category III goods are usually outside the export plan. Depending on the commodity, either the province or the county or city has the authority to issue the necessary export license.

Like the industrial ministries, the local authority is also permitted to retain a share of the foreign exchange earned by the locally controlled enterprises. The formula used to divide the foreign exchange varies from province to province, but apparently the locality may keep not only a share of its export earnings (including the earnings from the export of category I goods *produced locally*) but also a share of the foreign exchange earned from tourism and from overseas remittances.[42] The local authority has control over the allocation of the retained foreign exchange and uses it to satisfy some of its import needs and that of its subordinate units.

Under the present system, when a locally (centrally) controlled industrial enterprise has a need to import, it applies to its province (ministry) for foreign exchange allocation. If the request is approved, the provincial or ministerial department in charge of foreign trade is then authorized to issue an import license. Only then will the MFTC or PFTC assist the enterprise to seek out suppliers and negotiate the purchase. For example, the following procedure is used in Fujian. For the routine import of raw materials used to produce goods for export, the enterprises go to the Fujian Foreign Trade Corporation for the required import licenses. For the non-routine import of raw material, the enterprise submits its request to the Fujian Planning Commission for approval. Whether or not it is approved depends on FPC's judgment on whether the requested raw material is needed and whether raw material of similar quality is available domestically. If the request is approved, the FFTC is then authorized to issue the import license. If the needed import is a capital good (machinery or equipment), the enterprise submits its request to its immediate higher authority (usually an industrial corporation or possibly a provincial industrial bureau). If the superior unit approves and if the cost of the foreign equipment is not too high for the province, then the FPC, the FEC, and the FIEC jointly consider the request. If the request is approved, the enterprise and the FFTC (or Fujian's trade corporation in Hong Kong) are notified of the foreign exchange allocation, and the two parties then get together to arrange for the import. It should be noted that, in addition to its own foreign exchange budget, a ministry or a province may also apply to the SPC/SEC for additional foreign exchange to help finance a specific project. Of course, such an application must compete on a nation-wide basis with foreign exchange requests from other provinces and ministries.

All special trade projects must have the approval of MFERT.[43] However, MFERT has delegated the authority to approve projects to the provinces and to the industrial ministries and commissions under the State Council if they meet the following two conditions: 1) The project does not require the central allocation of additional material supplies, does not affect China's overall balance of fuel, power, and transport capacity, and does not produce goods that take up any part of China's export quota. 2) The project is below a certain size. The size threshold refers to the value of the total investment in the case of joint ventures and to the value of the foreign component in all other forms of special trade. There is no size limit on special trade projects that can be approved by the provinces of Guangdong and Fujian. The cut-off point is US$5 million for Liaoning, Beijing, and Tianjin, and US$3 million for other provinces and the industrial ministries and commissions under the State Council. In the case of Shanghai, a limit of US$5 million was originally imposed, but new guidelines announced in May 1983 raised the ceiling to US$10 million.[44]

Foreign firms, of course, may approach any Chinese enterprise to discuss special trade arrangements. Alternatively, they may approach CITIC, any of the PTICs, or the industrial ministries and their MFTCs for help in identifying Chinese enterprises that are suitable for and interested in special trade arrangements. However the initial approach is made, the central or local government organ responsible for the control of special trade arrangements will be brought into the process at a fairly early stage. In Shanghai, and probably elsewhere, the IEC (the local control unit) becomes involved at three stages: 1) Before the Chinese enterprise can begin formal negotiations, it must have the permission of its superior organs. The request for permission to negotiate flows from the enterprise to its company, then to one of Shanghai's industrial bureaus, and finally to Shanghai's IEC. 2) After preliminary discussion, feasibility studies are conducted and these are submitted to IEC for its review. If the feasibility study indicates that the project exceeds Shanghai's authority (for example, if total investment exceeds US$10 million), then at this point the project is turned over to MFERT. 3) The final agreement and contract must be approved by IEC. But if, at this stage, it is determined that the project exceeds Shanghai's authority, then the agreement is turned over to MFERT for review and approval.

It is important to note that even though under decentralization the industrial ministries and the provinces are playing a larger and more direct role in the conduct of normal and special trade, the head offices of NFTCs continue to perform some important functions on their behalf. Because many provinces and some industrial ministries are not familiar with foreign markets and international investment and trade practices, they still require the assistance of the head offices of NFTCs. This is particularly true for the inland provinces, which previously had conducted all their trade through coastal provinces and therefore have little experience in foreign trade. Thus, for example, from 1979 to the end of 1981, the China National Technical Import Corporation (TECHIMPORT), using a variety of special trade schemes, arranged the import of forty complete sets of equipment or production lines on behalf of localities and a few central departments.[45] In these instances, the end-user took the lead in the technical negotiation but left the commercial negotiation to TECHIMPORT. In effect, TECHIMPORT acted as an agent and received a fee for its services. Since even established commercial centers such as Shanghai may lack the expertise available at the NFTCs, enterprises in the more advanced regions may also find it necessary to seek the services of the head offices of NFTCs. One manifestation of this need is the recent formation of joint ventures between NFTCs and "key" industrial enterprises in such centers as Shanghai and Beijing for the purpose of promoting and developing foreign trade on behalf of the enterprises.

To summarize, China's foreign investment and trade system is now more decentralized in the sense that many departments other than MFERT and its NFTCs can now conduct economic relations and trade directly with foreign firms and that industrial ministries and provinces have been delegated limited authority to develop their own foreign trade and to approve special trade arrangements. Players have become more specialized, and fewer layers of bureaucracy now separate the foreign firms from the Chinese enterprises. However, some important features of the old system remain.

To facilitate economic planning and to maximize its export earnings, China continues to operate its export system as a state monopoly. Its most important exports are still marketed centrally, although in some instances by one of the newly created specialized MFTCs instead of the head office of one of the NFTCs. Many locally controlled exports are marketed through special corporations or associations that are in effect export cartels. In other words, as before, the system permits little price competition among producers. But because the specialized trade corporations, whether controlled locally or by one of the industrial ministries, are closer to the producing units and because some minor products can now be exported by county authorities (particularly in Guangdong and Fujian), the system is more responsive than before to consumers' needs and demand changes. Even more so than exports, imports continue to be tightly controlled. Although localities and industrial ministries now have discretionary spending power over a portion of the foreign exchange they earn, such power is not extended to their subordinate units. Therefore, to import, industrial enterprises still must apply for foreign exchange allocations on a case-by-case basis. The difference is that such applications are now processed more quickly since some of them require only ministerial or provincial approval. In addition, end-users of foreign machinery and equipment are now more likely to be directly involved in the technical negotiation of such imports and therefore are in somewhat closer contact with foreign producers.

But despite the fact that there are many more players involved in foreign trade and that there are fewer layers of bureaucracy between Chinese and foreign firms than before, very few Chinese industrial enterprises, except when involved in special trade arrangements, come into direct contact with foreign firms even though they may be involved in foreign trade. Since there is evidence that export firms in LDCs frequently receive from their foreign buyers free advice and technical assistance concerning quality control and product improvements[46] and since the diffusion of technology is dependent on direct contact, the continued isolation of most Chinese firms suggests that the present trade system is still deficient from the viewpoint of making the most effective use of trade as a vehicle for technology transfer.

A Pivotal Role for the Coastal Regions

Perhaps the most intriguing aspect of the present decentralized system is the greater authority and flexibility given to Guangdong and Fujian in the management of their economies, particularly of matters concerning foreign economic relations and trade. According to the provincial officials we interviewed, the two coastal provinces have been delegated greater planning authority, but they were not specific as to precisely what powers have been enlarged.[47] However, they gave us the impression that Guangdong and Fujian may now plan their economies autonomously as long as their activities do not violate the overall balance of the national plan, — that is, do not require the central authorities to rebalance supplies, fuel, and transportation. What is clear is that since 1980 Guangdong and Fujian have operated under a so-called "guarantee" (baogan) system, whereby the province and the central government share the revenue and the foreign exchange generated in the province according to a pre-determined formula that is supposed to remain fixed for five years (1980–84). For example, in Guangdong[48], the financial baogan system divides the revenues collected in the province as follows: a small number of taxes (for example, customs duties and the consolidated industrial and commercial tax on tobacco, sugar, watches, and alchoholic beverages) and the earnings of centrally controlled enterprises belong entirely to the central government, while the remaining taxes and the profits of local enterprises belong to Guangdong. However, from its revenues, Guangdong must remit annually RMB ¥1.1 billion to the center.[49] At the same time, the central government is supposed to maintain its allocation of investment funds to Guangdong (for example, for the development of transportation and communications) at the pre-baogan levels. The foreign exchange baogan system stipulates the following: Guangdong is responsible to turn over to the central government, at a minimum, foreign exchange equivalent to what it earned from exports and tourism in 1978, and at the same time its basic foreign exchange allocation is also fixed at the 1978 levels. In addition, Guangdong may retain 70 percent of the foreign exchange it earns from exports and tourism above the 1978 level as well as a share of the remittances it receives from abroad.[50] In turn, the province has an analogous baogan system with local authorities below the provincial level. In effect, the baogan system gives Guangdong and Fujian their own source of revenue and foreign exchange, thus making it possible for the provinces to plan their economic activities with greater assurance, since they now know more precisely what resources they can count on for five-year periods at a time. The system, of course, also gives Guangdong and Fujian a strong incentive to increase their local revenues and foreign exchange earnings since the province gets to keep a substantial share of any increments.

// To enhance their capability to attract foreign technology and capital, Guangdong and Fujian are also permitted the following flexibilities: 1) freedom to pay higher wages than in other parts of China, 2) greater authority to approve special trade agreements (see earlier discussion), 3) the authority to control the province's imports and exports as long as the commodities are not among those to be balanced centrally and as long as the province uses its own foreign exchange, 4) the authority to borrow directly from abroad,[51] and 5) the authority to operate Special Economic Zones (SEZs), where economic activities involving "foreign investments" are governed by regulations that are more liberal than those found in other parts of China. Of these measures, the creation of SEZs has stimulated the greatest interest among Chinese and foreigners alike. More important, SEZs have the potential to influence not only the economies of Guangdong and Fujian but the rest of China as well.

The Chinese define an SEZ as "an area . . . [where] controls are relaxed as compared with inland China for the purpose of promoting economic co-operation by all proper means with foreign businessmen, Overseas Chinese, as well as Hong Kong and Macao compartriots".[52] However, the original idea was only to create an industrial export zone at Shekou (twenty nautical miles from Hong Kong's Central District), to be developed and operated entirely by the China Merchants Steam Navigation Co. (CMSNC), a Hong Kong based company controlled by the Chinese Ministry of Communications. After the Shekou Special Industrial Zone (SSIZ) was established by the State Council in January 1979, Hong Kong business interests suggested that the zone be expanded to encompass property development and tourism and suggested the name "Special Economic Zone" to reflect the broader scope. Guangdong then made the same suggestion to the central government, and, in late 1979, it was authorized to develop certain areas in Shenzhen, Zhuhai, and Shantou as SEZs.[53] As a result of this development, SSIZ became one component of the larger Shenzhen SEZ, although it continues to be controlled and operated by CMSNC.[54] Subsequently, in October 1980, the State Council also authorized the creation of the Xiamen SEZ in Fujian.[55]

What makes SEZs special is that enterprises in the zones operate under a legal framework different from what exists in other parts of China. As of mid-1982 the following laws and regulations governing SEZs had been promulgated:[56] "Regulations of the People's Republic of China on Special Economic Zones in Guangdong Province"; "Guangdong Provisional Entry/Exit Rules for the Special Economic Zones"; "Guangdong Provisional Regulations for Enterprise Registration in Special Economic Zones"; "Guangdong Provisional Labor and Wage Regulations in Special Economic Zones"; and "Guangdong Provisional Land Regulations for Shenzhen Special Economic Zone." These special regulations allow market forces to play a more prominent role in SEZs and give enterprises in SEZs greater flexibility in management as well as greater incentives.

Foreign investors are invited to participate in a wide variety of economic activities in the SEZs, including agriculture, manufacturing, property development, tourism, research and development, as well as other activities "of common interest."[57] All forms of special trade are permitted, and in addition "foreign citizens, Overseas Chinese, compatriots in Hong Kong and Macao and their companies and enterprises are encouraged to open factories or set up enterprises and other establishments with their own investment" in SEZs.[58] In other words,

SEZs accept, indeed welcome, 100 percent foreign-owned enterprises (China contributes only the land, on which it receives a rent). However, products produced by enterprises in SEZs must be exported, unless the enterprise has permission to sell its products in China, and then the products are considered foreign goods and face Chinese customs duties and other taxes.[59]

Enterprises in SEZs are given a number of important incentives that are not available to foreign "investors" in other parts of China. The most important of these is that net earnings of enterprises in SEZs are taxed at a flat rate of 15 percent, as compared to 33 percent for joint ventures in other parts of China and progressive rates that range from 30 percent to 50 percent for foreign enterprises operating ouside SEZs.[60] In addition there is no remittance tax on after-tax profits remitted abroad. "Machinery, spare parts, raw materials, vehicles and other means of production for the enterprises in the special zones are exempted from import duties," and the duties on necessary consumer goods for use in SEZs may be lowered or exempted depending on "the merits of each case."[61] To encourage the use of Chinese products, domestic machinery and raw materials are available to enterprises in SEZs at the lower export prices, but they must be paid for with hard currencies.[62]

Investors in SEZs also have somewhat more flexibility and authority in the management of their enterprises. They may "operate their enterprises independently in the special zones and employ foreign personnel for technical and administrative work."[63] In principle, all enterprises in SEZs with foreign participation (that is, enterprises with 100 percent foreign investment, equity joint ventures, and co-operative ventures) employ workers under a contract system. Wages, length of employment, and work conditions are specified in the contracts. The enterprise may use whatever wage scale and wage system it wishes, and there is no regulation specifying the relationship between the wage paid in SEZs and that in similar industry outside the zones.[64] By not tying the wage paid in SEZs to that in state enterprises, the Chinese in effect are permitting enterprises in SEZs to rely more heavily on material incentives to increase productivity and improve product quality.[65] To introduce greater wage differentials among workers to reflect differences in their skills and productivity, the authorities have suggested that enterprises divide wages into two parts: a basic wage and a floating wage.[66] The basic wage is determined by the worker's position in the enterprise, while the floating wage is dependent on his skills, productivity, and work attitude. Besides the two-part wage, the worker is also eligible for bonuses. Like joint ventures, enterprises in SEZs with foreign participation have the authority to discharge redundant workers and to dismiss workers who have violated company rules.[67] Finally, since the law gives the SEZ administration the authority to review and approve investment projects[68] and to co-ordinate and supervise the work of other government units in the zone (banks, customs offices, tax offices, and so forth), there is also the possibility that foreign investors may face less red tape and bureaucracy in SEZs than in other parts of China.

An interesting question is why Guangdong and Fujian were singled out for these additional powers and flexibilities. The most frequent explanation we received in China was that the additional authority was requested by, and subsequently granted to, Guangdong and Fujian so that they may take full advantage of the open door policy and of their special circumstances — that historically both were more open to foreign trade and contacts, that large numbers of Overseas Chinese have roots in the two provinces, that both are close to Hong Kong and that Guangdong has had over thirty years of special relationship with Hong Kong. In other words, the special powers are to help Guangdong and Fujian tap an extremely important source of capital and skills, the Overseas Chinese communities in Southeast Asia. That most Overseas Chinese speak either the Guangdong or the Fujian dialect is an added advantage, since a common tongue facilitates communication and thus helps reduce the transactions costs of investing in China and the cost of transferring technology and skills to China. Of the Overseas Chinese communities, the closest, the largest, and the most dynamic is Hong Kong. China has long been fascinated by Hong Kong's economic success and is anxious to tap its capital, its entrepreneurship, its market know-how, and its managerial and technical skills. It is therefore not surprising that the incentive structure for the SEZs, most specifically the 15 percent tax rate, was devised primarily with Hong Kong in mind.[69]

The greater flexibility in Guangdong and Fujian also serves purposes other than to attract investments from Overseas Chinese. Ever since the Third Plenum, the Chinese have been experimenting with new ways of running enterprises and of managing the economy. Guangdong and Fujian, especially the SEZs, are therefore useful as a laboratory where reforms and new management methods (such as new incentive schemes and the greater use of the market) may be tried out. The SEZs are also useful as a way to control the introduction of foreign business and management methods (as well as foreign ideas and values more generally) by limiting them at first to a few restricted areas where they may be scrutinized and screened before permitting them to penetrate other parts of China. Finally, there are also political reasons for the special treatment of Guangdong and Fujian. It is becoming increasingly certain that China will claim sovereignty over Hong Kong in 1997 and that it hopes to regain Hong Kong as well as Macao and Taiwan under a special arrangement whereby they may continue to function under their present economic system — what the Chinese call "one society, two systems" (*yige shehui, liangge zhidu*).[70] To make such a scheme look plausible, the Chinese are anxious to demonstrate that capitalism and socialism can co-exist, if only in a few restricted SEZs. But, at a more practical level, it is clear that under whatever scheme eventually emerges, Hong Kong, Macao, and Taiwan are likely to interact with the Chinese economy primarily through Guangdong and Fujian. Indeed, the economies of Macao, Hong Kong, and Guangdong are already interdependent.[71] In anticipation of increased interaction in the future, it is only practical to permit Guangdong and Fujian greater flexibility in economic planning and management, in business practices, and in enterprise management so they can serve as a buffer between the rest of China and the more market-oriented economies in Hong Kong, Macao, and Taiwan. The hope is that the reduction of economic differences will also facilitate the reabsorption of Hong Kong, Macao, and Taiwan.

It was noted earlier that, besides Guangdong and Fujian, the three provincial-level municipalities (Beijing, Shanghai, and Tianjin) and Liaoning Province also have somewhat greater authority in arranging and approving special trade arrangements. Unlike Guangdong and Fujian, which were given greater flexibility largely because of their close ties to Overseas Chinese communities and their proximity to Hong Kong, Beijing, Shanghai, Tianjin, and Liaoning were granted greater authority because they are expected to take the lead in absorbing foreign capital and technology and because they have greater capacity to develop their own foreign economic relations and trade. The regional economic data in Table 2.2 suggest some of the reasons why these four regions are expected to play a pivotal role in the current open door strategy.

First of all, because the four are among the most developed regions in China, they have a greater capacity to absorb foreign technology and capital. In terms of the gross value of industrial output (GVIO), Shanghai and Liaoning rank first and second respectively in the country with Beijing and Tianjin not far behind. Together the four have 6 percent of the population but produce 28 percent of China's industrial output by value. The four have the highest GVIO per capita and per industrial worker in China. In particular, Shanghai stands out — its per capita GVIO is ten times the national average and about twice that in Beijing and Tianjin. Table 2.2 also indicates that the four have access to a considerable stock of human capital (scientists, engineers, and experienced technicians and skilled workers) and therefore have the necessary capacity to absorb new technology quickly and to do the research and development work that is often critical to the successful transfer and adaptation of foreign technology to a new environment.

Secondly, the four have had considerable commercial experience and therefore are in a strong position to take advantage of the open door policy and the decentralization of foreign trade. Shanghai and Tianjin, like Guangdong, have been central to China's international commercial relations since the mid-nineteenth century. In this century, Liaoning also has had considerable contact with the outside world, particularly Japan. Of the four, Beijing is the least outward oriented, and historically it was not a major commercial center. But being the capital, it has access to commercial expertise not easily available to other regions. In 1980, the four accounted for about 45 percent of China's total exports. Thus they are more confident, and, in terms of personnel and knowledge about international

Table 2.2 SELECTED ECONOMIC INDICATORS FOR CHINA'S COASTAL REGIONS 1981

	National	Shanghai	Beijing	Tianjin	Liaoning	Guangdong	Fujian
Population (million)	996.2	11.6	9.0	7.6	35.4	58.8	25.6
Industrial employment (thousand)	46,741	2,557	1,486	1,305	4,530	2,481	1,035
% in state enterprises[a]	69	77	71	69	63	60	63
Gross value of agricultural output 1980 RMB¥ billion)	231.1	3.3	1.8	1.8	8.4	12.0	5.8
Gross value of industrial output (1980 RMB¥ billion)	517.8	60.9	21.7	19.9	45.1	25.0	8.2
% light industry[b]	51	57	47	59	36	65	64
% state enterprises[a]	79	87	81	83	80	68	76
Number of industrial enterprises	381,500	8,000	3,800	4,300	16,800	23,200	10,700
% state enterprises[a]	22	42	29	23	21	25	25
% small enterprises[c]	99	95	93	97	97	99	99
Major industrial output							
Bicycles (million)	17.54	4.10	.16	3.32	1.47	1.30	.08
Sewing machines (million)	10.39	2.41	.55	.56	.78	.80	.24
Cloth (million metres)	14,268	1,666	291	424	635	268	137
Steel (million tons)	35.60	5.06	1.90	1.25	8.73	.40	.22
Cement (million tons)	82.89	2.01	2.30	.76	7.29	4.87	1.62
Electric power generated (billion kWh)	309.27	20.47	9.93	7.30	28.00	12.24	5.25
Investment in capital construction (RMB¥ billion)[d]	42.79	3.08	2.34	1.63	2.61	3.18	.87
% Non-productive construction[e]	41	24	64	59	49	44	42
1980 export earnings (US$ million)[f]	18,270	4,240	593	1,543	1,762	2,500[h]	361
1980 export structure (% total export)[f]							
Agricultural and sideline products	n.a.	11	n.a.	9	13	44	64
Textile and light industrial products	n.a.	70	n.a.	66	25	34	36[i]
Heavy industrial products	n.a.	19	n.a.	25	62	22	
Students enrolled in institutions of higher learning (thousand)	1,279	87	98	37	75	48	30
Technical personnel in state-owned units (thousand)[g]	5,714	260	308	137	361	234	118

Notes to Table 2.2

a. State enterprises are owned by "all the people"; collective enterprises are owned by those who work in them.

b. In general, light industry produces consumer goods, including consumer durables, chemicals for household use, chemical fibre and fabrics, and the processing of fuel for household use.

c. Chinese enterprises are classified as "small," "medium," or "large" depending on their production capacity. Each industry has its own criterion. For example, in the steel industry a small enterprise is one with an annual production capacity below 100,000 tons. However, in some industries, enterprises are classified by size according to the original value of their fixed assets.

d. Includes only the capital construction of state-owned units.

e. Non-productive construction includes all investments that do not serve material production directly, such as residential dwellings, hospitals, and educational and cultural facilities.

f. The export data are from BA Asia Limited, *Municipalities*, Vol. III: *China: Provincial Economic Briefing Series* (Hong Kong, 1982); *Beijing Review*, 4 January 1982, pp. 21–23 and 14 March 1983, pp. 18–19; *China Trade Report*, November, 1981, p. 9; Guangdong Provincial Statistical Bureau, "Communique," 6 May 1982; *China Business Review*, September-October, 1980, p. 16; and *Zhongguo Jingji Nianlan 1981* [Economic Yearbook of China 1981] (Beijing: Beijing Economic Management Monthly, 1981).

g. Includes engineers, scientists, teachers, medical doctors, and agricultural, industrial, and medical technicians.

h. Total foreign exchange earned.

i. Fujian exports very few heavy industrial products.

Sources: Unless otherwise noted, all data are from PRC, State Statistical Bureau, *Statistical Yearbook of China 1981* (Hong Kong: Economic Information & Agency, 1982).

commerce, they are also better prepared to deal with matters concerning foreign investment and trade. All four are expected to seek overseas contact aggressively.

Finally, the four are favored by China's current development strategy that stresses intensive growth, the renovation of existing facilities, and light industry. Under the current policy, old enterprises, particularly those in light industry, that can be upgraded through renovation and the acquisition of new technology are encouraged to participate in international economic co-operation. Many of the likely candidates are in the more developed coastal provinces, particularly the four main industrial centers: Beijing, Shanghai, Tianjin, and Liaoning. Shanghai and Tianjin are, of course, China's oldest industrial centers with many aging plants needing renovations. Beijing and Liaoning also have a disproportionate share of factories dating to the 1950s. Indeed, Shenyang (Liaoning's capital), Beijing, Shanghai, and Tianjin have been designated as centers for technological renovation, and considerable sums have been budgeted for industrial renovation in the four cities.[73] Given their greater involvement in the production of consumer goods, the emphasis on light industry should benefit Shanghai and Tianjin more than Beijing and Liaoning. Guangdong and Fujian, where light industry accounts for about 65 percent of the GVIO, are also major beneficiaries of China's current development strategy.

In principle, all regions in China may have overseas contact, but it is clear that, in view of their accessibility, favorable economic environment, and greater absorption capacity, the three great coastal cities, Liaoning Province, and the special provinces of Guangdong and Fujian are expected to play a leading role in China's absorption of foreign technology and capital in the 1980s. Thus, much of the initial impact and benefit of the Open Door are likely to fall on the coastal regions. However, several programs to diffuse the benefits to other regions have been introduced.

With Guangdong's permission, central industrial ministries and other provinces may establish a presence in Shenzen, by far the largest and the most developed SEZ in China.[74] The ministry or province is allocated land in the zone on which it may construct factories and establish economic co-operation arrangements with foreign companies. There may also be joint ventures involving the SEZ and enterprises from the interior as well as ventures that involve the SEZ, foreign enterprises, and enterprises from the interior.[75] In this way, enterprises from outside of Guangdong, through arrangements made by their superior units, can make use of the more favorable economic environment in the SEZ to attract foreign technology and capital through co-operation arrangements. Since Shenzhen does not have its own source of labor, industrial workers to operate the co-operation projects presumably must be transferred from elsewhere by the ministry or province concerned. As these workers are rotated back to their home plants, they will take with them the skills and know-how acquired in the SEZ. This is one of the ways by which foreign technology and skills attracted to SEZs will be diffused to other parts of China. Of course, from the viewpoint of the SEZs, economic co-operation with the interior is critical to their success since they do not as yet have the capacity to attract and to absorb large amounts of technology and capital on their own. Indeed, before the SEZs can become sources of new technology and skills for the interior, they must first acquire technology and skills from the more developed areas of China. For example, young workers from Shenzhen are currently being sent to cities such as Shanghai for training under veteran skilled workers.[76]

Since early 1981, as a part of its reform and readjustment program, the central government has called upon the less developed interior regions to learn from the older and more advanced industrial centers on the coast, particularly cities such as Shanghai and Tianjin, and upon the more developed coastal regions to assist the less developed regions.[77] The mechanisms used to transfer technology and skills from the coastal industrial centers to other provinces are similar to those employed to acquire new technology from abroad: compensation trade, technical co-operation, and joint ventures. In the first six months after the announcement of the policy in April 1981, 122 delegations from other provinces visited Shanghai to study its enterprises, and Shanghai enterprises signed 122 "co-operation" contracts with enterprises from twenty-six other regions.[78] In 1982 Tianjin had 410 such co-operation projects involving enterprises from twenty-two of China's provinces, and one interior city (Yichang, on the Yangzi River) reported having more than 60 co-operation arrangements with enterprises in Shanghai, Beijing,

Tianjin, and Jiangsu Province.[79] Through such interactions, established skills and technology are now being transferred from the coastal cities to the interior. Presumably, in time, the new skills and technology acquired from abroad by the coastal regions will also be diffused in the same manner.

As can readily be seen from the foregoing discussion, the new institutions surrounding the open door policy are rather complicated. Because of these complexities, and perhaps also because of a sense that the system is still in flux, some potential foreign participants in the Open Door have undoubtedly adopted a "wait-and-see" attitude. Nevertheless, a variety of open door projects have already been initiated, and we turn now to an examination of these early results.

3

The Initial Results: An Overview

The next three chapters examine in detail the experience to date of economic co-operation agreements and joint ventures in China. Here we present only a statistical overview of the initial results of the open door policy. First, the pace of development of international economic cooperation in China is reviewed. This is followed by a brief examination of developments in the Special Economic Zones (SEZs).

INTERNATIONAL ECONOMIC COOPERATION IN CHINA, 1979–1982

Table 3.1 presents the available data on "foreign investment" activities and special trade arrangements in China. Before discussing the evidence, a word about the data is perhaps in order.[1] Compared to but a few years ago, China is now making available a great deal more official economic and statistical data, but unfortunately foreign investment and special trade arrangements are areas where official data are still not published on a regular basis. Nevertheless, China does periodically release information concerning these topics. But because the data are made available through the mass media and for public relations purposes, they are usually handled carelessly, frequently with coverage, time period, and base year undefined. In consequence, the data are subject to differing interpretations.

Several aspects of the data in Table 3.1 should be noted. First, most economic co-operation agreements are not "pure" but involve features from several of the special trade arrangements identified in the table. For example, many processing arrangements have an element of compensation trade since the foreign participant frequently provides the Chinese with equipment which is repaid with end-products or a lower processing fee. At what point does a processing agreement becomes a compensation trade deal? In other words, what criteria are used to classify the special trade agreements? Do all regions use the same criteria? As yet, we do not have answers to these questions. Second, the value figures in Table 3.1 are not the amount of investment that actually arrived in China each year; rather, they are the pledges made by the foreign participants. Since pledges have a way of changing over time, some of the figures in Table 3.1 are bound to be in error. Finally, because there was a lag before the statistics relating to foreign investment and special trade were systematically collected and processed, the data for 1979 and 1980 are undoubtedly less reliable and complete than those for 1981 and 1982. Because of these and other shortcomings, we should not impute too great a degree of accuracy to the data in Table 3.1. Still they indicate the general order of magnitude and pattern of development of foreign investment and special trade in China.

From 1979 to the end of 1981, China approved "foreign investment" amounting to slightly more than US$3 billion. This figure refers to the cash and the value of equipment and technology pledged by foreign firms involved in economic co-operation projects in China. Actual arrival was considerably less. If the ratio of "investment" delivered to the amount pledged at the national level during 1979–1981 was no better than that reported in Guangdong (0.212),[2] then the actual amount of "foreign investment" that arrived by the end of 1981 may be as low as US$636 million. By the end of 1982, the amounts pledged to special trade projects (excluding processing agreements, equity joint ventures located in the SEZs, and wholly owned subsidiaries) totalled more than US$4.1 billion, of which about US$1.7 billion (or about 41 percent) represented actual arrivals.[3]

A variety of special trade arrangements have been used to absorb foreign technology and capital. At one extreme are the large, long-term offshore oil exploration projects, and at the other extreme are the numerous one-shot processing arrangements that are more important for the foreign exchange they generate than for the equipment and know-how they transfer. To judge by developments to the end of 1982, processing, compensation trade and cooperative ventures have developed more rapidly than equity joint ventures and co-operative development projects. The figures in Table 3.1 show that, in terms of numbers of contracts signed, simple processing and assembling agreements dominated the scene. However, the processing and assembling agreements have often been very small in scale, which explains why the few hundred compensation trade deals signed have provided three times as much equipment as all the thousands of processing and assembling agreements combined. Measured by the amount of capital pledged, co-operative ventures have been more important than either processing agreements or compensation trade, constituting barely 2 percent of the contracts signed and yet accounting for about 60 percent of the investment pledged. Significantly,

Table 3.1   INTERNATIONAL ECONOMIC COOPERATION IN CHINA USING FOREIGN FUNDS — AGREEMENTS APPROVED SINCE 1979

	1979[a]	1980	1981	Cumulative 1979–1981	Cumulative 1979–1982
A. Processing/Assembling					
Number of agreements	2980[c]	7120[d]	8900[e]	19,000+[e]	n.a.
Processing fee received (US$ million)[b]	29.6[f]	112.2[e]	188.2[e]	330[e]	n.a.
Value of equipment to be supplied by foreign participants (US$ million)	n.a.	n.a.	n.a.	156[g]	n.a.
B. Compensation trade					
Number of agreements	417[h]	(417[h])	173[h]	590[i]	872[o]
Value of equipment to be supplied by foreign participants (US$ million)	381[h]	(381[h])	79[h]	460[i]	700[p]
C. Cooperative ventures					
Number of agreements	n.a.	320[j]	70[j]	390[p]	792[o]
Foreign contribution pledged (US$ million)	n.a.	500[j]	1300[j]	1800[k]	2700[p]
D. Joint ventures in China					
Number of agreements	4	18	24	46	57
Foreign investment pledged (US$ million)	7	100	25	132	144
E. Joint Oil Exploration					
Number of agreements	9[m]	4[m]	0	13[m]	14[q]
Foreign contribution pledged (US$ million)	0	498[m]	0	498[m]	600[p]
F. Total foreign funds "absorbed" (US$ million)[n]					
Including processing	n.a.	1486	n.a.	3046	n.a.
Excluding processing			1404	2890	4144

Notes for Table 3.1

a. Except for processing, most of the other statistics for 1979 cover only the period from 1 July to 31 December. However, only processing was widely used prior to 1 July. The processing figures include a small number of agreements signed in the last half of 1978.

b. Fees deferred as repayment for equipment supplied by foreign participants are excluded.

c. 19,000 — (8,900 + 7,120). This includes a small number of agreements signed in the last half of 1978. *China's Foreign Trade*, May-June, 1980, p. 2, reports that over 2,000 processing contracts were signed in 1979.

d. *Shijie Jingji Daobao* [*World Economic Herald*], 17 May 1982, p. 1, reports that the number of processing agreements signed in 1981 was 25 percent higher than in 1980, implying that 7,120 (8,900/1.25) agreements were signed in 1980.

e. *Shijie Jingji Daobao*, 17 May 1982, p. 1, The cumulative figure includes a few agreements signed in the last half of 1978.

f. 330 — (188.2 + 112.2). *China's Foreign Trade*, April, 1982, p. 14, reports that more than US$28 million in processing fees were earned in 1979. This implies a 1978 figure of US$1.6 million.

g. *Shijie Jingji Daobao*, 17 May 1982, p. 1, reports that during 1979–1981 US$39 million in processing fees were deferred as repayment to foreign participants for equipment they supplied and that this figure represents about 25 percent of the total value of the equipment supplied. This implies that the total value was about US$156 million.

h. *China Business Review*, September-October, 1982, p. 25. In early 1981, Ji Chongwei reported that in 1980 China had signed more than 350 small and medium and three large compensation agreements, involving the import of equipment worth more than US$187 million. See *Beijing Review*, 20 April 1981, p. 11.

i. *Shijie Jingji Daobao*, 7 June 1982, p. 2.

j. Interview at MFERT. These are also the figures used by Ji Chongwei in "China's Utilization of Foreign Funds and Relevant Policies," *Beijing Review*, 20 April 1981, p. 16. However, the *China Business Review*, September-October, 1982, p. 25, reports somewhat different figures:
   1979–1980: number of agreements, 221; foreign contribution pledged, US$365 million, and 1981: number of agreements, 169; foreign contribution pledged, US$1,435 million.

k. *Shijie Jingji Daobao*, 7 June 1982, p. 2. The report also states that of the US$1.8 billion, Guangdong's share was US$1.5 billion. Ji Chongwei, "Utilization of Foreign Investment and Development of China's Economy," *China Market*, October, 1982, p. 11, also uses these figures and states explicitly that they refer to co-operative ventures approved during 1980–81. In our interview with the Guangdong Commission for Foreign Economic Work, we were told that from 1979 to 1981 the amount of foreign funds pledged to projects in this category in Guangdong was US$2,065 million.

l. Ministry of Foreign Economic Relations and Trade. See Table 3.2 for details.

m. *Shijie Jingji Daobao*, 7 June 1982, p. 2. The thirteen agreements include nine agreements for seismographic studies and four exploration contracts. The US$498 million represents the proposed expenditures specified in the exploration contracts.

n. The sum of the value of equipment to be supplied by foreign participants and the amount of foreign funds pledged in joint ventures, co-operative ventures, and joint oil exploration.

o. *Beijing Review*, 6 June 1983, p. 4.

p. *China Market*, May, 1983, p. 24.

q. *China Market*, May, 1983, p. 24, gives the cumulative number of offshore oil agreements as five (implicitly, the four exploration agreements of 1980 plus the ARCO agreement of 1982). For consistency of coverage, we show this as 14, to include the nine seismographic agreements of 1979.

the importance of co-operative ventures has also been on the rise. Of the foreign investment pledged in special trade agreements in 1981, between 80 and 90 percent (depending on the estimate used)[4] was accounted for by co-operative ventures.

The rapid development of schemes such as processing, compensation trade, and co-operative ventures is understandable. Both processing and compensation trade are relatively straightforward commercial arrangements that have been in use internationally (particularly in East-West trade) for some time and therefore are familiar to most Western traders. To the extent that a new technology is involved, it is frequently embodied in pieces of easily obtainable and relatively inexpensive equipment. Given their lack of marketing skills, the Chinese find these arrangements especially attractive since the foreign participants are responsible for finding outlets for the bulk of the finished products on the world market.

Co-operative ventures are attractive for several reasons. First, this is an extremely flexible and adaptable arrangement, and therefore it can be used for a wide variety of projects, everything from small manufacturing operations to large property development projects. Indeed, the dramatic increase in the average value of co-operative ventures in 1981 was caused primarily by the increasing use of this format to develop resorts and other commercial properties in Guangdong and Fujian. Second, it is an arrangement that permits the participants, if they wish, to work closely together for a short period of time to become better acquainted before entering into a more permanent relationship such as the equity joint venture. Finally, compared to the equity joint venture, co-operative ventures are restricted by fewer legal requirements and therefore may be easier to negotiate. Consequently, the co-operative venture is particularly suitable when the participants wish to share management and profit, but, because the project is a small one, find the transaction cost of arranging a joint venture too high. The experience to date with processing, compensation trade, and co-operative ventures is examined in greater depth in Chapter 5.

The equity joint venture, because of its greater legal complexity and economic involvement, has developed relatively slowly. Twenty-two joint ventures were approved in 1979–80, twenty-four in 1981, and another eleven received approval in 1982, bring the cumulative total to fifty-seven (Table 3.2). At the end of 1981, twenty-seven joint ventures were reported in operation. The total investment[5] in the fifty-five joint ventures that have released financial data amounts to US$305 million, of which foreign investment amounts to US$144 million. The average foreign investment in joint ventures was US$4.86 million in 1979–1980 and slightly more than US$1 million in 1981–1982.

Very little detailed information about these joint ventures has been released, but from press reports we know that they range in size from very small enterprises such as the Quanzhou Artificial Paper Flower Factory (total investment: US$226,000), the Dongfang Glasses (Opticals) Co., Ltd. (US$203,000), and the Yanhua Standard Battery Company (US$130,000), to large hotel development projects such as the Great Wall Hotel[6] (US$72 million), the Jianguo Hotel (US$17.6 million), the Palace Hotel (US$60 million), and the Fuzhou Hotel (US$16 million). However, most are small and medium size enterprises. We know the total investment figures for fifty-six of the fifty-seven joint ventures in existence at the end of 1982, and of these, eighteen have total investment of less than US$500,000, another thirteen have total investment between US$500,000 and US$2 million, and only eight have total investment in excess of US$10 million. Table 3.2 shows that the amount of foreign investment involved in joint ventures is relatively small, particularly if the hotel ventures are excluded. The average amount of foreign investment in manufacturing joint ventures from 1979 to 1982 is only US$1.42 million. Of the fifty-five joint ventures for which we have financial information, twenty-nine have less than US$500,000 in foreign investment and only two have US$10 million or more. Of the thirty-six manufacturing joint ventures for which data is available, nineteen have less than US$500,000 in foreign investment and none has US$10 million or more.

The distribution of joint ventures by economic sector shows that, at the end of 1982, four are in agriculture, thirty-seven in manufacturing, and the remaining sixteen in services (mostly tourism). Thirty-three (37 percent) of the eighty-nine joint ventures in existence in September 1983 are with Hong Kong firms, nineteen involved U.S. firms, and twelve involved Japanese firms.[7] However, in terms of the amount of investment, U.S. firms lead all other countries with 34 percent of the total value of foreign investment in joint ventures. Other foreign participants are from Great Britain, the Philippines, West Germany, France, Belgium, Switzerland, Sweden, Thailand, Norway, and Australia.[8]

One suspects that, in terms of the amount of foreign investment absorbed and the sophistication of technology and managerial know-how transferred, the Chinese must be a little disappointed by what was accomplished through the joint venture mechanism by the end of 1982. Earlier it was noted that equity joint ventures provided only US$132 million of the approximately US$3 billion of foreign funds pledged to China through the various forms of special trade at the end of 1981 and US$144 million of the more than US$4 billion at the end of 1982. This is a relatively small figure, particularly in view of the initial enthusiasm for joint ventures expressed by both China and foreign firms and when compared to the amounts of foreign funds other forms of special trade have attracted. What must also be disappointing to the Chinese is that few large industrial joint ventures involving substantial technology transfer have been established. At the end of 1982, China-Schindler Elevator Company (total investment: US$16 million) and Sino-Swedish Pharmaceutical Co., Ltd. (total investment: US$12 million) were the only two known industrial joint ventures in China with total investment greater than US$10 million.[9] China-Schindler is also one of the few existing joint ventures that is committed to the transfer of a substantial amount of sophisticated technology to China during the life of the agreement. Judging by the products manufac-

Table 3.2   INTERNATIONAL JOINT VENTURES IN CHINA[a]

	1979–1980	1981	1982	Cumulative Total 1982 year end	Jan.-Sept. 1983
1. Number of agreements approved[b]	22	24	11	57	31[e]
2. Total investment (US$ million)[c]	227.04 (22)	55.49 (23)	22.94 (10)	305.47 (55)	393.88 (20)
Agriculture	5.19 (2)	0.46 (1)	0.42 (1)	6.07 (4)	0
Manufacturing	46.75 (13)	51.04 (18)	19.15 (5)	116.94 (36)	248.76 (10)
Services	175.10 (7)	3.99 (4)	3.37 (4)	182.46 (15)	145.12 (10)
3. Total foreign investment[d] (US$ million)	106.99 (22)	25.54 (23)	11.56 (10)	144.09 (55)	152.46 (20)
Agriculture	2.59 (2)	0.23 (1)	0.32 (1)	3.14 (4)	0
Manufacturing	18.56 (13)	22.87 (18)	9.63 (5)	51.06 (36)	87.70 (10)
Services	85.84 (7)	2.44 (4)	1.61 (4)	89.89 (15)	64.76 (10)
4. Average size of foreign investment (US$ million)	4.86 (22)	1.11 (23)	1.16 (10)	2.62 (55)	7.62 (55)
Agriculture	1.29 (2)	0.23 (1)	0.32 (1)	0.78 (4)	0
Manufacturing	1.43 (13)	1.27 (18)	1.93 (5)	1.42 (36)	8.77 (10)
Services	12.26 (7)	0.61 (4)	0.40 (4)	5.99 (15)	6.48 (10)
5. Number of joint ventures distributed by					
A. Economic sector					
Agriculture	2	1	1	4	0
Manufacturing	13	18	6	37	12
Services	7	5	4	16	19
B. Size of foreign investment					
Below 0.5 US$ million	9	13	7	29	4
0.5–2.0 US$ million	3	7	1	11	4
2.0–10.0 US$ million	8	3	2	13	7
10.0+ US$ million	2	0	0	2	5
C. Location					
Beijing, Shanghai, Tianjin	10	5	6	21	11
Guangdong and Fujian	9	9	3	21	16
Other coastal areas	1	5	1	7	2
Interior	2	5	1	8	2
6. Number of manufacturing joint ventures by size of foreign investment					
Below 0.5 US$ million	7	9	3	19	2
0.5–2.0 US$ million	2	6	0	8	0
2.0–10.0 US$ million	4	3	2	9	5
10.0+ US$ million	0	0	0	0	3

a. The number of joint ventures included in calculating totals and averages is shown in the parenthesis. The value of investment in US$ is obtained by using the exchange rate in existence when the contract was signed.
b. Because the date of approval of one of the eighty-nine joint venture agreements is not known, only the characteristics of eighty-eight joint ventures are included in this table. The excluded joint venture is a manufacturing enterprise, located in Guangdong, and has an initial total investment of US$8.5 million (of which 50 percent was contributed by the foreign participant).
c. Total investment "refers to the sum [total] of the capital construction funds needed for the production scale specified in the contract . . . and the circulating funds for production. . . . Therefore, the total amount of investment of a joint venture may generally consist of two categories, funds provided by the parties to the venture themselves and loans obtained in the name of the venture" ("Regulations for the Implementation of the Law of The People's Republic of China on Joint Ventures Using Chinese and Foreign Investment," 20 September 1983). However, from other sources, it is clear that any hotel ventures relied heavily on loans.
d. Estimated as the product of the foreign party's equity share (%) and the reported total investment.
e. Some still awaiting approval.
Source: Based on information released by the Ministry of Foreign Economic Relations and Trade and reproduced in *The China Business Review,* September-October, 1983, pp 21–25.

tured by the other industrial joint ventures (for example, yarn, knitware, rattan products, batteries, watch bands, plastic flowers, abrasive paper, animal feed, and the assembly of television sets), the technology and managerial skills to be transferred are not particularly sophisticated. These disappointments notwithstanding, fifty-seven joint ventures negotiated and approved in three and a half years is still a significant accomplishment. This is all the more so considering the complete lack of experience in joint ventures between Chinese and foreign firms and the still uncertain investment climate that exists in China.

As indicated in Table 3.1, the co-operative development of energy resources is another area where progress was relatively slow during the early years of the Open Door. This was perhaps to be expected, given the risk, the technical complexity, and the magnitude of the investment involved. During 1982, however, the pace of co-operative developments accelerated somewhat, as China opened forty-three offshore blocks to bidding by the private oil companies and also negotiated a preliminary agreement with a subsidiary of Occidental Petroleum for the development of a large open-pit coal mine at Pingshuo in Shanxi Province.[10] By the fall of 1983, negotiations over the Pingshuo coal project were still continuing, and other coal projects, such as the Fluor Corporation participation in two open-pit mines in Inner Mongolia, were also at various stages of negotiation. In offshore oil, rather greater progress had occurred, as exploration contracts were signed with eighteen of the twenty-five foreign oil companies that were active bidders on the offshore tracts.

Despite their slow beginning, industrial joint ventures and the co-operative development of energy resources — in the longer term — have tremendous potential for transferring modern technology and for absorbing foreign capital. In Chapters 4 and 6 respectively we shall examine these two areas in greater detail.

Geographically, the regions most actively involved in special trade are those along China's coast, particularly Guangdong. In the period 1979–81, the foreign investment pledged in special trade agreements in Guangdong added up to about US$2,600 million,[11] or about 85 percent of the national total. Of the processing fees paid by foreign buyers in 1980–81, 58 percent was earned by Guangdong enterprises;[12] one-third of the equipment pledged to China as part of compensation trade deals is destined for Guangdong;[13] and 83 percent of all foreign funds pledged to co-operative ventures are also for Guangdong.[14] Joint ventures are less concentrated in Guangdong, but most are located along the coast. Of the 57 joint ventures in existence at the end of 1982, 42 are in Guangdong, Fujian, and the three provincial-level municipalities, and only eight are in the interior (Table 3.2).

In view of this preponderance of Guangdong in the national totals, it is inevitable that the pattern of activity in that province, in terms of types of projects favored, is much like the national pattern. In the years 1979–81, most of the agreements in Guangdong (about 95 percent of the contracts) were for simple processing and assembling, but co-operative ventures accounted for most of the investment generated. In terms of investment actually in place at the end of 1981 (as distinct from the substantially larger amounts pledged in the contracts), the pattern in Guangdong was as follows:[15]

Processing and assembling	US$ 23.18 million	(4.5%)
Compensation trade	23.69 million	(4.6%)
Equity joint ventures	7.16 million	(1.4%)
Co-operative ventures	410.45 million	(79.7%)
Sole ownership	50.31 million	(9.8%)
Total	US$514.79 million	(100%)

After Guangdong, Shanghai has probably been the next most active — earning 13 percent of the processing fees paid to China in 1980–81 and accounting for 11 percent of the equipment pledged as part of compensation trade agreements.[16] At the end of 1981, Shanghai claimed 2,800 processing contracts (contracted fees, US$83 million; cumulative fees received as of 1981 year end, US$43 million). 116 compensation trade deals (value of equipment pledged, US$49.6 million), 27 co-operative ventures (foreign contribution pledged, US$6 million), and 2 equity joint venture agreements (foreign investment, US$6.4 million).[17] Between 1979 and 1982, Beijing absorbed about US$399 million of foreign funds through special trade arrangements, mostly through 79 compensation trade projects (US$240 million) and 9 equity joint ventures (US$83.48 million).[18] In Tianjin about US$30 million was channelled to Chinese enterprises through special trade agreements from 1978 to the end of 1981.[19] Most agreements were for processing (total fees earned in 1980–81 were about US$4 million),[20] but at the end of 1981 Tianjin also had 13 compensation trade agreements (value of equipment pledged, more than US$15 million), 4 co-operative ventures (foreign contribution pledged, US$4.3 million), and 5 equity joint ventures (foreign investment, more than US$4 million).[21] Between 1979 and the end of 1981, Liaoning (another key coastal province) received US$70.12 million in "foreign investment" through special trade arrangements, mostly in the form of processing agreements, compensation trade deals, and co-operative ventures.[22] The cumulative figures for Fujian at the end of 1981 were: about 2,000 processing contracts (fees received, US$10.4 million), 98 compensation trade deals (equipment pledged, US$18.4 million), 26 co-operative ventures (foreign contribution, US$19.8 million), and 8 equity joint ventures (foreign investment, about US$11.11 million).[23] That the initial geographic impact of the Open Door has been confined largely to the coast is perhaps best indicated by the following statistic: the coastal provinces and the three provincial level municipalities together accounted for about 95 percent of the processing fees earned by all Chinese enterprises in 1981.[24]

DEVELOPMENT IN THE SEZS

The geographic impact of the Open Door was actually even more concentrated than the data in the last section suggest, for fully 60 percent of the US$3 billion of foreign funds pledged to China at the end of 1981 has been promised to projects in China's Special Economic Zones at Shenzhen, Zhuhai, Shantou, and Xiamen.[25] Of the foreign funds committed to the SEZs, 80 percent is pledged to projects in Shenzhen, located adjacent to Hong Kong and the largest of the four SEZs.[26] Thus it might be said that, in geographic terms, the most notable feature of the typical Open Door venture is its physical proximity to Hong Kong.

Economic Reporter, a Hong Kong publication with close connections to sources in China, has released the most detailed data on development in Shenzhen (Table 3.3). According to this source, as of 31 August 1981, Shenzhen had signed a cumulative total of 814 special trade contracts with pledged foreign contributions amounting to HK$2,764 million (in 1981, US$1 = HK$5.64). Of this amount, 91 percent was from Hong Kong, 5.5 percent from other Overseas Chinese communities, and the remaining 3.5 percent from foreign countries. The actual amount of foreign investment in place in August 1981 was HK$1,000 million, about 36 percent of the pledged total. The Chinese have since reported that by the end of 1981 the number of special trade contracts in Shenzhen had increased to 1,000 and pledged foreign contributions had climbed to HK$8,558 million.[27] The sharp increase in pledged contributions was owing to the signing of several large property development projects at the end of 1981 and the beginning of 1982. By the end of 1982, the number of signed special trade contracts reached 1,628 with a total planned investment of HK$10 billion,[28] and by mid-1983 Shenzhen had signed a cumulative total of 2,011 special trade contracts with a total planned investment of HK$12.4 billion (two-thirds of which was accounted for by 58 property development projects).[29] As of June 1983, the actual amount of foreign investment in place was HK$2 billion.[30] It should be noted that the August 1981 figures, provided by *Economic Reporter,* exclude investments in the Shekou Special Industrial Zone (SSIZ). One suspects that the 1981 year-end and the 1983 mid-year figures may also exclude investments in SSIZ. In June 1982 SSIZ reported 36 signed contracts with pledged foreign investment totalling HK$600 million.[31] Thus the total amount of pledged foreign contributions to projects in Shenzhen (including SSIZ) was probably around HK$9,500 million in mid-1982 and may have exceeded HK$13 billion in mid-1983. In 1978, the rural town of Shenzhen had about 10 small-scale industrial enterprises, a total non-agricultural employment of about 5,000 and a gross value of industrial output (GVIO) of RMB ¥610,000. By the end of 1981, Shenzhen had 267 industrial enterprises, a regular industrial labor force of more than 12,000, and a GVIO of RMB ¥240 million.[32] But despite the large amount of pledged foreign contributions and the obvious increased tempo of industrial activity, the SEZs must still overcome some serious difficulties.

All four SEZs are located in non-industrialized regions. Shenzhen and Zhuhai are small communities that were formerly parts of rural communes. Shantou is a port city famous for its traditional handicrafts (lace and pottery), but it has no industrial base and is not linked by rail with the rest of China. Xiamen is a city of 300,000,[33] but because of its location (across the strait from Taiwan), it received little industrial investment in the past three decades and has in consequence only a small industrial base.[34] Thus, at the time the four SEZs were formed, they did not have the minimum industrial infrastructure (power, transport facilities, water, telecommunication, and so on) to support the rapid increase in industrial activities through international economic co-operation that the Chinese wanted.

At present, the lack of infrastructure is probably the most serious obstacle to the rapid development of the SEZs. The problem is exacerbated by two factors. First, since they are located in rural areas, the SEZs require not only investments in industrial infrastructure but also investments in dwellings and other social overhead capital to support the workers and their families who will be moving to the zones.[35] Thus, what is involved is not just the development of industrial estates but rather the more costly development of new urban communities. Secondly, because the central government has apparently decided to limit its contribution to the development of the SEZs, the cost of development is to be borne largely by the local governments, and it is not clear that they have sufficient resources for the job.[36] For example, to enable Shenzhen City to develop its SEZ, it is permitted, under a *baogan* arrangement with the central and the provincial governments, to keep all its revenues and foreign exchange earnings for five years (until 1985). But the revenue bases in Shenzhen and in the other SEZs are not broad enough to generate sufficient funds to finance the large amount of infrastructure construction that is required. So for the past several years the local authorities have looked

Table 3.3   PROJECTS IN SHENZHEN MUNICIPALITY[a] INVOLVING FOREIGN
PARTICIPATION, 31 AUGUST 1981

	Number of Contracts Approved	Planned Foreign Contribution (HK$ million)
Total	814[d]	2,764[e]
Distributed by type of arrangement	100%	100%
Processing/assembling	62.1	2.3
Compensation trade	.6	1.8
Cooperative venture	34.4	60.1
Fish culture[b]	(25.4)	(3.3)
Others	(9.0)	(56.8)
Joint venture	1.0	2.8
Sole foreign management[c]	1.8	33.0
Distributed by industry	100%	100%
Industry	66.1	16.3
Agriculture (include livestock and fishery)	26.0	4.1
Commerce	1.5	7.9
Tourism	2.5	28.3
Housing	2.8	39.5
Transportation	.9	.2
Others	.2	3.6

a. The data exclude Shekou Industrial Zone but include projects outside the SEZ but within the
   territory administered by Shenzhen City. The data are from *Jingji Daobao* [*Economic Reporter*], 11
   November 1981, p. 8. In June 1982, Shekou Industrial Zone had signed thirty-six contracts, of
   which twenty-six were in industry and ten in commerce. The total planned foreign contribution in
   Shekou was about HK$600 million.
b. Fish culture [*lailiao zhongyang*] is the arrangement under which the Chinese contribute land and
   labor and the foreign participant contributes the capital for land preparation (the excavation of the
   fish pond) and some equipment. All the fish are exported, and the earnings after expenses are
   divided between the Chinese and the foreign party according to the terms stipulated in the contract.
   The usual length of the contract is seven years, and at the end of the contract, the fish pond and the
   equipment belong to the Chinese party. The Chinese usually classify fish culture under processing,
   but the arrangement is more like a co-operative venture. For a more detailed discussion of the
   arrangement, see *Shijie Jingji Daobao*, [*World Economic Herald*], 28 September 1981, p. 10.
c. Under this arrangement, China leases the land to the foreign enterprise. All other aspects of the
   venture are the sole responsibility of the foreign party.
d. 595 were in operation and 126 were preparing to begin operation.
e. Of this amount, HK$2,510 million came from Hong Kong (91%), HK$150 million from other
   Overseas Chinese communities (5.5%), and HK$104 million from foreign countries. As of 31
   August 1981, the actual amount arrived was HK$1,000 million, about 36 percent of the pledged
   amount.

abroad for help to develop the SEZs.[37] It now appears that the pace of development
in the SEZs will depend to a significant degree on the extent to which Hong Kong
and other Overseas Chinese business interests are willing to become financially
involved in infrastructure and property development in the zones. In the latter part
of 1981 and 1982, several agreements were reached under which Hong Kong
business groups will plan and finance the urban development of specific areas in

the Shenzhen SEZ.[38] These very large property development projects are the reason why Shenzhen accounts for such a large share of the "foreign investment" in China.

Given their rural locations, the SEZs must look to the surrounding rural communes for their primary source of labor. The experience to date is that workers from these communes are unskilled and unaccustomed to factory work.[39] The lack of a disciplined industrial work force is therefore another obstacle the SEZs must overcome. This problem is somewhat less serious in Xiamen because of its much larger population of high school graduates. But even in Xiamen the supply of experienced skilled workers is limited. To supply enterprises in its SEZ with skilled workers, Xiamen is planning to "borrow" them from established enterprises in the city. The "lenders" will receive from the city what the "borrowed" workers used to earn, partly to compensate for the loss of skilled workers and partly to ensure that slots will be held open for the "borrowed" workers should they need to return to their old jobs in the future.

Skilled workers and modern technology are complementary inputs, and if skilled workers are not available to the SEZs, then the zones will not be an effective channel for the transfer of modern technology, nor will they be very attractive to potential foreign investors. The Chinese recognize this problem and have promised that enterprises in the SEZs may recruit workers from other parts of the province. Presumably the central ministries and other provinces that are involved in the Shenzhen SEZ will also supply some of the skilled workers that are needed from enterprises they control in other parts of China. But, even with these flexibilities, the problem will not be solved easily. Chinese workers are not very mobile. For example, a Chinese worker cannot leave his enterprise without its permission, and very few enterprises are willing to part with skilled workers. In addition, the skilled workers themselves may be reluctant to move and give up the personal contacts and goodwill, so important to job security and welfare, in the old surroundings to begin another career in a totally new environment.

A third problem that has troubled the development of the SEZs is bureaucracy. The Chinese are hoping that the SEZs will become something like an "export processing zone." One major advantage of export processing zones in other parts of the world is that they are relatively free of government red tape and bureaucracy. It is as yet uncertain that the Chinese can achieve the same type of bureaucracy-free environment in the SEZs. In 1981, the Secretary of the Guangdong Communist Party spoke of the "selfish departmentalism" that was blocking the implementation of the open door policy in the SEZs.[40] Reorganization of the SEZ administration has reduced the red tape somewhat, but it is still the case that foreign investors must deal with many government departments.[41] Another problem is the lack of competent middle-level administrators with the authority and willingness to make decisions. Of course, if the problem of bureaucracy persists, it will defeat the very purpose of having SEZs.

The problems discussed above are reflected in the types of international economic co-operation projects that have been attracted to Shenzhen to date (see Table 3.3).[42] Because of the lack of industrial infrastructure, only 16 percent of the foreign funds pledged to Shenzhen as of 31 August 1981 involved industrial activities, and this share declined to 12 percent by mid-1983.[43] Most of the industrial projects are small, and many involve activities that could be contracted to rural households. In mid-1982, the only part of Shenzhen that was ready to receive medium and large industrial enterprises was the just completed SSIZ, the development of which was entirely financed by a central ministry through the CMSNC. In August 1981 nearly 40 percent of the foreign funds pledged to projects in Shenzhen were for property development, and by mid-1983 property development projects accounted for over two-thirds of the foreign funds pledged to Shenzhen. In terms of numbers, most international economic co-operation projects involved processing and fish culture, where technology transfer is extremely limited. In the long run, it will not be property development nor the small processing projects but rather the larger industrial co-operative and joint ventures that will determine the success or failure of the SEZs. The Chinese are keenly aware of this, and indeed the Shenzhen SEZ authority has repeatedly expressed its wish to have more skill- and capital-intensive manufacturing projects. In September 1983, this desire was made even more explicit when the Shenzhen authority, to encourage interests among potential foreign investors, released its list of sixty desired projects in nine priority areas (electronics, machinery, petrochemicals, food, construction materials, textiles, apparel, and light industries).[44]

The development cost and the potential impact of industrializing the SEZs are difficult to gauge, partly because the Chinese have said little about what they expect the cost to be and partly because overall plans for the SEZs have not been finalized.[45] Based on what little we do know, an attempt is made in Table 3.4 to make a rough-and-ready estimate of the infrastructure cost and the employment impact of industrializing the SEZs. The cost of developing the industrial estates that are currently in the Chinese plans and of developing the related urban facilities needed to support the workers who will be employed in these estates is estimated at about RMB ¥5.3 billion in 1981 prices. The most optimistic employment projection, assuming that the Chinese establish all the industrial estates currently in their plans and that they are fully utilized, is that about 189,000 industrial workers will be employed in the SEZs by the end of this century.

Given the economic conditions in South China, most, but not all, of the industrial workers who will be employed in the SEZs will be workers who otherwise would either be unemployed or employed in jobs of low productivity. Thus, in terms of employment, the SEZs represent a net gain to China. In addition, since all the industrial activities will be producing for the export market, the foreign exchange benefits will also be substantial. Finally, and most impor-

Table 3.4 ESTIMATED COST OF DEVELOPING INDUSTRIAL ZONES AND PROJECTED INDUSTRIAL EMPLOYMENT IN CHINA'S SEZs

	Size of designated industrial zones (km²)	Cost of infrastructure in industrial zones (RMB ¥ mil.)	Cost of related urban construction (RMB ¥ million)	Projected industrial employment in industrial zone (thous.)
Shenzhen	16.7[c]	2,088[d]	1,670[e]	80[f]
Zhuhai	3.11[g]	400[h]	300[e]	24[f]
Shantou (Longhu)[a]	1.6[a]	160[i]	240[i]	50[j]
Xiamen (Huli)[b]	2.0[k]	200[k]	300[k]	35[k]
Total	23.41	2,848	2,510	189

Notes

a. According to the *Beijing Review*, 14 December 1981, p. 20, the Shantou SEZ consists of the Longhu export processing zone (1.6 km²), a port area (1.7 km²), an integrated agricultural area (10 km²), and a tourist zone (Maya Island and parts of Chaoyang County).

b. In addition to enterprises in the Huli export processing zone, enterprises in other parts of Xiamen that have foreign participation and produce primarily for export may also enjoy SEZ privileges.

c. The Shenzhen SEZ measures 327.6 km². Of this, 16.7 km² is now reserved for industrial zones — 2 km² in Shekou, 2.7 km² in Shangbu, 6 km² in Shake, and 6 km² in locations yet to be decided. See Wang Zhengxian, "Special economic zones and our country's employment problem," *Jingji Tequ Dili Wenji* [Collected Essays on the Geography of SEZs], Zhongshan University, Department of Geography, October 1981, p. 33. Cai Renqun (quoted in David K. Y. Chu, "The Cost of the Four Special Economic Zones in China," Chinese University of Hong Kong, Department of Geography and Geographical Research Centre Occasional Paper No. 25, February 1982, p. 5) reports a total industrial area of 15 km². This figure, however, excludes the area reserved for roads and support facilities.

d. The cost of infrastructure (land preparation, roads, water, sewers, electricity, and telecommunications) is estimated to be RMB ¥125 million per km² (interview notes, Shenzhen SEZ Development Co.). 16.7 km² multiplied by RMB ¥125 million per km² equals RMB ¥2,088 million.

e. David K.Y. Chu, p. 10. Chu bases his estimates on the assumption that urban population in Shenzhen will reach 1 million in 2000 A.D. (urban population in 1979 was 30,000) and in Zhuhai County will reach 200,000 (25,000 in 1979). The Chinese estimate that it costs about RMB ¥1,700 per person to provide urban living accommodations of 6 m² per person. The estimates also include a small sum for the renovation of existing facilities.

f. Wang Zhengxian, pp. 33–34. For Shenzhen, Wang estimates employment to be 87,000, of which 7,000 will be engaged in the tourism industry. For Zhuhai, Wang estimates employment to be 25,000 of which 1,000 will be in tourism.

g. Zhuhai SEZ consists of 6.91 km², of which 45 percent (3.11 km²) is for industrial use. Wang Zhengxian cites a figure of 2.27 km² for the industrial area at Zhuhai, but this may be a net figure — that is, after deducting the area for roads and other support facilities.

h. Zhuhai SEZ Office, quoted in *Gang-Ao Jingji* [The Economies of Hong Kong and Macao], 1981, No. 6, p. 48.

i. Because conditions in Longhu and Huli are similar, we estimate the Longhu figure as 0.8 that of Huli (1.6 km²/2.0 km²).

j. *China's Foreign Trade*, April 1982, p. 10. The tentative plan for the Longhu processing zone projects that the zone — when completed — will have 250 enterprises with 50,000 employees.

k. Interview notes, Huli Export Processing Zone. The Huli processing zone is comprised of an industrial area of 2 km² and a wharf area of 0.5 km².

tant, China is expecting to derive some extremely important dynamic benefits from the foreign technology and skills attracted to the SEZs.

However, it should be noted that the amount of industrial employment that is likely to be generated in the SEZs, though important, will not be very large when viewed in the Chinese context. One also suspects that there are less costly ways to create industrial employment, earn foreign exchange, and acquire foreign technology than by developing SEZs from scratch in relatively remote locations. But, of course, these SEZs provide China with something it values highly — that is, a mechanism for absorbing foreign capital, modern technology, capitalist commercial practices, and foreign ideas that does not at the same time undermine its own institutions or expose a large number of its population to "undesirable" foreign influences. The zones become even more attractive from the Chinese viewpoint if a substantial share of the development cost is financed by foreign capital.

The time has now arrived to discuss some specific open door ventures on a case-by-case basis. The next three chapters will examine equity joint ventures, alternatives to the equity joint venture, and energy projects respectively.

4

The Development of Equity Joint Ventures in China: July 1979–June 1983

As early as mid-1978, reports were circulating that China would be willing to accept foreign direct investment. By early 1979 it was widely known that the Chinese government was drafting regulations for joint ventures. "The Law on Joint Ventures Using Chinese and Foreign Investment" was adopted on 1 July 1979 at the Second Session of the Fifth National People's Congress and promulgated on 8 July. Ten months later, when the joint venture agreement to establish the Beijing Air Catering Company was approved by the Chinese Foreign Investment Administration Commission, foreign direct investment in China became a reality.[1]

The reason for any joint venture is that each participant has something the other lacks and wants. What China lacks and wants is fairly clear. To develop its economy, China needs to import modern industrial technology and learn new marketing skills and managerial know-how, but it lacks sufficient foreign exchange to purchase what it needs outright. In joint ventures, China has a mechanism that allows it to acquire not only some of the technology it needs but also the foreign investment to help finance the acquisition. That the joint venture, because it involves local participation, gives the host country substantial control over its operation undoubtedly helps to make foreign investment more acceptable to the Chinese. China is also aware that successful transfer of complex technology, marketing know-how, and managerial skills requires a sustained relationship between the transferor and the recipient and that this is likely to occur extensively only under certain institutional arrangements, of which the joint venture is one of the most important.[2]

At the general level, one can think of at least four reasons why foreign firms may be interested in investing in joint ventures in China. The first is China's domestic market. Foreign businessmen have long dreamed of selling to China with its population of one billion. By now, this dream is tempered by the recognition that low per capita income, central planning, and a shortage of hard currency severely constrain what China is willing and able to import. But, in areas where China has assigned high priority, whether in manufacturing or in the services (for example, tourism), the joint venture mechanism is one way foreign firms may gain access to markets that would otherwise be closed to them. A second reason is China's potential as an export platform because of its proximity to the Asian markets that foreign firms want to serve and because of its abundant supply of unskilled and semi-skilled workers. The joint venture is a vehicle for technology transfer, so a third reason is the income foreign firms can expect from selling technology to China. Finally, foreign firms' interest in new stable sources of supply of fuels and minerals, coupled with China's vast undeveloped natural resources, provide a fourth reason for foreign businessmen's interest in joint ventures in China. Since natural resource development requires large initial investment and involves considerable risk, there are grounds to believe that in this area China may also be interested in the joint venture formula.

Of the many forms of international economic cooperation currently used by the Chinese, the joint venture departs most dramatically from China's previous practice of arm's-length trade. Its main characteristics are the sharing of management, of risk, and of ownership and profits by the participants. More than any of the other special trade arrangements, the joint venture intertwines the interests of the foreign firm and the local enterprise, and it can be presumed that the two parties share a common objective — the commercial success of the venture. Because of this similarity in objective, the joint venture is generally considered to be an effective vehicle for the transfer of technology and organizational and management skills from the foreign participant to the local enterprise. However, when the interests of the participants diverge, as they sometimes do in the course of the enterprise's development, the sharing of control and of ownership may create a serious problem because decision-making becomes difficult if not impossible. Given the inherent characteristics of the joint venture, its development in China depends critically on the ability of the Chinese and of the foreign businessmen to identify areas of mutual interest and to create ways to resolve conflicts.

The purpose of this chapter is to examine the environment for and the recent experience with joint ventures in China. It begins by discussing the emerging legal and economic framework for international joint ventures in China and then considers two case studies for the industrial realm.

THE EMERGING LEGAL AND ECONOMIC FRAMEWORK FOR JOINT VENTURES*

Because the viability of joint ventures depends on the political and economic systems in which they exist and must operate, the two most fundamental obstacles that stand in the way of their development in China are China's underdeveloped legal system and the significant differences between the Chinese and the Western economic systems. To foreign businessmen, direct investment implies ownership. But what does foreign ownership mean in China, where the means of production may be owned only by the whole people (that is, by the state) or collectively by the working people?[3] What protection do international joint ventures have under China's legal system, and how secure is that protection? Because the state has such extensive power in China, foreign investors are understandably concerned about the rules that govern the relationship between the joint venture and the state and between the joint venture and the rest of the economy. What degree of independence will international joint ventures have in China? When state interests and private interests conflict, how will this be resolved? To what extent will joint ventures be integrated into the centrally planned and managed economy? What authority will joint ventures have in such areas as finance and labour management? Since 1979 China has devoted much effort and energy to providing satisfactory answers to these and other questions and to working with foreign businessmen to bridge some of the differences between the Chinese and Western legal and economic systems.

The task of drafting a law to govern international joint ventures was greatly complicated by China's primitive legal system. In 1979, China did not have a company law, a contract law, or a commercial law, so that to create the legal framework for joint ventures in a single code would have been incredibly cumbersome and complex. Rather than drafting such a comprehensive law, China chose instead to produce a joint venture law of only fifteen broadly worded articles that declared a national policy of allowing foreign direct investment in China in the form of joint ventures but left the detailed rules and regulations to future legal pronouncements.[4] China has since supplemented its joint venture law with numer-

---

*The legal and economic environment described in this chapter is for the period from July 1979 to June 1983. In August-September 1983, China promulgated several new regulations concerning joint ventures in China and revised its joint venture tax law. As a consequence, the investment climate in China has improved somewhat. In our discussion, the areas affected by the new regulations or by the changes in the tax law are marked with an asterisk (*), and readers are referred to Chapter 7 for a discussion of the changes.

ous regulations and laws concerning joint ventures. As of June 1983, the following laws and regulations had been promulgated:[5] "The Law on Joint Ventures Using Chinese and Foreign Investment"; "Regulations on the Registration of Joint Ventures Using Chinese and Foreign Investment"; "Regulations on Labor Management in Joint Ventures Using Chinese and Foreign Investment"; "The Income Tax Law Concerning Joint Ventures with Chinese and Foreign Investment"; "Individual Income Tax Law"; "Detailed Rules and Regulations for the Implementation of the Income Tax Law Concerning Joint Ventures with Chinese and Foreign Investment"; "Detailed Rules and Regulations for the Implementation of the Income Tax Law Concerning Joint Ventures with Chinese and Foreign Investment"; "Detailed Rules and Regulations for the Implementation of the Individual Income Tax Law"; "Provisional Regulations for Exchange Control"; and "Provisional Regulations for Providing Loans to Joint Ventures of Chinese and Foreign Ownership by the Bank of China." These laws and regulations plus the official interpretations and policy statements constitute the emerging legal and economic framework that governs the formation, organization, and operation of joint ventures in China.

Formation and Organization

The rules governing the formation and the organization of joint ventures in China are, by now, well known and require only a brief summary. The joint venture law "permits foreign companies, enterprises, other economic entities or individuals . . . to incorporate themselves, within the territory of the People's Republic of China, into joint ventures with Chinese companies, enterprises or other economic entities."[6] The initiative to form a joint venture may be taken either by the Chinese or the foreign party. To proceed with formal negotiation, the Chinese participant must have the consent of its leading body. If the preliminary discussion proves fruitful, the participants then proceed to prepare economic and technical feasibility studies of the proposed venture. When agreement is reached, the signed contract, agreement, and articles of association along with the feasibility studies and other documents are submitted to the Ministry of Foreign Economic Relations and Trade (MFERT) for approval.[7] The joint venture contract should include, among other things, the amount and the form of investment, the main production equipment and technology to be used and their source of supply, how profit and losses are to be shared among the participants, how raw materials are to be supplied, the share of output to be sold within China and abroad, stipulations governing wages, labor welfare, and labor management, and procedures for dispute settlement. It should be noted, however, that MFERT is not only a review body; it also monitors the negotiation that precedes the agreement.[9] Within one month after the approval, the joint venture must register with the local administrative bureau for industry and commerce in the province or municipality where the venture is located, and it is considered officially established on the date the General Administration for Industry and Commerce issues its license.[10]

Joint ventures are to be organized as limited liability companies, and the foreign participant(s) shall in general contribute not less than 25 percent of the venture's registered capital.[11] The capital contribution may take a variety of forms, including cash, material goods (*shiwu*), industrial property rights, and (for the Chinese participant only) "the right to the use of a site." Except for the site, the value of all such contributions shall be jointly assessed or be determined by a mutually agreed third party.[12] The duration of the joint venture will depend on its "particular line of business and circumstances" and is to be negotiated between the participants.[13] If the participants agree, the length of the agreement may be extended. Early termination is also possible if the joint venture is suffering from heavy losses or if any participants fail to execute their obligations under the agreement. Each joint venture is to be headed by a board of directors composed of individuals appointed by the participants, but with the chairman appointed by the Chinese and one or two vice-chairmen by the foreign participant.[15] The remaining composition of the board, which is determined through consultation between the participants, is to be stipulated in the contract. The board of directors "is empowered to discuss and take action on . . . all fundamental issues concerning the venture," including the appointment of the general manager, the assistant manager(s), the chief engineer, the treasurer, and the auditors from "the various parties to the joint venture."[16] The Chinese describe the chairman of the board as the legal representative of the joint venture and the general manager as the person who implements the decisions of the board and administers the day-to-day operation of the enterprise.[17]

The above rules and regulations have raised numerous issues.[18] Most are legal points, but several have considerable general interest. First of all, does the fact that no maximum amount of foreign ownership is mentioned in the joint venture law imply that 100 percent foreign-owned enterprises are permitted in China? The answer appears to be a qualified yes. Eighteen enterprises that are entirely financed by foreigners already exist in the Guangdong Special Economic Zones[19], and the Chinese have not ruled out 100 percent foreign-financed projects in places other than the SEZs and indeed have stated that such proposals would be considered on a case-by-case basis.[20] However, it is unclear whether 100 percent foreign-owned enterprises outside the SEZs would be treated as joint ventures or be governed by new rules.[21] It also appears that 100 percent foreign ownership is still a politically sensitive issue so that even if it is permitted it is likely to occur only rarely outside the SEZs.

Second, the joint venture law permits the Chinese participant to a joint venture, if it already has the right to the use of a site, to include that right as part of its investment and stipulates that China is to determine unilaterally the value of the right. Subsequently, the Chinese have stated that the value of the right to the use of a site is to be set by local governments and is to be equivalent to the site use fees that the joint venture would otherwise have to pay.[22] However, it is unclear whether the value is the simple sum or the present value of the site use fees to be paid during the period of the joint venture agreement. In any case, since a genuine real estate market does not exist in China, the amount of the site use fee is likely to be a point of controversy between the Chinese and the foreign investors. However, it should be noted that the Chinese government does pay "negotiated" compensations for land it takes from communes that border the cities, so that it does have some idea of the "market value" of urban land.[23] The Chinese participant, of course, has the option of not including the site as part of its contribution. In this case, the joint venture pays the Chinese government an annual fee (rent) for the use of the site. While this option eliminates the need to assign a value to the right of using a site, it does not resolve the issue that an annual fee still needs to be set. Jerome Cohen and Owen Nee have noted that if China attempts to exploit its power to assess the value of the site unilaterally and the foreign investor protests, then even the valuation of the site may be negotiated.[24] Recent developments suggest that this may indeed happen. To calm prospective foreign investors troubled by reports that the Chinese have sometimes based the value of land rental upon prices in Europe, New York, and Hong Kong, a group of Chinese economists visiting Hong Kong in 1980 indicated that land rental value would be determined through "consultation."[25]

Third, the joint venture law does not give the criteria that China uses to judge investment applications nor does it give much guidance to potential investors as to the type of joint ventures preferred or the type of information they need to submit in support of their applications. The lack of specific information on these matters is partly owing to the fact that in 1979 China did not have a clear industrialization strategy and partly to a desire to remain as flexible as possible in an area where it has had no experience.[26] But the lack of guidance and information also increases the transaction cost of investing in China, since potential investors must devote an inordinate amount of time and resources to determining what the Chinese want and how proposals should be prepared. In response to persistent inquiries from aboard some general guidelines have emerged.

In terms of industry, the order of priority for joint venture investment in the first half of the 1980s is 1) light industry, textiles, foodstuffs, pharmaceuticals, and electronics; 2) coal, building materials, machine-building, iron and steel and chemical industries; 3) agriculture, animal husbandry, and aquatic products; and 4) tourism and services.[27] Within these industries, China desires joint ventures that 1) employ advanced technology and scientific management methods, increase product variety, and conserve energy and raw materials; 2) require small initial investment, have short gestation periods, and utilize existing enterprises as much as possible; 3) train technicians and managerial personnel; and 4) can export and earn foreign exchange. In other words what China is looking for is joint ventures that will help it to fill its capital, technology, and management gaps. It is also clear that China wants to avoid importing technology that it already has and to avoid joint ventures that are not feasible in terms of their raw material and energy requirements. The authorities are also interested in the project's *xiaoguo* or "effectiveness," a concept roughly equivalent to the rate of return. Employment creation through the use of labor-intensive technology is not a particularly important goal, since the Chinese take the view that the ability of joint ventures to influence the country's overall employment level is minimal. In any case, because the Chinese want joint ventures to export, they are concerned about product quality, which is often dependent on the use of a more capital-intensive technology. On the whole, these general criteria are consistent with China's current policy of economic readjustment. But they are not carved in stone, and one suspects that they will undergo alterations in the future if China's economic policy changes.

Finally, Article 5 of the joint venture law has raised considerable concern among potential foreign investors. In its English translation, the article reads in part: "The technology or equipment contributed by any foreign participant as investment shall be truly advanced and appropriate to China's needs. In cases of losses caused by deception through the intentional provision of outdated equipment or technology, compensation shall be paid for the losses." The obvious question is: by what standards will China judge technology to be "truly advanced and appropriate"? Technologies that are not up-to-date by world standards may nevertheless be very appropriate to China's needs. The confusion created by article 5 was largely the result of poor translation. The Chinese text of the joint venture law does not speak of "truly advanced and appropriate to China's needs" but "advanced and truly appropriate to China's needs" (*bixu queshi shi shihe wo guo xuyao de xianjin jishu*). The Chinese have since assured foreign investors that by advanced and truly appropriate they mean a technology that is advanced, dependable, and practical *in* China and that as long as the foreign participant has made clear to his Chinese counterpart the true vintage of the equipment he plans to supply he is not in jeopardy of violating Article 5.

Protection and Incentives

The Chinese recognize that unless foreign investors feel secure and have reasonable prospects of making profits, they are not likely to participate in joint ventures in China. At a general level, the Chinese government has seized every opportunity to underline its firm commitment to its current foreign investment policy, even to the extent of including the foreigners' right to invest in China in its revised constitution.[28] More specifically, the joint venture law protects the resources that foreigners invest in joint ventures and their right to dispose of their property and to remit their share of the after-tax profits and other funds abroad.[29]

The joint venture law does not directly address the issue of nationalization, but Chinese officials have gone to great pains to assure foreign investors that "under normal circumstances, the Chinese government will not requisition the industrial property of foreign investors" and that if it is "compelled by some irresistible factors or by the needs of public interests to requisition some [foreign] industrial property," it will be done according to law and that "reasonable compensation" will be made.[30] However, China has not as yet disclosed the procedure it will follow in case of nationalization or the legal relief that will be made available to foreign investors. Because industrial property rights are likely to make up a substantial share of the foreign participant's contributions to a joint venture, foreign investors are understandably disturbed that the joint venture law is silent on the issue of industrial property rights, particularly in view of the fact that China does not have a patent law and is not a signatory to the Paris Convention.[31] The inclusion of a "non-disclosure" clause in the joint venture agreement may provide a degree of protection, but the enforcement of such a clause may prove problematic in China.

In addition to its statutory guarantee, China has offered, through the People's Insurance Company of China, to insure joint ventures against political risk. It is curious that a state should offer insurance against its own actions, but with provincial governments gaining increasing power over economic matters, joint ventures may find the insurance useful as a protection against arbitrary actions at the local level. Perhaps more important was the signing on 30 October 1980 of an agreement between China and the United States under which China accepted the principal of subrogation, whereby the U.S. government, through the Overseas Private Investment Corporation (OPIC), "would acquire the right of an aggrieved [U.S.] company" with investment in China, thus transforming a "government-company dispute into a government-government dispute."[32] This, in turn, permitted OPIC to extend political risk insurance to private U.S. investment in China. A more recent development is the signing of a bilateral investment protection agreement between China and Sweden. Similar arrangements are currently under discussion between China and other capitalist countries.

With the announcement of the long-awaited income tax laws and foreign exchange regulations in 1980, the incentive framework for foreign direct investment in China became substantially clearer. The income of joint ventures "after deduction of costs, expenses, and losses" is taxed at a basic rate of 30 percent or an effective rate of 33 percent when the 10 percent local surtax is included.[33] In addition, a tax of 10 percent is levied on that portion of profits remitted abroad.[34] (The tax law, in both its Chinese text and its English translation, refers to this as an "income tax," but this is a clear misnomer.) Fixed assets are to be depreciated on a straight-line basis, with a minimum depreciation period of twenty years for buildings and ten years for machinery and equipment used in production.[35] However, the Ministry of Finance is willing to entertain requests to accelerate depreciation. Intangible assets such as the right to the use of a site, trademarks, and copyrights are to be amortized over ten years or the period of use as specified in the joint venture agreement.[36] Losses may be carried over for a maximum of five years, and foreign tax credits are possible.[37] As has already been discussed in Chapter 2, China's SEZs function under a legal regime separate from the framework governing foreign investment in other parts of China. In the area of taxes, the major differences are that joint ventures in the SEZs are taxed at 15 percent instead of 33 percent and do not pay the 10 percent tax on profits remitted abroad.[38]

Tax incentives available to joint ventures, as announced in 1980, include the following. Joint ventures scheduled to operate for ten years or more may be exempted from income tax in their first profitable year and be allowed a 50 percent tax reduction in the second and third profitable years.* Moreover, joint ventures in low profit sectors such as farming and forestry or located in underdeveloped regions may be allowed a 15 to 30 percent reduction of their income tax for a period of ten years beyond the initial exemption or reduction.[39] If a joint venture reinvests its profit in China for at least five years, it may be granted a 40 percent refund of the tax paid on the reinvested amount.[40] Finally, the joint venture law — but not the joint venture income tax law — mentions that joint ventures with "up-to-date technology by world standards may apply for a reduction of or exemption from income tax for the first two to three profit-making years."[41] What technology would qualify and how much reduction would be granted are not specified; presumably these are matters for negotiation. It is important to note that these tax reductions and exemptions are not automatically available to all qualified joint ventures. Rather they are granted at the discretion of the Chinese Ministry of Finance, suggesting that whether or not a joint venture's application for tax relief is approved will depend as much on China's fiscal needs at the time as on the merit of the application.

In addition to the income tax, the joint venture is also liable to other Chinese taxes including customs duties, the consolidated industrial and commercial tax (a broadly based turn-over tax imposed on import purchases and on sale and service proceeds)[42], the real estate tax (a local tax on urban real estate), and the vehicle license tax.[43] However, under certain circumstances, joint ventures are exempt from some of these taxes.[44] For example, joint ventures are exempt from import duties and the consolidated industrial and commercial tax (CICT) on advanced equipment imported as part of the foreign participant's contribution to the venture, provided the equipment cannot be purchased in China. Joint ventures may also apply to the Ministry of Finance and the General Administration of Customs for 1) the exemption of import duties and the CICT on raw materials, parts, components, and packing materials imported for the production of export goods* and 2) the exemption of the CICT on goods (excluding restricted export goods) exported. To complete the tax picture, it should be mentioned that, under the Chinese individual income tax law, foreign personnel working in China, depending on the length of residency, may be subject to China's income tax.[45]

To international investors what is relevant is not so much the Chinese taxes per se but how they compare with the tax environment found elsewhere. For potential investors interested in China, the relevant alternative is probably another developing economy in Asia. Table 4.1 presents the effective tax rate on profits found in selected parts of Asia. The comparison shows that the Chinese rate is about average — lower than that in Malaysia, the Philippines, and Singapore, higher than that in South Korea and Taiwan, and about the same as that in Thailand. However, substantial tax incentives are available in many of these economies, so that the tax environment for joint ventures may be significantly different than is suggested by the nominal tax rates on profits. Since in a high-risk environment foreign investors are anxious to recover their investments in as short a period of time as possible, the most important tax incentive is the tax holiday on corporate income tax. Because of differences in details, a precise comparison of this incentive for selected Asian economies is not possible. But a rough comparison of the length of tax holiday (Table 4.1) suggests that the Chinese incentive is less generous than what is available in other parts of Asia. From the comments they have received from foreign businessmen about the joint venture income tax law, the Chinese apparently have also come to the same conclusion.[46]

The unwritten rule that each joint venture must cover its own foreign exchange needs* and the policy of limiting foreign investment to fixed periods are two aspects of China's policy towards international joint ventures that have worked to reduce the incentives to foreigners to invest in China.

Table 4.1   EFFECTIVE TAX RATES ON PROFITS AND NUMBER OF YEARS OF TAX HOLIDAY IN SELECTED ASIAN ECONOMIES, 1981

	Effective tax rate on profits[a]	Tax holiday (number of years)
China	33%[b]	3[c] (exemption — 1 year, reduction — 2 years)
Malaysia	44.5%	2–5[d]
Philippines	35%	none
Republic of Korea	25%	8 (exemption — 5 years, reduction — 3 years)
Taiwan	maximum effective rate not to exceed 22%–25% (depending on industry)	5 (or the use of accelerated depreciation)
Singapore	40%	15 (exemption — 5 years, reduction — 10 years)
Thailand	29.5%	13 (exemption — 8 years, reduction — 5 years)

a. Assuming an industrial joint venture with a total investment of US$5 million and a 20 percent pre-tax rate of return on investment.

b. 30 percent if local surtax is excluded.

c. If the joint venture is located in an underdeveloped region or is engaged in a low profit industry, such as farming and forestry, a tax reduction of 15 percent to 30 percent for ten years beyond the original three may be granted.

d. The precise period depends on the size of the investment and the number of workers employed. Exemption may be extended to ten years if the enterprise produces a priority product, meets the local content requirement, or is located in a "development area."

Sources: Based on information in Federal Industrial Development Authority, *Malaysia, A Basic Guidebook for Potential Investors* (Kuala Lumpur, 1977); ROK, Economic Planning Board, *Guide to Investment in Korea* (Seoul, 1979); Industrial Development and Investment Center, *Investor's Guide* (Taipei, 1980); SGV & Co., *Doing Business in the Philippines* (Manila, 1982); and *Economic Bulletin for Asia and the Pacific*, v. 27, no. 2.

Although the joint venture law encourages joint ventures "to market their products outside of China,"[47] it does not require them to do so. Nor does the law require the joint venture to earn adequate foreign exchange before it can repatriate profits.[48] However, government statements issued since the announcement of the joint venture law and the negotiation experience so far suggest that unless a proposed venture is prepared to cover its foreign exchange needs (including profit repatriation) from its own foreign exchange earnings, it is unlike to receive approval.* The MFERT has made it quite clear that

in examining and approving a proposed joint venture, it is necessary to take into consideration the ability of the proposed enterprise to secure enough foreign exchange to pay the foreign participant his share of profits and the wages of the foreign employees, buy on the international market materials that have to be imported for its own use and cover the expenses of foreign exchange in its own day-to-day operation.[49]

In the same statement, the Ministry announced that "there are no fast rules on the proportion between domestic and overseas sales [by joint ventures]. The proportion should be worked out by the participants in the joint venture, on condition that the joint venture's foreign exchange balance is ensured." In fact, a joint venture may sell all its output in China only when the product is one that China is importing in large quantity, and even then the joint venture should sell part of its output to China's "foreign trade or other departments in exchange for foreign exchange to help balance"[50] its own foreign exchange earnings and outlays.

The requirement that the foreign exchange earned by a joint venture be at least equal to its foreign exchange outlays is likely to make many ventures in China look less inviting and certainly more risky to foreign investors. This is partly because the world market is more competitive than the Chinese domestic market and partly because it is uncertain that joint ventures, operating in the Chinese economic environment, can meet the quality standards and strict deadlines demanded by international buyers. From China's viewpoint, the requirement has at least two advantages. It helps to keep China's international trade in closer balance and thus reduces the pressure on its balance of payments, and by exposing joint ventures to international competition, it forces them to improve quality and become efficient more quickly. However, the rule (particularly if it is strictly enforced, as it currently appears to be),[51] is also likely to create inefficiency in the allocation of foreign exchange and to discourage worthwhile industrial joint ventures that are beneficial to China's long-term development but that cannot easily generate foreign exchange in the short run.

The Chinese have consistently expressed the view that the foreign participant's share in a joint venture must revert to Chinese ownership after a fixed period. Thus, during the negotiation of the joint venture agreement, two of the terms discussed must be 1) the duration of the joint venture and 2) the compensation to be paid to the foreign participant for his share of the venture at termination. While the first issue can be settled in a straightforward manner, the second is more difficult to resolve. Presumably both parties would be satisfied if the foreign participant is paid his share of the venture's worth (the present value of its future profits) at termination. But how can the worth of a venture at termination (or its future profits) be determined before it is even established? Obviously, it cannot. Thus, the two parties would either have to agree on a formula price based on the venture's book value (such as net worth as shown by the balance sheet at termination) or on negotiating the venture's worth at the end of the contract period. Neither approach is entirely satisfactory, the former because a firm's market value and its book value may differ substantially and in ways impossible to predict, and the latter because, with only one possible buyer, the foreign participant is dependent on the goodwill of the Chinese partner to negotiate fairly.[52] Therefore, it would appear that the limitation of foreign investment to a fixed period is likely to increase both the risk and the transaction cost to foreign investors, thus reducing their incentive to invest in China. It should also be noted that the Chinese consider the amount by which the liquidation value exceeds the registered capital of the joint venture at the time of liquidation as income, which is therefore taxable under the joint venture tax law.[53]

Management

China has a centrally planned economy, where industrial enterprises have limited decision-making authority and where resources are allocated by a bureaucratic command system. With an economic system that is so different from what they are familiar with, foreign firms are understandably cautious about investing in China. High on the list of questions that businessmen have concerning foreign investment in China are the following. How will joint ventures be integrated into China's command economy? Will the joint venture's autonomy be curtailed? and if so, in what ways and to what degrees? The beginning of an answer may be found in what the Chinese have said regarding the operation of joint ventures. Specifically, we examine below Chinese regulations and guidelines in four areas: production and marketing, labor management, finance, and dispute resolution.

Under Article 6 of the joint venture law, each joint venture (more precisely, its board of directors) has the power to formulate its own production and business programs. Raw materials, components, fuel, and other material inputs needed in production may either be purchased from Chinese sources or imported but only with the venture's own foreign exchange*; however when conditions are identical, joint ventures should "give first priority to Chinese sources." The joint venture must formulate an annual import plan and every six months apply for the necessary import licenses.[54] Since feasibility studies are conducted before the signing of the joint venture agreement, fuel and raw materials should be available. The Chinese also recommend that before the joint venture is established an agreement concerning fuel and raw material supply be concluded, presumably with the responsible department of the local government or the relevant ministry.[55] In accordance with "the relevant stipulations prescribed" in the joint venture contract, products produced by the joint venture may be sold either on the domestic market or on the world market.[56]

Because domestic product prices in China are administrative prices, they frequently reflect neither costs nor scarcity. China's severely distorted price structure, while not necessarily a problem when resources are centrally allocated by planners, is a major problem once profit-motivated joint ventures are permitted. Most importantly, price distortions are likely to result in joint ventures making socially sub-optimal decisions that waste scarce inputs, overproducing goods already in abundance and underproducng goods in short supply. To remedy this problem in part, the Chinese have decided to correct the worst price anomalies by introducing a two-price system for joint ventures.[57] On the input side, precious metals, petroleum, coal, and lumber used directly in production are to be supplied to joint venture at international prices but payable either in foreign currency or RMB ¥.* All other material inputs, including water, electricity, and gasoline used in vehicles, are to be supplied at domestic prices. As for output prices, goods produced by joint ventures for sale in China are generally priced similarly to those produced by other enterprises in China. However, with the approval of the local price bureau,[58] different prices may be charged to reflect quality differences. For products without domestic prices, the joint venture is allowed, after consultation with the local price bureau, to set its own price on the basis of costs plus reasonable profits and with reference to the price on the international market. However, joint ventures may set their own export prices.

The joint venture law calls for the "production and business programs of a joint venture to be filed with the authorities concerned and to be implemented through business contracts."[59] In fact, the authority in charge (the unit directly above the Chinese participant to the venture — usually a state corporation, an industrial ministry, or a local industrial bureau), through the Chinese directors on the board of the joint venture, plays an active role in the formulation of these programs. Indeed, the main function of the Chinese directors is to serve as the conduit through which information may flow between the joint venture and the Chinese planning bureaucracy. In other words, the joint venture interacts with the Chinese authority not only when it reports its annual programs but also on a continuing basis. The Chinese have stressed that the relationship between the joint venture and the Chinese authority in charge is one of guidance only.[60]

Once the board has finalized the program, it is forwarded to the authority in charge to be included in its annual plan. In this way the joint venture's output plans and input needs are integrated into the state's annual production and supply plans. Although the Chinese authority does not guarantee that the joint venture will receive all its allocated supplies, it does promise to notify the joint venture of supply problems in time for it to substitute imports for domestic supplies.[61] On the basis of its submitted output plans and its allocated supplies, the joint venture signs business contracts with suppliers and buyers. Products for the world market may be exported by the joint venture directly, through a foreign agent, or through one of China's foreign trade departments. The joint venture must formulate an annual export plan and every six months apply for export licenses if required by state regulations.[62] Products for the domestic market may be handled in one of several ways. If the product is one that is distributed according to the state plan or is one that is distributed by the state materials and commercial departments, then the output is turned over to the state for distribution to end-users. However, a joint venture may sell above-plan production and products that are not distributed by the state materials and commercial departments to end-users directly or through an agent. If the joint venture needs additional raw materials in order to produce above-plan output, it may (depending on what it needs) apply to a higher authority for the extra allocation or make the purchase directly from the supplier.

The "Regulations on Labour Management in Joint Ventures Using Chinese and Foreign Investment" define the authority that joint ventures have in labor management as well as the rights of workers employed by joint ventures. Of particular interest is the joint venture's authority in the following areas: labor selection, labor discipline, and wage incentives. The joint venture has the right to select Chinese workers from those it recruits or those recommended by the local labor bureau through examination.[63] The content of the examination and the standards used to select workers are to be decided by the joint venture. Surplus workers resulting from "changes in production and technical conditions" and workers "who fail to meet the requirements after training and are not suitable for other work" may be discharged, but they are entitled to severance pay.[65] The venture has complete control over the hiring and treatment of foreign personnel, and matters pertaining to their employment are to be negotiated and stipulated in their employment contracts.[66]

The joint venture has the power to discipline — and even dismiss — workers who have violated its rules and regulations. However, dismissals "must be reported to the authorities in charge of the joint venture and the labor management department for approval."[67] If the trade union, which exists in every joint venture, considers a disciplinary action unreasonable, it has the right to object and to seek a solution "through consultation with the board of directors." Should this fail, then the dispute goes to arbitration by the local labor bureau, and if either party disagrees with the decision, it may seek redress in the People's Court.[68] Because the trade union would normally consult with the Chinese members on the board of directors, it is unlikely that it would take a dispute to arbitration on its own initiative. The real conflict, if one exists, will most likely be between the Chinese and foreign members on the board of directors.[69]

The law allows the joint venture to establish its own wage and bonus system, but it also limits the take-home pay of workers employed by joint ventures to 120 to 150 percent of that earned by "workers and staff members of state owned enterprises of the same trade in the locality."[70] Apparently, the Chinese fear that if left unregulated the wage earned by workers in joint ventures may become substantially higher than that earned by state-employed workers. Wages, bonuses, and penalty schemes, work hours, and the other matters pertaining to employment discussed above are to be stipulated in a labor contract between the joint venture and the trade union representing the workers in the joint venture. The signed labor contract must be submitted to the local labor bureau for approval.[71] Apparently the approval procedure is used not to examine the merit of the contract, which presumably has been monitored throughout its negotiation, but to check whether it is properly executed and contains all the information required by law.[72]

Of the regulations concerning the finances of joint ventures, the following are worth noting. Joint ventures must open accounts with the Bank of China (or a bank it approves), and all foreign exchange transactions (export earnings, payments for imports, remittances, and so forth) are to be conducted through these accounts.[73] Unlike Chinese enterprises, joint ventures are allowed to borrow directly from foreign banks. This is hardly surprising since the Chinese see joint ventures as a mechanism for attracting foreign funds. Perhaps more important is the provision that a joint venture may also apply to the Bank of China for loans in RMB ¥ or in foreign currency to finance either current operation or planned expansion and technical improvements.[74] Thus, joint ventures are able to tap both the domestic and the international financial markets for funds.

The joint venture law stipulates that before after-tax profits may be distributed, contributions to the general reserve fund, the bonus and welfare fund, and the enterprise development fund must be deducted. The sizes of these contributions are to be negotiated and stipulated in the joint venture contract or decided by the board of directors. Judging from the agreements approved so far, contributions to these three funds account for between 10 and 15 percent of after-tax profits.[75] It should also be noted that the general reserve fund and the enterprise development fund may be used as working capital.[76] All other decisions regarding the distribution of after-tax profits are to be made by the board of directors. Joint ventures must apply to the Bank of China to remit after-tax profits and "other legitimate earnings" abroad and to the State General Administration of Foreign Exchange Control to remit capital funds out of China.[77] Although there is nothing in the regulations to indicate the readiness with which the authorities will approve these applications or the criteria used in making the decisions, the Chinese have assured foreign investors that "China will never stop a foreign participant in a joint venture from remitting abroad its share of profits even if the country should be struck by an imbalance in the international payments."[78]

Since the power of managing the joint venture is entrusted to its board of directors and since the composition of the board is based on the investment shares of the participants, a crucial issue is the protection of the minority owner (usually the foreign participant) against arbitrary actions by the majority. The joint venture law is quite vague on this issue saying merely that "in handling an important problem, the board of directors shall reach its decision through consultation by the participants on the principle of equality and mutual benefit."[79] The Chinese have since added that[80]

decisions on revising the articles of association of a joint venture, on terminating or disbanding the joint venture and on the increase, transfer and mortgage of its capital, as well as on the merger of the joint venture with other economic organizations must be taken unanimously at the meeting of the board of directors. Decisions on questions other than these may be taken by two-thirds or simple majority.

The Chinese are committed to the principle of management by consultation not only on questions of policy but apparently also in the day-to-day operation of the joint venture. Thus the general manager, who implements the policies set by the board, "must consult his deputies [among whom would usually be one representing the minority owner] in handling important decisions."[81] Of course, the minority participant to a joint venture can always negotiate for veto rights on major issues and include this in the joint venture contract and articles of association.

A framework for dispute settlement is also beginning to emerge. Joint ventures are likely to be involved in two types of dispute: internal disputes involving the participants to the venture and disputes between the joint venture and an external Chinese entity. Traditionally, the Chinese have preferred to resolve disputes through consultation and conciliation, and this continues to be an important part of China's current approach to dispute settlement. However, China is now more willing to accept arbitration. Article 14 of the joint venture law states that when the board of directors cannot resolve an internal dispute through consultation, it may submit the dispute for arbitration to the China Foreign Economic and Trade

Arbitration Commission or to an arbitral body agreeable to both parties (for example, an arbitral body in the defendant's country or one in a third country). The Chinese are also willing to use any international arbitration rules.[82] Most importantly, China has said that it will automatically abide by the decision of a foreign arbitral body as long as it does not violate "China's public order"(*gonggong zhixu*).[83] If the joint venture agreement does not specify arbitration, either party to an internal dispute may bring the case before the People's Court.[84]

Since joint ventures are required to implement their annual production and business programs through business contracts, disputes between joint ventures and Chinese enterprises over contract interpretation or contract fulfilment are inevitable. Procedures for the resolution of this type of dispute are stipulated in China's new "Economic Contract Law" announced in December, 1981.[85] As usual, the parties in dispute are encouraged to settle through consultation. However, if the parties cannot reach an agreement, then either party may ask the unit that governs the contract to mediate and arbitrate the dispute.[86] If either party is unsatisfied with the decision of the arbitral body, it may take the dispute to the Economic Tribunal of the People's Court.[87] Alternatively, the dispute may be taken directly to the Economic Tribunal for resolution.

On the whole, the laws and regulations concerning joint ventures provide a framework that most foreign investors can live with. As Cohen and Nee have remarked, "there is nothing in the [joint venture] law that is absolutely alien to a foreign businessman's way of earning profits."[88] The laws also leave considerable room for negotiation between the participants. This is as it should be. Joint venture projects can vary greatly, and it is important that the laws and regulations are sufficiently general to accommodate all types.

Although laws and regulations help define the environment for joint ventures, they are by no means the main determinant of the investment climate in China. Probably more important is how Chinese bureaucrats interpret and administer the regulations and how easily joint ventures adjust to China's planned economy. How readily will China permit profit repatriation? Will disputes be resolved promptly? Will the principle of management through consultation be followed in good faith? Will joint ventures need to "oil" the Chinese bureaucracy in order to get results? Will joint ventures be able to devise a wage scheme that will motivate the Chinese workers and still be acceptable to the government? Will joint ventures receive their supply allocations on schedule? These questions can be answered only by experience, of which unfortunately there is precious little at present. The following sections examine the experience of two of the earliest joint ventures in China: China-Schindler and Fujian-Hitachi. Neither has been in operation long enough to provide answers to all the questions raised above, but these admittedly incomplete case studies nevertheless do shed light on the negotiation process, the participants' motives for economic co-operation, and the types of problems joint ventures are likely to encounter.

CHINA-SCHINDLER ELEVATOR COMPANY, LTD.[89]

On 1 July 1980 the Chinese Foreign Investment Administration Commission approved an agreement between the China Construction Machinery Corporation (CCMC was then under the now-extinct State Capital Construction Commission), the Swiss elevator manufacturer Schindler Holdings AG, and the Hong Kong firm Jardine-Schindler (Far East) Holdings SA to form a joint venture, the China-Schindler Elevator Company, to manufacture elevators in China.[90] This is currently one of China's largest international joint ventures and is the channel through which China is acquiring sophisticated technology needed to modernize its elevator industry. Because it is an example of the type of joint venture that China is interested in and wishes to promote, the China-Schindler Elevator Company provides a particularly interesting case study.

History of Negotiation and Terms of Agreement

Of the various forms of economic co-operation, the joint venture is probably the most complex and timeconsuming to negotiate. However, China and Schindler came to terms fairly quickly. China first approached Schindler in December 1978 through its embassy in Bern.[91] Then in June 1979 Schindler and four other elevator producers were invited to present technical seminars in China and to make formal proposals for co-operation with China using the joint venture as the framework. The ensuing negotiation produced a preliminary agreement between China and Schindler in November 1979 and a final agreement in March 1980. The March agreement was revised, however, before receiving the final approval of the Foreign Investment Administration Commission. The China-Schindler Elevator Company was formally incorporated on 5 July 1980. The whole process, from the initial proposal to the incorporation, took about a year, a relatively short period of time considering that this was the first joint venture agreement in manufacturing negotiated between China and a foreign firm and that very little of China's legal framework for joint ventures was in place at the time.

A quick agreement was possible because a joint venture to produce elevators in China served the interests of both China and Schindler. In the late 1970s the Chinese construction industry began a major drive to correct the serious shortage of residential and office accommodations in China, the legacy of several decades of neglect. As part of this program, China was anxious to negotiate a joint venture agreement that would provide it with the technology and the skills to modernize its backward elevator industry. However, China wanted a joint venture that would be self-sufficient in foreign exchange. Thus, a side condition to any agreement was that the joint venture must export a share of its output. Of the five elevator producers China approached in 1979, only Schindler was interested in investing in a joint venture that would export a part of its output.[92]

Even before China approached Schindler, the company was considering establishing a production source in Asia in order to reduce its freight cost and thereby improve its competitiveness in the Asian market. Possible sites considered included South Korea, Taiwan, and Singapore. What kept Schindler from investing in any of these economies was the size of its market. In the late 1970s, Schindler's market (the Far East excluding Japan and China) was served by five major producers, each supplying about one-fifth of the estimated 2,500 to 3,000 elevators sold each year. Since a complete product line involved twenty to thirty models (even though many parts are similar), Schindler did not consider it economical to establish a plant in Asia that would produce only 500 to 600 elevators a year. However, once China approached the company, the picture changed. Schindler estimated that the joint venture could expect to supply 50 to 100 percent of the China market, and when this was added to the 20 percent of the Asian market that Schindler already served, the annual production run would be sufficiently large to justify investing in a plant.

Given the uncertain investment climate in China at the time, Schindler would have preferred some form of co-operation other than the joint venture. Compensation trade, for example, would have given Schindler the source in Asia it wanted without it having to risk large amounts of its own capital. The joint venture arrangement was considered only at China's insistence. However, Schindler decided at an early stage to limit its initial investment to a maximum of US$4 million. Basically, Schindler agreed to participate in the venture because it judged the risk of losing US$4 million worth taking considering the potential gains: a manufacturing source in Asia and profits from the sale of technology to China. Another but very subordinate motive for investing in China was Schindler's fear that if it did not go into China one of its competitors might have.

The China-Schindler joint venture agreement consists of a main agreement and five annexed documents: a license agreement, a consulting agreement, a maintenance franchise agreement, an export agency agreement, and a joint pro forma. In addition there are the articles of association. None of these documents has been released to the public. What is available for examination are the main agreement and the articles of association signed by the participants in March 1980 before they were revised by the Foreign Investment Administration Commission.[93] Both the Chinese and Schindler have said that the March agreement and the revised agreement differ only in minor details and that the spirit of the first agreement was not touched in the revision. In what follows we discuss the main terms of the China-Schindler ageement as we know it, based partly on the published March agreement, partly on the announced revisions, and partly on interviews with the participants.

China's original plan was apparently to form a joint venture involving Schindler, a factory in Beijing, and a factory in Tianjin. However, after a tour of China's manufacturing facilities that included a Shanghai plant, Schindler insisted that any joint venture must include the Shanghai facility. Since Schindler did not want to invest more than US$4 million and since the Chinese joint venture law requires that the foreign participant's investment share be not less than 25 percent, the maximum total investment in the joint venture was limited to US$16 million. Given the value of the facilities in Beijing, Tianjin, and Shanghai, this meant that the Chinese contribution could not include all three plants. Accordingly, the decision was made to proceed in two stages. In the first stage, the joint venture would involve only the Beijing and the Shanghai plants, and if everything went well then, in a second stage Schindler would increase its investment to permit the joint venture to include the Tianjin plant as well.[94]

The equity shares in the joint venture are as follows: CCMC, 75 percent; Schindler, 15 percent; and Jardine-Schindler, 10 percent. Schindler and Jardine-Schindler together contributed $4 million in cash and CCMC contributed $12 million in buildings, machinery, and inventory ($8 million from Shanghai and $4 million from Beijing). The two sites and the Beijing factory (the old building and a new building when completed) were not a part of the Chinese contribution, so the joint venture will pay an annual fee for their use. Apparently the fees were negotiated without much difficulty. Schindler felt it had no way to judge what rents in Beijing and Shanghai should be, and after some bargaining, it accepted what the Chinese offered.[95] If necessary, Schindler also agreed to provide additional financing in the second and the third year of the venture in the form of a long-term loan in Swiss francs (equivalent to RMB ¥5 million) at the most favorable market rates. The loan is to be totally repaid in the eighth year of the venture. The duration of the joint venture is twenty years, but it may be extended for periods of five years. However, the extension decision must be made in each case at least three years before the expiration of the agreement. At termination, CCMC will repurchase Schindler's share in the joint venture. The repurchase price is to be Schindler's share of the net equity of the joint venture according to the balance sheet on the date of termination plus a "premium" to be negotiated.[96]

The joint venture is to market its products both in China and abroad, with Schindler serving as the exclusive export agent for the period of the agreement plus five years. However, if the board of directors decides unanimously, China-Schindler may export directly to countries in which Schindler is not represented. Furthermore, the export agency agreement calls for sufficient exports to cover the joint venture's foreign exchange needs (including royalties and profit remittance), which works out to about 25 percent of the venture's projected output. Thus, in this agreement, the Chinese got what they wanted — that is, a joint venture that is self-sufficient in foreign exchange — and Schindler got its Asian source. For Schindler, this arrangement makes sense only if China-Schindler is competitive and its product is of good quality. Because its technicians will be working in China, Schindler was fairly confident that quality would not be a problem. And in any case Schindler felt it could always refuse to accept substandard goods from

China-Schindler. It was less certain that the joint venture would be able to control its production costs, so it negotiated a pricing formula to protect its global profits. What CCMC and Schindler agreed was 1) to tie the joint venture's export price to the world market price and 2) to set the joint venture's domestic price as low as is consistent with an after-tax profit of 15 percent of total turnover. With the joint venture's export price tied to the world price rather than cost, Schindler is assured that it will be able to maintain its export position in the competitive Southeast Asian market. And it does not matter if the joint venture exports at a loss since in the protected domestic market it can easily raise its price in order to earn the agreed after-tax profit of 15 percent of turnover. Thus, a respectable return on Schindler's investment in China is also assured.

For China, the underlying reason for participating in the joint venture was of course to acquire modern elevator technology. What it lacked and wanted to acquire was more reliable and sophisticated controls, the capacity to produce higher speed elevators to serve taller buildings, and better finishing. In the past Chinese elevator producers did not install or service the elevators they sold, and this is one reason why Chinese elevators have been unreliable. To correct this weakness, the Chinese also wanted to acquire Schindler's know-how in elevator installation and servicing. In short, China was interested in acquiring nearly the complete range of Schindler's production and maintenance know-how. Specifically, the joint venture agreement calls for Schindler to provide to the joint venture its product designs, manufacturing techniques and methods, production and quality control methods, factory construction and renovation designs, factory organization methods, elevator installation and maintenance methods, and engineering assistance.

The conditions governing this transfer are spelled out in three documents: a license agreement, a consulting agreement, and a maintenance franchise agreement. Under the license agreement, Schindler is to provide to China-Schindler during the duration of the joint venture agreement all its existing and future technology including technical assistance. Since elevator technology changes fairly rapidly and since Schindler spends a considerable sum each year on research and development of new technology, the transfer involved is substantial. The consulting agreement deals with technical assistance in areas not already covered by the license agreement — for example, plant dimensions and layout. Schindler is to provide this consulting service on request from China-Schindler and is to be paid a fixed fee. Under the maintenance franchise agreement, China-Schindler is to acquire Schindler's maintenance procedures and its help in developing a maintenance organization in China.

Of these documents, the license agreement is by far the most important, and it was also the most difficult to negotiate. As was to be expected, the sticking point was the price to be paid for the technology Schindler is to transfer to the joint venture. Traditionally, the Chinese have preferred to purchase technology for a fixed fee and avoided paying royalties (a "running license fee," tied to the annual output or sales of the licensee, payable over a specified time period). Schindler was clearly unwilling to accept a fixed payment only. What was finally agreed was that China-Schindler would pay for the transferred technology in two forms: 1) a fixed license (or disclosure) fee for five years and 2) a royalty to be calculated as a percentage of annual turnover (gross output), net of any imported Schindler-made components, and payable for the duration of the joint venture plus five years.[97] A second formula, in which the royalty would have been calculated as a percentage of the venture's annual output that is based on Schindler's technology, was also considered. Schindler was willing to accept the second formula as long as it yielded the minimum return that it wanted for the sale of its technology. To do this, the percent used in the second formula would have to be larger than the one used in the turnover formula. The difficulty was to estimate how quickly Schindler's share will rise from zero to 100 percent. If 100 percent is reached sooner (or later) than anticipated, then the second formula, over the life of the agreement, would result in a substantially larger (or smaller) royalty payment than the turnover formula. Because of this uncertainty, the two parties decided to use the turnover formula.

For several reasons, the lack of protection of industrial property rights in China did not cause Schindler much concern. The potential loss to Schindler if its technology is diffused to non-licensees in China is not great. China-Schindler already produces a major share of the elevators in China, and furthermore it was expected — at the time the agreement was signed — that the Tianjin plant might still become a part of the joint venture. In any case, as a part of the current economic reform, the Chinese are encouraging state enterprises to compete with one another. In this new environment, China-Schindler is not likely to pass on Schindler's technology to its domestic competitors.[98] Should the Chinese succeed in transferring Schindler's technology to third parties abroad, either in the form of exports or know-how, the potential damage to Schindler would be substantial. However, Schindler is also better protected outside of China. Its existing patents offer effective protection against the possibility that the Chinese might transfer its technology abroad. And China also will not find it easy to export elevators independently and compete against Schindler on the world market. The elevator industry supplies two products — elevators and after-sale maintenance. Competition in Southeast Asia is such that little profit is made on the sale of elevators. What makes the industry profitable is the earnings from after-sale servicing. But it is economical to maintain a servicing organization only if the seller has a large number of elevators to service. A new entrant to the Asian elevator market must therefore expect to operate in the red for many years until its maintenance volume is built up. Because of this barrier to entry, China is not likely to enter the export market on its own for some time to come.

As required by the joint venture, the overall management of China-Schindler is the responsibility of its eight-member board of directors (a chairman appointed by

CCMC, a vice-chairman appointed by Schindler, and six other members — five appointed by CCMC and one by Jardine-Schindler). Both Schindler and Jardine-Schindler wanted the board of directors to adopt resolutions only with the consent of both minority participants. The Chinese suggested that the consent of one minority participant is sufficient. Since the two minority participants have similar interests, this suggestion was accepted. The board of directors is to manage and supervise the operation of China-Schindler according to the objectives contained in the joint pro forma, a negotiated ten-year projection of key variables such as output, production costs, profits, and exports. Under the joint venture law, the board of directors also has the power to decide how much of the after-tax profits will be distributed as dividends. However, China-Schindler's dividend policy in the first six years is already stipulated in the joint venture agreement. In the first three years 100 percent of what is available for declaration as dividend shall be reinvested and in the following three years 50 percent shall be reinvested. Thereafter, the dividend policy will be determined by the board of directors.

Two other aspects of the China-Schindler agreement are worth mentioning: 1) While China-Schindler is subject to the same taxes as other joint ventures,[99] its taxable income is to be taxed at the effective rate of 31.5 percent, (30 percent for the central government and a 5 percent surtax for the local government) as compared to 33 percent for other joint ventures. China-Schindler is also granted exemption from income tax during its first three profit-making years. The reason for the difference in the tax rate is that the China-Schindler agreement was signed before China announced its joint venture income tax law. Profit remittance is taxed at 10 percent, but the China-Schindler agreement stipulates that this is to be paid by the joint venture so that in effect the Chinese pay 75 percent of this tax. 2) Disputes between the participants that cannot be settled by the board of directors will go to the Chinese Foreign Economic and Trade Arbitration Commission for arbitration. If its decision is unsatisfactory, the dispute then goes to the Stockholm Chamber of Commerce for arbitration under British rules.[100]

China-Schindler in Operation

It is useful to begin a discussion of China-Schindler's operation by describing briefly its internal organization. At the top of the enterprise is the board of directions. Under the board is a general manager who administers the enterprise from its Beijing head office. There are two plants, one in Beijing and the other in Shanghai.[101] Each plant is administered by a manager and is organized into functional sections and workshops. For example, the Shanghai plant has eleven functional sections (planning, labor, accounting, and so forth), four workshops (elevator doors and bodies, electronic controls, motors, and parts and tooling), and a repair team. The board meets at least once every three months and sets policies on all matters concerning production, marketing, research and development, expansion, budgeting, appointment, remuneration and dismissal of personnel, and finances. To implement its decisions, the board issues "management and operating instructions," which the general manager and his staff must carry out.

Each plant also has a labor union and a committee of the Chinese Communist Party. The party committee has no direct role in planning or in production and does primarily "political work." It also has a "watch dog" role, since it is supposed to make sure that the plant abides by China's laws and regulations. The union does educational and cultural work and sometimes conducts motivational propaganda. It also signs the labor contract on behalf of the workers in the plant. Union leaders, at least in the Shanghai plant, are representatives of the municipal general trade union and therefore are not on the enterprise's payroll.

Among the recurrent decisions the China-Schindler board makes, those concerning production and marketing are probably the most important. On the basis of the joint pro forma, the board sets quarterly production targets for the two plants. The manager of each plant then works out the detailed implementation with the planning and labor sections and the foremen of the workshops. At least in the Shanghai plant, the manager also consults with an elected "committee of experienced workers." Based on its output targets, each plant decides the amount of materials it requires.[102] The enterprise forwards the output targets and the required materials to the China Construction Machinery Corporation, which arranges for the allocation of supplies.[103] It is worth noting that some material inputs are controlled and allocated centrally, some are controlled centrally but allocated through the locality, and others are controlled and allocated locally.

Once the allocation is set, the plant signs contracts with suppliers for delivery. The choice of suppliers is up to the enterprise,[104] but basic supplies tend to come from well-established channels. If supplies are short, a higher authority (presumably CCMC or possibly its higher authority, the Ministry of Urban and Rural Construction and Environmental Protection) decides which enterprises are to receive supplies. If China-Schindler is not going to get its allocated supplies, it expects to be notified in time to import what it needs. Should the enterprise decide to exceed its production targets, it may look to three sources for additional material inputs: its own inventory, additional allocation from the appropriate authority, or direct purchase from suppliers with excess or above-plan production. China-Schindler pays the same prices for domestic raw materials as state enterprises do. Its working capital comes from its enterprise funds and from RMB loans from the Bank of China and the People's Bank of China.

The Shanghai plant uses over 100 suppliers and subcontractors, but its manager does not see supply as a problem. The Beijing head office appears to be equally confident that the enterprise will receive the supplies and parts it needs and on time. Considering the supply difficulties that have plagued Chinese enterprises, one wonders about the source of this confidence. Is it because China-Schindler is a "model" joint venture in a high priority sector and therefore can expect special considerations from the authorities? Is it because of the substantial excess capacity in China's heavy-industry sector since the start of the economic readjustment? Or is it because China-Schindler's major plant is in Shanghai close to all the important suppliers and therefore supply problems can be more easily sorted out? Perhaps all three factors contribute to the confidence.

In the distribution of its output, the enterprise gives exports first claim to ensure that its foreign exchange needs can be met. After exports, the Shanghai plant's next priority is to supply the planned needs of Shanghai. The remaining output is then marketed to domestic users outside Shanghai. If Shanghai wants more elevators than originally planned, it must negotiate the extra purchases with China-Schindler's board in Beijing. Presumably, in distribution, the Beijing plant also gives Beijing higher priority than the rest of China.

Before the plants became a joint venture, domestic distribution was done centrally; now it is handled by the enterprise directly. China-Schindler sees the entire country as its market. The Chinese feel that one of the most important things they have learned from Schindler is how to "do business" (*zuo shengyi*) — that is, to market their products more effectively. The enterprise now has sales and display offices in Beijing, Shanghai, and Guangzhou. Before it became a part of the joint venture, the Shanghai plant employed one part-time "salesman." Now thirty of its staff of ninety engineers are in sales. To improve local exposure and to help its reputation for quality, China-Schindler is also conducting maintenance classes in various parts of China. By mid-1982, it had completed two series of classes, one in Shandong and another in Jiangxi.

Since becoming a joint venture, the enterprise has introduced a new wage-bonus system. The joint pro forma provides for an average wage of about RMB ¥200 per month in the first year of the venture. In the subsequent four years, the average wage is to rise by 15 percent per year, and then it is to be renegotiated. A substantial portion of the RMB¥200 goes to compensate the government for various subsidies it provides to urban workers, for example, rent, food, medical care, and transportation. Workers at China-Schindler receive an average basic take-home wage of RMB ¥60–70 per month plus bonuses.[105] The size of the bonus that a worker receives depends on the amount and the quality of his work and on his attitude. The calculation is based on a complex point system. The staff is also eligible for bonuses. What is interesting about China-Schindler's bonus scheme is not the point system, which exists in some state enterprises as well, but the fact that the bonus is kept secret so that only the recipient and the supervisors know the amount awarded. The effect, of course, is to dilute the community pressure toward egalitarianism that is still prevalent in China. A second difference is that China-Schindler, because it is a joint venture, does not have to keep its total annual bonuses from exceeding two months of wages as do state enterprises. In 1981, its total bonuses were about 25 percent of its total wage fund. An average worker might earn about RMB ¥20–30 per month as bonus, while good workers might get RMB ¥50–60 per month. The average total take-home pay at the Shanghai plant is RMB ¥90 per month, about 25 percent more than the average earnings at comparable state enterprises.

A worker who violates China-Schindler's factory rules may be disciplined in several ways. The most obvious, of course, is to have the monthly bonus reduced or eliminated. The basic wage may also be reduced, although this has been done in only a few cases at China-Shindler. Besides economic discipline, there is also a graduated scale of administrative and political discipline, from recording the incident in the worker's file to warning, probation, and finally dismissal. Even the lightest administrative discipline — the recording of the violation — is a fairly serious matter in China since the record remains in the worker's file permanently and may have continuing and unpredictable consequences. In serious violations, both economic and administrative sanctions may be applied.

In accordance with the labor regulations concerning joint ventures, the basic wage and the discipline system just described are stipulated in the labor contract between China-Schindler and the union. Up to the present, the labor contract has been negotiated year by year. While the union does solicit the views of its membership before entering each year's negotiation, it does not take the signed contract back to the membership for ratification. The negotiation — perhaps a better term is consultation — between management and labor usually lasts three to five days. The Beijing and Shanghai plants are represented by different unions. The two unions negotiate together but sign separate contracts with China-Schindler. Presumably one matter that is discussed during the negotiation is the basic wage. When the general manager was asked whether China-Schindler will increase its basic wage from year to year, he responded that it will certainly match any wage increase received by the state enterprises but that in addition it may also make wage adjustments on its own initiative. However, wage increases will not necessarily occur every year but only from time to time. In any case, the ability of China-Schindler to increase its basic wage is limited since, by law, its average wage cannot be more than 50 percent higher than in comparable state enterprises. Because "comparable" is not precisely defined, this rule may be somewhat more flexible than it first appears.

Under the agreement, China-Schindler has the authority to adjust annually the size of its labor force according to its needs. At formation the enterprise had on its payroll about 2,400 workers, of which more than 25 percent were in technical or management positions. The one-to-four staff-worker ratio, while fairly common in China, is high by foreign standards and is one reason for the low labor productivity at the two plants. Not surprisingly, the joint pro forma calls for a gradual reduction of the staff-worker ratio over time, though so far no one has been laid off. The plan is to make the adjustment through attrition and a small increase in additional workers when production expands in the future.

Before the formation of the joint venture, the Beijing and the Shanghai plants together produced about 500 elevators a year. The agreement calls for annual production to double to 1,000 elevators by 1985 and to reach 2,000 units in 1988. The product-mix will shift gradually from elevators based entirely on Chinese designs to those based entirely on Schindler's technology. A greater division of labor will also be introduced. The Shanghai plant will specialize in motors, controls, and high finishing, and the Beijing plant will specialize in basic elevator bodies. Eventually each location will have the capacity to assemble 1,000 elevators a year. Whether these targets will be reached depends in part on how well the enterprise operates and in part on how quickly and smoothly Schindler's technology is transferred to and absorbed by China-Schindler.

China-Schindler produced 600 elevators in 1980 and about 700 (500 in Shanghai) in 1981. As of mid-1982 all of China-Schindler's elevators were still based entirely on Chinese designs although some imported Schindler-produced components were used and two Swiss technicians were on its staff. Most of the elevators produced were marketed domestically. A small (unspecified) number were exported but not as Schindler's product. The Chinese reported that China-Schindler's profit was RMB ¥3.2 million for its six months of operation in 1980 and RMB ¥7 million in 1981, both substantially higher than had been projected. These figures suggest an annual rate of return on investment of about 24 percent. However, the 1980–81 profit figures are somewhat misleading. First of all, profits in 1980–81 were apparently made larger by the fact that some earmarked funds (such as consulting fees) were not used because of management inertia. These funds will eventually have to be used. Secondly, the high profits partly reflected the fact that the royalty payments to Schindler were not fully implemented in 1980–81. Finally, China-Schindler exported only a small share of its output. Since export prices are lower than domestic prices, profits in the future are expected to be lower when, as agreed, a larger share of China-Schindler's output will be exported. It is interesting that China-Schindler expects its 1982 profits to be RMB ¥4 million, a 42 percent decline from the 1981 level.

As to why, after two years, China-Schindler still does not use Schindler's technology in its elevators, the Chinese have pointed to the fact that the five hundred binders of documents and thousands of blueprints they received from Schindler were all in French and German and on microfiche, and getting them enlarged and translated has taken longer than expected. In addition, some of the new technology is for China-Schindler's subcontractors, so time is needed to diffuse the technology. Undoubtedly these factors have contributed to the delay. But Schindler also attributes the slowness in part to the management's inability or unwillingness to make decisions promptly. It points to the Swiss Francs loan that sits in the bank unused because of decision-making delays concerning the renovation of the Shanghai plant and the construction of the new Beijing factory. The apparent need of the Chinese engineers to reinvent the wheel may be another reason for the delay. Chinese engineers have challenged nearly every technical suggestion that Schindler has put forward. There are two plausible reasons for this behavior: 1) the engineers want to make sure that the transferred technology is appropriate to Chinese conditions, and 2) they are afraid that if they do not thoroughly investigate the new technology they might be blamed if something goes wrong afterwards. If these are indeed the reasons, then the Chinese must learn to balance such concerns against the cost of delaying technology transfer. After all, foreign technical assistance is also a scarce resource that needs to be economized, and delay too has a cost.

It now appears that technology transfer may proceed somewhat more rapidly in the future. Because China-Schindler pays royalties on the basis of total turnover, it paid a royalty to Schindler in 1980–81 even though Schindler's technology was not employed. This has caused CCMC to come under considerable criticism in China for negotiating a poor contract. The implication that China has once again been outmaneuvered at the bargaining table has made CCMC and the Chinese members on China-Schindler's board exceedingly uncomfortable, [106] and may be the reason why China-Schindler recently decided to produce a 100 percent Schindler product by 1985, two years earlier than was originally planned.

What is Schindler's assessment of its two years of experience in China, and what problems has it encountered? The elevator industry employs a large number of craftsmen, and, in Schindler's view, the Chinese craftsmen at China-Schindler are as good as and perhaps better than their European counterparts, in part because with automation the number of European craftsmen has declined rapidly. Its assessment of Chinese engineers and technicians is equally favorable — they are competent and quick learners. Predictably, they are getting the most from China-Schindler's contact with Schindler. Some are already receiving, and many more will be receiving, additional training in Europe. The financial specialists, such as accountants, at China-Schindler are adequate if somewhat dated. One suspects the main problem is that in China accounting is seen as book-keeping and not as a management tool. Not surprisingly, Schindler found the Chinese very weak in commercial and managerial personnel. Until recently, there was no place in the Chinese enterprise for sales and marketing personnel. And, of course, a bureaucratic command system does not encourage the development of entrepreneurial talents.

In Schindler's view, slow decision-making is a major managerial problem at China-Schindler. Exhaustive discussions precede every board decision, even relatively minor ones. But an even more serious problem is the lack of a monitoring system that would make sure that managerial instructions are followed at the lower levels.[107] Apparently the Chinese manager, after he gives an order, seldom follows up to see if it has been carried out. Communication and co-ordination between departments within the enterprise are also relatively weak. It should be noted that the Chinese themselves admit to these short-comings and recognize that they need to be corrected. Because China-Schindler has plants at two locations, the chain of command is sometimes unclear. The manager of the Shanghai plant is appointed by the Shanghai Municipality and is also a director. Schindler is therefore apprehensive that the Shanghai plant may be more responsive to the Shanghai government than to its head office in Beijing. However, having a link with the Shanghai government can also be very useful, since the Shanghai plant depends on Shanghai for labor and some material inputs. Only time will tell whether this will develop into a serious management problem. Chinese managers are also insensitive to markets, and after two years of association with Schindler, they still have not adjusted to the fact that customers abroad have alternatives and do not accept delays as fatalistically as Chinese buyers.

While China-Schindler has control over production within its plants, it has little control when the activity involves other entities in the economy. Because it is involved in the export end of China-Schindler's business, Schindler is most aware of the shipping problem. Schindler pays c.i.f. prices for the elevators it purchases from China-Schindler, but because of transportation uncertainties in China it is spending twice the estimated time and resources in obtaining the elevators. One of Schindler's employees spends two-thirds of his time in China making sure that products, once manufactured, are shipped to Hong Kong. In effect, Schindler is doing much of the work that in other countries would be routinely done by the supplier. Pressuring China-Schindler to do more is not productive since the problem is largely outside its control.

An interesting development is that both participants are relying heavily on the joint pro forma not only to guide the management of China-Schindler but also as leverage to ensure that each participant is living up to its responsibility under the agreement. For example, if Schindler finds actual production cost is diverging sharply from the projection in the joint pro-forma and cannot persuade the Chinese to take corrective measures, it would consider the Chinese in violation of the joint venture agreement. Accordingly, Schindler would no longer be obligated to meet its responsibilities under the contract, such as fulfilling the export target. In other words, Schindler is using the joint pro forma to pressure the Chinese to make some of the needed changes in the operation and management of the enterprise. Similarly, the Chinese are using it to ensure that Schindler is living up to its obligations. After two years of operation, Schindler considers the joint pro forma the most important and useful component of the joint venture agreement, a view that is apparently shared by the Chinese.

The temporary exclusion of the Tianjin plant from the joint venture is now causing Schindler some concern. Offended that it was not invited to participate, the Tianjin plant, presumably with Tianjin's blessing, began to negotiate an arrangement with Otis.[108] Schindler then offered to reopen discussion with the Tianjin plant but was rejected. Schindler and China-Schindler also sought the intervention of the central government with the argument that an Otis-Tianjin deal will mean that China will pay twice for similar technology and that it will damage

China-Schindler economically. Though sympathetic, the central government was unable or unwilling to halt the Otis-Tianjin negotiation. With help from Otis, the Tianjin plant could give significant competition to China-Schindler both domestically and on the world market. This possibility is all the more troublesome to Schindler because, contrary to its original belief that the three plants it visited in Beijing, Tianjin, and Shanghai are China's entire elevator capacity, there are another major elevator plant in Shanghai (the Great Wall Co.), one in Guangzhou, and two or three smaller producers in other parts of China. Thus China-Schindler has to share the domestic market with these producers as well as the Tianjin plant. The Chinese told Schindler that should Otis and Tianjin reach an agreement, the contract will need MFERT's approval and that the central authority will protect China-Schindler's interests. However, Otis and Tianjin can by-pass central approval if they agree to a joint venture with total investment below US$5 million or a non-joint venture project (contractual co-operation or compensation trade) where the foreign involvement is less than US$5 million. In May 1982 Otis and the Tianjin plant signed an agreement to establish the China Tianjin Otis Elevator Co. Ltd., which will "sell, install and repair" elevators, escalators, and moving walkways, and the agreement received approval in December 1982.[109] The total investment in this joint venture, however, is only US$500,000, with Otis contributing 30 percent. Thus it appears that Otis's involvement with the Tianjin plant will be quite limited. At least in the near future Tianjin-Otis is not likely to become a serious threat to China-Schindler.

Another problem that Schindler had to face was its disagreement with the Chinese directors over salary policy. Under the agreement between CCMC and Schindler, the salaries of foreign staff are to be paid by the joint venture. When it came time to set the salaries for the two foreign technicians China-Schindler employed in 1981–82, the Chinese directors insisted that their Chinese counterparts receive the same salary. Foreign technicians are usually reluctant to work in China unless they are offered very high salaries to offset the hardships and the Chinese income tax. Thus, to Schindler, the "equal pay" demand is a Chinese attempt to "milk" the joint venture, particularly since the proposal will not increase the Chinese technicians' take-home pay. The Chinese directors argued for the equal pay on principle and on the grounds that it is required by the then unannounced regulations for the implementation of the joint venture law.[110] This dispute was temporarily resolved when the two sides agreed that for every foreign technician China-Schindler has on its payroll an equal number of Chinese technicians will receive the higher foreigner's salary. However, the higher salary will be disbursed only when the "equal pay rule" appears as an official government regulation.[111]

An overall assessment of the China-Schindler experience is probably not possible until at least the end of the 1980s. Schindler had hoped that the joint venture would be further developed after two years of operation than it is.

Nevertheless, taking everything into consideration, Schindler believes that what has been achieved is substantial. Numerous problems remain, of which probably the most fundamental is that the participants still do not fully trust one another. They are participants in a joint venture but not partners. Whether in time a feeling of partnership will develop so that China and Schindler can "sit on the same side of the table" is still an open question.

FUJIAN-HITACHI TELEVISION COMPANY, LTD.[112]

Negotiation History and Terms of Agreement

Fujian Province, which had been importing a large number of television sets from Hitachi, decided in 1979 to investigate the possibility of importing the components from the Japanese firm and then assembling the sets in Fuzhou. Its hope was that through import substitution it would save foreign exchange and at the same time acquire some new technology in electronics, an industry the province wanted to develop.[113] Originally, Fujian's intent was to arrange a processing agreement, but during its thirteen-month negotiation with Hitachi, the decision was made to take the joint venture route. Hitachi was motivated to participate in the joint venture by its desire to preserve its market in Fujian. It recognized that China will eventually restrict the import of television sets and hoped that the joint venture arrangement will enable it to circumvent the restriction by substituting the export of parts, components, and equipment for that of assembled television sets.[114] The agreement was signed on 13 December 1980.

Although the details of the Fujian-Hitachi agreement have not been released, some of the more important terms are known. The total investment was RMB ¥3.6 million (approximately US$2.4 million), with the contribution divided as follows: Fujian Electronic Import and Export Corporation, 40 percent; Fujian Enterprise Investment Corporation (Huafu), 10 percent; Hitachi Seisakusho, 38 percent; Hitachi Home Appliance Sales Co., 10 percent; and Toa Shoko Ltd., 2 percent.[115] Fujian's contribution consisted of the buildings and machinery (but not the site) of the Fujian Electrical Equipment Co., a five-hundred-worker enterprise that opened in 1965 as a repair establishment but has since developed the capacity to manufacture annually about twenty-seven thousand "mediocre quality" 12" black-and-white television sets. For the use of the site, Fujian-Hitachi will pay an annual land charge of RMB ¥15 per square meter.[116] Hitachi's contribution was in cash, which was used to import new machinery and equipment from Japan. The agreement is to last for ten years, but it can probably be extended.[117] At termination, the Japanese side is entitled to one-half of the net equity of the joint venture according to the final balance sheet.[118]

The enterprise is to be under the overall management and supervision of a seven-member board of directors, composed of four Chinese and three Japanese. The board chairman is to be Chinese (the current one is the president of Huafu), and one of the two vice-chairmen is to be Japanese. The agreement originally called for the general manager to be Japanese, but subsequently it became clear that a Chinese would be better able to work with the Chinese bureaucracy. Thus a Chinese (also from Huafu) was appointed general manager, and a Japanese, who is to deal primarily with production and technical matters, was appointed one of the two assistant managers. Both the general manager and the Japanese assistant manager are also directors of the company. The board may adopt resolutions concerning important matters only if both sides agree. Disputes between the participants that cannot be resolved by the board go to arbitration in Stockholm.

The enterprise will assemble Hitachi television sets under a license agreement, and for its technology Hitachi receives a royalty of J ¥830 for every set produced. During the term of the agreement Hitachi will transfer to Fujian-Hitachi whatever minor technical improvements it makes on the relevant models, but it is under no obligation to transfer major breakthroughs. The joint venture may not transfer Hitachi technology to third parties during the duration of the agreement plus five years. The joint venture is to market its products both domestically and abroad. The agreement calls for most of the output produced in the first three years of operation to be marketed domestically; thereafter, the export share is to rise and eventually to reach 50 percent or more. Profits made in the first three years of operation are to be reinvested in the joint venture. Interestingly, while the agreement does commit Fujian-Hitachi to employ all of the five-hundred workers of the Fujian Electrical Equipment Co., it does not require the enterprise to do so immediately. Instead, the workers will be gradually absorbed as production expands, with total absorption targeted for 1982. In the meantime the unabsorbed workers are to undergo training, and their wages are to be paid by Fujian Province.[119]

Fujian-Hitachi in Operation

Fujian-Hitachi's board of directors meets four times a year to make basic pricing, output-level, and product-mix decisions. From the general manager's description of the process, it is clear that these decisions are the results of an iterative process in which he is the key link between the Fujian government and the board. The general manager presents his suggestions concerning prices and output level to the board for consideration and approval. He also discusses the annual plans with the Fujian Television Industry Bureau.[120] Consultation with Fujian is crucial since most of Fujian-Hitachi's output is for the domestic market and is to be distributed through one of the provincial enterprises, the Fujian Television Import and Export Corporation. Quite clearly, the general manager plays a critical role in the planning process. As he said, he has to keep the interests of the state in mind, but he also has to protect the interests of the foreign partner. Once the output plans are finalized and approved by the board, they are forwarded to the Fujian Television Industry Bureau and integrated with the annual provincial plan. Output and price decisions are generally made at the beginning of each year, but mid-year adjustments are possible.

The problem of integrating Fujian-Hitachi into China's supply system is made simple by the fact that it currently uses mostly imported parts and components. At present, there are some Chinese components in its black-and-white sets (for example, the picture tubes are supplied by the National joint venture in Shanghai) but none in the color sets. The enterprise has arranged for on-site customs clearance of its imported parts and components, which are transported directly from the dock to the plant in container-trailers. However, the plan is to raise the local content of the black-and-white sets to 50 percent by value and that of the color sets to 30 percent by the end of 1982 and for overall local content to reach 50 percent by the end of 1983. Thus, in the future, Fujian-Hitachi will need to arrange an increasing share of its supplies through domestic channels. This should not be difficult since the number of suppliers involved will likely be small, and the bulk of the domestically made parts will probably be manufactured in Fujian or by plants that are currently under construction with Japanese assistance.[121]

Before the enterprise became a joint venture, its workers received an average basic wage of RMB ¥56 per month plus a small monthly bonus. The wage system has since changed in several important ways. The enterprise's wage outlay per worker was RMB ¥189 per month in 1982, of which slightly less than half went to the government to help pay for the many subsidies it provides to urban workers[122] and to the union to finance the construction of new housing, while 6 percent was allocated to the monthly bonus fund, and 2 percent went to the union to finance cultural activities for workers. This meant that, on the average, the basic take-home wage at Fujian-Hitachi was about RMB ¥82 per month in 1982.[123] The average worker also received a monthly bonus of about RMB ¥11. In addition, the workers at Fujian-Hitachi receive some special compensations. Because the general manager felt strongly that poor nutrition can adversely affect labor productivity, he persuaded the enterprise to provide a lunch subsidy of RMB ¥0.5 per worker per day. At first this subsidy was given in kind, but, subsequently, to give the workers greater flexibility, it was changed to cash. There is also a "cost-reduction bonus," whereby 20 percent of any cost savings is distributed as a special bonus to the unit that achieved the reduction. Finally, if the enterprise achieves its annual profit target, workers also receive a year-end bonus, which in 1981 averaged RMB ¥187 per worker (a few received as much as RMB ¥350). To lessen the pressure to distribute the bonuses along egalitarian lines, the amounts awarded to individuals are not announced publicly. If a worker is unsatisfied with his bonus, he may complain to the general manager directly. Thus far, there has been only one such complaint, which was settled quickly.

Hitachi is generally satisfied with the quality of the workers employed by the joint venture. It reports that the Chinese workers learn new skills fairly quickly, and it is also pleased by the lack of labor mobility in China. Workers at the Fuzhou plant are seldom late for work, and their morale is higher than that at similar plants in Southeast Asia.[124] In the first fifteen months of operation, the joint venture has had no serious problem with labor discipline. To promote responsibility among its workers, the enterprise installed time clocks and introduced a system whereby assembling errors may be traced to the person responsible.[125] The general manager has the authority to introduce minor factory rules and to take economic sanctions against those who violate them. For example, he announced that tardiness and spitting on the factory site would be fined.[126] There is also the usual graduated scale of administrative discipline. On more serious matters, he consults his two assistant managers and other relevant parties before taking action. The distinction between minor and major disciplinary matters is not explicitly explained in the labor contract, but depends on the judgment of the general manager. A worker who is disciplined may appeal the case to the local labor bureau or to the Fujian Television Industry Bureau, the provincial agency that oversees the joint venture's activities.

There is both a labor union and a committee of the Chinese Communist Party at Fujian-Hitachi. The union represents the worker in signing the labor contract, which contains provisions on hours, wages, bonus schemes, labor protection, and so forth. The current contract is for two years. In addition, the union does educational and cultural work, sponsors housing projects, and conducts friendly competition among workers and other motivational campaigns. While in principle union leaders are elected, they have been appointed at Fujian-Hitachi. In his discussion of the union's role, the general manager stressed that unions in China are unlike those in other countries because in China union and management are not adversaries. We were told that the party committee at Fujian-Hitachi does mainly "political work." When the general manager was asked about conflicts between the party committee and the management, he responded by saying that the party does not interfere with production or with other management matters, and should there be a conflict at Fujian-Hitachi, it can be easily resolved because he is also the party secretary.

Fujian-Hitachi's original projections of output, employment, and exports, its actual performance since production began in mid-April 1981, and its current targets are summarized in Table 4.2. What is notable about the 1981 performance is that the actual output of the new product (color tv) was very close to the original projection. It is unclear why the production of the 12″ black-and-white sets was so much lower than originally projected; perhaps it was the result of production difficulties or of a deliberate change in the product-mix. But whatever the reason, it was apparently temporary, since the 1982 target is higher than the original projection. A major problem that Fujian-Hitachi inherited was a surplus of managerial staff, and one of the first actions taken by the new general manger was to reduce the number of staff from over 140 to about 70.[127] Chinese technicians and managerial staff together totaled 120 in mid-1982. While the general manager felt that this number was still too high and that some on the staff were not well-trained, there was no plan to remove more staff members. The number of production workers in 1982 was substantially higher than originally projected but still below the number the enterprise expects to employ eventually. One obvious reason for the higher employment was the higher production targets, but without more information, it is impossible to judge whether all the additional workers are needed to achieve the higher output targets.

That Fujian-Hitachi only managed to export slightly more than one-half the target figures in 1981 does not augur well for its ability to reach the much higher 1982 export target, particularly in view of the depressed world market for consumer durables. The joint venture's exports are handled by Hitachi Home Appliance Sales Co., and it appears that the Chinese and Hitachi disagree strongly over export levels and export strategy. The Chinese want the joint venture to increase its exports quickly. In fact, they hope that 50 percent of its output will be exported by 1983–84, but at a minimum they want enough exports to cover the joint venture's foreign exchange requirements. Hitachi, on the other hand, feels that a rush to export by selling a bit here and a bit there is not a sound long-term strategy. The Japanese assistant manager at Fujian-Hitachi said that the enterprise is currently losing money on every television set exported and that the quality of the exports is not as yet sufficiently high. Hitachi, therefore, would like to concentrate on improving quality first and then aim to penetrate the North American market based on a reputation for quality. It is not difficult to understand why Hitachi prefers its approach. 1) It wants to protect its reputation for quality. 2) Because Southeast Asia is already served by Hitachi's other factories in Asia (in Singapore, Taiwan, South Korea, and so forth), the only long-term export markets open to Fujian-Hitachi are North America and Europe, and to penetrate these markets quality is extremely important.

The original projections were for Fujian-Hitachi to take a small loss in 1981, to break even in 1982, and to begin making profits in 1983. But in fact, in its first year of operation, the enterprise realized a profit of RMB ¥360,000, or approximately a 10 percent return on total investment. This profit, of course, is more a reflection of the protected domestic market and the joint venture's monopoly position in Fujian than an indication of efficiency.[128] Since unit cost is likely to decline as workers become more familiar with the new production technology, it would appear that profits are bound to increase in the future. However, working against this is the fact that Fujian-Hitachi will also export more in the future, and at present it is losing money on its exports.

The Chinese consider the most significant benefit of participating in the Fujian-Hitachi joint venture to be the up-grading of technology. The general manager told

Table 4.2   OUTPUT, EMPLOYMENT AND EXPORT AT FUJIAN-HITACHI: PROJECTIONS, ACHIEVEMENTS, AND TARGETS

	1981		1982		1985	
	Original Projection	Actual	Original Projection	Current[a] Target	Original Projection	Current Plan
Output (thousands)						
12" black & white tv	80	32.9	180	200	180	180
14" color tv	20	23.9	60	100	94	200
20" color tv	15	12.0	22	30	52	n.a.
Export (thousands)	5	2.7[b]	30	66[c]	100	n.a.
Employment						
Workers	141	n.a.	370	540	588	n.a.
Technicians & staff	100	n.a.	120	120	122	n.a.
Foreign staff	2	n.a.	2	2	2	n.a.
Total	243	n.a.	492	662	712	n.a.

a. The employment figures are the actual number of workers employed in mid-1982.
b. Fujian-Hitachi reported that 4% of its 1981 output was exported, or (.04)(68.6) = 2.7.
c. Fujian-Hitachi anticipates that 20% of its 1982 output will be exported, or (0.2)(330) = 66.
Sources: Fujian-Hitachi Television Company, Ltd. and JETRO *China Newsletter*, No. 36, pp. 19–20.

us that what the joint venture achieved in one year in terms of output increases and quality improvements could not have been accomplished by the Chinese themselves in five or even ten years. Much of the new technology was embodied in the machinery and equipment that the joint venture imported from Japan, of which the most important were two automatic assembly lines. Hitachi also provided the joint venture with considerable technical assistance. In addition to the two resident Japanese technicians, Hitachi sent numerous others to Fuzhou for short periods to teach the Chinese its production technology, quality control methods, and maintenance procedures. For example, Fujian-Hitachi's quality control system (line inspection, random sample checking of components, and total inspection of a small sample of the final product) was borrowed entirely from Hitachi. The enterprise has a technical section, but it is not involved in design or development work. Apparently the enterprise has not been successful in convincing the state to allocate it more university-trained engineers, and the technical people currently on staff were educated during the Cultural Revolution and are poorly trained. At the time of our visit, the enterprise was about to send eight of its engineers to Hitachi in Japan for training. Once they return, Fujian-Hitachi should be in a better position to absorb new technology. However, it will be some time before the enterprise acquires its own design and development capacity. Indeed, it has yet to begin to think about research and development.

In mid-1982, Fujian-Hitachi was still adjusting to its new legal status as a joint venture. Its workers had not as yet completely adapted to the new work rules. For example, one of the more important changes was the reduction of the traditional two-hour lunch break to one hour, a shift that was opposed by some workers. Understandably, time was needed for workers to adjust to the new arrangement. The local authorities also had not become totally familiar with the rules governing joint ventures, and this inexperience created problems. Because some of the rules concerning joint ventures lack precison, they create ambiguities and leave room for varying interpretations. The general manager cited two examples. The existing laws permit joint ventures to import and to dismiss workers, but he was uncertain about the conditions under which Fujian-Hitachi would be permitted to do so. His advice to those interested in investing in China is that they should realize that, since China has had so little experience with joint ventures, the participants must be prepared to develop everything from scratch and that this takes time. As an example, he mentioned the considerable time he and the other officers at Fujian-Hitachi spent settling just one relatively minor issue, the amount to be paid to Japanese technicians coming to China and to the Chinese going to Japan. Obviously with more experience these minor issues would consume less time, but meanwhile it is important that those involved in joint ventures be extremely patient.

Conflicts between the two economic systems are clearly visible at Fujian-Hitachi and are causing some difficulties. The Japanese assistant manager put forward the view that the company should be operated with the company's welfare in mind but that the Chinese tend to overemphasize the interests of the state. The Chinese general manager responded with the remark that the Chinese cannot do everything the Japanese way or else they would cease to be socialists. The Japanese assistant manager then replied that he was not interested in changing China from a socialist to a free enterprise system but feels that the government plays too heavy a role in the Chinese economy.

Without question, the equity joint venture is the least flexible of the special trade arrangements that, taken together, constitute the Open Door. It is probably also the most radical, in the sense that it goes the farthest toward permitting capitalist attitudes and institutions to intrude into China's domestic economy. Given these characteristics, it is hardly surprising that the equity joint venture has developed rather slowly, while the alternatives have spurted ahead. It is to these alternative forms of the Open Door that we now turn our attention.

5

Alternatives to the Equity Joint Venture in Light Industry

As can be seen from the discussion in the preceding chapter, the concept of the equity joint venture (*hezi jingying*) has been defined with reasonable clarity, and this form of co-operation is now governed by a relatively well-developed set of rules and regulations. By contrast, the other forms of special trade — such as processing and assembling agreements (*lailiao jiagong* and *laijian zhuangbei*), compensation trade (*buchang maoyi*), and co-operative ventures (*hezuo jingying*) — are not defined with as much precision. Indeed, as will be evident from the case studies described later in this chapter, it is sometimes difficult to say which category a particular venture belongs in. Thus, by comparison to the equity joint venture, these miscellaneous forms suffer from a considerable degree of ambiguity and imprecision, though by the same token it can be said that they benefit from a greater degree of flexibility. In general, this means that such agreements can be negotiated more quickly and also that they can more readily be adjusted to meet changing circumstances. As the data in Chapter 3 indicate, these flexible forms of special trade have proven to be more popular than the equity joint venture, which is more rigidly structured.

THE ROLE OF THE ALTERNATIVES IN CHINA'S CURRENT DEVELOPMENT STRATEGY

As already outlined in Chapter 1, China's current *neihan* ("intensive") development strategy places special emphasis on shifting the sectoral balance of the economy toward light industry, on upgrading existing enterprises, and on improving product quality and labor productivity. The strong tendency toward an unbalanced growth strategy in earlier periods can be seen in Table 5.1, which shows the allocation of investment between light and heavy industry over the years. In examining Table 5.1, it should be noted that even in the most recent period, when national policy has explicitly de-emphasized heavy industry, the lion's share of investment has still gone to that sector. As a supplement to Table 5.1, it should also be noted that the reports given at the National People's Congress in June 1983 suggest that in 1982 the heavy industrial sector managed to capture a larger proportion of total investment than had been intended.[1] This longstanding tendency to neglect light industry is reflected in the backward conditions that characterize this sector. According to a recent study, the average enterprise in light industry employs only about 160 workers and has fixed assets worth only about RMB ¥340,000. Even in the leading city of Shanghai, about half of the machinery currently in use in light industry embodies the technology of the 1940s.[2] China's neglect of light industry is also evident from the high regard now shown for imported consumer goods. To a degree, imported goods may enjoy a certain cachet simply because they are imported, but the more fundamental explanation is undoubtedly the recognition that foreign products generally meet higher quality control standards than their local counterparts.

Table 5.1   THE ALLOCATION OF INVESTMENT IN CAPITAL CONSTRUCTION BETWEEN LIGHT AND HEAVY INDUSTRY, 1953–1981

Time Period	Investment in heavy industry	Share	Investment in light industry	Share
	(RMB ¥ billion)	(%)	(RMB ¥ billion)	(%)
1953–1957	21.28	85.0	3.75	15.0
1958–1962	65.17	89.5	7.66	10.5
1963–1965	19.37	92.2	1.65	7.8
1966–1970	49.89	92.1	4.26	7.9
1971–1975	87.49	89.5	10.30	10.5
1976–1980	107.55	87.4	15.46	12.6
1981	17.26	80.2	4.26	19.8

Source: State Statistical Bureau, Statistical Yearbook of China 1981 (Hong Kong: Economic Information and Agency, 1982), pp. 302 and 304.

The miscellaneous forms of special trade discussed in this chapter are particularly well suited to China's current development strategy, for typically they are small in scale, labor-intensive, and geared to light industry, but at the same time they offer access to foreign technology, capital, and know-how. They are also export-oriented, which means not only that they help to generate scarce foreign exchange but also that they are exposed to the quality control standards of world markets. Even the processing and assembling agreements, which by definition involve very little foreign equipment, may make a significant contribution to the neihan growth strategy. During several of our interviews with Chinese economists and planners, we encountered a disdainful — almost derisive — attitude toward processing agreements, based on the apparent assumption that since so little equipment is involved, China acquires very little technology in these ventures. Yet in fact, as the case of the Xiamen boatyard (described below) illustrates, a technology can be fairly sophisticated even when the machinery is not. In the case of the boatyard, the imported equipment consists of nothing more than a few electrically powered hand tools, while the technology to be transferred involves the knowledge of how to lay up fiberglass sandwiching so as to achieve maximum hull strength. Thus, the critical ingredient is not the imported equipment but the skill and experience of the foreign shipwright. In the case of NIKE running shoes (also described below) the foreign participant's contribution is similar: a mastery of both production and marketing, neither of which is embodied in a machine. And, of course, even if it is true that some of the processing agreements involve little direct transfer of technology, they still have a valuable role to play in the Open Door, for they earn foreign exchange that can be used to import technology for other projects.

Like the processing agreements, the compensation trade agreements are mainly concentrated in small-scale ventures in light industry. Very often, the imported machinery consists of sewing machines and related equipment, used to produce clothing, shoes, handbags, and similar items. In a sense, the statistical averages on compensation trade are distorted by the fact that the data include a few large-scale ventures, such as the marine container factory near Guangzhou that the American firm of Container Transport International (CTI) is involved in. This facility, which began production in October 1980, utilizes foreign equipment worth US$12–13 million, which will be paid back over a five-year period by the sale of containers to CTI at concessional prices.[5] A far more typical compensation trade deal, in terms of size, is the agreement between East Asia Handbag Manufacturing of Hong Kong and a factory at Shenzhen, which uses plant and equipment worth about US$200,000 to produce handbags for sale through the K-Mart chain in the United States.[6]

Co-operative ventures, or contractual joint ventures as they are sometimes called, are typically larger in scale than either processing or compensation trade agreements, though — with the exception of some key projects in the energy sector — they too are often in the realm of light industry. This form of agreement is also popular for ventures in the service sector. At the smaller end of the scale are such projects as the Happy Home Furniture Factory in Shenzhen (described below) and the Zhan-Gang Cooperative Fishery Company. The latter venture, established in 1980, has used foreign capital of about US$1 million supplied by Hong Kong and Macao businessmen to buy boats and other equipment for fishermen operating out of the port of Zhanjiang. The catch is marketed in Hong Kong, and the profits or losses are divided between the participants according to the formula stipulated in the contract[3]. At the larger end of the scale is a project like the Hainan Chengmai

Oil Palm Plantation Company, a co-operative venture between the Guangdong authorities and Singapore business interests, in which the foreign investment has totaled US$30 million.[4] A similar large-scale farming venture, involving Japanese investment of about US$12 million, is now producing wheat and soybeans for export in Manchuria.[5] In the services sector, at least eight new tourist hotels, each involving foreign investment of US$20 million or more, are being built in China as co-operative ventures.[6]

The miscellaneous special trade ventures in light industry and the service sectors, in addition to their important role in transferring technology and earning foreign exchange, have also been significant in breaking down the pervasive tradition of "eating from one big pot." Precisely because most of these ventures are focused on exporting, they have had to make an effort to satisfy the production deadlines, quality control standards, packaging regulations and other requirements of overseas markets. This has not always been easy. For example, East Asia Handbag had to make a penalty payment of US$30,000 to K-Mart because some of the handbags produced in China were substandard.[7] American shoe importers have learned to compensate for dilatory shipments by ordering "spring shoes in fall colors."[8] One major Canadian importer of women's clothing has abandoned its China operations entirely because of the difficulty of getting Chinese enterprises to meet deadlines as promised.[9] And, as will be seen in the case study discussed below, the NIKE shoe company had serious difficulties getting Chinese factories to meet its quality control standards. In attempting to cure these problems, most of which hinge on the discipline and motivation of the labor force, Open Door ventures have often used piece-rate wages, productivity bonuses, and similar material incentives. In many cases, these incentive mechanisms seem to have resolved the quality control problems. These experiences in the Open Door ventures have in turn made it easier to introduce similar reforms in domestic enterprises.

THE LOCAL ECONOMIC ENVIRONMENT

Most Open Door ventures rely to a considerable extent on imported machinery and imported raw materials, and, of course, they also focus on foreign markets. This does not mean, however, that they are entirely insulated from the domestic economic system. All of them are linked to the local economy in various ways. Some have apparently encountered no difficulties because of this, while others have faced serious problems.

To varying degrees, the special trade enterprises must use local material inputs. All of them rely on local utilities, for example, and we heard many adverse comments about brownouts and blackouts in the supply of electricity. Many of the special trade enterprises have also made commitments to phase in the use of local raw materials where this is appropriate and feasible. In the process, they will inevitably become enmeshed in the problems of the local supply system. Understandably, many enterprises are reluctant to risk this. Recognizing the problem, the Chinese authorities are now reported to be developing a Foreign Economic Contract Law, analogous to the new Economic Contract Law that governs the relations between domestic enterprises.[10] The intent of both laws is to penalize suppliers who fail to deliver materials as promised. It is too soon to say how successful this innovation will be in resolving what is widely recognized to be a serious weakness of China's economic system.

Another very important avenue of linkage between the Open Door ventures and the local economic system is the use of the local labor force. Some of the managers we interviewed were rather critical of their workers, while others were evidently quite pleased. As might be expected, this variation is explained in part by the type of work being done. Workers who possess a well-established craft skill, such as woodworking or sewing, are often particularly valuable. The variation in the quality of workers is also a matter of age. Experienced older workers are naturally prized, and we also encountered praise for the newest generation of workers, whose educational levels and motivation are often quite good. Criticisms tend to focus on the in-between age group — that is, the group that grew up during the Cultural Revolution. Open Door ventures that have encountered problems with worker attitudes and motivation have experimented with a variety of bonus and incentive schemes as will be evident from the case studies discussed below.

A third important link between the Open Door enterprises and the domestic economy lies in the tax system. As indicated in Chapter 4, the formation of an equity joint venture creates a limited liability company (a new entity with a separate legal existence), the net earnings of which are subject to the 33 percent income tax plus the 10 percent tax on remitted profits stipulated in the "Income Tax Law of the People's Republic of China Concerning Joint Ventures with Chinese and Foreign Investment" of September 1980. (This summary description is subject to various exceptions and qualifications — the most important of which is that an equity joint venture located in a special economic zone is taxed at the 15 percent rate that applies to all ventures in an SEZ.) By contrast, the other forms of special trade do not generally create a separate legal entity that is subject to taxation in its own right.[11] Rather, these other forms of co-operation are treated simply as conduits through which income flows to the Chinese and foreign participants respectively, and the separate partners are then subject to various tax obligations on this income.[12] For the Chinese participant, the taxes that must be paid are similar to those levied on any other state enterprise — that is, typically, both the consolidated industrial and commercial tax and a steep tax on net earnings plus various minor imposts and fees.

The tax structure faced by the foreign participant in a special trade agreement other than an equity joint venture is spelled out primarily in two documents: the

"Income Tax Law of the People's Republic of China Concerning Foreign Enterprises" (promulgated 13 December 1981) and the supplemental "Regulations on Income Tax for Foreign Enterprises" (promulgated 21 February 1982). These statutes provide for a rather different tax regime from that governing equity joint ventures. Instead of the flat 33 percent rate that is applied to equity joint ventures, these laws stipulate a system of graduated tax rates, which — when the central and local rates are combined — run from a minimum rate of 30 percent on net incomes of less than RMB ¥250,000 per annum to a maximum marginal rate of 50 percent on that part of annual net income that exceeds RMB ¥1,000,000. (As with the income tax on equity joint ventures, these general provisions on the taxation of foreign enterprises are subject to various exceptions and qualifications, designed to encourage investment in certain favored sectors of the economy.)

In terms of the rates levied, the tax laws seem to favor the equity joint venture over the alternative forms of special trade, though this conclusion is weakened to a certain extent by the fact that only the equity joint venture is subject to the extra 10 percent tax on remitted profits. Interestingly enough, however, the Chinese tax experts whom we interviewed insisted quite vigorously and explicitly that these differing tax structures were not intended to favor the equity joint venture over other forms of special trade. Rather, they told us, a field survey of the actual pattern of foreign enterprise earnings was conducted before the tax rates were settled, and the rates were then chosen so that a median-sized enterprise would face the same tax burden regardless of its legal form.[13] The reason for this rather round-about approach appears to be that the tax law governing equity joint ventures, which provides for a simple proportional tax rate, was already in place when the Chinese began to study the tax requirements of the international oil companies. For the oil companies, a major concern was whether the Internal Revenue Service (IRS) would permit Chinese taxes to be credited against American tax obligations, thereby avoiding double taxation. The IRS ruling would depend, among other factors, on whether the Chinese applied the same tax law to the oil companies and to other foreign enterprises. By moving to a progressive, rather than proportional, tax structure in the foreign enterprise income tax law, China was able to accommodate the oil companies' desire to avoid double taxation, but at the same time it was able to tax the oil projects quite heavily while collecting much lighter taxes (proportionally) from small-scale ventures in light industry.

Of course, differences in tax rates are not the only tax issue that will be of concern to a foreign participant in a special trade venture. Just as important will be the definition of what constitutes income earned in China. Article 1 of the foreign enterprise income tax law calls for the taxation of income earned by three types of ventures operating in China: 1) an independent business operation (*duli jingying*), such as a wholly owned subsidiary of a foreign firm, 2) a co-production venture between Chinese and foreign partners (*hezuo shengchan*), and 3) the kind of business that has been variously translated as a co-operative venture, a joint business operation, or a contractual joint venture (*hezuo jingying*). Article 11 of the law covers the case of foreign firms that earn "income obtained from dividends, interest, rentals, royalties and other sources." For the kinds of non-operating income covered by Article 11, the law provides for a flat 20 percent tax withheld at source.[14]

For the most part the meaning of Article 11 seems straightforward enough, especially when read in conjunction with the definitions provided in the supplemental regulations, though the coverage of the phrase "other sources" is not clear, and the ambiguity is hardly eliminated by the explanation in Article 27 of the regulations that "income from other sources means the income which is decided by the Ministry of Finance to be taxable." The real difficulty, however, lies with Article 1. Conspicuously absent in this article's enumeration of the types of venture that are subject to income tax is any mention of either compensation trade or processing and assembling agreements. At a superficial level, this is understandable, since the foreign partners in these types of special trade earn their incomes by selling Chinese products in overseas markets and are not entitled to any share of the income of a production unit in China. Since on the surface it appears that these foreign firms derive no income from activities in China, it seems appropriate that they should pay no Chinese income tax.

At a more subtle level, however, the situation is not so clear. In many of these transactions, a central element is the transfer of technology from abroad. This transfer may take various forms (the foreign partner may supply machinery, provide blueprints, send employees as advisers, or whatever), and the compensation that the foreign firm receives for providing this technology may also take many forms, as the case studies below will illustrate. The point here is that the form of the compensation affects the foreign firm's tax liability. Suppose, for example, that the foreign partner provides a key piece of equipment to the Chinese enterprise and then later takes delivery of some of that machine's output. One possibility is that the foreign firm can receive a certain proportion of the output at no charge. A second possibility is that the foreign firm can be offered the output at a discounted price (that is to say, a price lower than it would have been in an arm's-length export transaction). A third possibility is that the foreign firm can pay full price for the product but receive a stipulated percentage of the Chinese enterprise's earnings. As can readily be seen, there may not be much substantive difference between these three arrangements, though only in the third does the compensation take the form of a visible stream of payments.

Under current semantic conventions, the first and second types of arrangement will usually be labelled compensation trade, though — if the foreign side provides raw materials in addition to the machinery — they are equally likely to be referred to as processing agreements. The third arrangement is now generally called a co-operative venture (or, in the older terminology, a contractual joint venture). The language of Article 1 of the foreign enterprise income tax law strongly suggests that only under the third arrangement will the foreign enterprise be taxed, and this indeed seems to be current Chinese practice. But the situation could change. The second category of venture listed in Article 1 (the co-production or *hezuo sheng-chan* venture) is not defined very clearly and could be interpreted to include most processing and compensation trade agreements. Furthermore, the language of the supplementary regulations moves some distance toward the inclusion of implicit income streams in taxable income, for Article 2 of the regulations speaks of "assembling . . . undertaken under contracts" as an activity that is subject to tax, and Article 26 makes provision for the imputation of income on the basis of arm's-length prices. Thus the statutes could be interpreted to mean that the various forms of implicit compensation for technology are subject to the foreign enterprise income tax, an interpretation that would lead to some tax being levied on many compensation trade and processing agreements. So far this has not happened, but it remains to be seen what the future will bring.

The discussion in the preceding paragraphs should not be construed as suggesting that there is anything illicit or unwise about the tax situation as it currently exists. Tax planning, after all, is not the same thing as tax evasion. Moreover, the taxation of implicit income streams is, at a practical level, a terrible headache to implement, and the Chinese may well feel that what they could gain in additional tax revenues would be more than offset by the extra administrative costs and by the potential loss of foreign goodwill. Also, it must be remembered that compensation trade and processing agreements do not entirely escape taxation under the current rules: the Chinese enterprise is still taxed, and any foreigners who live in China for more than ninety days are subject to a personal income tax.[15] Thus the Chinese authorities still receive some tax revenues, possibly substantial tax revenues, from these ventures. Furthermore, it is not generally correct to suggest that the foreign corporation escapes taxation on these implicit income streams, since this income will normally be taxed upon realization, either in the country where export sales take place or in the foreign partner's home jurisdiction.

THE INTERNATIONAL ECONOMIC ENVIRONMENT

As the domestic difficulties confronting special trade ventures have gradually been reduced (that is, as quality control has been improved, administrative hurdles simplified, tax regulations clarified, and so on), it has become increasingly evident that the Open Door faces a serious external problem as well — the rising tide of protectionism in major world markets. This recent change in the global economic climate is particularly threatening to Open Door projects because they stress exports so heavily. Generally speaking, the long period from 1947, when the General Agreement on Tariffs and Trade (GATT) was signed, until the Arab-Israeli war of 1973 and the subsequent quadrupling of world oil prices, was a period of significant liberalization in world trade. Under the auspices of GATT, many countries promised to negotiate substantial reductions in tariffs and to eliminate quotas and similar non-tariff barriers to trade altogether. These pledges were not always implemented with much enthusiasm (in particular, many countries continued to shield their agricultural sectors from the competition of imports), but on the whole this was an era of optimism and growth. Then, fed by the economic downturn of 1974–75, and the even deeper recession at the end of the decade, pessimism and protectionism re-emerged in world trade.

Having remained relatively isolated during the long era of trade liberalization, China had the misfortune to begin pursuing its open door strategy just when the outside world was becoming less sympathetic to such a move. The very industries that China would like to emphasize during the early stages of the Open Door (because they are labor-intensive and do not involve highly sophisticated technology) are often the same ones that seek protection in the developed economies. A good example can be found in the case of Chinese exports of porcelain dinnerware to the United States. In 1982 the American producers of dinnerware, alleging "significant injury" from Chinese exports, sought relief under Section 406 of the Trade Act of 1974. After investigating the situation, the International Trade Commission (the American government agency that is empowered to hear such complaints) ruled that Chinese dinnerware imports had merely displaced competing Japanese products in the American market and had therefore not caused the domestic manufacturers any significant injury.[16] Although the ITC found in China's favor in this instance, the grounds for the decision were protectionist in spirit. If the Chinese dinnerware had displaced American products rather than Japanese, the verdict could well have gone the other way. In another section 406 case heard by the ITC, American producers of canned mushrooms also argued that imports from China have caused significant injury to the domestic industry. In an initial determination, it was found that a 7.38 percent "margin of dumping" existed, but a later recalculation found that the margin was only 0.46 percent, and the ITC therefore ruled that no significant damage could have occurred.[17] Meanwhile, as Chinese exports grow, American producers of everything from shoes to manhole covers are contemplating the possibility of bring action against competing Chinese products.[18] It is perhaps worth noting that the tourism industry, for all of its dangers and difficulties from the Chinese point of view, is at least relatively immune from these protectionist developments, because it is politically awkward for Western governments to impose constraints on their citizens' holiday travel.

Regardless of the outcome where mushrooms or shoes or manhole covers are concerned, the true effect of protectionism will have to be judged for many years to come primarily in terms of the fate of textile and clothing exports, simply because these products account for such a large proportion of China's foreign exchange earnings. Furthermore, the textile and clothing industry has been a particularly attractive sector for processing agreements and other forms of Open

Door activity. As can be seen from Table 5.2, exports of textiles and clothing have in recent years provided about one-fourth of China's total earnings from commodity exports.[19] As can also be seen from Table 5.2, China's exports of textiles and clothing have been growing very rapidly in recent years — a development that has caused alarm on both sides of the Atlantic.

In Europe, the policy toward textile imports has been decidedly protectionist for a number of years.[20] On the whole, however, China's clothing and textile exports to the Common Market have grown rapidly in this same period — more than doubling between 1978 and 1981. The explanation for this anomaly is that the five-year textile agreement concluded between China and the European Economic Community (EEC) in 1979 allocated quotas to China that were large enough to permit substantial growth. In effect, the EEC accommodated China's desire for expanded exports by disappointing other, more established suppliers. Now, however, China has pretty well reached its quota limits, so any further growth of exports to Europe is unlikely. Indeed, on specific items that prove to be particularly sensitive, quota reductions may well be imposed by the EEC countries, as happened recently in the case of baby clothes going to Britain and of tents going to the Benelux countries.

On the other side of the Atlantic the situation is equally unpromising. In Canada, after a period of rapid growth between 1976 and 1978, China's textile exports were rolled back to 1975 levels by what is euphemistically labelled a voluntary restraint agreement.[21] In the United States, textile imports from China grew quite rapidly between 1972 and 1981, as shown in Table 5.3. A logarithmic trend line fitted to the data from Table 5.3 indicates an average growth rate of about 65 percent per annum over the decade covered. This rapid growth started from a negligible base, however, and therefore Chinese textiles did not appear worrisome to American producers until about 1978, a year in which imports from China still represented only about 2.1 percent of total American textile imports by value.[22] Attempted negotiations during 1979 failed utterly because the two sides were so far apart in their viewpoints, and the US responded by imposing quotas unilaterally on several key items. As Chinese products began to pile up in bonded warehouses, the Chinese realized that they had little choice but to adopt a more flexible stance. A new round of negotiations then began, which eventually led to the textile agreement signed by Bo Yibo and Jimmy Carter in September 1980.[23]

The 1980 agreement, which covered the three years from 1980 to 1982, provided for quotas on eight categories of textile products and stipulated that for these categories growth would on average be limited to 6 percent a year.[24] Compared to the growth rates of the preceding years, this limitation on growth represented a severe restraint. On the other hand, only eight categories were covered — a small number compared, for example, to the contemporaneous US textile agreement with Hong Kong, which imposed constraints of one sort or another on 105 categories.[25] As can be seen from Table 5.3, total Chinese textile

During the course of 1982, several rounds of negotiations were held attempting

Table 5.2 THE SHARE OF TEXTILES AND CLOTHING IN CHINA'S TOTAL EXPORTS, 1979–1981

(US$ billion)

	1979	1980	1981
Exports of yarn and fabrics	2.28	2.88	3.27
Exports of clothing	1.06	1.73	2.18
Textiles and clothing together	3.34	4.61	5.45
China's total exports	13.63	18.20	22.40
Share of textiles and clothing in total	24.5%	25.3%	24.3%

Sources and notes: CIA, *China: International Trade, Fourth Quarter, 1981* (June 1982), cited in *China Trade Report*, September, 1982, page 10, and *China Business Review*, March-April, 1982, page 59.

exports to the US continued to grow rapidly even after the 1980 agreement came into effect as China concentrated its efforts on unconstrained categories. By the close of the agreement period, products from China represented about 10 percent of all US textile imports and were rapidly approaching the levels enjoyed by the "big three" — Hong Kong, South Korea, and Taiwan.[26]

Table 5.3 CHINESE TEXTILE EXPORTS TO THE UNITED STATES 1972–1981
(US$ million)

Year	SITC No. 65	SITC No. 84	Total
1972	3	1	4
1973	10	2	12
1974	28	6	34
1975	33	9	42
1976	47	16	63
1977	35	26	61
1978	63	63	126
1979	65	153	218
1980	135	225	360
1981	237	378	615

Sources and Notes: SITC category number 65 covers yarns, fabrics, and floor coverings, while SITC category number 84 covers garments. Figures for 1972–1979 are from *U.S. General Imports, Country by Commodity* (microfiche). Figures for 1980–1981 are from CIA, *China: International Trade, Fourth Quarter, 1981*, June, 1982, p. 16.

to reach a new agreement before the old one expired, but to no avail. From the point of view of the Reagan administration, a sharp curtailment of the growth rate of Chinese textile imports was non-negotiable for at least three interconnected reasons: 1) the deep recession in the American economy generally, and in the textile industry more specifically, 2) the influence over the federal budget of certain key congressmen from textile states, and 3) the political danger of taking any action that would have an adverse impact on Taiwan. Thus, the US negotiators insisted that the number of categories covered by quotas must be substantially increased, that the current rules governing interim consultations must be changed to make it easier to impose new quotas during the life of the agreement, and that the average growth of quotas must be limited to about 1 or 2 percent per year.[27] The Chinese side characterized the American proposals as discriminatory and "extremely unfair" and rejected them out of hand.[28] China apparently hoped for a continuation of the 6 percent growth limits of the old agreement, at least until China's textile exports could achieve parity with the big three. In support of their position, the Chinese negotiators pointed out that in the broad perspective of total trade, US exports to China are far greater than China's exports to the US and that, even in the narrow perspective of the textile trade, China has been running a deficit in recent years, because it has been spending more for American cotton and synthetic fibers than it has earned from its exports of textiles and clothing.[29]

In the end no compromise was reached, and on 13 January 1983, the US announced that new, tighter controls on China's textile exports would once again be imposed unilaterally. The Chinese responded by sharply curtailing their purchases of American agricultural products, with the result that American sales of wheat, cotton, and soybeans in the first six months of 1983 plummeted to US$184.6 million from a level of US$855.3 million in the corresponding period of 1982.[30] This tactic succeeded in mobilizing the American farm lobby to counterbalance the textile lobby, and thus a new agreement was reached in July 1983. The new agreement, which runs until the end of 1987, will permit Chinese textile exports to increase by about 3.5 percent per year — less than the 6 percent limit the Chinese were asking for, but higher than the 1 percent limits currently imposed on the big three.[31] American textile interests responded to this agreement by launching a countervailing duty suit, an action which could undermine the five-year agreement.[32]

On both sides, these disputes involve fundamental structural adjustments, and thus tensions are unlikely to be eased as long as the world economy remains mired in recession. The dangers are evident. As the experience of the 1930s makes clear, a deep economic recession is an environment in which it is all too likely that one protectionist move will spawn succeeding rounds of "beggar-thy-neighbour" retaliation to the detriment of both countries. China can ill afford such a downward spiral. If the processing agreements, compensation trade, and co-operative ventures of the Open Door are to succeed, they must have access to export markets. Otherwise, they have no means to pay for their imported machinery and technology.

CASE STUDIES

The Beijing Radio Factory[33]

The Beijing Radio Factory had its beginnings in 1956, when ten small workshops, employing a total of about two-hundred workers, were merged to form the present enterprise. Originally housed in an old school building, the enterprise began by producing simple electronic components. Production of complete radios was begun on an experimental basis in 1958 and was firmly established by 1964. Since 1978 the enterprise has also produced cassette tape recorders. In 1981 the factory produced more than one million transistor radios, of which about 15 to 20 percent were exported, and about 100,000 tape recorders, of which a smaller percentage went to export. (For China as a whole, 1981 output levels were 36.3 million radio sets and 1.4 million tape recorders respectively.[34]) At the time of our visit in May 1982, output levels for the factory for 1982 were projected to be about 1,000,000 radios and about 160,000 tape recorders.

Under the state plan the factory is required to meet a wide variety of specified targets. In principle, the enterprise must achieve all of its targets or else forfeit its bonus, but in practice it seems that the bonus is dependent on four key targets: quantity, variety, quality, and profits. Though some negotiation takes place, the perception at the enterprise level is that the targets are essentially dictated by higher-level authorities. As an incentive to better performance, the enterprise bonus is structured as follows: if profits reach the target level and other key targets are also met, the enterprise gets to retain a specified percentage of the profit; of profits that exceed the target, the enterprise keeps a higher percentage. As a special incentive to export, the radio factory is allowed to keep about 20 percent of its foreign exchange earnings. (In fact, the enterprise does not really "keep" this foreign exchange in the sense of retaining direct signing authority over it; permission must still be obtained from the relevant authorities before it can be spent. But, as a factory spokesman explained, "the permission comes much more quickly.")

The enterprise now employs about 2,800 people, of whom about 2,000 are direct production workers and about 200 are engineers and technicians. The factory's technical staff has the capability to do some reverse engineering as indicated by their success at duplicating an imported heat-treating machine and selling copies to other factories. They would like to do more of this kind of technological borrowing, but the scarcity of skilled people hampers these efforts. On the assembly lines, by contrast, most of the work requires no special skill beyond simple manual dexterity. The typical pattern is for new employees to receive only two to four weeks of training before going to work on one of the lines. (The engineer who was our guide told us that he finds it easier to work with the middle-aged employees, who are more highly motivated. Shortly after he said this, we noticed one of the young women on an assembly line surreptitiously reading a magazine article about hair styling while she worked.)

Basic wage levels range from RMB ¥40 to over RMB ¥100 per month, but most of the workers are clustered toward the lower end of this scale because the average is about RMB ¥55. In addition to their basic wage, workers receive direct subsidies of about RMB ¥15 a month to cover transportation and similar expenses. Workers also receive an individual bonus which averages about RMB ¥10, though it can be as much as RMB ¥40 for the best workers. The bonuses are awarded according to a complex point scheme, recalculated each month, that covers such on-the-job attributes as productivity, attitude, and punctuality, but also encompasses off-the-job behavior (getting traffic tickets, for example). The effectiveness of this bonus system is probably diluted somewhat by the practice of publicly announcing the amount of each worker's bonus every month — an arrangement that creates social pressure for the bonuses to be disbursed in a relatively egalitarian pattern. Apart from the financial incentives of the bonus scheme, the factory also has a system of administrative sanctions to enforce labor discipline. These sanctions range from putting a note in the worker's employment dossier (the least serious step) up to outright dismissal (euphemistically called "transfer"). In fact, however, these administrative sanctions have such serious potential consequences for the worker that there is great reluctance to use them. In 1981 the factory experienced only one incident — a worker involved in a street fight — that was deemed significant enough to warrant administrative discipline and then only at the lightest level. (Of course, the fact that these sanctions are seldom invoked does not necessarily mean that they are ineffective; their mere existence may be enough to influence behavior.)

The "Peony" brand name, which is the exclusive property of this enterprise, is recognized throughout China as one of five brand names that signify high-quality radio products. Because the Chinese consumer is becoming increasingly finicky about quality, this brand-name identification is a valuable asset, and indeed cases have been reported in which famous brand names (like the "Flying Pigeon" bicycle) have been counterfeited by unscrupulous imitators.[35] To protect its reputation for quality, the Beijing Radio Factory has developed a three-level system of quality control inspections: first by the individual worker, then at the small group level, and finally at the workshop level. Of the million radios produced in 1981, only about one or two thousand were found to be defective; in most of these cases it was possible to identify the problem and repair it. The factory offers the consumer a six-month warranty on its less expensive models. On top-of-the-line models, each item is dated and numbered, so that if it is returned, the factory is able to identify the particular worker responsible for the defect. We were told that because of this attention to quality control, the Peony brand has been relatively unaffected by the recent recession, while producers of lower-quality radios have had to slash their prices by as much as 30 percent, or else "put everything into inventory."

When we asked our guide to identify aspects of the factory's mangement that posed problems or needed improvement, he replied that their main problem is with unreliable suppliers. The lack of a single tiny component can force them to shut down an entire assembly line. In his language, this is not a "subjective" problem but an "objective" one — that is, it is not a flaw in the factory's internal management but rather a shortcoming of the larger economic system within which the factory functions. The enterprise does have contracts with its suppliers, but in the past the enforcement of these contracts has been quite lax. So the managers spend a lot of time on the telephone, and in more serious cases they send representatives out to try to prod their suppliers into action. At the same time, however, their contracts with foreigners are very strict, so to protect themselves they order well ahead of need, carry large inventories of components, and so on. (During our tour, we saw one assembly line working on components that had been purchased two years earlier.)

Over the years, the factory's dealings with foreigners have been of several types. In earlier years their exports were handled by a foreign trade corporation, so they had little direct contact with the outside world. With the coming of the Open Door, however, the situation has changed. About four years ago they negotiated a simple processing agreement with a Japanese firm, but this arrangement proved unsatisfactory and is no longer functioning. More recently, the factory has entered into an agreement with the Hong Kong and Singapore affiliates of Philips, the well-known European electronics firm. This agreement, though not as elaborate or permanent in nature as the Fujian-Hitachi joint venture described in Chapter 4, is certainly something more than a simple processing arrangement. Furthermore, both sides have expressed the hope that a full-fledged joint venture may develop in due course.

Under the agreement with Philips, engineers from both sides have collaborated to design a radio and a cassette tape recorder which are intended mainly for the export market but which will also be permitted limited sales in the domestic market. Early prototypes were shipped abroad for testing, and a Philips team came to Beijing to inspect the first mass-produced models, but quality control does not appear to be a contentious issue since Philips does not have a resident inspector at the factory, nor does it send in outside inspectors on a regular basis. Planned export levels for 1982 were about 10,000 of the radios and a similar number of the tape recorders. Apart from the design work, Philips has provided certain specialized production equipment and also some components. In addition, about fifty of the factory's technicians have received two to four weeks of training at the Philips facilities in Hong Kong and Singapore. Finally, Philips has contributed its trademark and has taken responsibility for overseas distribution and marketing. The contract with Philips does not provide for separate compensation for these varied contributions. Rather, the price charged for the production equipment implicitly covers all the rest. Furthermore, since the equipment was not paid for at the time of delivery, but will be covered out of export earnings as they accrue, the agreement contains what is in effect a loan, and the price of the equipment was presumably set to provide for implicit interest payments on this loan.

The Beijing Radio-Philips agreement cannot easily be fitted into any of the regular categories of special trade, and thus it serves as a useful reminder that the possibilities of the Open Door are more complex and more flexible than the standardized vocabulary might suggest. Though Philips provides both technology and trademark, and receives compensation that is in effect a running royalty,[36] this is not really a licensing agreement in the usual sense. Though the Beijing factory does some assembling of components supplied by Philips, this is certainly not just a processing agreement. Though some machinery is supplied, this is not a normal compensation trade agreement either, since the contract can be renewed or terminated on a year-by-year basis at the pleasure of the two parties, which implies that the value of the machinery is not a major part of the package. Our informants at the Beijing factory did not use any of the standard labels to characterize their agreement with Philips, but rather called it simply "technical co-operation" (*jishu hezuo*).

Our guide stressed that, for a Chinese enterprise, the main reason for getting involved in a special trade venture should be to raise technical levels and improve quality control, while making profits should be secondary. In his judgment, the Beijing Radio-Philips co-operation has been a success by these standards. But although both sides have expressed an interest in forming an equity joint venture and the question has been discussed each year, Beijing Radio and Philips have so far been unable to reach an agreement on the larger-scale, longer term co-operation that a joint venture would entail. The basic problem is that the Chinese side wants to export as much as possible and certainly at least enough to cover the venture's foreign exchange needs, while Philips resists the idea of large-scale exports, preferring to concentrate sales in the domestic market. It remains to be seen whether a mutually acceptable compromise can be reached.

NIKE Athletic Shoes[37]

A decade ago the NIKE brand of athletic shoes was virtually unknown, and the company's annual sales totaled less than $2 million. Then the jogging and fitness boom swept North America. In fiscal 1982, NIKE's annual report showed revenues of $694 million on sales of 43 million pairs of shoes. NIKE's markets are concentrated in North America, but for the most part production is carried out in overseas locations — England, Ireland, Japan, Korea, Hong Kong, Taiwan, Malaysia, and several other places. Some of these overseas factories are owned directly by NIKE, but most are independent enterprises that work for NIKE on a contract basis. Although some of these facilities are quite large by shoe-industry standards (one key supplier in South Korea makes one million pairs of NIKE shoes a month), NIKE's explosive growth has forced it to continue looking for additional supply sources. The company made its first attempt to approach the Chinese at the Guangzhou Trade Fair in the autumn of 1979, but this initial effort ended in frustration — the company did not even obtain a visa to attend the fair.[38] Persistence paid off, however. A proposal submitted to China National Light Industrial Products Import and Export Corporation (INDUSTRY) in April 1980 produced results with remarkable speed: agreements in principle were signed with factories in Shanghai and Tianjin in September of that same year. These agreements covered two types of shoes: a canvas court shoe and a nylon running shoe. Initially, all the materials were to be imported, and the Chinese enterprises would be paid a certain fee for each pair of shoes manufactured. Thus, in essence, these were simple processing agreements, though with the understanding that Chinese materials would gradually be incorporated into the process when feasible. Reaching agreement on the fee per pair was not easy. NIKE's normal practice is to show a potential supplier a sample shoe and invite the supplier to submit a price quotation. In this case, however, it was felt that, because of China's unfamiliarity with the product, such a procedure might not be workable. As an alternative, therefore, NIKE simply opened its books to the Chinese and showed them that in the case of the canvas shoe, for example, suppliers in Taiwan and Korea were paid $5 per pair. The Chinese enterprises then offered to make the canvas model for $9 a pair! Understandably, NIKE demurred. Only after nine long months of negotiation was agreement reached on a fee of $5 per pair.

In addition to raw materials, NIKE has also supplied shoemaking machinery worth about $75,000,[39] which will gradually be repaid by discounting the processing fee for a certain number of pairs of shoes. Although this machinery came from Taiwan and was stamped "Made in the Republic of China," there were no adverse repercussions at first. Several months later, however, when the question of American arms sales to Taiwan became a point of increasing friction between Beijing and Washington, the shoe machinery was suddenly impounded and a fine of RMB ¥18,000 was imposed.

In addition to price disputes and political friction, the NIKE experience in China has also been troubled by quality control problems. As NIKE is well aware, serious joggers are a finicky group of consumers. Dissatisfaction with an inferior product spreads quickly by word of mouth, and no amount of glossy advertising is likely to offset the damage. This was graphically demonstrated in 1981 when one major manufacturer went bankrupt because the shoddy quality of its shoes had become an open secret in the running fraternity. Thus, NIKE has good reason to be fanatical about quality control. When a pair of shoes comes off the assembly line, a NIKE inspector grades it into one of three categories: A, B, or C. The grade A shoes are the only ones sold commercially. B-grade shoes (about 1 percent of global output) are those that meet all structural standards but have minor flaws in their appearance. These B-grade shoes are used for testing, donated to charitable groups, sold to NIKE's own employees, or otherwise disposed of outside of regular market channels. C-grade shoes are those that have some structural fault; standard procedure is to consign them to a shredding machine.

From the outset, NIKE insisted on stationing one of its own quality control inspectors at each Chinese factory. As a concession to the realities of the learning curve, however, NIKE agreed to buy 60,000 pairs of A-grade and B-grade shoes which, although identical to two standard NIKE models in other respects, would not carry the NIKE emblem, would not be marketed in normal channels, and therefore (by implication) would not need to be judged quite so rigorously by the inspectors. As a further sweetener to the contract, NIKE offered to pay 80 percent of the normal processing fee for any B-grade shoes, even though the standard contract with other suppliers specifies 60 percent. It was initially expected that these 60,000 pairs of non-brand shoes would be produced very quickly, but — because of quality control problems — this did not happen. At the nadir of NIKE's pessimism, in the summer of 1982, one of the factories in Tianjin had produced and stockpiled 6,000 pairs of shoes that NIKE judged to be C-grade and wanted to send to the shredder, to the dismay of the Chinese. In the past, these Chinese factories had had no trouble meeting the quality requirements of the state marketing network. Now, having allocated some portion (typically 20 or 25 percent) of their labor force, machinery, floor space, and other resources to the NIKE project, these same factories found that practically all of their intended export production was rejected by the foreign inspectors, even though the shoes in question were of much better quality than anything else they produced. Thus the enterprises were quickly getting into an untenable situation: the factory payroll was as large as ever, yet domestic earnings were truncated, while the anticipated foreign exchange earnings were looking more and more problematical.

Fortunately for both sides, these quality control problems were gradually resolved. (Part of the explanation may lie in the experimental bonus schemes that have been instituted in some of the factories, such as the Japanese-style end-of-year bonus that one factory distributed at the Chinese New Year in February 1983.) As of March 1983, production of the non-brand shoes had ceased, and two factories were producing shoes carrying the NIKE logo, with two more factories soon to come on stream and four others expected to begin making NIKE shoes before long. Not surprisingly, considering China's transportation bottlenecks, all eight of these enterprises are located in coastal cities, ranging from Tianjin in the north to Guangzhou in the south. Local raw materials and supplies, such as shoelaces and canvas fabric, have begun to be used, though no one seems to know when nylon fabric (which is a product of the petrochemical industry) will be available from domestic sources. In some respects, the NIKE relationship with China — despite all the troubles with quality control — has a more promising future than the Beijing Radio-Philips partnership, since NIKE wants to export all of the shoes produced and thus faces no potential clash of interests over access to the domestic Chinese market.

Xiamen (Amoy) Cigarette Factory[40]

This enterprise was established as a private concern in 1948 financed by Xiamen and Shanghai business interests. Changed to a joint public-private venture in 1954, it became a full-fledged state enterprise in 1958 when several smaller factories were merged with it. At the time of our visit, the enterprise was once again in a state of transition. Part of the change was physical since the buildings were being enlarged to permit the incorporation of a smaller branch factory that had previously been located elsewhere in Xiamen. The other part of the change was organizational. As the manager explained, their old status was that of an enterprise under "dual leadership": partly responsible to the local authorities and partly responsible to the national ministries of Light Industry and Commerce. For example, a request for foreign exchange would be directed to the local authorities, but the allocation of tobacco would be controlled by the national plan through the Ministry of Light Industry. (Not all of the factory's tobacco comes from the surrounding province of Fujian; the tobacco being unbaled during our tour came from Henan.) The factory's new status, which was still pending in the summer of 1982, will be that of a subsidiary unit to the newly created China Tobacco Company, which will reportedly have vertically integrated control over the production and marketing of all cigarettes in China when it is fully operational.

In the 1950s, cigarette manufacturing was extremely labor-intensive, but over the years production has gradually been mechanized. This is reflected in the factory's rising productivity figures: in 1954 average annual output was about 30 cases per employee (a case contains 10,000 cigarettes), while in 1981 the corresponding figure was about 640 cases per employee. From a production level of 15,000 cases in 1954, output gradually increased to about 200,000 cases a year during the 1960s and reached a level of about 600,000 cases a year in 1979 and 1980. The near-term goal, once the branch factory has been integrated with the parent enterprise, is to produce about 800,000 cases per year. (For China as a whole, cigarette production was 15.2 million cases in 1980 and 17.0 million cases in 1981.)[41]

At present the factory employs about 900 production-line workers plus about 60 technicians and other staff. The current work force — which is about equally divided between men and women — is generally quite young. About 200 older workers retired recently and now receive pensions from the enterprise. The manager who was our guide views the young workers quite favorably and says that they learn quickly and work hard. A new worker, after graduation from middle or senior secondary school, enters the factory as an apprentice at a wage of RMB ¥28 a month, plus bonuses. A month of training is followed by assignment to a regular production-line position. After a year of experience, the apprentice takes a test (part written, part applied) and, if successful, moves up to the position of journeyman at RMB ¥31 per month. Only in the third year does a journeyman become an entry-level regular worker. The average wage in the factory is about RMB ¥67 per month, which includes about RMB ¥20 of direct subsidies for such things as haircuts, transportation, and so on. Like other urban workers in China, these employees also receive substantial indirect subsidies, since the market prices of basic foodstuffs and several other important consumer items do not fully cover costs of production. These subsidies are financed through the central government's budget, which underwrites the losses of the retail marketing system.

Individual monthly bonuses average about RMB ¥15 to 20, with good workers usually receiving about RMB ¥30, though the bonus may be as much as RMB ¥50 in exceptional cases. These bonuses are calculated on a small-group basis (that is, all the workers on a particular machine receive the same amount), according to a complicated formula that makes adjustments for the lower productivity of older machines. Each small group is given targets for such things as cost level, quality, and maintenance. Failure to meet any target means a reduction in the group's bonus. In effect, this bonus scheme builds a piece-work component into the wage system, which may be one explanation for the generally high level of motivation among the workers. The enterprise is thinking of changing its present bonus system to a new scheme that it calls "economic reckoning" (*jingji hesuan*), under which each unit is given a cost control figure and then receives as its bonus any saving beyond the control figure that the group can achieve. So far, however, this proposal is only at the discussion stage. (Described superficially, the proposed reform seems to create a perverse incentive for groups to neglect maintenance in order to keep apparent costs as low as possible, but perhaps the details of the proposal provide some safeguards against this danger.)

If the factory succeeds in meeting its targets under the annual plan, it is permitted to retain 22 percent of its profit (net earnings) for internal purposes, such as renovating the factory, providing for collective welfare, and paying the workers' individual bonuses. At the cigarette factory we were not told what fraction of retained earnings is allocated to paying individual bonuses, but in other factories we visited the figure given was always in the range of 20 to 30 percent of retained earnings. Since the factory's average monthly bonus is RMB ¥15–20, the annual total for bonuses is about RMB ¥180,000 to RMB ¥220,000. Thus it can reasonably be inferred that retained earnings range between RMB ¥600,000 and RMB ¥1,100,000. Because retained earnings are 22 percent of profits, the factory's annual profit for 1981 was, by implication, between RMB ¥2,700,000 and RMB ¥5,000,000, or about RMB ¥4.5 to 8.5 per case of cigarettes.

The information provided in the *Statistical Yearbook of China* implies that in 1981 the tobacco needed to produce a typical case of cigarettes was purchased by the state for about RMB ¥120, and that a case of cigarettes sold at retail for about RMB ¥775.[42] The Xiamen factory's annual payroll, including bonuses and some allowance for pension costs, can be calculated to be about RMB ¥1,100,000 to 1,200,000, or about RMB ¥1.8 to 2.0 per case. If we allow a generous RMB ¥30 per case as an estimate of other costs (paper, electricity, depreciation charges on machinery, and so forth), the following rough but revealing picture emerges of the financial anatomy of the cigarette business in 1981:

Cost of tobacco	RMB ¥120 per case
Labor costs	2
Estimated other costs	30
Factory profit	6
(net of bonuses)	
Subtotal (price ex-factory)	RMB ¥158
Mark-up	617
Retail price	RMB ¥775

Transportation costs have been omitted from this analysis, but — for a product with such a high value per unit weight — they would be relatively small. Whether the mark-up is taken as an excise tax on cigarettes or as the profit of the marketing network makes little difference; it is revenue to the state either way. In addition, of course, 78 percent of the factory's profit also accrues to the state, though the amounts involved are more modest. All in all, it is little wonder that — according to several of the economists and planners we interviewed — control over the cigarette industry has been a persistent source of conflict between local and central authorities.

The Xiamen Cigarette Factory's relationsip with the American tobacco firm of Reynolds has equally interesting financial implications. This relationship traces its origins to April 1978 when Reynolds representatives from Hong Kong made their first visit to Xiamen. After two years of discussions and negotiations, a detailed agreement was signed in April 1980 between Reynolds and the Ministry of Light Industry and the Fujian authorities. A two-stage development is envisioned: the current processing agreement, to be followed by a more complex joint production agreement or perhaps an equity joint venture at some time in the future.[43] Under the current agreement, the Xiamen factory produced 14,000 cases of Camel brand filter cigarettes in 1981. (Taking Camels and domestic brands together, the factory's output was about 615,000 cases in 1981.) A portion of the 1981 Camel production went to Hong Kong, with marketing handled by Reynolds, while the rest was sold for foreign exchange in such domestic outlets as the Friendship Stores and tourist hotels, with marketing handled by the China National Native Produce and Animal By-Products Import and Export Corporation, or CHINATUHSU as it is more commonly known.[44] Production of Camels for 1982 was expected to be considerably larger than for 1981 (the machinery in question has a capacity of 50,000 cases a year), and 1982 output was to be divided about equally between Hong Kong and the local tourist market.

Under the current agreement, Reynolds provides three things: machinery, technical assistance, and raw materials. The machinery is of two sorts: production-line equipment capable of producing about 2,000 cigarettes per minute and sophisticated quality control devices that check dimensions, porosity, moisture content, and other relevant characteristics of the product. This imported equipment is reported to be worth about US$1 million, an extraordinarily high figure for a processing agreement. Yet this venture is not referred to as compensation trade because the machinery is only on loan to the Chinese. Reynolds retains the option to sell it or remove it at the termination of the agreement.[45] Quite deliberately, the imported production-line equipment is of 1960s vintage. The Chinese considered the possibility of installing later-generation machinery, capable of manufacturing 4,000 to 6,000 cigarettes per minute, but decided that the newer machinery, because of its higher paper tension, more sophisticated gluing, and greater maintenance requirements, was too advanced for local conditions. (The equipment already in the factory before the agreement with Reynolds was built in China and has a speed of about 1,000 cigarettes per minute.) The technical assistance provided by Reynolds has been of several types: advice on plant layout, instruction in the use and maintenance of the imported machinery, and training in the random sampling techniques necessary for better quality control. During the first seven or eight months of the agreement, several Reynolds people stayed in Xiamen almost continuously, but during 1982 only occasional visits were necessary. At present the raw materials for the Camel cigarettes — tobacco, paper, filter material, cartons, and so forth — are entirely imported. The local manager expects that it will be possible to use Chinese tobacco and paper for the Camels in due course but expressed pessimism about obtaining filter materials domestically. (Like nylon for the NIKE running shoes, the filter material is a product of the petrochemical industry.)

The Chinese side supplies buildings, labor, utilities, and some ancillary equipment. In return, Reynolds reportedly pays the Chinese US$30 for each case of Camels produced.[46] We were told that the factory gets 20 percent of any foreign exchange earned, with 30 percent going to the Fujian authorities and 50 percent to the central government, but this arrangement may now be changed, because the new Fujian rules provide for foreign exchange to be divided 40 percent to the enterprise, 30 percent to the province, and 30 percent for the central authorities. In any event, even if the factory retains only 20 percent of the US$30, or about RMB ¥16.8 at the internal settlement exchange rate, the gap between this processing fee and the factory's unit labor costs means that the enterprise makes a significant profit on each case of Camels. When asked about the benefits of the link with Reynolds, however, the manager emphasized the opportunity for technological and managerial upgrading and did not mention profit. At the same time, with Camels selling at retail for RMB ¥1.7 per pack,[47] or about US$475 per case at the tourists' rate of exchange, it is evident that the factory is not capturing very much of the total profit in the situation — although higher-level authorities may be, since CHINATUHSU presumably receives a share of the retail mark-up for its role in distribution.

The agreement with Reynolds has no fixed termination date, and pricing and production plans are settled by negotiation on a year-to-year basis. The two sides have discussed the possibility of producing other Reynolds brands in Xiamen. They have also talked about developing and producing an entirely new brand on a joint venture basis, but these more ambitious plans have not progressed as rapidly as was first hoped. The fundamental difficulty is that — as with Philips and Peony — the Chinese side wants to concentrate on exports, while Reynolds is mainly interested in marketing within China, since exports to other parts of Asia would have to compete with cigarettes that Reynolds is already producing in Malaysia, the Philippines, and elsewhere. Whether the two sides will be able to reach a compromise on this issue at some time in the future remains to be seen.

Celestial Yachts and the Xiamen Boatyard[48]

In 1958 several ship repair facilities were merged to form the Xiamen boatyard. Initially, the boatyard had the capacity to build about eight large wooden junks (250-h.p., 120-ton displacement) per year. In 1970 the yard was enlarged to permit construction of two steel vessels (600-h.p., 350-ton displacement) each year in addition to the wooden boats. At the time of our visit, the enterprise employed 530 workers, who received an average wage of RMB ¥50 per month plus an average bonus of RMB ¥5 per month.

In 1980 the boatyard sent a technician and five workers to Japan to learn how to work with fiberglass. (Because of the heavy wooden framing of a traditional Chinese junk, a fiberglass vessel of equivalent cargo capacity is only half as large and therefore uses only about half as much fuel.) Unfortunately, the Japanese company that was supposed to provide the fiberglass technology proved to be undercapitalized, and the deal collapsed. Shortly after this the Xiamen Development Corporation, an arm of the Xiamen SEZ administration, introduced the boatyard to Celestial Yachts. (Celestial is registered in Hong Kong, though its principals are Americans.[49]) In October 1981 the two sides signed a fifteen-year agreement under which the boatyard will build fiberglass yachts with materials and specifications provided by Celestial, and Celestial will market the boats, primarily in North America. The contract itself is a very simple, flexible document, only about three pages long, but it does express the hope that this processing agreement will evolve into a joint venture in due course.

The first vessel to be built under the agreement will be a forty-eight foot center-cockpit ketch. Celestial sent an experienced American shipwright to Xiamen in February 1983 to look after construction of the hull, with the expectation that other foreigners might have to be added later to supervise certain specialized aspects of the work, such as engine-mounting and electrical wiring. When we visited the shipyard in June, the full-scale wooden mockup of the hull (from which the fiberglass hulls are in turn molded) was just reaching completion, and the projected timetable was that the first yacht would go into the water in October or

November. The American shipwright told us that he was extremely pleased with the quality of workmanship at the yard and that in four months in Xiamen he had achieved what he failed to accomplish in nine frustrating months on a similar venture in Sri Lanka.

According to the manager of the shipyard, Celestial will pay a processing fee of US$10,500 apiece for the first ten ketches. This fee was derived in the following fashion: Celestial told the shipyard that construction of a similar vessel requires about 3,000 hours of labor in North America, 4,500 in Taiwan, 5,000 in Korea, and 5,500 in Thailand. The shipyard management felt that an average of the Korean and Thai figures, or 5,250 hours, could be taken as a conservative estimate of their own capabilities. The minimum rate that the shipyard was prepared to accept was US$2 per hour. Taken together, these figures implied the fee of US$10,500 per yacht. For boats after the first ten, the contract provides for a gradual escalation of the fee. Since the enterprise has a priority claim on 40 percent of the foreign exchange it earns, each of the first ten ketches will be worth US$4,200 to the shipyard — or about RMB ¥11,760 at the internal settlement exchange rate. At the same time, direct labor costs for 5,250 hours of labor would be less than RMB ¥1,800 at current wage and bonus rates. Thus, if the yacht-building project succeeds, it will be financially feasible for the shipyard to grant significant wage increases to its workers, and it seems likely that this will be done, especially since these highly skilled craftsmen are currently earning about the same wage as an entry-level worker at the nearby cigarette factory.

Eventually, Celestial hopes to be building as many as eight ketches per month at Xiamen and then to begin producing a twenty-five-foot racing dinghy as well. The shipyard seems quite supportive of these ambitious plans and has even taken out a bank loan of RMB ¥400,000 to construct a new workshed and launching area for the Celestial project. From the Chinese point of view, the main payoff to this investment will not be the fees earned by building luxury yachts, though this foreign exchange is undoubtedly useful. The real payoff will come when the shipyard begins to build fiberglass fishing and commercial vessels for local fleets. Simultaneously, these developments should be a stimulus to Chinese suppliers. Already, Chinese lead is being used for ballast, and the use of Chinese bronze fittings is under discussion. Resin and fiberglass fabrics will probably come from Chinese sources at some time in the future as well. (China already makes these materials, but so far the price is well above world levels and the quality is not up to world standards.) As the literature of economic development would put it, this is a project that has a variety of beneficial forward and backward linkages.

It remains to be seen, however, whether these ambitious plans will be fulfilled. Two potential problem areas are easily identified. First, the production of eight ketches a month will require a labor force of about 250 highly skilled craftsmen. Is the local pool of traditional shipwright skills large enough to support this expansion? Alternatively, can new workers be trained quickly enough? Second, even if these production questions are solved satisfactorily, the problem of finding buyers will remain. Celestial's expectation is that the ketch will be priced at about US$100,000 to $110,000 f.o.b. at Xiamen or about US$112,000 to $122,000 c.i.f. on the west coast of the United States. There is no doubt that, if quality is satisfactory, such pricing would permit aggressive market penetration, since a high-quality forty-eight-foot center-cockpit ketch currently being built in Hong Kong by Kong and Halvorsen is priced at about US$228,000 at the shipyard or US$245,000 delivered in New York.[50] With the American economy in deep recession, however, the market for luxury yachts has gone quite soft, and therefore even a rapidly growing share of this shrinking market may not sustain the production levels that Celestial is hoping for. Furthermore, some of Celestial's competitors — including Kong and Halvorsen — are also developing yacht-building facilities in China,[51] so the price gap on which Celestial's marketing hopes are based may not persist for long. In the end, this processing agreement may bring substantial rewards to both Celestial Yachts and the local shipyard, but it is evident that the risks are substantial as well.

Shenzhen Printing Company[52]

This enterprise, located in the Shenzhen SEZ in Guangdong Province, has a compensation trade agreement with a Hong Kong firm. The Hong Kong side contributed HK$15 million (about US$2.5 million) worth of equipment, while the Chinese side contributed RMB ¥2.8 million for the buildings. Construction of the factory and a workers' dormitory was begun in August 1979, trial production began in September 1980, and regular production began in October 1981. The factory, divided into four workshops, has the capacity to produce printed materials, packaging, and paper boxes worth about HK$30 million annually. The initial plan was to use about 80 percent of the plant's capacity to produce items for the Hong Kong partner, with raw materials brought in from Hong Kong, and to use the other 20 percent of capacity to process Chinese raw materials for the domestic market. At these projected levels of output, the Hong Kong side would incur an annual obligation of about HK$4 million in processing fees, and these sums would then be applied toward repayment of the equipment loan over a five-year period. In fact, however, the factory was running well below capacity in the summer of 1982 owing both to start-up problems and to the recession in Hong Kong, and projected output for the year was only about HK$20 million. If, as now seems likely, the equipment has not been fully paid for at the end of the five years, the agreement will continue until repayment is complete.

The enterprise has 224 workers and staff, plus 18 skilled workers from Hong Kong (the latter paid by the Hong Kong side). Like all enterprises in the Shenzhen SEZ, this factory is governed by the "Provisional Labor and Wage Regulations for Enterprises in the Special Economic Zones of Guangdong Province," adopted on

17 November 1981, which stipulate that all the workers in such enterprises must be hired on a contract basis.[53] Part of the reason for this regulation is that a formal contract can specify the circumstances under which dismissal is warranted, can provide for lay-off when economic conditions are depressed, and can in general put the workers on explicit notice that they do not enjoy an "iron rice bowl." Because the factory was established before the labor regulations were announced, however, about 140 of the workers are still not on contract, and for them "the old customs" apply, which means that it would be difficult to lay them off for economic reasons, though they could still be dismissed for serious infractions of discipline.

In 1982 an entry-level worker at the factory was paid a basic wage of RMB ¥39 per month, plus cash subsidies of about RMB ¥20, plus a bonus that averaged about RMB ¥40, for a total of about RMB ¥99 per month. The factory's average wage in 1982, including cash subsidies and bonuses, was RMB ¥109 per month, scarcely more than the entry-level wage, which reflects the fact that the workers are very young, most of them just out of school. (Average wages in the Shenzhen SEZ at the end of 1982 were reported to be about RMB ¥150 per month, excluding bonuses.[54]) In addition to the cash subsidies, the workers also receive significant subsidies in kind. For example, their housing in the dormitory costs them only RMB ¥0.4 per month. It is understood that bonuses in the SEZ can be higher than in other parts of China, but — because of an unwillingness to rely too heavily on material incentives — there is said to be a rule that the average monthly bonus should not exceed RMB ¥30. In fact, however, most enterprises in Shenzhen (including this one) violate the rule.

When asked about labor problems, the enterprise spokesman noted that this is a difficulty that exists everywhere and that its causes are complex: in part, it is a result of the Cultural Revolution, when the social environment instilled no discipline. The factory tries to deal with this issue through "education and political work." Workers with a bad attitude are removed from their workshop (where they are unwelcome) and given other work to do. If all else fails, unsatisfactory workers are dismissed (this happened to two or three workers in 1981). In such an event, the local Labor Bureau may recommend the dismissed workers to other enterprises, but most units will not want them, and most likely they will end up doing some kind of temporary work.

Pepsi-Cola[55]

The Happiness Soft Drinks Factory in Shenzhen is engaged in a co-operative venture (or contractual joint venture) with the Hong Kong subsidiary of Pepsi-Cola. Like almost everything else in the Shenzhen SEZ, the prefabricated metal building that houses the enterprise was constructed very recently. The American side paid for the building and its two sets of equipment: one set that produces bottled soft drinks, and the other that produces soft drinks in cans. The American side also contributes the Pepsi brand name, of course. The Chinese side provided the land and some auxiliary buildings. The bottles and cans and the flavoring syrup are imported, while electricity and water are purchased locally for RMB ¥0.20 per kwh and RMB ¥0.18 per cubic metre respectively, paid in foreign exchange certificates. Production of bottled soft drinks began in February 1982 and runs about 5,000 cases a day (24 bottles per case). About 80 percent of this output is marketed in Hong Kong, and the rest is marketed for foreign exchange certificates in China. Production of canned drinks began in April 1982 and runs about 7,000 cases per day (24 cans per case). The canned product is sold entirely in Hong Kong.

At the time of our visit, the workforce at the enterprise consisted of about eighty workers plus a manager and an accountant from the Chinese side and five managerial people from the American side. The contract with Pepsi runs for fifteen years. At the end of that period, the equipment will still belong to the American side, but there seems to be a strong expectation that it will be sold or given to the Chinese when the time comes. During the first five years of the contract, all profits are to be split equally between the two sides. Then, during the final ten years, the Chinese side will receive 60 percent of the venture's profits and the American side 40 percent.

In most respects, this co-operative venture is not discernibly different from the processing and compensation trade agreements already described in this chapter. They are similar in scale, in complexity of technology, in their focus on exporting, and so on. The one difference is that this is a profit-sharing arrangement, and hence the earnings of the Chinese side may be subject to greater volatility than would be the case under a fixed-fee processing agreement. In practice, however, this may not be a significant difference, since the earnings from processing fees may not be particularly stable either — because the volume of work done depends on market conditions and also because the fee per unit is subject to periodic renegotiation.

The Happy Home Furniture Factory[56]

Like the Happiness Soft Drinks Factory, the Happy Home (*Jia-Le*) Furniture Factory in Shenzhen has a co-operative venture agreement with a Hong Kong partner signed in 1979. Under the terms of this five-year contract, both sides contributed cash (about half and half), and the money was then used to purchase equipment and materials for the production of sofas. The agreement stipulates an f.o.b. price at the factory, and the net earnings based on this price are split equally between the two sides. The foreign partner then markets a share of the output in Hong Kong at whatever price can be gotten and keeps all additional profits from these sales. Similarly, the Chinese side markets a share of the output domestically (mainly to hotels) and keeps the incremental profits. Domestic sales are sometimes for foreign exchange certificates and sometimes for RMB; in the latter case, a higher price is charged. In addition to the sofas, the factory produces mattresses for export under a processing agreement with a Hong Kong firm, and it produces carved wooden furniture and other items for the domestic market on its own account. The pattern of production fluctuates from month to month, depending on market conditions in Hong Kong and locally. In 1981, the total value of the factory's output was RMB ¥3.25 million.[58]

This factory is a collective, not a state-owned enterprise, and consequently its wage system is quite different from the other factories described in this chapter. The 135 workers in the factory are divided into three categories: 57 regular workers and the remainder either contract or probationary workers. Probationary workers are paid RMB ¥2 per day for three to six months and then — if they prove satisfactory — are promoted to contract workers. Because these new recruits are skilled wood carvers from the interior of Guangdong, virtually all of them are promoted in due course. Contract workers are given a one-year contract, which is renewed if the worker is still needed. The worker promises to obey factory discipline, to avoid any illegal activity, and to remain at work for a full year (unless special circumstances arise). In return, the worker is protected from lay-off during the year. The 57 regular workers were "inherited" from earlier days. Despite the provisions of the SEZ labor regulations, they are not on contract and still enjoy what is essentially an "iron rice bowl." Both the contract workers and the permanent workers are paid entirely on a piece-work basis, with no bonuses. Monthly wages range from RMB ¥100 to RMB ¥300, with an average of about RMB ¥170, which includes a daily food subsidy of RMB ¥0.30. The manager gave us the impression that the enterprise could afford to increase its piece-rates but that the government authorities are reluctant to see wage levels go too much higher. As an alternative, therefore, the enterprise uses its extra profits to expand productive capacity.

What can be said in summary about the Open Door in light industry, whether embodied in an equity joint venture or in one of the myriad alternative forms? Despite their modest scale and the general absence of the most sophisticated technology, these ventures seem to have much to offer that is directly relevant to China's current needs: new production methods, better quality control techniques, new product ideas, access to foreign capital, assistance with export marketing, and a chance to experiment with a variety of worker incentive systems — to name only some of the possibilities. At the same time, these Open Door projects undoubtedly also have vulnerabilities, and it is rather easy to anticipate some of the criticisms that may emerge in the future. For example, from the public health point of view, is it a good idea to improve the productivity of the cigarette industry, or even the soft drinks industry?[59] Without the iron rice bowl, how much difference is there between socialism and capitalism for the average worker? As the Chinese economy becomes more export-oriented, will it not also be more vulnerable to the downswings of the capitalist business cycle? Despite these potentially awkward questions, however, there seems to be a strong consensus in favor of an improvement in the standard of living, and this creates a natural constituency for the Open Door idea where light industry is concerned.

6

The Energy Sector

The idea of opening the energy sector to the outside world (by bartering fuel exports for technology imports) has been an explosive political issue in China. As indicated in Chapter 1, in the 1970s Deng Xiaoping and others were accused of "selling off China's natural resources" and "opening the door to imperialist plunder" for daring to suggest such a policy. These caustic criticisms have now been muted, and China's official policy is to welcome foreign participation in the development of its energy resources. But the debate is by no means ended, for many difficult decisions must still be made. The sheer size of most energy projects and the inherent complexity of the engineering and economic issues involved virtually guarantee that energy policy will continue to be a controversial topic. Indeed, China's energy sector is so important, both as political symbol and as economic resource, that the success or failure of the Open Door in this one sector, by whatever yardstick the results may eventually come to be measured, may well determine the fate of the Open Door more generally.

THE IMPORTANCE OF ENERGY IN CHINA'S DEVELOPMENT PLANS

In the mid-1970s, China's leaders were bitterly divided over the question of whether China ought to export such resources as coal and oil. But apparently they agreed on one point: China's energy sector, led by the petroleum industry, was on a secure and rapid growth path, and this in turn made an ambitious program of economic development feasible. In terms of the production increases achieved by that time, this optimism was understandable. As can be seen in Table 6.1 and Table 6.2, all components of the energy sector displayed rapid growth in the 1950s, but

Table 6.1 ENERGY PRODUCTION IN CHINA, 1949–1982

Year	Coal	Crude Oil	Natural Gas	Electricity	Hydro-Electricity
1949	32	0.1	0.01	4.3	0.7
1950	43	0.2	0.01	4.6	0.8
1951	53	0.3	0.00	5.7	0.9
1952	66	0.4	0.01	7.3	1.3
1953	70	0.6	0.01	9.2	1.5
1954	84	0.8	0.02	11.0	2.2
1955	98	1.0	0.02	12.3	2.4
1956	110	1.2	0.03	16.6	3.5
1957	131	1.5	0.07	19.3	4.8
1958	270	2.3	0.11	27.5	4.1
1959	369	3.7	0.29	42.3	4.4
1960	397	5.2	1.04	59.4	7.4
1961	278	5.3	1.47	48.0	7.4
1962	220	5.8	1.21	45.8	9.0
1963	217	6.5	1.02	49.0	8.7
1964	215	8.5	1.06	56.0	10.6
1965	232	11.3	1.10	67.6	10.4
1966	252	14.6	1.34	82.5	12.6
1967	206	13.9	1.46	77.4	13.1
1968	220	16.0	1.40	71.6	11.5
1969	266	21.7	1.96	94.0	16.0
1970	354	30.7	2.87	115.9	20.5
1971	392	39.4	3.74	138.4	25.1
1972	410	45.7	4.84	152.4	28.8
1973	417	53.6	5.98	166.8	38.9
1974	413	64.9	7.53	168.8	41.4
1975	482	77.1	8.85	195.8	47.6
1976	483	86.8	10.10	203.1	45.6
1977	550	93.6	12.12	223.4	47.6
1978	618	104.1	13.73	256.6	44.6
1979	635	106.2	14.51	282.0	50.1
1980	620	106.0	14.27	300.6	58.2
1981	622	101.2	12.74	309.3	65.5
1982	666	102.1	11.93	327.7	74.4

Units:

Coal:	million metric tons of raw coal
Crude Oil:	million metric tons
Natural Gas:	billion cubic metres
Electricity and	
Hydroelectricity:	billion kilowatt-hours

Sources: For 1949–1981, State Statistical Bureau, *Statistical Yearbook of China, 1981* (Hong Kong: Economic Information Agency, 1982), p. 227. For 1982, State Statistical Bureau, "Communique on Fulfilment of China's 1982 National Economic Plan," *Beijing Review*, May 9, 1983, p. v.

Table 6.2   ANNUAL GROWTH RATES OF ENERGY SUPPLIES (percent)

	1950–1959	1960–1969	1970–1977
Coal	24.1	3.0	5.6
Crude Oil	34.0	18.3	17.5
Natural Gas	55.0	4.4	22.6
Total electricity	25.7	7.1	9.0
Hydroelectricity	23.7	8.2	13.2

Note: These average annual growth rates for the periods indicated were calculated by fitting least-squares logarithmic trend lines to the data of Table 6.1.

performance in the 1960s was mixed. Coal and natural gas production grew only fitfully. Electricity fared somewhat better, because hydro power expanded rather steadily (apart from the Cultural Revolution year of 1968), though thermal power was adversely affected by the problems in the coal industry. At the same time, however, the 1960s were a period of great triumph for China's oil industry. Despite the difficulties caused by the abrupt withdrawal of Soviet technical assistance, the major oil field at Daqing was brought into production, and oil output for the country as a whole grew at an average rate of nearly 20 percent a year over the decade. In the 1970s the rapid growth of oil continued, natural gas production improved dramatically, hydroelectricity achieved double-digit growth (though

Table 6.3   EXPORTS OF CRUDE OIL (thousand metric tons)

1962	63
1963	75
1964	92
1965	196
1966	199
1967	161
1968	131
1969	107
1970	192
1971	263
1972	636
1973	1,834
1974	5,069
1975	9,878
1976	8,496
1977	9,107
1978	11,313
1979	13,432
1980	13,309
1981	13,754

Sources: For 1962–1980, State Statistical Bureau, *Statistical Yearbook of China, 1981* (Hong Kong: Economic Information and Agency, 1982), p. 383. For 1981, Ministry of Foreign Economic Relations and Trade.

thermal grew more slowly), and even the laggard coal industry showed significant improvement compared to the 1960s.

As the output of crude oil increased, China gradually curtailed petroleum imports and then began to export. All through the 1950s, Chinese imports of petroleum products exceeded domestic production, but this pattern of import dependency began to change about 1960, and by 1966 China's petroleum imports had dropped to negligible levels.[1] As can be seen from Table 6.3, China began exporting crude oil as early as 1962, but at first the amounts involved were minuscule, and China did not become a *net* exporter until about 1972.[2] Only in 1973, when China first entered the hard currency oil market in a significant way, did oil exports exceed one million tons per year. As already indicated, this decision to sell oil to capitalist countries was bitterly critized by the ultra-Left. Interestingly enough, the Chinese decision to export was made *before* the first OPEC price shock. But the increase in the posted price of Saudi Arabian marker crude from $2.898 per barrel in June 1973 to $11.651 per barrel in January 1974,[3] fortuitous though it was, must have made the strategy of exporting oil seem all the more attractive in many eyes.

As the petroleum industry prospered, Chinese attitudes toward the energy sector became increasingly optimistic, even euphoric. In 1970 "Iron Man" Wang, the hero of Daqing, expressed the belief that oil production could reach 400 million metric tons by 1990.[4] (This implied a growth rate of about 12 percent a year, which seemed realistic — indeed, almost conservative — when compared to the rates achieved in the 1960s.) In 1974 the chairman of the Japan-China Oil Import Council, influenced by what he had been told on a trip to China, predicted that oil output would reach the 400 million target by 1980.[5] In the spring of 1977, Hua Guofeng announced that China would build "ten more oilfields as big as Daqing" (implying an output level of about 500 million tons) by the turn of the century, and the minister of petroleum endorsed this "new great leap forward" in the oil industry.[6]

The successes of the energy sector were instrumental in shaping the ambitious goals of the Ten-Year Plan of 1976–1985, first announced by Hua Guofeng at the National People's Congress in February 1978. As indicated in Chapter 1, this plan called for agricultural output to increase at a rate of 4 to 5 percent a year and for industrial production to rise at an annual rate of 10 percent or better. The key symbolic target of the plan, which was closely linked to the Baoshan project, was to increase steel production to 60 million tons by 1985. Such ambitious goals obviously assumed that energy supplies would pose no constraints. Yet in fact, for reasons to be discussed below, both the coal and oil industries were losing their growth momentum just as the Ten-Year Plan was getting under way. In less than a year, the plan had effectively been discarded — replaced by the Third Plenum's decision to pursue "readjustment, restructuring, consolidation, and improvement." Only a few years before, Chinese commentators had delighted in heaping scorn and ridicule on the "so-called energy crisis" in the capitalist countries,[7] but before the end of the decade China had entered a major energy crisis of its own as the key projects of the third and fourth waves of technology import ran afoul of serious energy shortages. Furthermore, the problem has not been limited to a few key projects; it is widespread throughout the economy. According to data from the State Planning Commission, the industrial output lost in a recent (unspecified) year owing to the idle capacity caused by energy shortages would be worth more than RMB ¥70 billion.[8] In terms of the value of industrial output reported for recent years, this sum represents a loss of about 12 to 15 percent of total industrial output.[9]

In the short term it will not be easy to relieve these shortages by increasing China's energy supplies. A few energy sources, such as the biogas digesters and mini-hydro projects that are becoming increasingly common in the rural areas of China,[10] are viable as small-scale operations, but most energy sources are inherently of the mega-project variety. Because of their size, they have lengthy gestation periods even under favorable circumstances — that is, even when political conflicts, technical problems, and financial constraints do not conspire to cause additional delays. As Zhao Ziyang said in late 1982, "energy output cannot be increased significantly in the near future."[11] In the short run, then, only two alternatives seem to be available. The first is to shift the pattern of production away from activities that are particularly heavy consumers of energy. This option is already being pursued quite vigorously under the rubric of readjustment, with its emphasis on consumption over accumulation and on light industry over heavy. It is reported that in 1982 alone over 20 million metric tons of standard coal were saved as a result of this readjustment of the economy's product mix.[12] But there are limits to what can be accomplished by this approach. For one thing, some consumer goods, such as housing, food grains, synthetic textiles, and tourist travel, are quite energy-intensive. Furthermore, the vested interests in heavy industry have demonstrated a considerable capacity to resist readjustment.

The second alternative is to use the available supplies of energy more efficiently. The possibilities here are numerous. For example, China has about 180,000 industrial boilers, most of which have been in service for many years. It is estimated that on average they utilize only 50 percent of the calories in the fuel they burn, whereas boilers of the latest foreign design have an energy efficiency of about 80 percent. If all of China's boilers were of the most efficient type, the annual saving of fuel would be more than 50 million metric tons of standard coal.[13] Other examples can be found in transportation. Over 90 percent of China's trucks are of the four-ton, gasoline-engine type, rather than the energy-saving eight-ton, diesel-engine model.[14] And on the railroads, 77 percent of the locomotives are still old-fashioned steam engines, which have the advantage that they can burn coal, thereby conserving petroleum, but which have the disadvantage that they burn the coal very inefficiently. (Recent Chinese policy statements have stressed the need to shift the railroads over to diesel or electric locomotives, but in China's circumstances a more appropriate solution might be to develop a sophisticated steam locomotive to replace the Qianjin 2-10-2.[15]) The difficulty with all of these suggestions for energy conservation is that, although many opportunities can readily be identified, the proposed improvements often require costly investment. Thus, the goal of saving energy runs into direct conflict with the goal of emphasizing consumption and curtailing accumulation.

In view of these near-term difficulties with energy, it is not surprising that the industrial growth targets of the Sixth Five-Year Plan are substantially less ambitious than those of the abortive Ten-Year Plan that it replaces. Instead of the 10 percent annual growth rate for industrial output specified in the Ten-Year Plan, the new Five-Year Plan sets a target of only about 4 percent a year.[16] Yet the longer-term goal of achieving a gross value of industrial and agricultural output of RMB ¥2,800 billion by the year 2000 — the "doubling and redoubling" target first announced by Zhao Ziyang in 1981 — has not been abandoned. Rather, it is now expected that economic growth will accelerate in the late 1980s and more especially in the 1990s and, therefore, that the original target of quadrupling industrial and agricultural output is still within reach. Since the agricultural sector cannot be expected to grow by more than 4 or 5 percent a year (a rate that is in fact faster than the rate actually achieved between 1953 and 1980[17]), the industrial sector will have to grow by more than 9 percent a year between 1985 and 2000 if the quadrupling target is to be achieved.[18]

Will energy shortages prevent this target from being reached? Zhao Ziyang's answer, already quoted in Chapter 1, is unabashedly equivocal: perhaps they will, and perhaps they will not. Total production of energy is expected to reach about 1,200 million metric tons of standard coal equivalent by the turn of the century — that is, to do no more than double the 1981 figure of 632 million tons.[19] Thus it will be essential that the efficiency of energy utilization be dramatically improved, so that a 2 percent increase in output can be achieved with each 1 percent increase in the energy supply. In the jargon of economics, the "energy-output elasticity" will have to be brought down to a value of 0.5, a striking improvement over the experience of the years from 1953 to 1980, when the energy-output elasticity exhibited an average value of 1.1.[20] As already suggested, this improvement will be very difficult to achieve, for at least three reasons. First, investment in energy-saving technology can be quite costly, and it is therefore hampered by China's shortage of savings. Second, some of the most energy-guzzling activities in the economy (such as steel production and nuclear weapons development) are difficult to curtail because of the power of the vested interests involved. Third, and perhaps most important, China's agriculture has reached a point where crop increases can probably be achieved only by using substantial amounts of energy. For all these reasons, it will be extremely difficult for China to bring the energy-output elasticity down to 0.5.

What about the other half of the energy equation? That is, what is the likelihood that energy output can be increased to the equivalent of 1,200 million metric tons of standard coal by the year 2000? The answer depends on the growth prospects of the various subsectors of the energy industry, and these subsectors need to be examined on a case-by-case basis since each faces its own special circumstances. In their turn, the growth prospects of the subsectors depend — among other things — on the extent to which foreign capital and technology are utilized. Furthermore, it must be remembered that any energy exported to repay this foreign contribution will constitute a reduction in the domestic supply. Thus total energy output will have to exceed 1,200 million tons by enough to provide this foreign exchange, or else — even if China manages to reduce the energy-output elasticity to 0.5 — the goal of quadrupling the gross value of industrial and agricultural output by the end of the century will still be unattainable.

THE SUPPLY OF ELECTRICITY

Despite the substantial growth rates of electricity shown in Table 6.1 and Table 6.2, the supply of electricity has never caught up with the increasing demand for this form of power, and rationing by means of rotating brownouts and blackouts (of both residential and industrial users) is readily apparent even to casual visitors. Neither small enterprises like the cigarette factory in Xiamen nor giant enterprises like the Wuhan steel mill have been spared. A good indication of the severity of the problem can be seen in the allocation of investment under the current Five-Year Plan: the electric power industry is scheduled to receive RMB ¥20.7 billion, significantly more than the amounts planned for either the coal industry (RMB ¥17.9 billion) or the petroleum industry (RMB ¥15.4 billion) — even though the latter two are identified as high-priority bottleneck areas.[21] The production target for electricity by the end of the century is 1,200 billion kwh, or four times the 1980 figure.[22] It has been estimated that this expansion will require a total investment of about RMB ¥123 billion over the 1980s and 1990s,[23] so it appears that — despite the already high level of investment in electricity under the Sixth Plan — the annual investment allocations will have to be doubled during succeeding plan periods if the output goal is to be reached.

The bulk of China's electricity is generated in thermal plants, with coal the predominant fuel. As can be seen from Table 6.1, the proportion of hydro power in total electricity output has been rising gradually, but it still constitutes only about 20 percent of the total. So far there is no significant nuclear generation of electricity. Because of the long gestation periods on major hydro and nuclear plants, thermal plants will have to continue to provide most of China's electricity for the foreseeable future. In the past the general pattern was to ship coal by rail from mining areas to thermal generating plants located near the end-users. Now, in order to ease the traffic burden on the railroads, greater emphasis is being given to large-scale pithead thermal generation in plants such as the new 1.2 million kw power station at Datong and the 800,000 kw power station at Tangshan.[24] This in turn requires the building of high-tension transmission lines, which are expensive and involve a relatively sophisticated technology. Only recently has China built its first two super high-voltage (500 kv) transmission lines. The first, which incorporates equipment from France, Sweden, and Japan, connects the coal-mining areas of Pingdingshan with the city of Wuhan (610 kilometres). The second, which uses only Chinese equipment, connects the coal mine at Yuanbaoshan with the industrial city of Liaoyang in Manchuria (380 kilometres).[25]

Unlike thermal electricity, which can create kilowatt-hours only by burning up coal or oil, hydro and nuclear power represent net additions to China's overall energy supply. They have other advantages as well: low operating costs, no air pollution, reduced railway traffic, and so on. But hydro and nuclear power have disadvantages, too.

China's potential for hydro power is enormous. Despite the rapid development of hydro capacity over the past three decades, the present output of hydroelectric power (74.4 billion kwh in 1982) still represents only about 3.9 percent of China's estimated potential output of 1,900 billion kwh per year.[26] Recent policy statements have called for a gradual shift from thermal to hydro, and current plans call for the completion of twenty major hydro projects (with an aggregate capacity of 10 million kw) by 1990, which would add about 50 billion kwh to the annual supply of hydroelectricity.[27] The largest of these twenty projects is the hydro station at Gezhouba on the Yangzi River.[28] The giant project (2.715 million kw capacity), which was started in 1970 and is scheduled to reach full capacity in 1986, illustrates several of the controversial aspects of hydro power development. The first problem, which is immediately evident, is the lengthy gestation period. (Even much smaller projects than Gezhouba — with capacities in the 1 million kw range — have a construction period of about a decade.[29]) Hydro projects are also expensive. The total cost of Gezhouba is about RMB ¥3.5 billion, or about RMB ¥1300 per kilowatt of capacity. By contrast, investment in a thermal plant is reported to be only about RMB ¥600 per kilowatt of capacity.[30] A thermal plant has the additional advantage that its capacity is available year-round, while most hydro facilities experience substantial seasonal fluctuations in their water supply. Gezhouba, for example, is expected to produce only about 58 percent of its theoretical maximum annual output, while the Liujiaxia and Longyangxia hydro stations on the Yellow River can only achieve ratios of 53 percent and 46 percent respectively.[31]

Another problem with hydro power is the accumulation of sediment behind the dam. In the case of the Sanmen dam on the Yellow River, designed by the Soviets in the 1950s, the reservoir silted up so fast that the project had to be entirely revamped and is now expected to have a capacity of only 200,000 or 250,000 kw, instead of the 1,080,000 kw originally intended.[32] The problem of silt is potentially serious at Gezhouba, too, for the Yangzi River at that point carries a load of about 520 million tons of sediment annually, though the Chinese seem confident that this silt can be flushed away periodically. Yet another problem with hydro power is that the reservoirs sometimes flood valuable resources. For example, it is estimated that the colossal Three Gorges project (which, if it is ever built, will have ten times the capacity of Gezhouba) would inundate 44,000 hectares of farmland and force the emigration of 1.4 million upstream residents.[33] Hydro projects in more isolated (and hence more sparsely populated) regions are preferable from this point of view, but they have the corresponding liability that they require greater investment in transmission networks. The choice between thermal and hydro is further complicated by the fact that some hydro projects yield flood control and navigation benefits, which thermal plants do not provide. And of course the running costs of hydro plants (fuel costs in particular) are negligible by comparison to those of a thermal plant.

It should be evident, even from this brief discussion, that project evaluation in the electric power industry is fraught with difficulties. The choices are rendered even more complicated by the fact that China is also developing a nuclear option. China's first nuclear power plant (a small experimental unit with a capacity of 125,000 kw) was brought on stream in Sichuan province early in 1981.[34] At the end of 1982 it was announced that a 300,000 kw nuclear plant will be built near Shanghai and is scheduled to be in operation by 1988.[35] The "728," as it is called, takes its name from the date (8 February 1970) when Zhou Enlai authorized domestic R&D in this field. Both in name and in design the "728" reflects a strong commitment to self-reliance, and the project will utilize only a few imported components. Yet it is also reported that $100 million in foreign exchange has been allocated to the "728." There is not necessarily any contradiction here, however, for a nuclear power plant is so expensive that purchases of $100 million can indeed represent only a small part of the investment needed.

A much larger nuclear power plant, to be located near Hong Kong, has also been under discussion for several years, but its fate is still problematical.[36] As designed, the plant would use two nuclear reactors and would have a capacity of 1.8 million kw. The original decision to build this plant was announced by Deng Xiaoping in 1978, but within a few months these plans were postponed because of the policy of readjustment. Then in August 1982, the Chinese government gave approval in principle for the project to be resumed. Recent estimates place the total cost at about $5 billion, of which (by contrast to the "728") a major proportion would be for imported equipment. In the spring of 1983, China signed agreements in principle to buy the nuclear technology from France and the power-generating turbines from Britain, but there are indications that the Chinese would prefer to acquire American nuclear technology from Westinghouse, and — as of mid-summer 1983 — American officials were still saying that "there is nothing irreversible in the agreement with the French."[37]

When the project was first discussed, it was expected to be structured as a cooperative venture between Guangdong Electric Company (holding 60 percent) and China Light and Power of Hong Kong (holding 40 percent). This proposal is now being re-studied on the Hong Kong side, to see if it is still economically sensible in the light of lower world prices for oil and coal.[38] Even if Hong Kong decides not to participate, there still seems to be a good chance that China can obtain financial help in the form of Ex-Im Bank loans or similar assistance from the governments of the countries supplying the equipment. Without a firm commitment from Hong Kong to buy a share of the electricity, however, the project will lack foreign exchange to repay its loans. Under the circumstances, China may decide to postpone the venture until Hong Kong can be induced to participate. Even if the project is approved in the near future, it cannot be brought on stream until sometime in the 1990s. Furthermore, even operating at full capacity, the plant — after supplying, say, half of its electricity to Hong Kong to cover debt repayment — would add only about 2 percent to the supply of electricity in China. It seems fair to conclude, therefore, that nuclear power is not destined to make a significant contribution to China's energy supply before the turn of the century at the earliest.

In summary, the electric power industry faces several difficult problems. The choice between thermal and hydro generation, to say nothing of the nuclear option, is a complex one, and the very complexity of the decision means that the planning process takes time. Furthermore, the capital costs involved place serious constraints on the number of projects that can be financed at one time. In certain aspects of electricity generation, foreign technology has a useful contribution to make, as exemplified by recent agreements concerning turbine technology, high-tension transmission systems, dam design, and so on.[39] But, because electricity exports are physically possible only to a few nearby destinations, these agreements may be hampered by the general policy guideline that expects Open Door projects to cover their own foreign exchange requirements in most cases. All in all, it will not be easy for the electric power industry to reach its goal of producing 1,200 billion kwh by the end of the century.

THE COAL INDUSTRY

In the coal industry, as in hydroelectricity, China has enormous potential. A recent report indicates that verified reserves exceed 640 billion tons[40] — that is, enough coal for one thousand years of production at present output levels. Unverified reserves are even larger. Thus the ultimate supply of coal is certainly no problem. Yet the industry has had major difficulties. As can be seen from Table 6.1, coal production grew rather fitfully in the early 1970s. By contrast, the years from 1975 to 1978 (with the understandable exception of 1976, when a severe earthquake struck the key mining center of Tangshan) were years of rapid growth in output, and in 1978 production of raw coal exceeded 600 million metric tons for the first time. In that same year the minister of coal announced that output would double by 1987.[41] But in fact the spurt was already over, and this optimistic projection was soon jettisoned, as was the minister who voiced it.

It is now argued that this brief spurt was accomplished only by a myopic policy of overemphasizing extraction to the neglect of tunnelling work.[42] (Tunnelling diverts labor and machinery from current production but provides the necessary base for continued extraction in later years.) A further criticism that is now voiced is that for many years the coal industry was handicapped by the Maoist exhortation to make south China self-sufficient in coal, even though coal from Shanxi province (transport costs included) was much cheaper.[43] Investment was chan-nelled to low-quality mines in the south, while rich veins in Shanxi went un-developed. Furthermore, it is now said, the railroads of north and east China (the main coal routes) were starved of expansion funds in order to finance much less productive railroads in more remote areas of the country. A recent article in *Jingji Yanjiu* has suggested that, on fourteen recently built railway lines, each RMB ¥1,000 of investment led to 7,600 ton-kilometres of new traffic annually, while on eight heavily used older lines an equivalent investment permitted a traffic increase of 30,700 ton-kilometres.[44] Because of the traffic congestion on the railroads out of Shanxi, many mines have been forced to "set production accord-ing to the availability of transport" (*yi yun ding chan*). Even with production curtailed in this manner, a backlog of 17 million tons of coal had piled up in Shanxi by the end of 1981, and some of this coal sat around so long that it began to catch fire by spontaneous combustion.[45]

These recent criticisms are reflected in the policies laid down in the Sixth Five-Year Plan. Investment in the coal industry was only RMB ¥3.2 billion in 1979 and RMB ¥2.5 billion in 1980, but the planned investment for 1981–85 is RMB ¥17.9 billion, or an average of RMB ¥3.58 billion per year — concentrated mostly in Shanxi and other coal-rich areas of the north.[46] Furthermore, the Sixth Plan also allocates RMB ¥29.8 billion to transportation and communications, mainly for the railways and harbors that handle coal. At the same time, the growth targets for coal have been pared back substantially. Output is now expected to reach 700 million metric tons by 1985, 840 million by 1990, and 1,200 million only by the year 2000 (rather than by 1987).[47] In percentage terms, these targets represent increases of about 2.5 percent per year during the Sixth Plan and then about 3.7 percent per year for the remaining fifteen years of this century.

Measured against historic growth rates, these targets seem quite cautious. (A trend line fitted to the coal output figures of Table 6.1 reveals an average annual growth rate of nearly 11 percent over the three decades from 1952 to 1981.) Even so, however, this planned expansion of output will require substantial investment. According to a recent discussion in *Jingji Yanjiu*, each increment of one million tons added to annual coal production requires an investment of about RMB ¥200 million.[48] Naturally, this figure is only an approximate one, since the precise amount required depends on the geology and geography of the coal deposit in question. But the figure is consistent with the investment levels and production targets of the Sixth Plan, which imply an investment of about RMB ¥225 per ton of new capacity. The announced target of increasing coal production by 500 million tons between 1985 and the end of the century therefore implies a total investment of about RMB ¥100 billion, or an average of RMB ¥6.7 billion per year — nearly double the annual level allocated under the Sixth Plan. Furthermore, this figure covers only the direct investment in mining; the complementary funds required for railroads and other infrastructure are not included. Thus the investment in coal, like the investment in electricity, is expected to accelerate sharply after 1985.

These bottlenecks in coal production seem to offer a promising field for Open Door ventures. In 1972–74, during China's third wave of technology import, coal mining equipment worth about $95 million was purchased from Poland, England, and West Germany, but these transactions were of the traditional arm's-length variety, involving only a minimal amount of foreign technical advice.[49] Another surge of machinery imports began during 1978, at the time of the fourth wave.[50] Some of these imports were straight cash purchases, but the transition to "special trade" and the Open Door was already beginning to emerge. One early sign came in August 1978, when China announced tht it would accept a $4 billion loan from West Germany to buy coal mining equipment.[51] Later that year China began to hint that the Japanese contracts signed during the spending spree of the fourth wave, including the Baoshan Steel contracts, would be jeopardized if financing could not be arranged. On 16 February 1979, China's Ministry of Finance formally notified the Japanese companies that contracts worth $2.6 billion had failed to receive Bank of China approval and were being suspended.[52] Although these contracts did not involve coal mining equipment directly, there was an intimate indirect link to the coal industry, for the contracts of the fourth wave had been negotiated within the general framework of the Japan-China Long-Term Trade Agreement of February 1978 — an agreement specifying that China's plant and equipment imports during the early years of the agreement would be balanced by coal and oil exports to Japan during the later years.[53]

This first crisis over the Baoshan contracts was resolved in May 1979, when the Japanese commercial banks arranged two syndicated Eurodollar loans (at ½ percent over LIBOR) to finance the contracts suspended in February. As an added enticement to China, Japan's industrialists persuaded their government to extend a 420 billion yen ($1.8 billion) line of credit from Japan's Export-Import Bank to several resource development projects that would improve China's capacity to produce the coal and oil exports called for by the Long-Term Trade Agreement. These Ex-Im Bank loans were for fifteen years at the concessional rate of 6.25 percent per year.[54] Of this Ex-Im Bank financing, China requested that about $940 million be allocated to coal mining. The first three mines to receive assistance were selected in April 1980, and another four were approved later.[55] (For details of these seven projects, see Table 6.4).

At the same time as this financial package for the seven coal mines was being arranged, both China and Japan were becoming concerned about the infrastructure (railroads and harbors) that would be needed to handle the planned coal exports. In September 1979 China asked for loans of about $5.5 billion from Japan's Overseas Economic Cooperation Fund (OECF), to finance eight key projects that had been shelved when the overambitious Ten-Year Plan was abandoned. Of these projects, four were directly related to the anticipated coal export bottleneck: double-tracking and electrification of the railroad between Beijing and the port of Qinhuangdao, expansion of the coal docks at Qinhuangdao, construction of a new railroad from the coal field at Yanzhou to the port of Shijiusuo in Shandong province, and development of the docks at Shijiusuo.[56] After extensive negotiations, it was announced in December 1979 that OECF could provide only about $1.5 billion, but that the four coal-related projects would receive the bulk of this money. The OECF loan will run for thirty years, with a ten-year grace period, and carry an interest rate of 3 percent per year.[57] According to Japanese reports, the following commitments have been made for these four projects (in billion yen):[58]

	1979	1980	1981	1982
Shijiusuo Port	7.1	9.9	18.5	2.3
Yanzhou-Shijiusuo RR	10.1	3.1	3.2	11.8
Qinhuandao Port	4.9	13.8	9.1	0
Beijing-Qinhuangdao RR	2.5	11.2	9.2	30.9
Totals	24.6	38.0	40.0	45.0

Thus, a total of 147.6 billion yen (about $630 million) had been committed by the end of 1982, but it is reported that relatively little of this money has actually been spent.[59] A variety of problems have hampered the work, including a conflict between the Ministry of Railways and the Ministry of Communications over the layout and administration of the coal yards at Qinhuangdao.[60] The four OECF projects were originally scheduled for completion in 1985, but a knowledgeable American visitor remarked not long ago that 1986 is "a more likely date."[61]

As Table 6.4 shows, the seven mines financed by Japan's Ex-Im Bank are not the only coal projects that are expected to receive foreign funds. One of the others is the giant open-pit mine at Pingshuo in Shanxi, which has a planned annual output level of 15 million metric tons of thermal coal.[62] By contrast to the seven Ex-Im Bank projects, where the foreign involvement is limited to providing loans, the mine at Pingshuo will be structured as a co-operative venture (contractual joint venture), and therefore the foreign partner will be directly involved in management and will share in the financial risk. The foreign partner in this case is the American firm of Island Creek Coal, a subsidiary of Occidental Petroleum. An agreement to conduct a feasibility study of the project was signed in March 1982. When we visited the Ministry of Coal in the summer of 1982, we were told that Pingshuo would start exporting by 1985, but the dramatic drop in world coal prices has forced a delay in this timetable, since the projected after-tax rate of return on Island Creek's investment has fallen well below the original target of 20 percent.[63] Construction was to begin in April 1983, but this target was pushed back to July 1983 and was then postponed even further, as the partners pursued intensive renegotiations of the financial details. As of early November 1983, a final agreement had still not been reached. Thus, if construction requires thirty-eight months, as Occidental expects, coal production will not begin until early 1987, even if a final agreement can be concluded by the end of 1983.

Once production reaches the capacity level of fifteen million tons of raw coal a year, what fraction will be required to repay Island Creek? The answer depends on the precise terms of the contract, which may never be made public, but an approximate answer can still be constructed from the information that is available, which is done in Table 6.5. Under the terms of the proposed contract, Island Creek will receive 50 percent of the project's net earnings until its original $230 million investment has been amortized; after that it will receive 40 percent of the net earnings.[64] If this means, as it appears to mean, that only the incremental 10 percent will be applied to amortization, then it can be seen from the data of Table 6.5 that — at US$37 per ton — it will take about twenty-six years before amortization is completed. Once the incremental 10 percent has been subtracted, the after-tax share accruing to Island Creek will be about $35.5 million a year, yielding a return of about 15.4 percent on the $230 million investment.

The estimates in Table 6.5 are of course only approximations. However, they do indicate that, at an export price of $37 per ton f.o.b., it would require exports of about 1.2 million metric tons a year to cover the payments of $44.4 million to Island Creek. This is only about 10 percent of Pingshuo's projected annual output of 12.5 million metric tons of clean coal. Interestingly enough, this percentage does not vary significantly as coal prices fluctuate: high prices means higher

Table 6.4   COAL MINING PROJECTS WITH POSSIBLE FOREIGN LINKS

Mine (Province)	Planned Annual Capacity Increase (million metric tons)	Foreign Link	Expected Date of First Production
Yanzhou (Shandong)	3	Japan's Ex-Im Bank	1983
Zaozhuang (Shandong)	1.5	Japan's Ex-Im Bank	1984
Xiqu (Shanxi)	3	Japan's Ex-Im Bank	1984
Kailuan (Hebei)	4	Japan's Ex-Im Bank	1987
Zhenchengdi (Shanxi)	1.5	Japan's Ex-Im Bank	1987
Malan (Shanxi)	4	Japan's Ex-Im Bank	1988
Sitaigou (Shanxi)	4	Japan's Ex-Im Bank	1990
Pingshuo (Shanxi)	15	Occidental Petroleum	?
Xuzhou (Jiangsu)	0.75	Lotus Corp. (USA)	1987
Liupanshui (Guizhou)	3.8	(European?)	?
Changcun (Shanxi)	4	World Bank	?
Jiangzhuang (Shanxi)	4	World Bank	?

Sources: Kenji Hattori, ''Sino-Japanese Coal Cooperation,'' JETRO *China Newsletter*, No. 36 (Jan.-Feb., 1982), pp. 2–17; Martin Weil, ''China's Troubled Coal Sector,'' *China Business Review*, (March-April, 1982), pp. 23–34; Dori Jones, ''The Dawning of Coal's 'Second Golden Age,' '' *China Business Review*, (May-June, 1980), pp. 38–48; *China Trade Report*, August, 1982, p. 3, and December, 1982, p. 14; *Economic Reporter*, March, 1981, p. 26; *China Market*, July, 1982, pp. 54–55; Amanda Bennett, ''Occidental's Giant China Mine Project Hits Snag as World Coal Price Plummets,'' *Wall Street Journal*, August 10, 1983, p. 29.

profits and hence larger payments to Island Creek, but this is largely offset by the higher revenue per ton, so that even at a price of $55 per ton, the export tonnage needed to cover payments to the foreign partner would be only about 12 percent of total output.

Table 6.5   FINANCIAL ESTIMATES FOR THE PINGSHUO PROJECT, AT A COAL PRICE OF US$37/METRIC TON F.O.B.

		(US$ million)
Domestic Sales Revenues[a]	$ 44.8	
(3.8 mmt at RMB ¥23.6/ton; US$1 = RMB ¥2)		
Export Revenues[b]	321.9	
(8.7 mmt at US$37/ton f.o.b.)		
Total Revenues		$ 366.7
Rail Transport Costs[c]		(39.2)
(8.7 mmt; 900 km; RMB ¥0.01/ton-km)		
Revenues at the Mine		327.5
Estimated Operating Costs		
Labor (1500 workers at US$12/hour)[d]	(50.0)	
Non-Labor[e]	(100.0)	
Total		(150.0)
Net Earnings (Pre-Tax)		177.5
Island Creek's 50% Share[d]		88.8
Island Creek's Share After Tax[f]		$ 44.4

Notes and Sources:
a. Of Pingshuo's projected output of 12.5 mmt of clean coal per year, 8.7 mmt will be exported and 3.8 mmt will be retained for domestic use. See *Coal Outlook*, 14 March 1983, p. 1. The domestic price of coal is estimated from data in *Statistical Yearbook of China 1981*, pp. 212 and 227.
b. Vancouver *Province*, 12 October 1983.
c. *Coal Outlook*, 14 March 1983, p. 1, gives the distance as 558 miles from Pingshuo to Qinhuangdao. For the rate of RMB ¥0.01 per ton-km, see Martin Weil, "Coal Slurry in China," *The China Business Review*, July-August 1983, p. 21.
d. Amanda Bennett, "Occidental's Giant China Mine Project Hits Snag as World Coal Price Plummets," *The Wall Street Journal*, 10 August 1983, p. 29.
e. The estimate that non-labor costs are about twice labor costs is based on the cost pattern in mining in western Canada and must be considered quite rough. See *The British Columbia Mining Industry in 1982* (Vancouver: The Mining Association of British Columbia, 1983), p. 33.
f. The Foreign Enterprise Income Tax Law, Article 5, and the accompanying Regulations, Article 7, provide for the possibility of a brief tax holiday for foreign ventures in coal mining. Once these tax holidays have passed, the tax rate applied to ventures of the size of Pingshuo is essentially 50 percent, which is the rate used here.

Another, but much smaller, coal project that also involves an American partner is the Zhangji mine near Xuzhou in Jiangsu province.[65] The American partner in this case is the Lotus Corporation, and the agreement has been referred to as a compensation trade deal. Lotus will provide a loan of $35.6 million to renovate the mine, increasing its annual output from the current 450,000 tons per year to 1.2 million tons. Of the annual increment of 750,000 tons, Lotus will receive about 25 percent (about 190,000 tons) for seven years. Thus, the rate of return on Lotus's investment will depend on world coal prices and of course on the tax situation as well. It could be argued that the coal allocated to Lotus represents the repayment of a loan and that therefore the portion representing principal should be tax free, while the portion representing interest should be subject only to the 20 percent withholding tax on interest income set forth in Article 11 of the foreign enterprise income tax law. However, Article 11 specifies that this 20 percent tax rate applies only to foreign companies which "have no establishments in China," and Article 2 of the accompanying regulations explicitly identifies "places where natural resources are being exploited" as constituting an "establishment" within the meaning of Article 11. Thus, even though many Chinese discussions have described compensation trade ventures as mere loans (repaid in kind rather than in cash), it seems clear that the tax laws view these payments as operating income and make no real distinction between compensation trade agreements and contractual joint ventures. Therefore, despite the differing labels, it seems likely that Lotus will face the same tax structure as Island Creek. Assuming that Lotus qualifies for the relevant tax holidays, it can be calculated that the rate of return on its $35.6 million (after Chinese taxes, but before U.S. taxes, if any) will be about 10.6 percent at a coal price of $45 per ton, but would be 21.4 percent at a price of $65 per ton.

Yet another coal project for which foreign participation has been discussed is the Liupanshui district of Guizhou province.[66] This is already a well-established mining region; the proposal is to increase its annual output by 3.8 million tons, of which 2 million tons would be exported (through the port of Zhanjiang). This would entail an investment of RMB ¥560 million, of which RMB ¥120 million would be used to improve the mines, RMB ¥20 million would be spent on the port of Zhanjiang, and RMB ¥420 million would be used to upgrade the 1,400-kilometer, single-track railway that connects the mining region to tide-water. Early in 1982 it was reported that this investment might be provided by a group of Hong Kong businessmen. A few months later it was reported that a group of six European countries (Italy, Belgium, France, West Germany, Britain, and Spain) had committed themselves to investing in the project, though no formal contracts seem to have been signed. In May 1983, it was reported that Malta had agreed to make a twenty-five year loan to finance coal development in Guizhou.

The final projects listed in Table 6.4 are two coal mines in southern Shanxi that have been selected for possible World Bank assistance.[67] Although feasibility studies and other preparations for these two projects are now well advanced, formal approval has not yet been announced, though it is expected within a few months.

If all of the projects listed in Table 6.4 are actually carried out, what will the implications be for China's coal situation? Japanese sources estimate that the seven mines financed by the Ex-Im Bank will be producing only about 1.9 million tons of raw coal by 1985,[68] while it is reasonably certain that none of the other projects in Table 6.4 will come on stream by that date. Thus, of the 34 million tons of coal that China hopes to add to total output between 1982 and 1985, only about 5 percent would come from Open Door projects. By 1990, however, it is entirely possible that all of the projects of Table 6.4 will be in production, though perhaps some would not yet be at full capacity. At most, then, this would add about 48.5 million tons to annual output, or about 28 percent of the increment of 174 million tons by which total coal output is expected to rise between 1982 and 1990. In addition to the projects listed in Table 6.4, several other major coal ventures are also reported to be under negotiation, but it seems unlikely that they will be brought into production quickly enough to make much difference to the 1990 figures.[69] In short, if the target of 840 million tons by 1990 is achieved, about three-quarters of the growth in output will have to come from mines that do not have an outside partner. Thus, even with the impact of the Open Door, China's coal industry will still have to rely primarily on its own efforts to achieve its goals.

In 1980 China exported 6.6 million tons of coal and coke.[70] During our visit to the Ministry of Coal, we were told that by 1990 China plans to export about 30 million tons a year, a figure that is substantially higher than recent predictions made by outside observers but that is at the same time much more realistic than the target of 60 million tons by 1985 that was announced in the late 1970s.[71] In terms of harbor capacity, this target for 1990 seems quite feasible, because the two phases of expansion at Qinhuangdao and the first phase of development at Shijiusuo, taken together, will add 25 million tons to the existing annual coal export capacity, while the second phase at Shijiusuo, plus the developments at Zhanjiang, will add another 7 million tons of capacity — if these latter projects are completed by 1990.[72] As for rail capacity, the OECF-financed rail projects, combined with the recent upgrading of two key lines out of Shanxi (now double-tracked and electrified) should greatly facilitate coal shipments, though the rolling stock problem must still be dealt with.[73] Since total output is expected to reach 840 million tons by 1990, there will certainly be no problem supplying exports of 30 million tons.

But what about demand? Can markets be found for exports of this magnitude? In large measure the answer depends on developments in Japan, though Chinese exports to other markets are not insignificant. Of Japan's coal imports of 78 million tons in fiscal 1981, Australia provided nearly 42 percent and the United States provided about 33 percent. Canada and South Africa were also major suppliers. China stood a poor fifth on the list, supplying only about 3.3 percent of Japan's coal imports.[74] The Japanese market for coking coal is not expected to grow in the foreseeable future because of the depressed state of the steel industry, but recent Japanese projections of thermal coal imports anticipate rapid growth of this segment of the market, rising from 12 million tons in 1981 to 50 or 60 million tons in 1990.[75] This projected growth of thermal coal imports may not take place because the recent softening of world oil prices has reduced the pressure for Japan to switch from oil to coal. (One Japanese expert has called the 1990 projections "mere meditations."[76]) Furthermore, Japanese end-users have not always been satisfied with the quality of Chinese coal,[77] which suggests that even if Japan increases its thermal coal imports dramatically, it may not buy from China.

In brief, it may not be easy for China to find markets for coal exports of 30 million tons by 1990, though the mutual expectations and obligations created by the Long-Term Trade Agreement with Japan should help — if the price is right. In this context it should be noted that during our interviews in 1982, we were told by Yin Shujing, the deputy managing director of the China National Coal Development Corporation, that in his opinion the internal problem of getting the coal mined and shipped is more serious than the external problem of finding export markets.[78] The apparent implication of this remark is that China is willing to set its coal prices so as to achieve the desired market share in Japan and elsewhere. In March 1983 China accepted a drastic reduction in the price of its coal exports to Japan (from $61.75 to $47.75 per ton),[79] but this was paralleled by reductions in the prices paid to Japan's other suppliers, so further price cuts will be necessary if China is to expand its market share. In terms of the domestic price of coal, there is still a substantial margin for further price bargaining because the retail price of coal in 1981 was RMB ¥32.6 per ton ($18.11 at a $1/RMB ¥1.8 exchange rate).[80] It must be remembered, however, that the pervasive problem of a distorted domestic price structure may make such calculations an unreliable guide for policy decisions.

Measured in tons of coal, how much will the Open Door projects of Table 6.4 cost China? Assuming that all of the projects are close to full production by 1990 (which will make total output about 48 million tons), the situation in that year can be summarized as follows:

Seven Ex-Im Bank Mines. A debt of $940 million at 6.25 percent, repayable over fifteen years, requires an annual amortizing payment (principal and interest together) of about $98.4 million, which translates into coal shipments of 2,800 thousand tons at $35 per ton or 1,800 thousand tons at $55 per ton. The OECF financing should probably be included here as well, which (at 3 percent on $1.5 billion) adds another 700 to 1,000 thousand tons of coal, depending on world prices.

Pingshuo. As already indicated, the coal payments to Island Creek can be estimated at 1,200 to 1,500 thousand tons.

Xuzhou. Here the contract specified the amount of coal: about 190 thousand tons.

Liupanshui. At the official exchange rate, the projected investment of RMB ¥560 million equals about $280 million. If the financing is on commercial terms, like those at Pingshuo, the required annual coal exports would be 1,500 to 1,800 thousand tons. If concessional financing like the Ex-Im Bank loans can be arranged, the required shipments would be 500 to 800 thousand tons.

World Bank. Assuming that the World Bank's terms are not too different from the Ex-Im Bank financing, the coal payments on a loan of $200 million would be 300 to 500 thousand tons annually.

In total, then, the projects of Table 6.4 require coal exports of between 4.7 million and 7.8 million tons in 1990. Thus, even if 1990 coal exports fall well short of the target level of 30 million tons, there should be no problem covering the minimum export requirements created by the Open Door projects. What is more, the foreign partners in these projects have a direct incentive to help China find export markets for this coal.

If the calculations of the preceding pages are approximately correct, the Open Door projects in the coal industry appear to be quite beneficial to China. Even if the necessary foreign repayments run on the high side (because of low coal prices), the amount involved in 1990 seems to be about 7 or 8 million tons a year, compared to a total output for these mines of about 48 million tons a year. If the situation continues to develop in the same proportions until the end of the century, Open Door ventures in coal mining would then be producing about 160 million tons annually, of which about 25 million tons would be needed for foreign repayments. The difference accrues to China to use either to earn foreign exchange or to supply domestic energy needs. Furthermore, the agreements will expire long before the mines are exhausted, and at that point the full output accrues to China. Perhaps even more importantly, these projects will provide direct contact with foreign mining technology, both underground and open-pit. If this outside technology can be successfully adapted and assimilated, the pay-off will be substantial.

THE PETROLEUM INDUSTRY

As shown in Table 6.1, the rapid growth of China's crude oil and natural gas production began to decelerate from about 1976 onward, and output actually declined after 1979. As already indicated, these problems appeared just as the ambitious Ten-Year Plan and the associated Long-Term Trade Agreement with Japan were coming into force. As a consequence, the Ten-Year Plan was soon abandoned, and the Long-Term Agreement had to be modified significantly. When the Trade Agreement was originally negotiated, the Japanese oil importers were reluctant to accept increased supplies of Chinese crude both because of the heavy quality and high wax content of the Chinese oil and because of their scepticism about China's ability to fulfil larger export commitments.[81] The Japanese proposed that oil imports should rise only gradually, to an annual level of 11.3 million tons by 1982, but the Chinese counterproposal called for 15 million tons by 1982. Li Xiannian reportedly assured the Japanese that "China is capable of exporting 15 million tons of crude oil. We will guarantee it."[82] The Chinese view eventually prevailed — a result that presumably reflects the pressure that Japanese exporters of plant and equipment exerted on Japanese oil importers. Ironically, these Japanese attitudes were completely reversed within a few months for the renegotiation of the Baoshan contracts destroyed the euphoria of the machinery manufacturers, while the overthrow of the Shah of Iran and the subsequent second OPEC "price shokku" made Chinese crude oil more attractive to the oil importers. At the same time, however, the production difficulties in China's oil industry were becoming increasingly evident, and by early 1980 high-ranking Chinese officials were warning the Japanese that the original export commitments would be difficult to meet.[83] In the end, actual Chinese crude oil exports to Japan in 1982 measured only about 9 million metric tons, and exports planned for 1983 are even less.[84]

The problems of the petroleum industry are evident in the recently announced Sixth Five-Year Plan and the discussion that has accompanied it. A total of RMB ¥15.4 billion will be invested in the sector over the years from 1981 to 1985, and it is predicted that this investment will lead to new production of 35 million tons of crude oil and 2.5 billion cubic metres of natural gas annually by 1985. Despite this investment, however, total output is expected to remain flat (at about 100 million tons of oil and 10 billion cubic metres of gas) until 1985 because of the depletion of existing wells.[85] At the present time, about 80 percent of China's crude oil comes from just three onshore fields: the famous Daqing field in Heilongjiang, which supplies about 50 percent of China's oil, and the Renqiu and Shengli fields in the Bohai basin of Hebei and Shandong, which supply about 15 percent each.[86] In all three of these fields, output levels are now characterized as "stable," which is a euphemistic way of saying that it is proving difficult to increase their output. In part, this levelling off is a natural pattern that occurs in all oil fields as they mature, but it has also been suggested that the fields have been damaged by excessive water injection — that is, that output was maximized in the short run at the expense of eventual long-term yield.[87] As for natural gas, about half of China's output is produced in association with oil and therefore reflects the pattern of oil production rather closely. But even the gas produced separately (almost all of it in the province of Sichuan) has not increased much in recent years. It is now said that in the past too much stress was laid on meeting current output targets, while development of future gas reserves was neglected. The Sixth Five-Year Plan therefore gives greater emphasis to prospecting for new fields.[88]

In response to the recent plateau in petroleum production, the Chinese have sought enhanced recovery methods for existing fields and have also increased the pace of exploration and development of new onshore fields. Both efforts have involved foreign technology. An example of the former is the new program at Daqing, financed in part by a World Bank loan of $162.4 million, to increase the output of oil from the Gaotaizi oil-bearing strata.[89] Another example is the computerized analysis of wells at the Dagang and Renqiu oilfields done by the

French logging firm of Schlumberger.[90] In the realm of onshore exploration and development, notable examples of foreign participation include the recent work of French seismic teams in the Junggar basin in Xinjiang and of American seismic teams in the Qaidam basin in Qinghai, as well as the exploratory drilling being undertaken in the Ordos Desert of Inner Mongolia by the Japan National Oil Corporation.[91] The obvious disadvantage of all of these exploration areas is their remote location and inhospitable environment, which means that "transport and logistics are very difficult."[92] Although other onshore fields in more accessible locations are also being developed, their production capacity appears to be relatively limited. For example, the new Zhongyuan oilfield that straddles the Henan-Shandong border produced only 2.15 million metric tons of oil and 0.5 million cubic metres of natural gas in 1982.[93]

In the face of these problems with onshore oil and gas, it was natural for China to look offshore as well. The search for offshore hydrocarbon deposits in Asia began in the 1950s. The Japanese initiated serious seismic and gravimetric surveys of areas near Japan in 1956, and Asia's first offshore well was drilled near Borneo in 1957.[94] But interest in the offshore possibilities remained relatively dormant until 1968 when an extensive seismic survey under the auspices of the U.N. Economic Commission for Asia and the Far East (ECAFE) concluded that "the continental shelf between Taiwan and Japan may be one of the most prolific oil reservoirs in the world."[95] A follow-up survey the next year, which covered wide areas of the South China Sea, the Gulf of Thailand, and the coastal area of Indonesia, served to reinforce the excitement that the earlier report had generated.[96] Predictably, all the littoral states soon came forward to stake conflicting claims to this potential bonanza. Between 1972 and 1977, at least 110 exploratory wells were drilled offshore in concession areas granted by authorities other than China. Of these 110 wells, only 22 showed significant oil or gas deposits, and few if any of these were commercially viable at the prices of the day.[97] These disappointing results tended to confirm the geologists' suspicions that the hydrocarbon structures on China's continental shelf, much like the onshore fields at Daqing and Dagang, are highly fractured and hence expensive to exploit.[98] At the same time, however, it must be noted that for technical and economic reasons this early drilling avoided the areas of deeper water and for political reasons avoided the areas of the most contentious territorial claims — which happen also to be the areas where the thickest and most promising sediments are located.[99]

It is reported that China's first offshore well (in the Bohai Gulf) was drilled in 1967, but this early well was located on a pier extending from the shore line and therefore did not really involve offshore technology.[100] China's more significant offshore efforts came only in the 1970s, spurred no doubt by the ECAFE surveys of 1968 and 1969. China's early offshore rigs were simple barges, suitable only for shallow, sheltered waters, but the "Bohai I" (the first domestically built jack-up rig) was completed in 1972.[101] This rig was soon supplemented by a foreign jack-up purchased from Japan in 1973 and renamed the "Bohai II." (This vessel capsized and sank in November 1979 — an accident that cost the lives of 72 crew members.[102]) The decision to purchase the "Bohai II" from Japan was only one of several clear signals indicating that the meaning of self-reliance was undergoing a reinterpretation at this time. The first exports of crude oil to Japan also occurred in 1973, and the following year a French firm was hired to carry out a more sophisticated analysis of the Bohai Gulf than the Chinese were able to do alone.[103] It is hardly coincidental that Deng Xiaoping's first political rehabilitation occurred in April 1973.

By 1975 China was buying even more sophisticated and expensive drilling rigs, "loaded with the latest American offshore drilling equipment."[104] These purchases suggest that the Chinese thought the offshore prospects quite promising, and certainly the information leaked to foreign visitors in this period was extremely optimistic. The appraisals of foreign experts were generally more cautious, though their estimates of China's offshore reserves ranged all the way from 1.4 billion to about 40 billion metric tons.[105] As was widely recognized, however, such estimates — based only on indirect seismic evidence — could be badly off the mark. Furthermore, in offshore oilfields appraisal drilling is too expensive to be carried to the point where it eliminates uncertainty altogether. As one Western expert commented with respect to North Sea oil, "It is virtually a truism to say that the reserve of a field is not properly known until the last barrel has been produced."[106]

Deng Xiaoping fell from power for the second time in April 1976, as his critics castigated him for betraying the principle of self-reliance and for selling off China's natural resources to the imperialists. But offshore drilling continued, and by the time of Deng's second rehabilitation in August 1977, there were persistent reports of oil strikes in the South China Sea, both in the Pearl River delta and in the Beibu Gulf (the Gulf of Tonkin). The stage was set for the dramatic events of 1978.

The Long-Term Trade Agreement with Japan, which was signed in February 1978 and which committed China to substantial oil exports, has already been described. Equally significant was the mid-year decision to invite Japanese and French oil companies to participate in the development of the Bohai Gulf.[107] But even more important was the blossoming of co-operation between China and the United States, which was symbolized by the visit of a high-level Chinese petroleum delegation to the U.S. in January and by the reciprocal visit of an American delegation led by Secretary of Energy James Schlesinger in October and November. As Kim Woodard has noted, "The political framework of the Schlesinger visit became clear just one month later when, on December 15, 1978, President Carter announced the normalization of diplomatic relations between China and the United States."[108] It is worth noting that December 1978 was also the date of the pivotal Third Plenum.

What the Open Door has meant for offshore petroleum since 1978 can most easily be summarized by dividing developments into three broad geographic regions: north, central, and south. In the north, as already indicated, the Chinese began drilling in the Bohai Gulf about 1967, but they accelerated this work substantially in the early 1970s. French and Japanese firms were involved at a fairly early stage, supplying equipment and services, though still on the basis of traditional arm's-length contracts. Over the course of the decade, the Chinese drilled about 100 exploratory wells in the Bohai, of which 22 are reported to have been oil and gas shows.[109] The first significant find was in 1974, and by the end of the decade production in this region, concentrated in the small Chengbei, Haisi, and Shijiutuo fields, had reached about half a million tons of oil a year.[110] These results were not deemed satisfactory and — coupled with the sinking of the "Bohai II" and other failings — led to a major shake-up in October 1980 in which the minister of petroleum, Song Zhenming, was fired and the vice-premier in charge of the industry, Kang Shien, was given a "public demerit, first grade."[111] Even before these startling events, the Bohai Gulf situation had been fundamentally altered by the May 1980 signing of co-operative venture (contractual joint venture) agreements that brought the French and Japanese into exploration and development activities as partners rather than just arm's-length suppliers. The French contract, about which relatively little is known, is with Société Nationale Elf Aquitaine (SNEA or Elf), a company in which the French government is the majority shareholder. Elf drilled two dry holes in 1981, and after a year of inactivity in 1982, it is scheduled to drill two more wells in 1983. It is reported that the Elf project "has been hampered by morale and operational problems on its Chinese-owned rig (the "Bohai X") as well as by disappointing drilling results."[112]

By contrast, the Japanese projects in the Bohai Gulf have been quite successful. The first of these, which is concerned only with development of the existing Chengbei field, is relatively unimportant, because Chengbei is a small field with estimated reserves of only about 3 million tons.[113] But the second Japanese venture, which is involved in exploration and development activities over an area of 25,400 km², is a different matter altogether. The available reports give only a garbled description of the contract, but apparently the general structure is a co-operative venture in which China holds a 51 percent interest and the other 49 percent is held by the Japan-China Oil Development Corporation (JCODC), a consortium in which both public and private Japanese interests are represented but which is government controlled through the Japan National Oil Corporation.[114] According to the original contract, the exploration and appraisal phase would last for five years. During this phase the survey work done prior to 1980 would be counted as China's contribution, while JCODC would spend $210 million. Toward the end of 1982, however, the contract was revised by mutual agreement to extend the exploration phase by two years and to increase the expenditures to $600 million (all of this to be contributed, apparently, by the Japanese).[115] Once the exploration phase is completed, the production phase begins, and at that point all expenditures are to be shared in the 51/49 ratio. However, the Japanese have also agreed to cover 49 of China's 51 percent with a loan from the Japan Ex-Im Bank and to accept the remaining 2 percent in Renminbi. Thus, even at the production stage, the drain on China's budget will be negligible. The other side of the coin is, of course, that this agreement is mortgaged to the hilt, which creates the possibility of a debt crisis if the project should be unsuccessful. In fact, however, such a danger is virtually eliminated by three important considerations: 1) the debt does not cover the expenditures of the riskier exploration phase, 2) the loan from the Ex-Im Bank will presumably carry concessional interest rates, and 3) under a thin veneer, this is essentially a government-to-government agreement, and it therefore seems probable that — if a problem should develop — Tokyo would accept some modification of the contract rather than jeopardize Japan's larger diplomatic goals. In short, this is an agreement from which China stands to gain both oil and technology transfer at very little expense or risk. To say this is not to suggest, however, that the Chinese are getting something for nothing. The essence of the situation is that a non-renewable resource is being depleted, and it is only reasonable that the owner should receive some compensation.

In any event the Japanese seem quite satisfied since they have agreed to pump an extra $390 million into the venture. This attitude reflects the success of the exploration to date. The very first well, spudded in December 1980, hit a promising structure in March 1981. When a flow test was conducted in April, the well put out an estimated 7,000 barrels a day of "the best quality oil China has yet produced."[116] By the end of 1982 a total of five wells had been drilled, and four of the five are reported to be of commercial value (1,800 barrels per day or better).[117] In the spring of 1983 JCODC predicted that, when full production is established, oil output in the Bohai Gulf will "greatly exceed ten million tons a year."[118]

One important advantage of the Bohai Gulf is that it is entirely surrounded by Chinese territory and is therefore untroubled by conflicting ownership claims. By contrast, the overlapping territorial claims in the central part of the continental shelf (in the Yellow Sea and the East China Sea) are extremely complex and contentious.[119] China has asserted a claim to the entire shelf area, right out to the Ryūkyū Trench, on the basis of the principle of "the natural prolongation of the land territory," while Taiwan, viewing itself as the legitimate government of all of China, has asserted similarly expansive claims. At the same time, Japan and South Korea have staked positions based on a different legal principle, the median-line rule. Naturally, North Korea has its own view of the situation. Lying right in the middle of these conflicting claims is a large sedimentary basin called the Taiwan-Sinzi Folded Zone, which is "the thickest and potentially the richest basin on the Chinese continental shelf."[120] Because of these political complexities, this area — despite its seductive geophysical characteristics — has been explored only rather slowly and fitfully. A few wells have been drilled by American operators in concessions granted by Taiwan and South Korea, but the results have been disappointing. After several years of foot-dragging in the Japanese Diet (where many members were worried about antagonizing Beijing), Japan and South Korea ratified an agreement in 1978 to establish the Japan-Korea Joint Development Zone, but the test wells drilled in this zone since 1978 have also been dry holes. China's response to these developments has been to protest vigorously and simultaneously to launch exploratory drilling of its own in the same general area. These efforts date from 1974, when the catamaran drillship "Kantan I" sank its first well in the Yellow Sea, but success came only in August 1981, when the jack-up "Kantan II" drilled a wildcat well in the East China Sea that tested at 2,628 barrels a day of high quality crude.[121] By announcing the precise geographic co-ordinates of this well, the Chinese made sure that everyone got the message: the well is located in a concession area that Taiwan had previously granted to an American company, and it is only a few kilometres west of the Japan-Korea Joint Development Zone.[122] The Chinese have since drilled at least three other wildcats in the same region. It is noteworthy that this exploration has been carried out by the Ministry of Geology and Minerals, not by the Ministry of Petroleum Industry, though what this interministerial rivalry portends is not clear. When Tokyo has complained about this drilling, Beijing has answered that it is only doing explora-tory work and that it will refrain from any production until the territorial disputes have been settled.[123] It remains to be seen how these conflicts will ultimately be resolved, but one thing seems clear: the Taiwan question is central to the dispute, and it is an issue that will not easily be settled. Therefore, significant oil production from the Taiwan-Sinzi Folded Zone is not likely to occur in the foreseeable future, though — as will be described below — developments are moving ahead in regions of the Yellow Sea that are closer to China's coast and therefore not contested by Japan or Korea.

In the South China Sea the conflicting territorial claims of the littoral states are, if anything, even more complex and contentious than those in the East China Sea. In the Gulf of Tonkin, the dispute is a bilateral one. Vietnam argues that the proper division is along the north-south line at 108° 3'13" East, as established by an 1887 treaty between France and China. China rejects this boundary as an illegitimate legacy of the colonial era, but it has offered no clear alternative.[124] Else-where in the South China Sea the disputes are multilateral, involving China Vietnam, Taiwan, the Philippines, Malaysia, Brunei, and Indonesia. These dis-putes thrive amidst a welter of conflicting legalisms: the median-line rule, the natural prolongation principle, the archipelagic concept, the 200-mile economic zone, and so on — as well as the time-honored principle that possession is nine points of the law.[125] Of particular importance to these conflicting claims are two groups of tiny islands, known in English as the Paracels and the Spratlys (known in Chinese as the Xisha and the Nansha respectively). China seized the Paracels from South Vietnam in 1974, and Hanoi moved troops on to some islands of the Spratly group when Saigon fell in 1975. (These Vietnamese troops enjoy an uneasy coexistence with military units from Taiwan and the Philippines that were already occupying other islands in the same group. In the summer of 1983, a group of Malaysian commandos also occupied one of the atolls in the group.)

As in the East China Sea, interest in the South China Sea became more acute after the ECAFE surveys of 1968 and 1969, though offshore oil activity near Indonesia was already underway in the 1960s.[126] In 1974 and 1975 significant but subcommercial deposits were found by Shell and Mobil in concession areas granted by the Saigon government.[127] In 1976 a successful wildcat well was drilled off the coast of the Philippines in what soon became the major Nido field.[128] Amidst this activity, China was also busy in the mid-1970s with extensive seismic surveying and with negotiations for the purchase of several sophisticated offshore drilling rigs. Two jack-ups, purchased from Robin Loh in Singapore at a reported price of $18 million apiece, had begun drilling in the Gulf of Tonkin and the Pearl River estuary by late 1976 or early 1977.[129] China encountered some difficulty putting these rigs into operation, and American technicians had to be flown in to deal with the lubrication and misalignment problems that arose from Chinese inexperience.[130] Within a few months, however, China was able to send samples of "Hainan crude" and "Pearl River crude" to Japan for analysis. These samples aroused particular interest because they were lighter and less waxy than the crudes coming from northeast China.[131] This exploration, carried out by the Chinese themselves (though with imported equipment), continued into 1979 and led to at least one significant discovery in the Gulf of Tonkin.[132]

As in the Bohai, however, these results were not entirely satisfactory, and in 1980 a contract was signed that brought in Total Chine (a company controlled by the French government) as a partner in the Tonkin Gulf activities on terms similar to the contract with Elf in the North. Unlike Elf, however, Total has been quite successful in its drilling. Total's very first well, early in 1981, hit what appeared to be a big discovery, though later wells demonstrated that the structure was only a small pocket. But late in 1982 a field with good commercial potential was located.[133]

At the same time that China was pursuing its joint ventures with government-controlled oil firms (JCODC, Elf, and Total), it was also taking significant steps toward co-operation with the private oil companies. Not long after the normalization of diplomatic relations between Beijing and Washington, the oil majors were given permission to shoot extensive seismic surveys over eight large tracts of ocean, six in the South China Sea and two in the Yellow Sea. The results of these surveys, which cost the oil companies an estimated $200 million to carry out, were delivered to the Chinese in June 1981.[134] After evaluating these surveys, China opened forty-three offshore blocks to bidding in February and March 1982. To express an interest in one of the twelve blocks in the Yellow Sea, a company was required to submit $10,000, while an expression of interest in one of the thirty-one blocks in the South China Sea cost $40,000.[135] Forty firms responded by the April 25 deadline, and on 10 May these companies were given complete bidding documents, including the crucial eighty-page model contract. The companies were then allowed one hundred days to formulate and submit their detailed bid proposals, along with a $1 million signature bonus.[136] When the 17 August deadline had passed, a total of 102 bids had been received — some from individual companies, some from groups of companies acting together.[137] (Two of the forty-three blocks being offered overlap the disputed 108°3'13" line by three miles, and it is reported that Chinese wildcat wells found oil just beyond this line in 1979.[138] It will be interesting to see whether any bids have been submitted on either of these two disputed blocks.) After several more months of intense negotiations, the first contracts — covering five of the forty-three blocks — were finally signed in May 1983 with a consortium led by British Petroleum.[139] In August, contracts were signed with two consortia led by Occidental Petroleum and also with an Esso-Shell consortium. In September, contracts were signed with the Japan National Oil Company and with a consortium led by Idemitsu. The result of this flurry of contract signings is that, of the twenty-five foreign oil companies that bid for offshore exploration rights, eighteen have been included in one or more of the contracts signed.[140]

Simultaneous with this complex bidding process, China was also conducting separate negotiations with Atlantic Richfield (ARCO) and its junior partner, Santa Fe Minerals, over a concession area southwest of Hainan Island. An agreement in principle had been reached in June 1981, and a final contract was eventually concluded in August 1982.[141] According to the Chinese, the decision to deal with ARCO separately came about essentially as an accident of history and has no special significance.[142]

How soon will offshore oil be produced in substantial amounts, and at what cost? Because of the uncertainties of offshore drilling, these are difficult questions to answer, but it can be noted that toward the end of 1982 Tang Ke, the minister of petroleum industry, expressed the view that "oil production in these offshore fields will begin after 1986 and by 1990 production could be quite substantial."[143] Where offshore oil is concerned, official Chinese pronouncements have consistently been unduly optimistic about the deadlines that could be achieved, but foreign observers seem to agree with Tang that substantial commercial production is likely in the South China Sea by the end of the 1980s, and sooner in the Bohai.[144]

China's target for annual crude oil production by the year 2000 is 200 million metric tons.[145] Since it is proving difficult to sustain onshore production at its current level of about 100 million tons a year, the implied target for offshore oil is at least 100 million tons annually. From the engineering point of view (that is, in terms of the time that it takes to build offshore platforms and other infrastructure), such a goal seems to be feasible. Recent estimates of offshore reserves (2–4 billion tons in the South China Sea alone)[146] also suggest that such a goal is feasible, although — despite the promising evidence from the seismic surveys and early drilling — the amounts of recoverable oil will not really be known until considerably more drilling has been done. Furthermore, the cost will depend critically on the nature of the deposits located: their size, their distance from shore, the depth of the ocean, and so on. The First National Bank of Chicago and the Hong Kong and Shanghai Banking Corporation have both estimated that expenditures on exploration and production could total $20 billion by the early 1990s.[147] Other knowledgeable commentators have suggested that an offshore production capacity of 100 million tons a year could require investment of perhaps $40 to 60 billion.[148] The model contract calls for the foreign oil companies to pay all the exploration costs, but at the production stage the Chinese side will assume 51 percent of costs.[149] Therefore, the Chinese share of total investments could be roughly $20 billion, or about RMB ¥40 billion at the current exchange rate. Spread over the remaining years of this century, this sum translates into annual expenditures of about RMB ¥2.5 billion — which seems to be a feasible order of magnitude from the fiscal point of view because the Sixth Five-Year Plan allocates about RMB ¥3.1 billion annually to the petroleum sector.

Apart from questions of engineering and finance, another factor that may affect the pace of offshore oil development is the problem of "dual-use" technology — that is, technology that has industrial applications but that also has important military uses. In the realm of offshore petroleum, examples of dual-use technology include satellite navigation equipment, precision devices for measuring magnetic fields (which are used in oil exploration but are also used for submarine detection), and large-scale computers (which are needed to process seismic data but also have a variety of military applications).[150] Technology of this sort from the West has been subject to significant export restrictions, administered either by the U.S. Department of Commerce or by the agency known as COCOM (the Coordinating Committee for the Control of Strategic Trade with Communist Countries). Ever since the U.S. government placed China in its own unique "category P" for the purposes of export control in 1980, it has been the stated intent of American policy to apply less stringent controls to China than to Soviet Bloc countries. Chinese officials have complained, however, that "category P" status made little difference in practice.[151] In response, the Reagan administration has informed the Chinese that China will be moved to the category of countries considered to be "friendly or allied with the U.S." In part, this change is being made in order to make it possible for American oil companies like Occidental and Exxon to carry out their offshore oil contracts.[152]

Assuming that the potential engineering, financial, and political problems can all be dealt with satisfactorily as they arise and assuming, therefore, that offshore oil production reaches 100 million tons a year or better by 2000 A.D., what will this mean for China's *net* energy supplies? That is, how much of this oil will accrue to China and how much to the foreign partners? And, to view the matter in financial terms, what rate of return will the two sides earn on their respective investments? Precise answers to such questions will depend on the specific details of the contracts negotiated (which are closely guarded secrets) and on the future course of oil prices and other variables (which are inherently uncertain). What is reasonably certain, however, is that the model contract sets the upper limits of what the foreign participants can hope to attain. For this reason, a careful examination of the model contract is quite illuminating.

It is obviously difficult to summarize an eighty-page document adequately in a paragraph, but some of the key features can be mentioned.[153] As indicated above, the foreign partner pays all costs during the exploration stage, which is limited to either five or seven years, depending on the size of the area being explored. If the exploration results indicate that development is warranted, the Chinese will then contribute 51 percent of the development costs (or less, at their discretion). The model contract specifies a fifteen-year production period, but provides for an extension of time if the field is still producing at the end of fifteen years. Since the lifespan of a large offshore field is typically twenty years or more and since the model contract specifies that "good oilfield practice" must be followed (which means that the rate of extraction cannot be pushed too hard, because this diminishes the ultimate recovery ratio), it seems probable that extensions will be needed. The oil produced will be divided as follows: 50 percent will be set aside as "cost oil," 17.5 percent will go directly to China as turnover tax and royalty, and the remaining 32.5 percent is divided into "share oil" and "allocable profit oil." The share oil goes entirely to China, while the allocable profit oil is divided between the partners in proportion to their shares in the development costs (thus, normally, 51/49). The foreign partner's share of allocable profit oil is then subject to the foreign enterprise income tax, at a tax rate that approaches 50 percent. The proportion of the 32.5 percent that goes to share oil rather than to allocable profit oil (the so-called "x factor") is one of the three key elements around which the competitive bidding process is focused — the other two being the pace of exploration and a vague category called "other contributions," which could include personnel training programs, financial assistance, or anything else that is mutually agreeable. The 50 percent of output set aside as cost oil will be allocated year-by-year to cover operating expenses first, then exploration costs, and finally development costs. Once the exploration and development costs are fully recaptured, which is expected to take roughly five years, the cost oil not needed to cover operating expenses will be added to allocable profit oil.

Computer simulations of the complexities of the model contract suggest several important conclusions. First, the rate of return earned by the foreign partner is extremely sensitive to the fine details of the situation, particularly to three key parameters: the time lags between expenditures and revenues, the precise characteristics of the offshore structures, and the market price of oil and gas over the next three decades. From the private oil companies' point of view, the after-tax rate of return can easily be quite attractive (30 percent or better) or quite dismal (10 percent or worse), and this outcome is dependent on factors that cannot be known in advance. In short, the situation contains a substantial element of real risk, and the anticipated private rate of return will have to reflect this.

Second, the rate of return earned by the foreigner is *not* particularly affected by variations in operating costs. The explanation for this seeming paradox lies in the structure of the model contract, which — in its treatment of cost oil — has many of the characteristics of a "cost-plus" contract. Because the profit oil is split 51/49 and because the marginal corporate tax rate is 50 percent, about seventy-five cents of every extra dollar of operating expenses ends up being paid by the Chinese side. This point is worth emphasizing, because the foreign oil companies have recently begun to complain privately about the exorbitant rates being charged by China for accommodations, telephones, duties on imports, and so on. [154] Given the structure of the contract, any attempt of this sort by the Chinese to squeeze extra profit out of the foreign partner is likely to create resentment without generating much extra revenue. (Part of the explanation for this situation is, of course, the fiscal tug-of-war between central and local authorities in China.)

Third, the rate of return earned by the Chinese on their share of the investment is substantially better than what the foreign partner earns. For example, in one simulation that posited rather gloomy conditions (high development costs, a low price of oil, and so forth) the after-tax rate of return to the foreign partner was about 11.7 percent, while the return on the Chinese share was about 29.9 percent — even though it was assumed in this simulation that the contract made no provision for share oil. Thus, if an "x factor" had been built in, the differential between the foreign partner and the Chinese would have been even wider. It is important to reiterate, however, that the return to the Chinese is really a blending of what are, in principle, two quite distinct items: a return to capital and a royalty payment for the depletion of a non-renewable resource. What the chairman of Burmah Oil has said with respect to North Sea oil is well worth repeating where China's offshore resources are concerned:

> No matter whether you are a Saudi, a Scotsman or a Shetlander, the question must be the same — how long will it last and what can I do with it while it does so that I am economically strong when it runs down? . . . If we are not quick to determine the best long term use of the North Sea revenues, then by the early part of next century not even an oily rag will remain to remind us of it. [155]

Fourth, and finally, computer simulations of the model contract suggest that the fraction of total oil production that accrues to the foreign partner is surprisingly insensitive to variations in the details of the situation. For a wide range of values of the key parameters, the foreigners' share of the oil remains quite stable, at between 21 and 25 percent of the total. Thus, in terms of China's larger growth strategies, the lesson that emerges from all of this arithmetic is as follows: if 100 million tons of offshore oil are needed for domestic energy requirements in the year 2000, then total offshore oil production will need to be about 125 to 130 million tons per annum.

ENERGY IN CHINA'S DEVELOPMENT STRATEGY AND BALANCE OF PAYMENTS

The time has come to try to put the separate pieces of the energy picture together into a coherent whole. As already indicated, China's general economic objective is to quadruple the gross annual value of industrial and agricultural output during the last two decades of the century — or, to be more precise, to increase the output figure from its 1980 level of RMB ¥710 billion to a projected level of RMB ¥2,800 billion by the year 2000. Assuming that the energy-output elasticity can be brought down to the target value of 0.5, this output target implies that energy supplies will have to be nearly doubled, which is exactly consistent with the projection that energy production will rise from its 1980 level of 620 million tons of standard coal equivalent to 1200 million tons by 2000 A.D.[156]

Interestingly enough, however, the industry-by-industry output projections do not add up to 1200 million tons of standard coal equivalent. We have already noted that coal output in 2000 A.D. is expected to be 1200 million metric tons, and crude oil output, 200 million metric tons. Natural gas output is projected to be 34.5 billion cubic metres.[157] Nuclear power seems unlikely to be making much of a contribution to the aggregate energy picture by the end of the century. The situation with respect to hydro electricity is somewhat cloudy. One recent authoritative discussion projected an output of 150 billion kwh in 2000 A.D., but other discussions have suggested that, out of the projected total electricity supply of 1200 billion kwh, hydro should supply at least as great a proportion as it does now. This would imply hydro output of at least 240 billion kwh by the end of the century.[158] What all of these projections mean in the aggregate is as follows:[159]

Industry	Projected Output	Standard Coal Equivalent
Coal	1200 mil. tons	856.8 mil. tons
Oil	200 mil. tons	286.0 mil. tons
Gas	34.5 bil. m³	45.9 mil. tons
Hydro	150-240 bil. kwh	63.3-101.3 mil. tons
Total		1252-1290 mil. tons

In view of the stated goal, what is to be made of this discrepancy of 50 to 90 million tons? One interesting possibility is that China's planners see this amount as the quantity that will be needed to cover repayments on the Open Door projects in the energy sector and have therefore subtracted this amount to reach a net figure of

1200 million tons. We should hasten to add, however, that we have encountered no Chinese discussions that argue along these lines or indeed that even recognize the existence of the discrepancy. But the order of magnitude is consistent with our own calculations, presented earlier in this chapter, of the coal and oil exports needed in 2000 A.D. to cover the foreign obligations in these industries. Thus, despite the seeming contradictions in the projections, the total picture is not really inconsistent.

If 1200 million tons of standard coal equivalent are needed for domestic industry and 50 to 90 million tons are needed to repay Open Door projects, there seems at first glance to be little margin left to export for purposes of earning extra foreign exchange. On closer examination, however, this turns out not to be so. In the early 1980s, exports of coal, electricity, and natural gas (measured as percentages of domestic production) were all negligible, but the exports of crude oil and refined petroleum products amounted to about 20 percent of the total output of 100 million metric tons.[160] Thus the oil industry's contribution to domestic energy supplies was really only about 80 million metric tons, and the projected doubling of oil's contribution therefore requires only 160 million tons. If net oil output actually reaches 200 million tons, as expected, this leaves about 40 million tons a year available for export, over and above the amounts needed to repay Open Door obligations. Even at the relatively soft price of $25 a barrel, this translates into foreign exchange earnings of $7.5 billion a year. Chen Muhua, the minister of foreign economic relations and trade, has recently stated that China's strategy for at least the near term will be to export increasing amounts of coal, not oil, but this shift does not alter the general conclusion that there is enough slack within the projected figures to permit fairly significant energy exports.[161]

In summary, the production levels projected for the various energy industries by the end of the century seem to be reasonably conservative, and — if attained — they should be adequate to provide a doubling of domestic energy supplies with something left over to earn foreign exchange. What appears to be much less conservative is the goal of reducing the energy-output elasticity to 0.5. This seems to us to be a point of great vulnerability in the larger development strategy, though it is also an area where the Open Door may have a particularly constructive role to play.

Appendix to Chapter 6   Analysis of the Model Contract

The simulation used to analyse the model contract is scaled to an output of 750 barrels (100 tons) a year. The scale chosen makes no difference to the final rate of return calculations. The complexities of the model contract are best understood in terms of four phases in the life of the oil field: a period of n years of construction, and then three consecutive periods of production: m years while exploration costs are repaid, p years while development costs are repaid, and then q remaining years before the field is depleted. Thus, the full production period runs for $(m + p + q)$ years. In the full simulation, fractions of a year can be accommodated (that is, n, m, p, and q need not be integers), but for ease of exposition they are treated as integers in this discussion.

Throughout the period of production, operating costs (OC) have a first claim on the 50 percent of output set aside as cost oil. Thus, the number of barrels required to cover operating costs is just OC/P, where P is the price per barrel. Therefore, of the 375 barrels of cost oil each year, $[375 - (OC/P)]$ barrels are available for purposes other than covering operating costs.

During the construction phase, the foreign partner pays all of the exploration costs (EC) and 49 percent of the development costs (DC). Thus, during the construction phase of n years, the foreign partner's average expenditures per year are given by

$$[EC + 0.49(DC)]/n,$$

an expression which for ease of notation will later be referred to simply as A.

During phase one of production, the foreign partner has net receipts (after operating costs and taxes) of

$$P\{[375 - (OC/P)] + [(0.5 \text{ tax rate})(0.49 \text{ share})(0.75)(1 - x)(375)]\},$$

an expression which for ease of notation will be referred to below simply as B. In the latter part of expression B, the factor (0.75) is an adjustment for the royalty-type taxes, and the factor $(1 - x)$ is the adjustment for the so-called "x factor."

During the second phase of production, the foreign partner has net receipts of

$$0.49P\{[375 - (OC/P)] + [(0.5)(0.75)(1 - x)(375)]\},$$

an expression referred to below as C.

During the final phase of production, the foreign partner has net receipts of

$$P(0.5)(0.49)(1 - x)[(375 - OC/P) + (0.75)(375)],$$

an expression referred to below as D.

The rate of return to the foreign partner's investment can now be calculated by finding the (unique) solution to the following polynomial equation:

$$\sum_{i=1}^{n} A/(1+r)^{i-1} - \sum_{j=1}^{m} B/(1+r)^{n+j-1} - \sum_{k=1}^{p} C/(1+r)^{n+m+k-1}$$
$$- \sum_{l=1}^{q} D/(1+r)^{n+m+p+l-1} = 0.$$

7

Problems and Prospects

Developments to date suggest that even though qualitatively the Open Door has significantly altered China's approach to technology transfer and the utilization of foreign capital, the quantitative impact has been relatively modest. Of course, the door has been ajar for only a short period of time, so the process of creating lasting economic relations between China and countries of the capitalist world is just beginning. It is therefore much too early to assess the impact of the Open Door or to judge its success. Indeed, it can be argued that the real test of whether China will attract, assimilate, and absorb a significant amount of foreign technology and capital is only about to begin. However, the experience of the five years since the Third Plenum does provide a clearer view of the likely opportunities, problems, and prospects of international economic co-operation in China. In what follows, those factors that have emerged to date as having had particularly important influences on slowing the pace of development and reducing the impact of the Open Door are first examined. The prospects for success of the open door policy are then considered. Finally, because the open door policy and domestic economic reforms are functionally related, the chapter concludes with a brief discussion of the difficulties facing economic reforms.

PROBLEMS EXPERIENCED TO DATE

It is not difficult to identify the main reasons why development of international economic co-operation in China has proceeded so far at a slower pace than both sides had originally hoped for and anticipated. Unfounded high expectations are one reason. But there are other, more tangible contributory factors. While the constraining influence of some of the factors discussed below is likely to become less important in time, some will continue to have a dampening effect on the pace of development of international economic co-operation in China in the foreseeable future.

In the early 1980s, uncertainty over development strategy and high interest rates have made Chinese planners and policy-makers more cautious about rushing into a large number of new international co-operation projects. When China abandoned its Ten-Year Plan in 1979, the economy entered a period of adjustment and reform, and the country had to pause to sort out its priorities. Until late 1982 China operated without a long-term plan to guide its decision-makers. This lack of direction has undoubtedly slowed negotiation of international projects.

China's reluctance to use large amounts of foreign credit has also limited the impact of the Open Door. Between 1979 and 1981, a substantial amount of foreign credit was made available to China. At the end of 1981 China had access to official export credits of about US$17 billion at concessionary interest rates of between 7.25 and 8.75 percent.[1] In addition, slightly over US$10 billion of private commercial credits were also available to China at rates slightly above the London Inter-Bank Offered Rate (LIBOR).[2] The precise amount of credit that China has used in the past four years is not clear, but the evidence suggests that whatever the amount, it was not large. In early 1982, Ji Chongwei announced that China's cumulative use of foreign loans in recent years amounted to about US$2,335 million, of which US$1,000 million were foreign government loans, US$1,135 million were loans from international agencies (IMF, World Bank, and UN), and only US$200 million were from the lines of credit arranged by the Bank of China.[3] Recently, the *Beijing Review* reported that, between 1979 and the end of 1982, China used foreign loans (presumably including short term suppliers' credit) totalling US$10.8 billion, of which US$7.1 billion had been repaid.[4]

It is not difficult to understand why China has not been more aggressive in the use of credit to finance the import of technology and the growth of international economic co-operation projects in China. Most of the official low-interest credits that China arranged were restricted to export financing from specific countries, and when China's import plans were altered by changes in its development strategy and cutbacks in investment projects, these credits were no longer required and could not easily be transferred to other uses. The terms of the commercial credits, at about 0.5 percent above LIBOR, are quite generous. But with LIBOR in 1981 and early 1982 above 10 percent, borrowing even on these terms looked expensive to the Chinese who, until recently, questioned the legitimacy of interest payments on ideological grounds. Because of high interest rates, the Chinese have become, in the past few years, more reluctant to incur external debts, recognizing as they do that a large debt, if not managed judiciously, can lead to the kinds of repayment problems that now confront Poland, Mexico, and Brazil.

The reluctance of foreign countries, particularly the United States, to share certain types of technology with China has also not helped development. As noted in the previous chapter, in 1980 the American government placed China in its own special "category P" for the purpose of export control, which in principle should have liberalized trade between the two countries. In reality, however, there were still serious problems. As a Chinese trade official remarked recently, "The U.S. places restrictions on our exports of textiles, mushrooms, and porcelain, and when China wants to import technology and equipment, the U.S. refuses to issue a license."[5] The ambiguities of American policy toward the export of sophisticated technology to China can be seen in the recent attempt to block the sale of computer-controlled telephone equipment by a Belgian affiliate of ITT and also in the equivocation over permission to sell nuclear power technology.[6]

For businessmen, the attractiveness of any venture must be assessed in terms of its risk, transaction costs, and rate of return. That the development of international co-operation projects in China has proceeded relatively slowly suggests that, in terms of these criteria, many foreign businessmen still consider investment conditions in China to be less than favorable. Why? Several reasons come to mind.

For a foreign firm interested in participating in the Open Door, a major objective — indeed, the major objective — is profit. The Chinese recognize this and are willing to permit foreigners to make profits. But there are constraints. Government officials and departments are vulnerable to the criticism that they have allowed China to be exploited if international economic co-operation projects appear too successful — that is, if foreign profits from such projects appear too large. Added to these political pressures, there is also a fiscal pressure to squeeze the profits accruing to foreigners. Even if the central authorities intend one policy, local authorities may pursue another, especially under the new *baogan* arrangements, which create a strong incentive for local authorities to invent additional revenue-gathering mechanisms. This central-local tug-of-war over revenues is certainly one important explanation for the high fees (high by international standards, that is) charged for car rentals, telephone service, helicopter charters, hotel accommodations, and a variety of other services supplied to the foreign business community in China.

The exploitation issue is also relevant to the question of wage levels. One of the main reasons why foreign firms are attracted to China is the low cost of labor. But "low wages" can easily be equated with the "exploitation of Chinese workers." The Chinese insistence that wages and prices be "just" and that profits be "reasonable" means that there are political limits to the size of profits that can be made in China. Such restrictions are, of course, likely to make projects in China less attractive to foreign firms, particularly if the risk involved is high. That high returns are needed to compensate for high risks is a concept that many Chinese cadres do not as yet fully appreciate.

It should be noted that foreign participants who are concerned about the return on their investments are not so much worried about wages per se as about unit labor costs. Wages are low in China in part because labor productivity is low. In our interviews, Chinese cadres and foreign businessmen alike indicated that many potential foreign participants in international economic co-operation projects in China would actually like to see an increase in the take-home pay of Chinese workers in the belief that higher wages will motivate workers to perform more efficiently and thus reduce unit labor cost and increase profits. But here too there are political constraints. Motivation schemes that rely heavily on wage incentives are bound to increase income inequality among Chinese workers. Although the current political line is that income should be distributed according to labor, the degree of dispersion that will be tolerated is still uncertain. That the wages of workers in equity joint ventures cannot exceed those of state enterprises in similar industries by more than 50 percent suggests that the politically tolerable limit on economic differences may not be very large. In addition, the less competent workers and cadres may also resist a wage scheme that ties income closely to performance and productivity. The realization that it may be difficult to improve labor productivity quickly in the Chinese environment has undoubtedly made projects in China less attractive to some foreign firms.

For many foreign firms, the most attractive aspect of participating in international economic co-operation projects in China is the possibility of penetrating its domestic market. But, quite naturally, the Chinese have insisted that such projects be outward-oriented and that a large part, if not all, of the annual output be marketed abroad. This is certainly the case for processing and assembling agreements and compensation trade arrangements, but other forms of special trade must also be at least self-sufficient in foreign exchange. As was noted earlier, the advantage to China of making such projects outward-oriented goes beyond the direct effects on the balance of payments. It is also a way to ensure that the projects are economically viable and that the resultant products are of sufficiently high quality to compete internationally. Finally, it shifts part of the burden of marketing the output from the Chinese to the foreign participants.

But the insistence that these projects be generally outward-oriented has made such projects less attractive. In part this is because the international market is more competitive than the Chinese domestic market. That China opened its door just when the Western economies entered their deepest recession since the Great Depression has not helped. Protectionism has been on the rise, making it more difficult for products made in China to enter the major world markets. But it is to be hoped that this is a temporary phenomenon. A more permanent concern to foreign firms is that many already have sources to supply the major world markets and therefore are not particularly anxious to help develop another source in China that will compete with their existing sources. Potential foreign participants are also less attracted to the more outward-oriented projects because they are still uncertain that the Chinese will be able to meet the quality standards and strict deadlines required by the international market.

Our interviews suggest that the Chinese and foreign participants look at co-operative and equity joint ventures somewhat differently. Foreign businessmen generally believe that in making decisions the interests of the joint venture should be put first. However, to the Chinese, the interests of the joint venture, though important, should not necessarily take precedence over state interests. In other words, foreign participants are primarily concerned about profits, while their Chinese counterparts must also consider the interests of the state and are therefore more willing to sacrifice profits in order to achieve other objectives. Obviously, this realization has made joint ventures less attractive to foreign firms.

International economic co-operation in China has developed slowly in part also because many foreign businessmen continue to consider it risky to make sizeable financial commitments to projects in China. Because the open door policy is the direct result of political changes in China and is closely tied to Deng Xiaoping and his supporters, the question uppermost in the minds of Western businessmen is how long the door will remain open and whether future political shifts will adversely affect the profitability of international economic co-operation in China. The Chinese government has tried to reassure foreign businessmen, both through the promulgation of laws and through public pronouncements, that their investments and financial interests in China will be protected and that the internal political environment has stabilized. Such assurances have emanated from the highest level. As Deng Xiaoping has emphasized: "We in China have suffered too much from political turbulence and we have gained a very deep impression from this experience; deeper than any similar experience you may have had. There is now a situation of political tranquility and stability." But past political turbulence has also left a deep impression in the minds of foreign businessmen so that some still consider China a high political risk.

Political risks aside, there are other reasons why doing business in China has been perceived as risky. One serious problem has been the significant differences between the Chinese and Western legal systems. Because of China's underdeveloped legal system, foreign businessmen, until recently, operated essentially in a legal vacuum. In such an environment, the perceived risk of lending to or investing in Chinese enterprises was extremely high and was a major obstacle to the development of international economic co-operation. In the past four years, a large number of statutes concerning economic matters have been enacted and special economic divisions and organs to enforce these laws have been established, so a clearer picture of the legal environment has emerged. But businessmen still worry about how these laws and regulations will be interpreted. That many Chinese laws and regulations are kept secret is also worrisome to foreign businessmen. Until there is more experience with how the Chinese legal system will work and more is known about how the Chinese will interpret the enacted laws, foreign businessmen will continue to be uneasy about making large financial commitments. However, it is important to emphasize that the experience of the past few years suggests that, in the current environment in China, it is possible to challenge the legal interpretation of a Chinese government organ and to receive a favorable ruling from a higher body.[9] To foreign businessmen, this is surely an encouraging sign. If development continues along this line, some of the fears about the Chinese legal system that have been expressed by foreign businessmen will be allayed.

Differences between the Chinese and Western economic systems have also increased the perceived risk of doing business in China. Part of the problem is that, with economic reform just beginning, it is still too soon to know what changes will actually be introduced or how quickly and forcefully they will be implemented. In any case, some of the risk is traceable to problems that may be systemic, and foreign observers are not as yet convinced that the Chinese leadership can solve these problems with the type of reform currently under discussion. For example, supplies are allocated primarily by administrative means according to the annual plan.[10] The Chinese see this as being superior to the "anarchy of the market." But the command system has proven (in China as well as in other socialist countries) to be much less efficient than the market in allocating resources, and the supply problems created by such a system have frequently been exacerbated by poor planning. The result is increased supply uncertainty for the individual enterprise, something that all foreign businessmen abhor. Of course, the more a special trade project is integrated with the Chinese domestic supply system, the more it is subject to this type of risk.

Unfamiliarity with China's economic system, its administrative practices, and the Chinese work style are also problems that foreign businessmen must overcome. In time and with more experience, this type of problem will be reduced. But, to date, this unfamiliarity has tended to increase the foreigners' perceived risk of doing business with China. The lack of information about the Chinese economy, both at the macro and the micro levels, makes it extremely difficult for foreign businessmen to form sound judgments about market size, profit opportunities, and the feasibility of proposed projects.[11] From the foreign businessman's viewpoint, making decisions without adequate information increases the risk of a project. The problem is owing in part to the reluctance of the Chinese to make information public, but in part it is also owing to the fact that in China statistics are not collected and processed as systematically as they could be. Since 1979, the Chinese government has published more economic data, so, in time, the information problem will probably be reduced. But, as of now, the information gap is still immense.

Another obstacle experienced to date is the unusually high transaction costs of doing business with China. Differences in language, in economic system, and in cultural background have all contributed, and this comes as no surprise to those who traded with China prior to the Open Door. But the transaction costs of special trade may be even higher, in part because these agreements are generally more complex than arm's-length trade and in part because they frequently involve issues that are politically more sensitive to the Chinese. The difficulty of obtaining information about China has meant that the average foreign businessman must spend a great deal more time and resources on information gathering and preliminary assessment of business opportunities in China than in most other countries. Because of differences in the Chinese and Western legal and economic systems, many more issues need to be clarified and negotiated. The need to establish limits to prices and profits also complicates the negotiations.

Communication costs are also high. Part of the problem is that communication facilities in China are relatively backward. But foreign businessmen have also found it difficult to communicate with their Chinese counterparts. The problem is more than just a difference in language as the communication problem exists for experienced Hong Kong Chinese businessmen as well. Indeed, differences in background, experience, values, and attitudes between the foreign businessmen and their Chinese counterparts have all contributed to make communication and negotiation difficult.[12] It is the middle echelon of the Chinese bureaucracy that carries the burden of the negotiation with foreign businessmen, and the shortage of competent and experienced cadres at this level and the fact that many of the new players on the Chinese side are relatively inexperienced in international business have also added to the search and negotiation costs experienced by foreigners. Afraid of criticism, which may come from almost any quarter, Chinese bureaucrats are exceedingly cautious and risk averse. Thus, decisions, even relatively minor ones, are taken only after exhaustive consultations among many parties. Unlike foreign businessmen, Chinese cadres do not derive direct economic benefits from the business under discussion. Accordingly, the Chinese are less willing to take risks and bring the discussion to a successful conclusion quickly. The large size of the Chinese bureaucracy, and its multiple layers, also contributes to delays. Because of these problems, foreign businessmen have found it necessary to make numerous trips to China, and the time they spend in China is often used unproductively.[13]

Two groups of foreign businessmen appear to have found the transaction costs of doing business with China less burdensome. The first group is those Overseas Chinese who are interested in small and simple special trade arrangements. For them the transaction costs are somewhat lower, in part because they face no language barrier. In addition, because their business is usually with their native province of Guangdong or Fujian and because of the greater autonomy in international economic relations granted to these two provinces, their special trade deals can often be arranged without involving the senior government. Indeed, in Guangdong and Fujian, many small processing arrangements require only the approval of the city or county (*xian*) foreign trade office.[14] An Overseas Chinese businessman may further reduce the transaction cost if the arrangement involves his native village where he has friends and relatives and may be known personally to the local cadres. In fact, we were told in Guangdong that Overseas Chinese generally prefer to locate their special trade projects in their native villages.

The second group is the large multinational corporations. For them, the transaction costs are less burdensome because, unlike small and medium size companies, multinationals can afford to allocate the necessary financial resources and executive time to develop economic relations with China. For example, few small or medium size companies can afford to place a company representative in Beijing to follow developments in China, to assign a senior executive to specialize on China, or even to subscribe to the services of the national trade groups that specialize on China. Furthermore, because multinationals are generally interested in the larger projects, they are likely to deal directly with Chinese officials who are more senior and more experienced in international business. Thus, multinationals need to penetrate fewer layers of bureaucracy to reach those in China in decision-making positions.

That it is the small and medium size companies that are finding the transaction costs of doing business in China particularly burdensome is unfortunate because it is probably these companies that may be most interested in the type of economic co-operation projects that the Chinese are currently promoting — that is, relatively small projects to up-grade the production capacity of existing Chinese manufacturing enterprises, particularly those in light industry. Furthermore, in some technologies, it is the small and medium size firms that are the leaders in the field.

It is important to emphasize that one reason why transaction costs are high is the lack of experience in special trade arrangements. In time and with more experience, one may expect the transaction costs to decline. Guidelines for prices and profits may be established so that in the future both sides will know roughly the permissible limits, thus eliminating the need to negotiate every contract from scratch. In time, local cadres, who do much of the negotiation on China's behalf, will also become more familiar with the policies and guidelines of the central government as well as with international trade practices. And, of course, in time both sides will become more familiar with each other's objectives, values, and work style. In other words, with more experience and with each side more familiar with the other, the transaction costs of doing business will decline.

The Chinese are also aware that high transaction costs have discouraged some foreign businesses (particularly the small and medium size companies) from considering economic co-operation with China, and they are anxious to lower this barrier. There is also a growing recognition in China that if the country is to attract more investment from abroad, it must offer foreign investors a more favorable rate of return. As a recent editorial in the *People's Daily* noted, "Capital in the international markets always goes after profits. It will not come if it has no prospects of gain, or will gain a lower profit than the international average."[15]

In mid- and late-1983, the Chinese government announced several changes that measurably improve the business climate. In May 1983 the joint venture income tax law was revised to provide a somewhat more generous tax holiday (the revisions received formal approval at the Second Session of the Standing Committee of the Sixth NPC in August 1983 and were promulgated on 25 September

1983).[16] Joint ventures will now be exempted from the income tax in the first two profit-making years and will have their income tax reduced by one-half in the third, fourth, and fifth profitable years (the original provision provided only a one-year tax exemption plus a two-year 50 percent reduction in income tax), so that China's tax incentive for foreign investment is now closer to what is available in other parts of Asia (see Table 4.1).

Then, in September 1983, the long-awaited detailed regulations for the implementation of the joint venture law were promulgated, and they contained several clauses that provide some additional incentives to joint ventures. For example, the rules governing the exemption of import duties and the consolidated industrial and commercial tax (CICT) on goods imported by joint ventures were liberalized marginally.[17] Furthermore, during its initial period of operation, a joint venture may now apply for an exemption from the CICT for that part of its output sold in China if it is experiencing financial difficulties.[18] The two-price system imposed on joint ventures was also changed slightly. Hereafter, they will have to pay the higher international prices for Chinese precious metals, oil, coal, and timber only on that portion used to produce products for export.[19] The new regulations also relaxed the rule on the amount of income foreign workers employed by joint ventures may remit home. Now, foreign staff and workers may request permission to remit abroad all (instead of only 50 percent) of their income after living expenses.[20]

From the viewpoint of the foreign businessman, the most interesting, and potentially the most significant, change is China's announcement that it plans to relax its insistence that each joint venture must export at least enough to satisfy its own foreign exchange needs (see Chapter 4). The recently released "Regulations for the Implementation of the Joint Venture Law" include the following three articles:

Article 60: The Chinese Government encourages joint ventures to sell their products on the international market.

Article 61: Products of joint ventures that China urgently needs or imports can be mainly sold on the Chinese market.

Article 75: A joint venture shall in general keep [a] balance between its foreign exchange income and expenses.

These rules are not very different from the ones in existence from 1979 to September 1983. Thus, apparently, what has changed is how China intends to apply these rules. China has announced that it will not "mechanically demand that all joint ventures market the major part of their products abroad or balance their foreign receipts and payments."[21] In other words, although access to the domestic market will still be granted only on a case-by-case basis, joint ventures may now find it easier to get permission to sell their products in China.

The "Regulations for the Implementation of the Joint Venture Law" further stipulate that, when a joint venture produces primarily for the domestic market and therefore is not self-sufficient in foreign exchange, its foreign exchange needs will be met first of all from the foreign exchange retained by the senior unit in charge of the Chinese participants in the joint venture (that is, the province, the municipality, or the ministry that controls the Chinese participant), and only if the senior unit has insufficient foreign exchange will the joint venture's foreign exchange needs be considered by MFERT and the State Planning Commission for inclusion in the country's foreign exchange plan.[22] Given this rule, Chinese units will continue to be very careful about entering into a joint venture that will produce primarily for the domestic market. Nevertheless, the additional tax incentives and the improved prospect of selling to the domestic market are likely to make the equity joint venture a more attractive form of international economic co-operation in the eyes of foreign businessmen. However, whether many joint ventures will be given access to China's domestic market remains to be seen.

PROSPECTS FOR SUCCESS

To evaluate the prospects, one must first define the meaning of "success." Among the criteria that might be incorporated into such a definition two are most obvious. The first is size — that is, how much foreign technology and capital China attracts. But size alone is not a sufficient indicator of success. The imported technology and capital must be properly assimilated and effectively used. Thus the second relevant criterion of success is *jingji xiaoguo* (economic effectiveness).

The Potential Magnitude of the Open Door

How much technology China will import and how extensively it will utilize foreign capital to help finance its modernization will be determined by many factors, some within its control and some not. Among the main factors that China says it will consider in deciding how much technology and foreign funds it will use is its ability to absorb technology and to use foreign capital effectively. Ultimately, the magnitude of the transfer will also depend on the mutual capacity to devise ways to reduce some of the problems discussed in the previous section, on China's development policy in the 1980s, on its ability to export and its willingness to borrow from abroad, and on external factors such as U.S. policy relating to technology export and the trade policies of the major developed countries. As well, the success of the Open Door will be influenced by how quickly and how smoothly the Hong Kong problem is resolved. The purpose of the discussion below is not to project what the eventual magnitude of the Open Door will be but only to consider in greater detail a few of the main factors that are likely to influence the amount of technology and foreign capital that China will utilize in the 1980s and 1990s.

Some of the problems contributing to the slow development of international economic co-operation from 1979 to 1982 appear to be in the process of being resolved and may cease to be important obstacles to the development of commercial relations between China and the West in the 1980s. We have already noted the steps taken recently by the Chinese government to improve the business climate in China.[23] Another significant development was the clarification and the further liberalization of U.S. rules governing technology transfer to China. In 1983, China was removed from its own unique "category P" and placed in "category V" along with countries "friendly or allied with the U.S." such as India and Japan. In September 1983 U.S. Defense Secretary Weinberger informed the Chinese that the United States has approved the export to China of forty-three items of high technology, including some advanced "dual-use" technology.

But numerous problems remain. The many differences between the Chinese and the Western legal and economic systems will continue to be a major obstacle. Thus, the magnitude of the Open Door in the 1980s will be determined in part by how successfully China and the international business community find ways to bridge these differences. Many of the conflicts will not be easy to resolve. For example, ever since the open door policy was announced, foreign companies have been urging China to adopt a patent law so that they will have legal protection against unauthorized use of their technology once it has been transferred to China. But China must move carefully because in drafting such a law it must be concerned not only with the interests of patent holders (in this case, foreign companies) but also with China's interests and needs. How quickly and how smoothly these differences will be worked out will depend on the flexibility and goodwill on both sides. Experience so far suggests that, while progress can be expected, both sides will need to be patient and persistent. Even though China has recently expressed its willingness to allow some joint ventures to market their products in China, patience will also be necessary in resolving the conflict between China's desire to export and the foreign participants' desire to focus on China.

Perhaps more than anything else, balance of payments considerations will determine the size of the Open Door in the 1980s. How much technology China will import and how actively it will participate in international economic co-operation projects will depend on how rapidly China's exports grow and on China's ability and willingness to borrow and to accept foreign investment. These factors are interconnected, for the amount of debt and equity that China can prudently accept will be determined by its ability to repay, which in turn depends on its export potential.

Between 1978 and 1982, despite world-wide recession, China's foreign exchange earnings from commodity exports more than doubled, growing at an average annual rate of about 25 percent (Table 1.3). The current export composition is: primary products (excluding mineral fuels and products), 25 percent;

mineral fuels and products, 24 percent; and manufactured products, 51 percent.[24] Of the manufactured exports, two-thirds are light industrial and textile products. For both demand and supply reasons, China's exports of primary products (excluding mineral fuels and products) are not likely to increase significantly, if at all, in the future.[25] Thus, future increases in exports will have to come from mineral fuels and products and from manufactured products. Indeed, the recent rapid increase in exports was largely owing to the expansion of exports in these two categories.

One reason for the rapid increase in industrial exports is that it began from a relatively small base, so it is unlikely that exports can continue to increase at the same rate in the future. In any case, with protectionism on the rise, resistance to Chinese industrial exports, particularly light manufactured products, has increased.[26] Now that the major capitalist economies are beginning to show signs of economic recovery, the rising tide of protectionism may begin to ebb. However, the strength and duration of the current recovery are still uncertain, so it will not diminish very quickly. With the world market expanding rather slowly and with many developing countries sharing China's economic characteristics (so that their comparative advantage in trade also lies in textiles, clothing, and other light manufactures), China will not find it easy to expand its industrial exports dramatically. This has adverse implications for the future development of special trade arrangements, particularly those that are almost totally export-oriented, such as processing agreements and compensation trade. Unlike some developing countries, however, China also has the potential to become a major exporter of natural resources, especially petroleum and coal. Indeed, developments in the energy sector may well determine the overall success of the Open Door. But, because of the current weak state of the world economy, the demand for coal and oil on the international market is still relatively soft.

The above assessment of market conditions suggests that while there is potential for China to expand its exports of industrial products, coal, and petroleum in the long term, rapid export growth in the short and medium term will be difficult. Furthermore, our discussion of domestic demand and supply conditions in chapters 5 and 6 suggests that before China's energy industry and its manufacturing sector can increase their production and exports significantly, China will need to import technology and capital to develop and upgrade these industries as well as the infrastructure needed to bring these products to world market and to conserve the consumption of energy at home. Thus, foreign capital, either equity or debt, must play a role if the Open Door is to succeed.

It was noted earlier that, in recent years, China's opportunities to borrow have been substantial. To date, however, China has not utilized very much of this potential credit. Its outstanding foreign debt increased from US$2.5 billion at the end of 1978 to US$5.1 billion in 1979 and reached a peak of US$6 billion in 1980.[27] As Table 7.1 shows, some of this credit was used to cover the current account deficits in its balance of payments. With the shift in economic policy and the

Table 7.1   CHINA'S INTERNATIONAL BALANCE OF PAYMENTS, 1978–1981
(US$ billion)

	1978	1979	1980	1981
Current Account	0	−1.1	−1.0	3.5
Trade balance	−0.2	−0.9	−0.4	3.2
Exports (fob)	10.2	13.5	18.9	21.4
Imports (fob)	10.3	14.4	19.4	18.2
Services (Net)	−0.3	−0.7	−1.1	−0.3
Earnings (Total)	1.0	1.7	2.5	3.5
Interest (incl. earnings from HK)	0.2	0.3	0.6	0.8
Tourism	0.3	0.4	0.6	0.8
Labor	0.1	0.2	0.2	0.4
Freight and other	0.4	0.7	1.1	1.5
Expenditures (Total)	−1.4	−2.5	−3.6	−3.8
Technology payments	−0.2	−0.5	−0.8	−0.4
Interest	−0.2	−0.5	−0.4	−0.6
Freight and other	−1.0	−1.5	−2.4	−2.8
Unrequited transfer (Net)	0.5	0.6	0.6	0.6
Capital Account	−1.0	2.3	1.8	−0.9
Direct investment	0	0	0.1	0.3
Government-backed loans	0	0	0.4	0.5
Supplier credits	0.1	0	−0.1	−0.4
Processing and compensation trade arrangements	0	0	0.2	0
IMF trust fund loan	0	0	0	0.4
Commercial, and other	−1.1	2.3	1.2	−1.7
Reserves (Negative sign indicates increase)	0.7	−0.6	−0.2	−1.8
Monetary gold	0	0	0	0.1
Special Drawing Rights	0	0	0.1	0
Total change in holdings	0	0	−0.1	−0.2
Counterpart to allocation to SDRs	0	0	0.1	0.1
Reserve position in IMF	0	0	−0.2	0.2
Use of IMF credit	0	0	0	0.5
Foreign exchange assets	0.8	−0.6	−0.1	−2.5
Net Errors and Omissions	0.3	−0.6	−0.7	−0.8

Source: These are US government estimates, released December 1982. The estimates were published in *China Business Review*, January-February, 1983, pp. 48–49.

adoption of readjustment and reform, China curtailed its import program. The value of imports (f.o.b.) declined from a peak of US$19.4 billion in 1980 to US$18.2 billion in 1981 and to US$17 billion in 1982. Thus, despite a slow-down in its export growth, China's trade balance improved dramatically, and the country enjoyed an import surplus of US$3.2 billion in 1981 and over US$4.6 billion in 1982. This strong surplus in commodity trade, when added to increased earnings from invisible trade (services), gave China a current account surplus of US$3.5 billion in 1981 and an estimated US$5.0 billion plus in 1982, and permitted China to reduce its already low external debt and to build up its hard currency reserves. It is estimated that at the end of 1982, China's external debt was reduced to US$3.7 billion, and its foreign exchange reserves stood at an all time high of over US$8 billion (compared to US$2.2 billion in 1979).[28] Thus, even if its exports do not increase significantly in the short run, China is now in a strong financial position to increase its import of technology, particularly if it is willing to use foreign credits. However, there are indications that China, to ensure future supplies of raw materials for its industry, may be planning to use some of its reserves of hard currency to invest in overseas resource development. Possibilities include investments in iron ore and alumina mines in Australia, forest industries in New Zealand and Canada, and the potash industry in Canada.[29]

How much more can China prudently borrow? The conventional wisdom is that a country's scheduled payments for interest and principal together should not exceed 20 or at most 25 percent of export earnings. Chinese spokesmen have indicated, however, that China intends to observe a more cautious 15 percent limit (even though in 1980, when its external debt was at peak, the debt-service ratio was only about 8 percent).[30] The balance of payments information in Table 7.1 suggests that in a typical year China's earnings from invisibles run about 15 percent of earnings from commodity exports. Therefore, it seems reasonable to assume that the 1982 commodity exports of US$21.6 billion imply total foreign exchange receipts on current account of about US$25 billion in that year.[31] China's self-imposed 15 percent debt-service ratio thus provides for maximum annual payments of about US$3.7 billion, which could increase over time if export earnings continue to grow. How much debt can be serviced by such an amount depends on the interest rate and the terms on which principal is repaid. At commercial rates, with LIBOR currently (July 1983) running at about 10 percent, annual payments of US$3.7 billion could service a debt of about US$20 billion quite comfortably, even allowing for some exchange rate fluctuation. At concessional terms — and most of the credit extended to China has been on concessional terms, though not all of it has matched the 3 percent interest rate on the loan from Japan's Overseas Economic Cooperation Fund[32] — the prudent debt load could be even larger. Clearly China can afford to increase its external debt substantially.

Now that interest rates are lower than in 1980–82 (although in real terms they are still quite high), China may be willing to borrow more. However, in financial matters, the Chinese will probably continue to be conservative. It is not likely that, in the foreseeable future, China will finance a major import program by increasing its external debt from its current level by, say, five- or sixfold — even though the conventional guidelines say that this would be safe. That the Sixth Five-Year Plan (1981–85) projects the average annual growth of imports, at 9.2 percent, to exceed that of exports by only 1.1 percent confirms our belief that a major import program based heavily on external borrowing is unlikely.[33] Indeed the Sixth Five-Year Plan estimates that the annual average payment for external debt servicing during 1981–85 will be RMB ¥4.9 billion (US$2.45 billion at US$1 = RMB ¥2.0), which implies a debt-service ratio below the self-imposed limit of 15 percent.[34]

It would appear that we should not expect to see in the next few years a dramatic quickening of the pace of development in international economic co-operation projects in China (unless, of course, the current off-shore oil exploration results in a major oil boom in the near future). However, the size of the Open Door will increase steadily in the 1980s. Where are the likely areas for international economic co-operation? Some clues may be found in the investment priorities of the Sixth Five-Year Plan announced in November 1982.[35] As Table 7.2 shows, planned state investment in fixed assets is projected to be RMB ¥360 billion, of which about 64 percent is for new capital construction and about 36 percent for the renovation of existing enterprises. The total amount of investment in new capital construction during 1981–85 is about the same as that in 1976–80.[36] But, considering that from 1953 to 1980 only 20 percent of the total investment in fixed assets was allocated to the upgrading of existing facilities, the increase to 36 percent during the Sixth Plan represents a major shift in emphasis.

Table 7.2   PLANNED STATE INVESTMENT IN FIXED CAPITAL, 1981–1985
(RMB ¥ billion)

	Amount	% of Total
Total fixed asset investment	360.0	100.0
New capital construction	230.0	63.9
Updating of existing facilities	130.0	36.1
New capital construction by sector	230.0	100.0
Agriculture, forestry, water conservancy	14.1	6.1
Textiles and light industry	14.0	6.1
Heavy industry other than energy	39.1	17.0
Building materials	7.3	3.2
Metallurgical industry	17.5	7.6
Chemicals	11.4	4.9
Machine building	2.9	1.3
Energy	58.6	25.5
Transport and communications	29.8	12.9
Commerce	6.3	2.7
Housing and other construction	17.9	7.8
Education, health, culture	9.4	4.1
Geological prospecting	1.5	0.6
Other industries	8.5	3.7
Other projects not included elsewhere[a]	30.8	13.4

a. Includes rehabilitation of Tangshan and Tianjin from the 1976 earthquake.
Source: "The 6th Five-Year Plan (1981–85) of The People's Republic of China for Economic and Social Development (Excerpts)," Beijing Review, May 23, 1983.

Although no breakdown of the investment to renovate existing enterprises has been given, a substantial share will no doubt be allocated to light industry where enterprises are generally older and in greater need of rejuvenation. The main focus of the upgrading program will be on energy conservation, which is understandable, for the goal of reducing the energy-output elasticity to 0.5 by the end of the century is a point of serious vulnerability in China's long-term growth plans.

Table 7.2 shows that, of the investment for new capital construction, nearly 40 percent will be used to develop China's energy and transportation sectors, currently identified as key bottlenecks. Thus, the priorities for 1981–1985 appear to be energy, transportation, and the technical transformation of older enterprises.[37] These then are the areas where international economic co-operation will most likely occur. Indeed, the Sixth Five-Year Plan states explicitly that "we should use foreign funds mainly to develop energy and transportation, and to modernize our equipment so that foreign funds are used in such a way as to finance the introduction of foreign technology and for technical transformation."[38] Because the policy of readjustment is expected to have achieved its objectives by 1985, the current emphasis on technical transformation and light industry may in the future be less noticeable even though the Open Door is described in more permanent terms. However, international economic co-operation in the development of energy resources is likely to continue beyond 1985.

The success of the Open Door may be threatened by developments in Hong Kong. An important feature of the Open Door is its regional orientation, specifically the special role assigned to the coastal provinces of Guangdong and Fujian. Because of its proximity to Guangdong and Fujian and because of its special relationship with China, Hong Kong has been extremely active in the development of international economic co-operation in China. Currently, Hong Kong accounts for a preponderant share of the foreign funds pledged to special trade projects in China, perhaps 50 percent of the national total. Indeed, a major reason why the central government granted Guangdong and Fujian greater flexibility and authority in the area of special trade is to enable them to tap the resources of Hong Kong. An indication of Hong Kong's importance to the success of the Open Door is that when its economy weakened in 1982, the number of international economic co-operation agreements being signed declined significantly.[39] One reason the Hong Kong economy declined was, of course, the world-wide recession. Another was the erosion of business confidence in the face of increasing uncertainty over Hong Kong's political future.[40] Thus, how quickly and how smoothly the political future of Hong Kong is resolved will affect the success and the impact of the Open Door.

In 1979 when Sir Murray MacLehose, then the British governor of Hong Kong, visited Beijing and raised the subject of Hong Kong's future, Deng Xiaoping responded by saying that "investors should put their hearts at ease."[41] The issue was again discussed when British Prime Minister Margaret Thatcher visited China in September 1982. This time the two sides agreed to "enter into talks through diplomatic channels with the common aim of maintaining the stability and prosperity of Hong Kong."[42] However, from the comments made by Mrs. Thatcher and by the Chinese after the visit, it is apparent that the two sides held very different points of view. Mrs. Thatcher's position was that the nineteenth century treaties that created Hong Kong were valid in international law and that while these treaties could be changed, it must be by mutual consent. It should be noted that, even if China were to accept this view, the lease on the New Territories would still end in 1997, so that over 90 percent of the territory in Hong Kong will revert to Chinese rule in that year. China's position is that "Hong Kong . . . is the outcome of a series of unequal treaties which were imposed on China by imperialism. Hong Kong . . . [is a] part of Chinese territory. . . . The settlement of the [question] of Hong Kong . . . is entirely within China's sovereign right and does not at all fall under the ordinary category of colonial territories."[43] In other words, China does not recognize the unequal treaties that established Hong Kong and takes the position that its sovereignty over the entire territory of Hong Kong is not negotiable. However, the Chinese have also made it clear that in the interests of all parties Hong Kong should continue to exist as a free port and an international financial center.

The prospects for meaningful negotiations improved somewhat when in the spring of 1983 Mrs. Thatcher wrote a personal letter to Zhao Ziyang that apparently signalled a shift in her earlier position on the Hong Kong issue, and in turn the Chinese stopped insisting on British recognition of China's sovereignty over Hong Kong as a precondition for further negotiation.[44] Following this breakthrough, substantive negotiations were begun in July.[45] Meanwhile, a Chinese solution to the Hong Kong problem, known as the sixteen character policy, emerged in late 1982. The solution calls for regaining sovereignty, preserving the original system, letting the people of Hong Kong govern themselves, and maintaining prosperity and stability.[46] In the first four rounds of the negotiation between Britain and China, the discussion apparently focused not on the question of sovereignty but on how best to maintain Hong Kong's stability and prosperity after 1997 — that is on how Hong Kong will be administered.[47] It is reported that the British position is that since socialism and capitalism are basically incompatible, the best way to ensure continued stability and prosperity in Hong Kong is for the British to act as a buffer between the two systems by continuing to play an administrative role in Hong Kong after 1997.[48] China, on the other hand, takes the view that "sovereignty without administrative power is meaningless[49] and has countered with its proposal to "let the people of Hong Kong govern themselves (gangren zhigang)."

Because Britain derives few (if any) economic benefits from Hong Kong, because politically and strategically Hong Kong is more important to China than to Britain, because China now ranks the recovery of Hong Kong as one of its major national objectives, and because Hong Kong, once the New Territories are returned to China in 1997, is not a viable economic entity, most Hong Kong residents believe that ultimately China will reestablish its sovereignty over the entire territory. Indeed, few Hong Kong residents would dispute China's claim of sovereignty. For its part, China has made clear its intention to reclaim Hong Kong. Perhaps the clearest statement on this point is the one Hu Yaobang gave to a group of visiting Japanese reporters on 15 August 1983:

We consider the so-called three Hong Kong treaties to be unequal. But it is a fact that the treaties exist. Moreover, it is clearly written in the treaty that the expiry date is June 30, 1997. Therefore we do not intend to bring forward or postpone this date. We will recover Hong Kong on July 1, 1997. As far as China is concerned, our attitude is one of respect for history.[50]

What concerns the people of Hong Kong is how China will administer the territory after 1997. More specifically, they wonder whether the present economic system and their current lifestyle and standards of living can survive under the proposed Chinese scheme of *gangren zhigang*.

Article 31 of China's new constitution, adopted on 4 December 1982, permits the state to establish special administrative regions (SARs) when necessary. It is clear that this article was designed specifically with Hong Kong and Taiwan in mind and that *gangren zhigang* is to operate within the SAR framework. In July 1983, Beijing gave to a group of visiting post-secondary students from Hong Kong a vaguely worded ten-point guideline that outlines its plan for Hong Kong.[51] According to this plan Hong Kong will enjoy a high degree of autonomy as a special administrative region. For example, the statement promises that, apart from defense and foreign affairs, China will not interfere in Hong Kong's internal affairs and that existing social, economic, and legal institutions may remain unchanged.

But despite such promises, Hong Kong continues to be uneasy about *gangren zhigang*. The reasons for Hong Kong's prosperity and stability are its openness, its flexible wage system that is highly responsive to market forces, the non-interference economic policy of its government, the autonomy its government enjoys under the arrangement with Britain, and the stock of human capital (entrepreneurs, skills and talents) that it has gradually developed. Given the history of the People's Republic of China, it is difficult for some Hong Kong residents to believe that the Hong Kong government will have the same degree of autonomy under *gangren zhigang* as it does today or that it will be as committed to non-interference in economic matters as the present government.[52] There is also the fear that China will be unable to keep its promise of minimum change so that Hong Kong may only enjoy its SAR status for a short transitional period before it is absorbed into China's socialist system. Therefore, many Hong Kong residents strongly hope that the negotiation between China and Britain will produce a guarantee against arbitrary Chinese interference or changes to Hong Kong's special status. Indeed, some believe that confidence in Hong Kong's future can only be retained if Britain, while accepting Chinese sovereignty over Hong Kong, is permitted to continue to play an administrative role until a time when the local residents have greater confidence in the Chinese government's commitment to non-interference. But, of course, it is unclear whether the Chinese position of *gangren zhigang* is sufficiently flexible to permit such an arrangement.

Much of the skill, talent, and capital in Hong Kong is mobile, so that if China and Britain do not come to a solution that is satisfactory to Hong Kong and do not do so relatively quickly, then there is the danger that resources will flow out of Hong Kong in large quantities.[53] It should be noted that during the 1970s, the fastest growing activity in Hong Kong was not manufacturing but banking and financial services, and resources in this sector are extremely mobile. If resources do leave, it will have farreaching effects on the future development of China's SEZs and the pace of development in international economic co-operation in China, particularly in Guangdong and Fujian. Hong Kong as it exists today is an important source of skills, technology, and capital for China. This source may vanish if political uncertainty drives these scarce resources to a more attractive environment elsewhere. Already, governments in Thailand, Singapore, the Philippines, and Taiwan have all announced policies which aim to attract Hong Kong businessmen and entrepreneurs who may be thinking about relocation to move to their jurisdictions.

The current uneasiness over Hong Kong's future is perhaps best reflected in the decline in the value of the HK dollar. At the end of 1982, the exchange rate stood at about US$1 = HK$6.5. By July 1983, shortly before the beginning of substantive negotiations between China and Britain, the value of the HK dollar had declined to US$1 = HK$7.5. Since the beginning of negotiation, the HK dollar has continued to weaken. When the fourth round of negotiation ended on 23 September 1983 without visible signs of progress and with the Chinese still firmly insisting that Britain cannot play an administrative role after 1997, the value of the HK dollar dropped the next day from HK$8.35 to an all time low of HK$9.55 against the US dollar. This pressured the government to intervene in the foreign exchange market and convinced the Hong Kong Association of Banks, the government backed cartel of local banks that sets interest rates, to raise the prime lending rate by three points to 16 percent.[54] Then on 15 October 1983, the government announced that the two note-issuing local banks will have to back the HK dollars they issue by depositing US dollars in the Government Exchange Fund at the rate of US$1 = HK$7.8.[55] In response to these measures, the HK dollar rebounded, and at the end of October its value stabilized at around HK$7.8-8.0 against the US dollar. But these recent events have clearly demonstrated just how nervous and volatile the mood is in Hong Kong.

Since it is to the mutual interest of China and Britain to find a solution to the Hong Kong problem that is acceptable to the people of Hong Kong, since neither side would benefit if confidence is permitted to deteriorate further and since it is in

China's interest to make the 1997 transition as smooth as possible to ensure Hong Kong's future prosperity and stability and thus improve the prospects for an eventual peaceful reunion with Taiwan, there are reasons for cautious optimism. Apparently some progress was made during the fifth round of talks between Britain and China that took place on 19–20 October 1983.[56] However, it remains to be seen whether agreement can be reached on this very delicate issue.

The Economic Effectiveness of the Open Door

The success of the open door strategy must be judged not only be the size of the open door but also by how effectively the foreign funds and technology are absorbed and used to develop the Chinese economy. Indeed, given the current emphasis in China on "better economic results," Chinese policy-makers may consider economic effectiveness a more important success criterion than size. For this reason, China has repeatedly emphasized that how much foreign technology and capital it will utilize in the future will be determined in part by how effectively it can make use of foreign resources.

As noted in Chapter 1, commentaries on China's own experience with technology transfer are replete with examples of waste, unfulfilled potential, and low effectiveness. The Chinese have offered many reasons for the poor results in the past. Because the investment level was too high and because too many capital construction projects were undertaken at the same time, China's resources were stretched beyond their limits, thus wasting resources and prolonging the gestation period of capital construction. Foreign technology and capital equipment are unproductive unless combined with complementary domestic inputs, such as skilled workers, competent technicians and managers, a smoothly operating infrastructure, and industrial raw materials. Because of poor planning and because of scarcities of complementary domestic inputs in China, imported foreign technology and equipment in the past often could not achieve their full potential. Another criticism frequently heard is that some of the technology imported in the past has been inappropriate — that is, too mechanized, too capital-intensive, and unnecessarily sophisticated for China's needs and factor endowment. Will China be able to avoid these problems in the 1980s?

The readjustment policies introduced after 1979 are in part an attempt to come to grips with some of these problems. Investment and import programs were scaled down to more realistic levels. Attempts are now underway to impose strict controls over investment.[57] More resources have been allocated to the bottleneck sectors, energy and transportation. To alleviate the shortage of skills needed by an industrializing society, technical and higher educational systems are being expanded, including the training of managers. The government is also paying greater attention to planning and is emphasizing the use of feasibility studies. These current efforts will undoubtedly reduce some of the problems noted above and thus help increase China's capacity to absorb foreign technology and capital. But one should not expect these problems to disappear altogether.

That it is necessary for Chinese leaders to emphasize repeatedly the need to control overall investment and to warn against increasing investment in "misplaced projects" is but the most visible sign that the problem has not disappeared and indeed may be endemic.[58] The source of the problem is that to enterprises and to individual departments investment appears to be almost a free good. True, investment funds are now allocated to enterprises as interest-bearing bank loans rather than as free grants from the state budget. But the interest rate charged is nowhere near the scarcity value of investment funds. Since the interest rate does not perform the same rationing function in China that it does in market economies, investment funds must still be controlled and allocated administratively from above. This is a nearly impossible task unless enterprise and local flexibility and autonomy are severely restricted. But, for other reasons discussed in Chapter 1, China is also committed to increasing the degree of local and enterprise autonomy. Thus, a serious contradiction emerges. Local autonomy is desired, but it leads to excessive investment, which undermines morale and motivation by squeezing consumption levels and which also tends to exacerbate the energy bottleneck.

The problem of choosing inappropriate technology is not unique to China. Many economists and policy-makers outside of China have also expressed concern that the technology being imported by Third World countries is too capital-intensive for their factor endowment.[59] There are two possible explanations for this phenomenon. One possibility is that industrial technology may be inherently rigid, in the sense that more labor-intensive ways of doing things are simply not feasible. The other possibility is that the wrong technology is chosen even though something more appropriate is also available.

The available empirical evidence suggests that China and other developing countries face a rather wide range of possibilities for factor substitution, especially if product quality and scale of operation are allowed to vary.[60] It appears that the use of capital-intensive techniques is frequently the result of erroneous choices. Why do such errors occur? One explanation sometimes suggested is that developing countries favor technology of the latest vintage simply because it is the latest and hence more prestigious, even when it is also capital-intensive, inappropriately large in scale, designed for high quality intermediate inputs, dependent on sophisticated operating and maintenance skills, or otherwise ill-suited to the local environment. In the Chinese case, the criticisms of the Baoshan and Wuhan steel mills raise this issue, and it is illuminating to note that during our tour of the Baoshan site our engineer guide turned to us and asked, "Is this big enough for you?" (*Gou da le ma?*). Other Chinese technocrats, however, are well aware that the most advanced and largest scale technology may not necessarily be the most appropriate for China. Indeed, in our discussions with trade officials in Beijing, we were told that China is even willing to import second-hand equipment in some instances, and this is borne out by the example of the machinery chosen for the cigarette factory in Xiamen.

In general, however, there is a definite tendency in China to favor the latest and the largest — a tendency that has institutional as well as psychological causes. As we were reminded during a discussion in Beijing, the decision to import plant and equipment involves so many different agencies and layers of approval that there is a strong incentive to minimize the hassle and red tape by asking for one big, complete plant in a single package. (Of course, the expression "complete plant" is a relative term since even the Wuhan rolling mill involved local costs equal to the foreign exchange costs. However, what the critics mean by "big and complete" is clear enough in the context.) Furthermore, even in recent years more than 80 percent of the foreign exchange devoted to importing technology was still being allocated to building new facilities, not to renovating existing enterprises.[61] When expenditures for renovation and upgrading receive only the crumbs from the investment loaf, there is a clear incentive to ask for the most advanced technology available, thereby postponing obsolescence as long as possible. No doubt it is correct to say, as an official of the State Planning Commission did in 1979, that "we should not import complete plants if importing key equipment will solve the problem. If importing technology [that is, designs and specifications] will solve the problem, we should not import equipment at all." But the pressures to import the latest, the biggest, and the most complete remain very strong.[62]

It is also widely believed that the tendency to import excessively capital-intensive technology frequently arises from distorted factor prices. Specifically, it is suggested that government intervention has kept currencies overvalued and interest rates artificially low, which in turn has made imported machinery of the latest vintage seem more attractive than it really is. Professor Ranis of Yale University, summarizing the available evidence from Third World countries, has concluded that "the thicker the veil between an economy's equilibrium or shadow prices for factors of production, as well as for finished goods, and the prices which appear in the market as a consequence of various kinds of government intervention, the more distorted the technologies that actually emerge from the selection process."[63] There is no doubt that this veil is extremely thick in China where the official exchange rate is overvalued and the nominal interest rate charged to enterprises has, until recently, been essentially zero and is still much below the shadow rate.

There is an even more fundamental issue that needs to be raised. Even if a project is technically feasible, even if complementary domestic inputs are available, and even if the project uses appropriate technology, there is still the question of whether another project may not be better. In other words, given the scarcity of investment funds and of foreign exchange in China, economic effectiveness requires the selection of the most valuable projects from a long list of attractive possibilities. It is a truism to say that China's needs are limitless. But as Li Qiang has pointed out, "a distinction should be made between what is important and what is less important, between what is in urgent need and what can wait."[64] How, then, is such a ranking to be accomplished? What yardstick should be used to measure economic urgency?

To these questions, neoclassical economics offers a seemingly simple answer: calculate the rate of return on the investment in each project (and, ideally, for several variants of each project), and then use these rates of return to rank the choices. The logic behind this answer is worth reviewing briefly. In competitive markets, the pressures of supply and demand push up the prices of goods and services that are scarce and push down the prices of items that are more plentiful. Under these circumstances a high rate of return identifies a project which is using low-priced (relatively plentiful) inputs to produce high-priced (relatively scarce) outputs. For this reason, allocating investment to the projects with the highest rate of return is just what economic efficiency requires.

That most open door projects must now undergo technical and economic feasibility studies and that *jingji xiaoguo* (economic effectiveness) is stressed in economic decisions are evidence that the Chinese do give some consideration to rates of return on investment. Yet our impression is that the rate of return is not given the emphasis that it would get in Western project analysis. And it is usually measured only in the form of a payback period, rather than a true rate of return calculation. In this situation a visiting economist, asked to offer constructive criticisms, is tempted to reply in the following terms. First, the use of payback period calculations should be avoided, since these calculations are an unreliable proxy for a proper rate of return measurement.[65] And, second, the economic rate of return, once it has been estimated as carefully as possible, should be given more weight in the project evaluation process.

Although *jingji xiaoguo* is now given greater stress, the discussions we had in China and current Chinese assessments of past investment projects both suggest that measures of economic effectiveness have not in fact been given a great deal of weight in China's decision-making process. Critics of past projects usually give primary emphasis to shortcomings of implementation and administration. Even when the discussion is focused explicitly on economic effectiveness, it often ends up talking about mismanagement, which is a different issue.[66] An important issue, to be sure, but a different one.

Why do the Chinese exhibit such reluctance to rely on a rate of return criterion in project evaluations? Part of the answer is that, to the untutored, emphasizing the rate of return smacks of "putting profits in command" and "taking the capitalist road." Sophisticated Marxists know better than this, but they may still have reason to fear the political and personal consequences of questioning popular dogmas.[67] Another part of the answer is probably that the Chinese recognize that the rate of return, for all of its theoretical relevance to project evaluation, can sometimes be quite unsatisfactory in practice — for at least four different reasons.

The first potential source of difficulty is that the best available expertise on a particular question often resides in institutions that have a vested interest in the answer. Only the congenitally naive would accept the findings of such experts without skepticism. The second source of difficulty is that project evaluation is, of necessity, an exercise in anticipating the future. Since no one's crystal ball is unclouded, the result is never entirely reliable. The third difficulty arises from the fact that some projects have substantial "externalities" — that is, they have economic effects that are not reflected in their own costs and revenues. These effects may be harmful (environmental pollution, for example) or beneficial (technical training of the labor force). Externalities of both types are, by their very nature, easy to overlook in project evaluation, and when this happens the calculated rate of return provides a distorted measure of a project's economic worth.[68]

The fourth difficulty with using the rate of return as the yardstick for economic effectiveness arises when prices do not provide accurate signals about relative scarcities. As an article in *Jingji Yanjiu* put the point in 1979, "the profits and losses brought about by irrational pricing cannot be used to assess economic results."[69] In China most prices are administered by the state, and the structure of prices for the past thirty years has been quite rigid and slow to change. This extreme price rigidity derives from two sources: memories of the terrifying hyperinflation of the 1940s and attitudes shaped by the bureaucratic requirements of the planning apparatus. In the Chinese context, both are understandable. But, as Chinese economists are now arguing with increasing clarity and force, this longstanding preoccupation with price stability has led to a badly distorted price structure, which in turn has caused substantial economic harm.[70] A Price Research Commission has been established and is currently carrying out an investigation of the price problem. In the meantime, investment decisions must still be made. Since actual prices yield distorted results, the sensible alternative, at least in principle, is to carry out rate of return calculations in terms of "shadow prices" — that is, artificial prices that attempt to reflect the relative scarcity of resources.[71] In fact, Chinese economists are already using shadow prices as an applied tool in project evaluation.[72]

These four problems taken together mean that a rate of return must always be estimated with care and accepted with caution. This does not mean, however, that the rate of return can be rejected as the yardstick in project selection. As long as the goal is to improve economic effectiveness, then the rate of return, for all of its potential shortcomings, is still the relevant criterion, and China's policy-makers must continue to stress its importance and encourage its use, particularly at the lower administrative levels. It is too much to hope that in the Chinese environment, indeed in any environment, optimality can be attained. But the search for optimality is, in itself, likely to improve economic results. Because China is now stressing economic results more and because it is giving economic effectiveness (whether measured as a payback period or as a rate of return on investment) a greater weight when selecting investment projects, the likelihood of making major investment mistakes of the magnitude of Baoshan in the future is reduced. There may still be white elephants, but one now has hope that they will be fewer in number and smaller in size.

What economic results the international economic co-operation projects will achieve in China will depend on how effectively the Chinese participants absorb the technology and know-how of the foreign participants and adapt them to Chinese conditions. On this question, the following two points based on our field observations may be relevant. Effective transfer and diffusion of technology requires close contact between the transferor and the recipient. This is particularly important when the process involves disembodied technology, such as managerial and maintenance know-how as well as other technical skills that are stored in the minds of individuals. Although China is interested in acquiring technology from abroad and its current leaders have expressed the desire to learn from and to co-operate with foreign businesses, the Chinese are still somewhat ambivalent about using foreign managers and experts in Chinese enterprises. On the one hand, at least some Chinese leaders recognize that foreign business and technical specialists are crucial to the effective transfer of technology and therefore to the success of international economic co-operation projects in China. On the other hand, they worry about the social and political impact of a large number of foreigners working in China. One constraint is nationalism. Permitting "too many" foreigners to work as managers or senior engineers in China may lead to criticism that the country is becoming dependent on foreigners. The presence of a group which lives substantially better than the average Chinese also runs counter to socialist egalitarian principles. Of course, paying foreigners wages that appear extraordinarily high by Chinese standards (though not internationally) also opens the door to criticism that the government is permitting foreign interests to exploit China. Our impression is that up to now the Chinese have not been particularly anxious to have many foreign managers or specialists, except for short visits and when they are needed to trouble shoot.[73] This, of course, defeats one of the main purposes of having international economic co-operation projects — namely, to use them as a conduit for technology transfer.

Our second observation is that Chinese enterprises do not in general take a dynamic view of technology. In most countries, developed as well as developing, enterprises generally make some effort at improving productivity through adaptive research and development. Because of these activities, some plants imported by Third World countries are able to exceed their original capacity relatively quickly. However, our impression is that Chinese enterprises do not in general engage in adaptive R&D or have the capacity to extend or make improvements on newly acquired technology. Even for a huge project like the 1.7-metre rolling mill at Wuhan there is the implicit assumption, made by both its defenders and its critics, that just because the equipment was imported in the 1970s, it will be forever frozen into a 1970s pattern of activity. The lack of adaptive research capability at the enterprise level not only makes technology transfer more difficult but also lessens the impact of a new technology. What is it in the Chinese environment that encourages such a static, non-innovative point of view? Part of the problem is that Chinese enterprises, like their Soviet role models, have until recently been given few resources and even fewer incentives to pursue technical improvement and innovation.[74] And, even today, the resources that may be used for innovation at the enterprise level are exceedingly meager. A contributory factor is that R&D in China is highly centralized. During our visit to Baoshan, we were told that R&D for the enterprise will be the responsibility of a unit in Beijing. That even huge enterprises like the Baoshan steel complex do not have their own R&D units suggests how difficult it is for enterprises to make innovative modifications. Another part of the problem is the shortage of competent personnel and the adverse impact of the Cultural Revolution, both on technical education and on the prestige and influence of experts at all levels. If the Open Door is to have its full potential impact, greater attention will need to be paid to these problems.

ECONOMIC REFORM AND THE OPEN DOOR

The above discussion suggests that the economic effectiveness, and therefore ultimately the size, of the Open Door will be determined largely by China's ability to correct some of the major distortions and deficiencies in its economy. Until enterprises are given greater incentive and authority to adapt and innovate, until enterprises and government departments are charged the scarcity value of investment funds, until feasibility studies and rate of return calculations are given greater emphasis in project selection at all administrative levels, until prices better reflect the scarcity values of commodities, until workers and managers are better motivated to improve quality and productivity, until resources are given greater mobility to move from low to high productive uses, and so on, the economic impact of the Open Door will be less than the potential maximum. In other words, the connection between the Open Door and the domestic economic reforms is an intimate one. The two are functionally linked in the sense that the failure of the reform will seriously reduce the economic effectiveness of the Open Door. The two are also linked politically since the same leaders are committed to both so that anything that discredits one will inevitably also undermine the other to some degree. Political questions aside, what are the prospects for economic reform?

As noted in Chapter 1, China's leaders are hoping 1) to replace "the convention of 'everyone eating from the same big pot' and 'giving everyone an iron rice bowl' " with a new motivation and incentive system that ties rewards more directly to results, 2) to move away from a command economy towards a mixed economy of state enterprises, co-operatives, and small private enterprises, where planning will rely more heavily on the Law of Value (prices) and will be supplemented by market regulation, and 3) to reduce the irrationalities in the country's enterprise management and commercial systems. What is the likelihood that these changes will come about and that they will produce the desired improvements in efficiency and productivity? The answer depends on the willingness of China's leaders to tackle some very difficult problems, which can only be sketched rather briefly here.[75]

Any attempt at reform must come to grips with China's irrational price system. A meaningful price reform must not only correct the existing distorted price structure but must also allow prices to play an allocative function. While Chinese leaders appear to be ready to accept the first change, at least partially, they are not, as yet, willing to permit the second. Even the first is not easy to implement. There seems to be fairly wide agreement among Chinese planners and economists that the price of a commodity should be set equal to average cost plus a reasonable mark-up for profit. But this apparent answer only begs the question, for "costs" are themselves simply the prices of other commodities, which must somehow also be determined — simultaneously or iteratively. Furthermore, the concept of a reasonable mark-up for profit offers a fertile field for controversy. A price reform based on such principles is likely to end up canonizing a new set of rigid, non-optimal prices. From the point of view of economic efficiency, a better approach would be to institute a set of flexible prices that shift frequently to keep supply and demand in balance, as the Polish economist Oskar Lange suggested half a century ago.[76]

Such a proposal faces a fundamental obstacle, however, for it would undoubtedly permit repressed inflationary pressures to emerge. For the Chinese, who have experienced extremely stable prices for several decades, and many of whom still remember the chaos that resulted from the hyperinflation in the late 1940s, any increase in price levels can be unsettling. After the price of cotton textiles was increased by 20 percent in January 1983, panic buying was reported in some parts of China, following rumors that prices of other consumer staples would also be increased.[77] But, even if inflation could be controlled satisfactorily, price reform would still face political obstacles since it has implications for the distribution of income. In the past it has been the prices of daily necessities that have been kept artificially low, which means that low-income groups are likely to be the most adversely affected by price reforms.

To inject more incentive into the economic system and to make rewards more dependent on results, the government is committed to reforms. One of the clear implications is that workers with special skills and education should receive more pay, and indeed Chinese leaders have stated quite explicitly that "the wages of scientific and technical personnel are too low" and "the needs of highly-educated mental workers in their work and daily life call for special attention."[78] Another clear implication is that income differentials will probably increase, not merely within factories, but between factories as well — and even between geographic regions. This is likely not only because, with bonuses and piece rates, the variation in take-home pay is bound to widen, but also because of the importance of fringe benefits and social services in a Chinese worker's real income. Many of the amenities that urban workers enjoy, such as housing, education, and recreation and health facilities, are provided by the enterprise. As enterprises are permitted to retain a greater share of their own earnings, the variation in amenities will also widen. Furthermore, now that the revival of the private and collective sectors is being encouraged, private entrepreneurs may emerge to take advantage of the opportunities inherent in the disequilibria present in the economy, and some of them may earn substantial incomes from such activities.

Although China's current leaders have denounced the ultra-Left egalitarianism that was practised in the past, it is still uncertain how much income dispersion the system will tolerate. Judging by the numerous newspaper articles that have been published to reassure the population that the government now encourages people to become rich through labor, the central government is probably willing to see a significant increase in income differentials. However, this may not be the view of cadres at the local level. There are many reports that enterprises have distributed bonuses equally among workers, thereby subverting the desired incentive effect. Many cases of local officials obstructing private entrepreneurship or imposing arbitrary fees on income earned from private activities have also been reported. In fact, in March 1983, the Ministry of Public Security felt compelled to issue a "circular on protecting households which have acquired wealth through labor." As an article in *Nanfang Ribao* explained, "these people [local cadres] have become used to poverty . . . to them, poverty is the badge of socialism."[79] Given the deep-rooted resistance within the Party to visible wealth and income differentials, it is not at all certain that current efforts to inject more incentive into the economic system will succeed. For this reason, the success of economic reform will also depend on whether the current attempt at structural reform of the Party and of the bureaucracy will succeed in removing the unqualified, the inefficient, and those who resist economic reform from their positions of power.

Enterprise managers and workers may also resist the reforms. It is true that enterprise managers would like to have larger enterprise funds and greater authority, but few are willing to assume the increased risk that goes with enlarged autonomy in a more market-oriented economy. Similarly, workers want higher income, but they also want job security. Furthermore, it is not certain that the government will really permit many poorly run enterprises to go bankrupt. After all, an enterprise in China not only plays an economic role but also has political and social functions. As already indicated, the Chinese are currently experimenting with a contract employment system. But will the government permit enterprises to lay off redundant workers in order to increase profit and productivity? If it does, then unemployment, with all its adverse social and political implications, will emerge as a major problem. If it does not, as is more likely, then the practice of giving everyone an iron rice bowl will in effect continue. Furthermore, closing down an enterprise entirely is even more difficult than laying off a few of its workers. The perception that socialism is planned and stable, while capitalism is anarchic and erratic, is absolutely central to orthodox Marxism. From such a perspective, the bankruptcy of an enterprise becomes a symbol, not just of economic error, but of political and moral failure as well, and it is therefore almost unthinkable.

In the light of all these problems, it is not clear how quickly, if at all, significant economic reform will occur in China. The present target is that an overall plan to reform the economic system will be ready by the end of the Sixth Five-Year Plan (1985) and will be implemented during the Seventh Plan (1986–90). There is tremendous inertia in the system, so changes are likely to come gradually and only after extensive experimentation. However, the recognized shortcomings of the Stalinist extensive strategy of industrialization and of the ultra-Left strategy of frenetic mass mobilization seem to leave few alternatives to an intensive growth strategy. Since the proposed reforms of the economic system are an essential element of the intensive strategy, they cannot easily be abandoned. But neither can they be easily carried out.[80] How this dilemma is resolved will ultimately determine the future and the likely impact of the Open Door.

It would be almost impossible to exaggerate the drama or the importance of the changes that have occurred in China in the past five years or so. Furthermore, it is clear that the Open Door is a central element in the story. At the same time, however, it is important to keep these remarkable developments in perspective. In statistical terms, China remains one of the most isolated economies in the world, with exports averaging only about 3 or 4 percent of GNP in recent years. This modest level of foreign trade, coupled with China's great size, makes one conclusion inescapable: China's future economic development will have to rely mainly on domestic resources and domestic efforts. In this sense, *zili gengsheng* has always been the only viable policy choice for China.

At the same time, however, it is our firm belief that foreign technology and capital — though they will always be unimportant in the aggregate statistics — can make a vital contribution to China's economic growth. As a mechanism for transferring technical skills and innovative attitudes, special trade has a potential importance that is out of all proportion to its modest quantitative scope. It is our hope, therefore, that the Open Door will remain ajar for many years to come.

Appendix A

Principal Chinese Laws and Regulations Governing Foreign Economic Activities in China

The following laws and regulations are the more important statutes governing foreign economic activities in China adopted in the five years since the Third Plenum. The purpose of this appendix is not to examine these statutes but only to identify them and to provide the English translation of a few of the more important articles. When there is more than one translated version, the version provided by the Chinese is used. The Chinese have stated that the English translation of Chinese laws and regulations is for reference only. English translation of the full texts of many of these laws can be found in such publications as *Beijing Review, China Business Review, China Trade Report, China's Foreign Trade*, and *China-International Business*.

The Law of the People's Republic of China on Joint Ventures Using Chinese and Foreign Investment

Adopted on 1 July 1979 at the Second Session of the Fifth National People's Congress; promulgated on 8 July 1979; and came into force on the date of its promulgation. The law contains fifteen broadly worded articles that lay down the general principles governing equity joint ventures. The full text is reproduced below:

Article 1
    With a view to expanding international economic co-operation and technological exchange, the People's Republic of China permits foreign companies, enterprises, other economic entities or individuals (hereinafter

referred to as foreign participants) to incorporate themselves, within the territory of the People's Republic of China, into joint ventures with Chinese companies, enterprises or other economic entities (hereinafter referred to as Chinese participants) on the principle of equality and mutual benefit and subject to authorization by the Chinese Government.

Article 2

The Chinese Government protects, by the legislation in force, the resources invested by a foreign participant in a joint venture and the profits due him pursuant to the agreements, contracts and articles of association authorized by the Chinese Government as well as his other lawful rights and interests.

All the activities of a joint venture shall be governed by the laws, decrees and pertinent rules and regulations of the People's Republic of China.

Article 3

A joint venture shall apply to the Foreign Investment Commission of the People's Republic of China for authorization of the agreements and contracts concluded between the parties to the venture and the articles of association of the venture formulated by them, and the commission shall authorize or reject these documents within three months. When authorized, the joint venture shall register with the General Administration for Industry and Commerce of the People's Republic of China and start operations under license.

Article 4

A joint venture shall take the form of a limited liability company.

In the registered capital of a joint venture, the proportion of the investment contributed by the foreign participant(s) shall in general not be less than 25 per cent.

The profits, risks and losses of a joint venture shall be shared by the parties to the venture in proportion to their contributions to the registered capital.

The transfer of one party's share in the registered capital shall be effected only with the consent of the other parties to the venture.

Article 5

Each party to a joint venture may contribute cash, capital goods, industrial property rights, etc., as its investment in the venture.

The technology or equipment contributed by any foreign participant as investment shall be truly advanced and appropriate to China's needs. In cases of losses caused by deception through the intentional provision of outdated equipment or technology, compensation shall be paid for the losses.

The investment contributed by a Chinese participant may include the right to the use of a site provided for the joint venture during the period of its operation. In case such a contribution does not constitute a part of the investment from the Chinese participant, the joint venture shall pay the Chinese Government for its use.

The various contributions referred to in the present article shall be specified in the contracts concerning the joint venture or in its articles of association, and the value of each contribution (excluding that of the site) shall be ascertained by the parties to the venture through joint assessment.

Article 6

A joint venture shall have a board of directors with a composition stipulated in the contracts and the articles of association after consultation between the parties to the venture, and each director shall be appointed or removed by his own side. The board of directors shall have a chairman appointed by the Chinese participants and one or two vice-chairmen appointed by the foreign participant(s). In handling an important problem, the board of directors shall reach decision through consultation by the participants on the principle of equality and mutual benefit.

The board of directors is empowered to discuss and take action on, pursuant to the provisions of the articles of association of the joint venture, all fundamental issues concerning the venture, namely, expansion projects, production and business programmes, the budget, distribution of profits, plans concerning manpower and pay scales, the termination of business, the appointment or hiring of the president, the vice-president(s), the chief engineer, the treasurer and the auditors as well as as their functions and powers and their remuneration, etc.

The president and vice-president(s) (or the general manager and assistant general manager(s) in a factory) shall be chosen from the various parties to the joint venture.

Procedures covering the employment and discharge of the workers and staff members of a joint venture shall be stipulated according to law in the agreement or contract concluded between the parties to the venture.

Article 7

The net profit of a joint venture shall be distributed between the parties to the venture in proportion to their respective shares in the registered capital after the payment of a joint venture income tax on its gross profit pursuant to the tax laws of the People's Republic of China and after the deductions therefrom as stipulated in the articles of association of the venture for the reserve funds, the bonus and welfare funds for the workers and staff members and the expansion funds of the venture.

A joint venture equipped with up-to-date technology by world standards may apply for a reduction of or exemption from income tax for the first two to three profit making years.

A foreign participant who re-invests any part of his share of the net profit within Chinese territory may apply for the restitution of a part of the income taxes paid.

Article 8

A joint venture shall open an account with the Bank of China or a bank approved by the Bank of China.

A joint venture shall conduct its foreign exchange transactions in accordance with the Foreign Exchange Regulations of the People's Republic of China.

A joint venture may, in its business operations, obtain funds from foreign banks directly.

The insurances appropriate to a joint venture shall be furnished by Chinese insurance companies.

Article 9

The production and business programmes of a joint venture shall be filed with the authorities concerned and shall be implemented through business contracts.

In its purchase of required raw and semi-processed materials, fuels, auxiliary equipment, etc., a joint venture should give first priority to Chinese sources, but may also acquire them directly from the world market with its own foreign exchange funds.

A joint venture is encouraged to market its products outside China. It may distribute its export products on foreign markets through direct channels or its associated agencies or China's foreign trade establishments. Its products may also be distributed on the Chinese market.

Wherever necessary, a joint venture may set up affiliated agencies outside China.

Article 10

The net profit which a foreign participant receives as his share after executing his obligations under the pertinent laws and agreements and contracts, the funds he receives at the time when the joint venture terminates or winds up its operations, and his other funds may be remitted abroad through the Bank of China in accordance with the foreign exchange regulations and in the currency or currencies specified in the contracts concerning the joint venture.

A foreign participant shall receive encouragements for depositing in the Bank of China any part of the foreign exchange which he is entitled to remit abroad.

Article 11

The wages, salaries or other legitimate income earned by a foreign worker or staff member of a joint venture, after payment of the personal income tax under the tax laws of the People's Republic of China, may be remitted abroad through the Bank of China in accordance with the foreign exchange regulations.

Article 12

The contract period of a joint venture may be agreed upon between the parties to the venture according to its particular line of business and circumstances. The period may be extended upon expiration through agreement between the parties, subject to authorization by the Foreign Investment

Commission of the People's Republic of China. Any application for such extension shall be made six months before the expiration of the contract.

Article 13

In cases of heavy losses, the failure of any party to a joint venture to execute its obligations under the contracts or the articles of association of the venture, force majeure, etc., prior to the expiration of the contract period of a joint venture, the contract may be terminated before the date of expiration by consultation and agreement between the parties and through authorization by the Foreign Investment Commission of the People's Republic of China and registration with the General Administration for Industry and Commerce. In cases of losses caused by breach of the contract(s) by a party to the venture, the financial responsibility shall be borne by the said party.

Article 14

Disputes arising between the parties to a joint venture which the board of directors fails to settle through consultation may be settled through conciliation or arbitration by an arbitral body of China or through arbitration by an arbitral body agreed upon by the parties.

Article 15

The present law comes into force on the date of its promulgation. The power of amendment is vested in the National People's Congress.

Regulations of the People's Republic of China on the Registration of Joint Ventures Using Chinese and Foreign Investment

Promulgated by the State Council on 26 July 1980, and came into force on the date of its promulgation. Article 1 reads in part that "A joint venture using Chinese and foreign investment should, within one month of approval . . . register with the General Administration for Industry and Commerce of the People's Republic of China."

Regulations of the People's Republic of China on Labour Management in Joint Ventures Using Chinese and Foreign Investment

Promulgated by the State Council on 26 July 1980 and came into force on the date of its promulgation. Article 2 reads in part that "matters pertaining to employment, dismissal and resignation . . . wage and awards and punishment . . . labour protection and labour discipline in joint venture shall be stipulated in the labour contract." Article 4 states that "surplus workers and . . . those who fail to meet the requirements after training and are not suitable for other work can be discharged." Article 5 states that "the joint venture may . . . take action against those workers or staff members who have violated rules and regulations of the enterprise." Article 8 states that "the wage level of the workers and staff members in a joint venture will be determined at 120 to 150% of the real wages of the workers and staff members of state-owned enterprises of the same trade in the locality."

Regulations of the People's Republic of China on Special Economic Zones in Guangdong Province

Submitted by the State Council and approved by the 15th Session of the Standing Committee of the Fifth National People's Congress on 26 August 1980. Article 1 states that

> In the special zones, foreign citizens, Overseas Chinese, compatriots in Hong Kong and Macao and their companies and enterprises . . . are encouraged to open factories or set up enterprises and other establishments with their own investment or undertake joint ventures with Chinese investment, and their assets, due profits and other legitimate rights and interests are legally protected.

Article 4 states that

> All items of industry, agriculture, livestock breeding, fish breeding and poultry farming, tourism, housing and construction, research and manufacture involving high technologies and techniques that have positive significance in international economic cooperation and technical exchange, as well as other trades of common interest to investors and the Chinese side, can be established with foreign investment or in joint venture with Chinese investment.

Article 14 states that

> The rate of income tax levied on the enterprises in the special zones is to be 15%. Special preferential treatment will be given to . . . enterprises with an investment of US$5 million or more, and enterprises involving higher technologies or having a longer cycle of capital turnover.

The Income Tax Law of the People's Republic of China Concerning Joint Ventures with Chinese and Foreign Investment

Adopted at the Third Session of the Fifth National People's Congress (30

August-10 September 1980); promulgated on 10 September 1980 and came into force on the date of its promulgation. Article 3 states that "the income tax rate on joint ventures shall be 30%. In addition, a local surtax of 10% of the assessed income tax shall be levied. The income tax rates on joint ventures exploiting petroleum, natural gas and other resources shall be stipulated separately." Article 4 states that "in the case of a foreign participant in a joint venture remitting its share of profit from China, an income tax of 10% shall be levied on the remitted amount."

Individual Income Tax Law of the People's Republic of China

Adopted at the Third Session of the Fifth National People's Congress (30 August-10 September 1980), promulgated on 10 September 1980 and came into force on the date of its promulgation. Article 1 reads in part that "an individual income tax shall be levied . . . on the incomes gained within or outside China by any individual residing for one year or more in the People's Republic of China. For individuals not residing in the People's Republic of China or individuals residing in China less than one year, individual income tax shall be levied only on that income gained within China."

Detailed Rules and Regulations for the Implementation of the Income Tax Law of the People's Republic of China Concerning Joint Venture with Chinese and Foreign Investment

Approved by the State Council on 10 December 1980; promulgated by the Ministry of Finance on 14 December 1980 and came "into force from the same date as the 'Income Tax Law of the People's Republic of China Concerning Joint Ventures with Chinese and Foreign Investment' " (10 September 1980).

Detailed Rules and Regulations for the Implementation of the Individual Income Tax Law of the People's Republic of China

Approved by the State Council on 10 December 1980; promulgated by the Ministry of Finance on 14 December 1980 and came "into force from the same date as the 'Individual Income Tax Law of the People's Republic of China' " (10 September 1980).

Interim Regulations of the People's Republic of China Concerning the Control of Resident Offices of Foreign Enterprises

Promulgated by the State Council on 30 October 1980 and took effect on the date of promulgation. Article 2 states that "any foreign enterprise desiring to establish [a] resident office in China should first of all apply for permission and after securing approval go through the registration procedure."

Provisional Regulations for Exchange Control of the People's Republic of China

Adopted at the Regular Session of the State Council on 5 December 1980; promulgated by the State Council on 18 December 1980 and came into force on 1 March 1981. Article 2 reads in part that "all foreign exchange receipts of enterprises with Overseas Chinese capital, enterprises with foreign capital and Chinese and foreign joint ventures, must be deposited with the Bank of China, and all their foreign exchange disbursements must be paid from their foreign exchange deposit accounts." Article 25 states that "an amount not exceeding 50 percent of their net wages and other legitimate earnings after tax may be remitted or taken out of China in foreign currency by staff members and workers of foreign nationality and those from the Hong Kong and Macao regions employed by enterprises with Overseas Chinese capital, enterprises with foreign capital and Chinese and foreign joint ventures."

Provisional Regulations for Providing Loans to Joint Ventures of Chinese and Foreign Ownership by the Bank of China

Came into force on 13 March 1981. Article 2 states that "any joint venture that has been approved . . . according to The Law of the People's Republic of China on Joint Ventures Using Chinese and Foreign Investment, registered with the General Administration of Industry and Commerce of the PRC and granted a business licence is qualified to apply for loans."

Additional Regulations Concerning the Registration of Resident Offices of Foreign Enterprises

Circular issued by the General Administration of Industry and Commerce and announced on 1 June 1981.

Rules Governing the Carrying of Foreign Exchange, Precious Metals, and Payment Instruments in Convertible Currency Into or Out of China

Promulgated by the State General Administration of Exchange Control and published on 10 August 1981.

Rules for the Implementation of Foreign Exchange Control Relating to Foreign Representations in China and Their Personnel

Promulgated by the State General Administration of Exchange Control and published on 10 August 1981.

Particulars of Making Investment in SKIZ [Shekou Industrial Zone]

Published in September 1981. This supersedes "Particulars of Joint Ventures in SKIZ," published in 1979. Article 5 reads in part that

All enterprises in SKIZ shall qualify for a 3–5 year tax holiday from the date of their commissioning. Afterwards, a 15 percent Corporation Profit Tax shall apply. (With agreements signed before August 27, 1980, when the Regulations on Special Economic Zones in Guangdong Province . . . was promulgated, the Corporation Profit Tax rate originally agreed upon [10%] remains effective.)

Detailed Rules for the Approval of Applications for Foreign Exchange by Individuals

Promulgated by the State General Administration of Exchange Control and took effect on 1 January 1982.

Detailed Rules Concerning Foreign Exchange Control Relating to Individuals

Promulgated by the State General Administration of Exchange Control and took effect on 1 January 1982.

Provisional Entry/Exit Rules for the Special Economic Zones in Guangdong Province

Adopted at the 13th Session of the Standing Committee of the Fifth Guangdong Provincial People's Congress on 17 November 1981, and came into force on 1 January 1982. Article 3 reads in part that "foreigners and Overseas Chinese who invest and set-up factories or run various business undertakings or buy houses or reside permanently in the special economic zones shall apply, against certificates granted by the development company of the special zones, for multiple entry/exit visas."

Provisional Regulations on Registration of Enterprises in Special Economic Zones of Guangdong Province

Adopted at the 13th Session of the Standing Committee of the Fifth Guangdong Provincial People's Congress on 17 November 1981 and came into force on 1 January 1982.

Provisional Provisions on Wages in the Enterprises in Special Economic Zones in Guangdong Province

Adopted at the 13th Session of the Standing Committee of the Fifth Guangdong Provincial People's Congress on 17 November 1981 and came into force on 1 January 1982. Article 2 states that

All enterprises with exclusive foreign investment, joint ventures with Chinese and foreign investment and cooperative enterprises in the special zones shall use the contract system in employing workers and staff, and labor contracts will be signed between the enterprise and the workers and staff. The labor contract should include the following: employment, dismissal and resignation of the workers and staff; production and work tasks; labor service fees and stipulations on rewards and punishments; work time and vacation; labor insurance and welfare benefits; labor protection; and labor discipline.

Provisional Provisions on Land Control in Shenzhen Special Economic Zone

Adopted at the 13th Session of the Standing Committee of the Fifth Guangdong

Provincial People's Congress on 17 November 1981 and came into force on 1 January 1982. Article 15 states that

The time limit for the land used by overseas investors shall be determined through consultations according to the amount of the investment in the projects and actual needs. The longest time limit is as follows:
1. 30 years for industrial use;
2. 20 years for commercial use . . .;
3. 50 years for residential property development;
4. 50 years for educational, scientific . . ., medical and health use;
5. 30 years for tourist undertakings;
6. 20 years for planting, animal husbandry, poultry raising and fish breeding.

Article 16 states that

The standards for annual fees (RMB) per square meter of land are:
RMB 10 to 30 for industrial use;
RMB 70 to 200 for commercial use;
RMB 30 to 60 for residential property development, and
RMB 60 to 100 for construction of tourist undertakings.
From the day when these regulations are made public, land use fees shall be readjusted once every three years, and the change shall not exceed 30%.

Income Tax Law of the People's Republic of China Concerning Foreign Enterprises

Adopted at the Fourth Session of the Fifth National People's Congress on 13 December 1981; promulgated on the same date; and came into force on 1 January 1982. Article 1 states that

"Foreign enterprises" mentioned in this law refer, with the exception of those for whom separate provisions are stipulated in Article 11, to foreign companies, enterprises and other economic organizations which have establishments in the People's Republic of China engaged in independent business operation or cooperative production or joint business operation with Chinese enterprises.

Article 3 states that

> Income tax on foreign enterprises shall be assessed at progressive rates for the parts in excess of a specific amount of taxable income. The tax rates are as follows:

Range of income	Tax rate (%)
Annual income below 250,000 yuan	20
That part of annual income from 250,000 to 500,000 yuan	25
That part of annual income from 500,000 to 750,000 yuan	30
That part of annual income from 750,000 to 1,000,000 yuan	35
That part of annual income above 1,000,000 yuan	40

Article 4 states that "in addition to the income tax levied on foreign enterprises in accordance with the provisions of the preceding article, a local income tax of 10 percent of the same taxable income shall be levied." Article 11 states that "a 20 percent income tax shall be levied on the income obtained from dividends, interest, rentals, royalties and other sources in China by foreign companies, enterprises and other economic organizations which have no establishments in China. Such tax shall be withheld by the paying unit in each of its payments."

Detailed Rules and Regulations for the Implementation of the Income Tax Law of the PRC Concerning Foreign Enterprises

Approved by the State Council on 16 February 1982; promulgated by the Ministry of Finance on 21 February 1982; and came into force on the same date as the publication and enforcement of the Income Tax Law of the PRC Concerning Foreign Enterprises (1 January 1982). Article 2 states that

> The establishments mentioned in Article 1 of the tax law refer to organizations, places or business agents established by foreign enterprises in China engaged in production or business operations. . . . [These] include management organizations, branch organizations, representative organizations, factories, places where natural resources are being exploited and places where building, installation, assembling, exploration and other projects are being undertaken under contracts.

Regulations of the People's Republic of China on the Exploitation of Offshore Petroleum Resources in Cooperation with Foreign Enterprises

Promulgated by the State Council on 30 January 1982 and came into force on the date of its promulgation. Article 3 states that

The Government of the People's Republic of China protects, in accordance with the legislation in force, investments by foreign enterprises participating in the exploitation of offshore petroleum resources, their share of profit and other legitimate rights and interests, and their activities in cooperative exploitation.

Article 7 states that

CNOOC [The China National Offshore Oil Corporation] shall exploit offshore petroleum resources in cooperation with foreign enterprises by entering into petroleum contracts. Unless otherwise specified . . . the foreign enterprise that is one party to the contract (hereinafter foreign contractor) shall provide exploration investment, undertake exploration operations and bear all exploration risks. After a commercial oil and/or gas field is discovered, both the foreign contractor and CNOOC shall make investment in the cooperative development. The foreign contractor shall be responsible for the development and production operations until CNOOC takes over the production operations when conditions permit under the petroleum contract. The foreign contractor may recover its investment and expenses and receive remuneration out of the petroleum produced according to the provisions of the petroleum contract.

Article 12 states that

In implementing the petroleum contract, the foreign contractor shall use appropriate and advanced technology and managerial experience and is obliged to transfer the technology and pass on the experience to the personnel of the Chinese side involved in the implementation (hereinafter Chinese personnel). In the course of the petroleum operations, the foreign contractor must give preference to the Chinese personnel in employment, keep the percentage of Chinese steadily rising, and train the Chinese personnel in a planned way.

Article 19 states that

The operator must give preference to manufacturers and engineering companies within the territory of the People's Republic of China in concluding subcontracts for all facilities to be built in implementing the petroleum contracts . . . provided that they are competitive in quality, price, term of delivery and services.

Provisional Regulations of the General Administration of Industry and Commerce of the People's Republic of China on the Payment of Registration Fees by Joint Ventures Using Chinese and Foreign Investment

Issued by the General Administration of Industry and Commerce in March 1982.

Rules Concerning the Levy and Exemption of Customs Duties and Consolidated Industrial and Commercial Tax on Imports and Exports for the Chinese-Foreign Cooperative Exploitation of Offshore Petroleum.

Approved on 28 February 1982 by the State Council and promulgated on 1 April 1982 by the General Administration of Customs and the Ministry of Finance.

Temporary Provisions on Tax Registration for Foreign Enterprises That Begin Operation or Close Down

Promulgated on 15 April 1982 by the General Tax Bureau, Ministry of Finance.

Provisional Articles on Control of Advertising

Promulgated on 17 February 1982 and came into force on 1 May 1982.

The Economic Contract Law of the People's Republic of China

Adopted at the Fourth Session of the Fifth National People's Congress on 18 December 1981 and came into force on 1 July 1982. Article 2 states that "an economic contract is an agreement between legal persons for achieving a certain economic purpose and for defining each other's rights and obligations."

The Civil Procedure Law of the People's Republic of China

Approved at the 22nd Session of the Standing Committee of the Fifth National People's Congress on 8 March 1982 and promulgated for trial implementation on 1 October 1982.

The Trademark Law of the People's Republic of China

Announced on 25 August 1982 and came into force on 1 March 1983.

Rules for the Implementation of Exchange Control Regulations Relating to Enterprises with Foreign Capital, and Chinese and Foreign Joint Ventures

Approved by the State Council on 19 July 1983 and promulgated by the State Administration of Exchange Control on 1 August 1983. Article 1 states that "these rules are formulated for implementing the provisions of Chapter V of Provisional Regulations for Exchange Control of the People's Republic of China." Article 15 states that

Staff members and workers of foreign nationality and those from Xianggang and Aomen areas employed by enterprises with overseas Chinese capital, enterprises with foreign capital and Chinese and foreign joint ventures may remit abroad their wages and other legitimate earnings after tax deductions . . . . For the remittance of amounts exceeding 50% of their wages and other earnings, they may apply to the SAEC or its branch offices.

Regulations for the Implementation of the Law of The People's Republic of China on Joint Ventures Using Chinese and Foreign Investment

Promulgated by the State Council on 20 September 1983 and came into force on the date of its promulgation. This document contains the detailed regulations that govern the formation and operation of joint ventures in China. There are 118 articles, which are organized into the following 16 chapters: general provisions, establishment and registration, form of organization and registered capital, ways of contributing investment, board of directors and management office, acquisition of technology, right to the use of site and its fee, planning, purchasing and selling, taxes, foreign exchange control, financial affairs and accounting, staff and workers, trade union, duration, dissolution and liquidation, settlement of disputes, and supplementary articles.

Notes

NOTES TO CHAPTER 1

1. For illuminating discussions of the origins of CASS and its role as a brain trust for economic policy-making, see Cyril Chihren Lin, "The Reinstatement of Economics in China Today," *China Quarterly* 85 (March, 1981): 1–48, and Michel Oksenberg, "Economic Policy-Making in China: Summer 1981," *China Quarterly* 90 (June, 1982): 165–94.
2. *Beijing Review*, 10 November 1978, pp. 10–11.
3. For the text of the communique of the Third Plenum, see *Beijing Review*, 29 December 1978, pp. 6–16. For the assessment of the Third Plenum as the critical turning point, see, for example, "On the Question of our Country's Foreign Economic Relations," *Hong Qi* [Red Flag], 16 April 1982, pp. 2–3, and Hu Yaobang's report to the 12th Party Congress, *Beijing Review*, 13 September 1982, p. 11.
4. This is, of course, a simplification. For a more complete discussion, see Kjeld Erik Brodsgaard, "Paradigmatic Change: Readjustment and Reform in the Chinese Economy, 1953–1981," *Modern China* 9 (January, 1983): 37–83 and 9 (April, 1983): 253–72; Alexander Eckstein, *China's Economic Revolution* (London, New York, and Melbourne: Cambridge University Pres, 1977); Stephan Feuchtwang and Athar Hussain, eds., *The Chinese Economic Reforms* (London and Canberra: Croom Helm, and New York: St. Martin's Press, 1983); and the very useful compendium volumes issued by the Joint Economic Committee of the U.S. Congress: *People's Republic of China: An Economic Assessment* (1972), *China: A Reassessment of the Economy* (1975), *Chinese Economy Post-Mao* (1978), and *China under the Four Modernizations* (1982).
5. Marxist economics identifies productive forces and productive relations as the two main aspects of social production. Productive forces are the technology, skills, and resources available to the society. Productive relations are the relationships formed by people during the production process, including the pattern of property ownership and product distribution.
6. The Chinese discussion of this issue is usually couched in terms of the relative importance of the Law of Value and the Law of Balanced and Proportional Development.
7. Gao Lu and Chang Ge, "A Critique of Deng Xiaoping's Comprador-Bourgeois Economic Thought," *Hong Qi* [Red Flag], 1 July 1976, pp. 25–30.
8. The essay to which this quotation is attributed was first written by Mao in 1942, but the sentences quoted are missing from early published versions. They appear, however, in the 1953 edition. For further discussion of these textual variations, see Andrew Watson, ed. and transl., *Mao Zedong and the Political Economy of the Border Region* (Cambridge: Cambridge University Press, 1980), pp. vii and 60.
9. Mao Zedong, "On the Ten Major Relationships," *Beijing Review*, 1 January 1977, pp. 23–25.
10. Zhou Enlai first suggested the Four Modernizations as a long-term goal in 1964 and again in 1975.
11. The current constitution, adopted on 4 December 1982, also mentions the Four Modernizations, but, significantly, the year 2000 is no longer cited as the target date.
12. Other specific targets announced included the following: steel production was to reach 60 million

tons in 1985 (twice the 1978 output), light industrial production was to rise at a 12 percent annual rate, and "the state plans to build or complete 120 large-scale projects, including 10 iron and steel complexes, nine nonferrous metals complexes, eight coal mines, 10 oil and gas fields, 30 power stations, six new trunk railways, and five key harbors." See Hua Guofeng, "Report on the Work of the Government," delivered at the Fifth National People's Congress, 26 February 1978.

13. The first indication that all was not well came in February 1979, when the Chinese government informed several Japanese trading firms that it would not give final approval to twenty-two contracts (involving the sale of twenty-nine plants) that the Japanese had signed with various Chinese foreign trade corporations. After renegotiation that modified the method of payment (from cash to deferred payment over five years), the contracts for all but one of the plants were reinstated by July 1979.

14. The full text was published in Renmin Ribao [People's Daily] on 14 December 1981, pp. 1–4. For an English translation, see Beijing Review, 21 December 1981, pp. 6–36.

15. See, for example, Josef Goldmann and Karel Kouba, Economic Growth in Czechoslovakia (White Plains, NY: International Arts and Sciences Press, 1969), chapter 4, and Ferenc Janossy, The End of the Economic Miracle (White Plains, NY: International Arts and Sciences Press, 1971), chapter 1.

16. See, for example, Edward F. Denison, Accounting for United States Economic Growth (Washington, DC: Brookings Institution, 1974), and Edward F. Denison and William K. Chung, "Economic Growth and Its Sources," in Hugh Patrick and Henry Rosovsky, eds., Asia's New Giant (Washington, DC: Brookings Institution, 1976).

17. Dong Fureng, "The Relationship between Accumulation and Consumption in China's Economic Development," in George C. Wang, ed. and transl., Economic Reform in the PRC (Boulder, CO: Westview Press, 1982), p. 59. See also Shen Yue, "Vigorously Increase Economic Results, Bring About Genuine Speed," Jingji Guanli [Economic Management], July, 1982, p. 10.

18. Beijing Review, 5 May 1980, p. 7; 30 June 1980, p. 3; and 21 December 1981, p. 11.

19. Beijing Review, 13 September 1982, p. 12; and 8 November 1982, p. 18.

20. Beijing Review, 27 October 1980, p. 16.

21. Beijing Review, 21 December 1981, p. 31. Zhao's goal is more conservative than Deng's for two reasons: 1) it is not measured in per capita terms, and 2) gross industrial and agricultural production has grown faster than GNP in the past.

22. Beijing Review, 15 November 1982, pp. 13–14.

23. World Bank, China: Socialist Economic Development, 1 June 1981, Annex E, p. 14.

24. One consequence of this shift in emphasis is that since 1978 light industry has expanded much more rapidly than heavy industry. According to official government statistics, the average annual growth rate of the gross value of production in light industry between 1979 and 1982 was 11.7 percent, while that for heavy industry was 3.6 percent.

25. Procurement prices for agricultural products increased by about 24 percent between 1978 and 1981. The average annual wage of urban workers increased about 26 percent over the same period. See State Statistical Bureau, Statistical Yearbook of China 1981 (Hong Kong: Economic Information & Agency, 1981), pp. 414 and 429.

26. These and the following figures are from Zhao Ziyang, "Report on the Sixth Five-Year Plan," delivered at the Fifth Session of the Fifth NPC on 30 November 1982. For a slightly abridged English translation of this speech, see Beijing Review, 20 December 1982, pp. 10–35.

27. Compared to 20 percent for the period 1953–80.

28. In agriculture this takes the form of allocating work points by the type of work performed (e.g., weeding) rather than by effort or results.

29. Beijing Review, 20 December 1982, p. 30.

30. For discussions of the responsibility system in agriculture, see Su Xing. "The Responsibility System and the Development of the Collective Economy in Rural Areas," Jingji Yanjiu [Economic Research], November, 1982, pp. 3–9; and Jack Gray and Maisie Gray, "China's New Agricultural Revolution," in Stephan Feuchtwang and Athan Hussain, eds., The Chinese Economic Reform, (London and Canberra: Croom Helm, and New York: St. Martin's Press, 1983), pp. 151–84.

31. From Zhao Ziyang's report to the Fourth Session of the Fifth NPC on 30 November and 1 December 1981. See Beijing Review, 21 December 1981, p. 25.

32. China Reconstructs, 32 (May, 1983): 9.

33. Beijing Review, 6 April 1981, pp. 21–29.

34. *Beijing Review*, 18 August 1980, p. 3.
35. For discussions, see the forum of articles in *Jingji Yanjiu* [Economic Research], August, 1982; Xue Muqiao, *China's Socialist Economy* (Beijing: Foreign Languages Press, 1981), especially chapters 7 and 8; Xue Muqiao, "The System of Economic Management in a Socialist Country," and Liao Jili, "The Restructuring of the Management of China's Economic System," both in George C. Wang, ed. and transl., *Economic Reform in the PRC*; *Beijing Review*, 6 April 1981, pp. 21–29; and Yao Jianyou, "An Enquiry into the Expanding of Enterprises' Retained Profits," *Jingji Guanli* [Economic Management], August, 1981, pp. 69–71.
36. Under the old system, the Shanghai Non-Ferrous Metal Rolling Works had applied for a grant of RMB ¥6.85 million to expand its production capacity. When loans were instituted, the manager reduced his request to RMB ¥2 million but still achieved the planned increase in output. See Liao Jili, "The Restructuring of the Management of China's Economic System," p. 85. See also *Beijing Review*, 15 December 1980, pp. 1–4.
37. See Zhao Ziyang's Ten-Point Program, *Renmin Ribao* [People's Daily], 14 December 1981, pp. 1–4.
38. James B. Stepanek, "China's Economic Experiments meet Stiff Opposition," *China Business Review*, January-February, 1980, pp. 68–69.
39. Yao Jianyou, "An Enquiry into the Expanding of Enterprises' Retained Profits," p. 70.
40. Hu Yaobang, "Create a New Situation in All Fields of Socialist Modernization," *Beijing Review*, 13 September 1982, p. 17.
41. Zhao Ziyang, "Report on the Sixth Five-Year Plan," *Beijing Review*, 20 December 1982, p. 25.
42. Ibid., p. 30.
43. For authoritative discussions, see Zhao Ziyang's speeches to the Fourth and Fifth Sessions of the Fifth NPC, *Beijing Review*, 21 December 1981, and 20 December 1982, and Hu Yaobang's report to the 12th National Congress of the CCP, *Beijing Review*, 13 September 1982.
44. Besides the commentaries on China's own experience, much attention was focused on the benefits of borrowing technology from abroad as demonstrated by the success stories of economic history. Predictably, the example most often cited is Japan's decision in the Meiji era to abandon seclusion and "to seek knowledge throughout the world." One pamphlet published in Shanghai in 1980, after discussion of the Japanese case, goes on to make the interesting point that technology from the capitalist countries was also a significant element in the development of the Soviet Union — so much so, in fact, that Soviet imports accounted for one-third of world exports of machinery and equipment in 1931 and nearly one-half of world exports in that category in 1932. See Cao Linzhang, Wu Shaozhong, Xu Ying, and Gu Guangqing, *Yinjin Jishu he Liyong Waizi* [Importing Technology and Using Foreign Capital] (Shanghai: People's Press, 1980), pp. 10–15.
45. Hans Heymann, Jr., quoted in A. Doak Barnett, *China's Economy in Global Perspective* (Washington, DC: Brookings Institution, 1981), p. 189.
46. Richard E. Batsavage and John L. Davie, "China's International Trade and Finance," U.S. Congress, Joint Economic Committee, *Chinese Economy Post-Mao* (Washington, DC: Government Printing Office, 1978), p. 710.
47. Gu Nianliang, "China's Current Effort to Import Technology and Its Prospects," *Chinese Economic Studies* 14 (Fall, 1980): 56.
48. Robert F. Dernberger, "Economic Development and Modernization in Contemporary China: The Attempt to Limit Dependence on the Transfer of Modern Industrial Technology from Abroad and Control Its Corruption of the Maoist Social Revolution," U.S. Congress, Joint Economic Committee, *Issues in East-West Commercial Relations* (Washington, DC: Government Printing Office, 1979), p. 109; A. Doak Barnett, p. 193; and Gu Ming, "Plans Readjusted, Policy Unchanged," *Beijing Review*, 27 July 1979, p. 9.
49. A. Doak Barnett, p. 205; Gu Nianliang, p. 57.
50. Batsavage and Davie, p. 712.
51. Chen Huiqin, "The Orientation of Technology Transfer Must Be Changed," *Jingji Guanli* [Economic Management], April, 1981, p. 22.
52. Chen Huiqin, pp. 22–23. To facilitate exposition in this excerpted form, the sequence of Chen's discussion has been rearranged somewhat. The Chinese phrase *jingji xiaoguo* ("economic effectiveness") is in this context just a euphemism for "rate of return on investment," but to translate it

in this direct fashion is to distort the flavor of the original. For an interesting further discussion of *jingji xiaoguo*, see Cyril Chihren Lin, pp. 23–26.

53. Meng Xiancheng, "Some Questions on the Building of the 1.7-Meter Rolling Mill," *Beijing Review*, 25 August 1980, p. 26.

54. Xu Zhiying, "Wuhan's Steel Rolling Mills — Mastering Advanced Foreign Technology," *China Reconstructs*, November, 1982, pp. 33–39.

55. Chen Huiqin, p. 23.

56. Lin Senmu, "The Lessons of the 22 Imported Complete Plant Projects," *Jingji Guanli* [Economic Management], June, 1981, pp. 13–14.

57. For details of the complicated off-again, on-again history of Baoshan, see "When the Chinese Suspend Your Contract," *China Business Review*, September-October, 1979, pp. 58–60; Dori Jones, "The Baoshan Contracts," *China Business Review*, July-August, 1980, pp. 47–49; "The Collapse of Construction Projects," *China Business Review*, January-February, 1981, pp. 9–13; "Baoshan Pays Its Bills," *China Business Review*, March-April, 1982, p. 4; David Bonavia and John Lewis, "The Battle of Baoshan," *Far Eastern Economic Review*, 20 February 1981, pp. 49–50 and 57; "China Takes a Hatchet to the Baoshan Project," JETRO *China Newsletter* 30 (February, 1981): 10–11; William Hwang, "Prospects for Solution to Contract Issue," JETRO *China Newsletter* 31 (March-April, 1981): 2–5; and Keiichi Koshiro, "Another Look at the Baoshan Complex," JETRO *China Newsletter* 32 (May-June, 1981): 8–13.

58. *Beijing Review*, 18 April 1983, pp. 9–10; *Far Eastern Economic Review*, 5 May 1983, pp. 128–31.

59. Bonavia and Lewis, "The Battle of Baoshan," pp. 49–50.

60. Jones, "The Baoshan Contracts," p. 49.

61. *Beijing Review*, 28 July 1980, pp. 15–18.

62. Lin Senmu, p. 13.

63. *Renmin Ribao* [People's Daily], 21 March 1980, p. 3.

64. *Renmin Ribao* [People's Daily], 24 February 1979, p. 1.

65. *Beijing Review*, 15 June 1981, p. 3.

66. Forum by members of the Chinese Academy of Sciences, reported in *Beijing Review*, 8 December 1980, p. 5.

67. See, for example, *Renmin Ribao* [People's Daily], 8 May 1979, p. 1; and *Hong Qi* [Red Flag], 16 April 1982, p. 6.

68. *Far Eastern Economic Review*, 7 May 1982, pp. 54–55, and 21 May 1982, p. 8.

69. *Beijing Review*, 24 May 1982, p. 3.

70. See, for example, Hu Yaobang, *Beijing Review*, 13 September 1982, p. 20.

71. *Hong Qi* [Red Flag], 16 April 1982, p. 6; and *Renmin Ribao* [People's Daily], 14 December 1981, pp. 1–4.

72. *Beijing Review*, 21 December 1981, p. 23.

73. *Hong Qi* [Red Flag], 16 April 1982, p. 6; and *Shijie Jingji Daobao* [World Economic Herald], 7 June 1982, p. 4.

74. Ralph Miller, quoted in Richard Baum, ed., *China's Four Modernizations: The New Technological Revolution* (Boulder, CO: Westview Press, 1980), p. 205.

75. *Beijing Review*, 21 December 1981, p. 24.

76. For 1974 quote, see U.S. Congress, Joint Economic Committee, *Chinese Economy Post-Mao*, Vol. 1 (Washington, DC: Government Printing Office, 1978), p. 722; for 1979 quote, see *Beijing Review*, 27 April 1979, pp. 15–16.

77. *Beijing Review*, 21 December 1981, p. 24.

78. Ji Chongwei, "China's Utilization of Foreign Funds and Relevant Policies," *Beijing Review*, 20 April 1981, p. 19.

79. *Beijing Review*, 21 December 1981, p. 24.

80. Ibid.

81. Ibid.

82. For Liaoning list, see JETRO *China Newsletter* 29 (December, 1980): 21–22; for Hubei, see *Jingji Daobao* [Economic Reporter], 24 May 1982, p. 7; for Fujian, see *Jingji Daobao* [Economic Reporter], 4 November 1981, pp. 6–7, and *Economic Reporter*, December, 1981, pp. 14–17; for Anhui, see *China Economic News*, 17 May 1982, pp. 9–12; for Tianjin, see mimeographed list

issued by Tianjin Foreign Investment Commission; for Shanghai, see *Brief Introduction of Projects for Economic and Technical Cooperation*, published by Shanghai Investment and Trust Corporation; for the Guangzhou meeting, see *Economic Reporter*, April, 1982, pp. 10–13, May, 1982, pp. 6–12, and June, 1982, pp. 21–25.

83. The total value for the 130 projects is US$1,650 million, of which US$900 million is sought from foreign investors. Thus, the typical project will have about 54 percent foreign funding.

84. *Beijing Review*, 26 July 1982, p. 3.

NOTES TO CHAPTER 2

1. Under progress payments, China usually gave the supplier 20 percent advance payment, 70 percent upon shipment, 5 percent on delivery, and the remaining 5 percent at the end of the test or guarantee period. Under deferred payments, the usual terms were for China to give the supplier a downpayment of 20 percent and to pay the remaining 80 percent in equal installments over a five-year period after the equipment was delivered and installed. Under progress payments, China did not pay an interest charge, so to the extent that the cost of financing was not incorporated into the price of the equipment, it came out of the supplier's profits. In the case of deferred payments, the supplier usually obtained the credit, often financed through a government export incentive program, and then passed the cost of financing on to China in the form of a higher price.

2. In addition to the commercial practices discussed in this section, China has of course greatly expanded its scientific and technological contacts through non-commercial channels. For example, China has signed numerous government-to-government agreements to promote scientific and technical exchanges with the more developed countries. China has also strengthened its ties with multilateral scientific and technological organizations.

3. From 1979 to 1981, China signed 116 licensing contracts with foreign firms as compared to only 16 in the six-year period from 1973 to 1978. See *China's Foreign Trade*, April, 1982, p. 11.

4. Much has been written about these special trade arrangements. One of the clearer official descriptions is in Ministry of Foreign Economic Relations and Trade, *Guide to Investment in China* (Hong Kong: Economic Information & Agency, 1982). Similar arrangements have been used in East-West trade since the 1960s. For a discussion of the Eastern European experience in this realm, see United Nations, Economic Commission for Europe, *East-West Industrial Cooperation* (New York, 1979).

5. The Chinese often translate *hezuo jingying* as contractual joint venture, which — when shortened — becomes joint venture. To avoid confusion, we use instead the term co-operative venture, which is a closer translation of *hezuo jingying*.

6. *Beijing Review*, 14 December 1981, p. 16; and *Economic Reporter*, April 1982, p. 21.

7. If the import is new equipment, then presumably the original supplier's invoice can be used to establish the value of the equipment. Otherwise, the negotiation can be quite timeconsuming.

8. Probably the largest compensation trade agreement to date is that between Container Transport International (CTI) and the Guangzhou Shipyard. Under the agreement, CTI supplied the shipyard with US$110 million to build and equip a container manufacturing plant. In return, the Chinese are obligated to sell the entire output (about 800 plus containers a month) to CTI for five years at reduced prices. See Dori Jones, "Competition, Socialist Style," *China Business Review*, November-December, 1980, pp. 47–48; and Stephen Markscheid, "Compensation Trade: The China Perspective," *China Business Review*, January-February, 1982, pp. 50–52.

9. The Chinese attach considerable importance to this. Included in their description of compensation trade is the statement that "the technology and equipment purchased by compensation trade must be applicable and advanced. It must be helpful to the reformation of the existing enterprises in China as well as to raising productive capabilities and technical standards." See *Guide to Investment in China*, p. 49

10. For example, co-operative ventures have been established to bring tourists to China from Hong Kong. The Chinese contribution to these arrangements, besides a bit of office space in Guangdong, consists of an intangible — the right to operate a tour in China. The foreigner's contribution is the capital to finance the operation (that is, to purchase equipment such as tour buses), the marketing

connection in Hong Kong to supply the tourists, and the organizational skills to plan and manage a tour. These arrangements are useful to China primarily because they earn foreign exchange, though they also offer some exposure to management and marketing practices.

11. For example, one such venture is that involving the Shanghai Aircraft Factory and McDonnell Douglas. The Shanghai factory is to produce aircraft doors with technical assistance (two quality control personnel and one tool engineer) from Douglas. The arrangement exposes Chinese technicians and workers to sophisticated welding techniques and chemical treatment of sheet metal surfaces, both technologies that are critical to the development of the Chinese aircraft industry. See Carol S. Goldsmith, "Countertrade, Inc.," *China Business Review*, January-February, 1982, pp. 48–50; and Helen Kauder, "Subcontracting in China," *China Business Review*, September-October, 1982, pp. 37–39.

12. Quoted in James B. Stepanek, "Direct Investment in China," *China Business Review*, September-October, 1982, p. 21. That the Chinese want foreign firms to become more involved in the management of co-operative ventures was emphasized in the speech by the vice-minister of the Ministry of Foreign Economic Relations and Trade at the China Investment Promotion Meeting in Guangzhou in June 1982. See *Beijing Review*, 26 July 1982, p. 19. But nearly all the specifics mentioned by the vice-minister are for the joint venture arrangement.

13. Control is used here to mean the ability of the supplier firm to influence the recipient's behavior in ways beneficial to itself. For an interesting discussion of control in this context, see V. N. Balasubramanyam, *International Transfer of Technology to India* (New York: Praeger, 1973), pp. 17–21.

14. However, it is important to note that, depending on the nature of the technology, effective control over the recipient can be achieved in ways other than through full ownership.

15. The number of FTCs varied from period to period. For example, they numbered between sixteen and eighteen before 1961, declined to twelve in 1961, and increased to thirteen in 1966. In the mid-1970s, they numbered ten. For a more detailed discussion of China's trade organization before 1979, see Audrey Donnithorne, *China's Economic System* (New York: Praeger, 1967), chapter 12: and U.S. Department of Commerce, *Doing Business with China*, various editions.

16. Edith Terry, "Decentralizing Foreign Trade," *China-International Business* 1 (1981): 447. For exceptions to this rule, see Audrey Donnithorne, p. 326.

17. *Far Eastern Economic Review*, 1 September 1983, p. 108.

18. According to one of its officials, FICC's responsibilities include the following: 1) examine and approve joint venture projects; 2) research and formulate laws, decrees, and regulations; 3) organize, consider, and conclude foreign economic co-operation arrangements; and 4) investigate and research the general state of international economic development and trade. See Sally Lord Ellis, "Decentralization of China's Foreign Trade Structure," *Georgia Journal of International and Comparative Law 11* (1981): 291.

19. CITIC has since participated in joint ventures involving foreign and Chinese participants as well as in joint ventures involving only Chinese participants. What is interesting is that because CITIC's investment involves funds borrowed abroad, its joint ventures with purely Chinese enterprises apparently meet the letter of the law and operate as "joint ventures using Chinese and foreign investment."

20. Under its 1962 Articles of Association, the BOC was a joint state-private enterprise and was supervised by the People's Bank of China.

21. In November 1979, Chinese officials stated that Beijing, Shanghai, Tianjin, Guangdong, and Fujian had authority to approve special trade projects up to a limit of RMB ¥3 million. Subsequently, in 1980, the cut-off point was raised to US$3 million. See *China Business Review*, September-October, 1980, p. 18.

22. *China Trade Report*, April, 1980, p. 5.

23. For reports of competition between provinces, see *China Trade Report*, May, 1980, p. 13; and JETRO *China Newsletter* 29 (December, 1980): 23–25. We were also told of such competition in our interviews with local trade officials.

24. *Hong Qi* [Red Flag], 16 April 1982, p. 5.

25. JETRO *China Newsletter* 31 (April, 1981): p. 29.

26. Unless otherwise noted, the information in the following sections is based on interviews with central and local trade officials during May-July, 1982.

27. In mid-1982 there were twelve such corporations: China National Cereals, Oils and Foodstuffs Import & Export Corporation; China National Native Produce and Animal By-Products Import & Export Corporation; China National Textiles Import & Export Corporation; China National Light Industrial Products Import & Export Corporation; China National Arts and Crafts Import & Export Corporation; China National Chemicals Import & Export Corporation; China National Metals and Minerals Import & Export Corporation; China National Machinery Import & Export Corporation; China National Instruments Import & Export Corporation; China National Technical Import Corporation; China National Packaging Import & Export Corporation; and China National Silk Corporation. In addition, five other corporations that provide services to the foreign trade sector were under the direct supervision of MFERT.

28. In mid-1982 there were eighteen such corporations: China National Machinery and Equipment Import & Export Corporation, XINSHIDAI Company of China, China National Aero-Technology Import & Export Corporation, China Electronics Import & Export Corporation, China Precision Machinery Import & Export Corporation, China Northern Industrial Corporation, China State Shipbuilding Corporation, China Scientific Instruments and Materials Corporation, China National Metallurgical Import & Export Corporation, China Nuclear Energy Industry Corporation, China Great Wall Industrial Corporation, Oriental Scientific Instruments Import & Export Corporation, China National New Building Materials Corporation, China National Seeds Corporation, China National Tree Seed Corporation, China National Breeding Stock Import & Export Corporation, China National Agricultural Machinery Import & Export Corporation, and China National Coal Import & Export Corporation.

29. Zhong Wen, "Reforming the Structure of China's Foreign Trade," *China's Foreign Trade*, January 1981, p. 3.

30. The 1982 edition of CCPIT's *China's Foreign Trade Corporations and Organization* lists Beijing, Tianjin, Shanghai, Guangdong, and Fujian as localities with PFTCs. However, since the publication of this edition, PFTCs (or provincial import corporations) have been established in the following localities: Liaoning, Guangxi, Jilin, Zhejiang, Yunnan, Henan, and Hubei. There may be others as well.

31. They are Beijing, Tianjin, Shanxi, Shanghai, Jiangsu, Zhejiang, Anhui, Fujian, Jiangxi, Henan, Hubei, Hunan, Guangdong, and Sichuan. There are also five corporations that specialize in dealing with investments from Overseas Chinese.

32. The 1982 edition of *China's Foreign Trade Corporations and Organization* lists five IECs: China Abrasive and Grinder Export Corporation, China National Electric Wire and Cable Export Corporation, China National Bearings Export Corporation, China Electro-Ceramic Allied Corporation, and China United Electric Export Corporation. But there are others, such as the Shanghai Toys Import & Export Corporation, that operate like an "export association" and should be considered IECs.

33. *China's Foreign Trade*, April, 1982, p. 3.

34. This is a somewhat simplified diagram, as several of the less important players are not shown. The following description of how the system works is based largely on our interviews with various central and local trade organizations, such as CCPIT, MFERT, and local IECs.

35. *Guide to Investment in China*, p. 163.

36. A brief description of the other departments may be useful. The Treaties and Law Department examines the laws and regulations concerning foreign economic relations and trade; the Foreign Aid Department is in charge of China's foreign economic aid; the Foreign Economic Cooperation Bureau is responsible for economic projects and joint ventures in foreign countries; the International Organization Liaison Department administers economic technical co-operation with international organizations; and the titles of the other units provide a good description of their respective responsibilities.

37. *Guide to Investment in China*, p. 163.

38. Hereafter, "province" is used to include the three cities that have provincial status: Beijing, Shanghai, and Tianjin.

39. This body goes by many names. In some provinces it is called the Provincial Commission for Foreign Economic Work, and in others it is called the Provincial Import-Export Office.

40. At least in Tianjin, the actual work is done by the PFTB with the collaboration of the branch offices of the NFTCs.

41. The number of commodities in this category changes from time to time. In mid-1982, category I commodities included the following: hog bristles, feathers and down, sausage casings, cotton, cotton and polyester fabrics, silk thread, miscellaneous silk products, rice, edible vegetable oil, steel products, tungsten, antimony, tin, crude oil and petroleum products, and complete sets of equipment.

42. According to the FICC, the official guideline is that provinces are permitted "to retain 20% of the previous year's earnings from the export of locally produced but centrally controlled commodities and 40% for commodities under local jurisdiction." See Edith Terry, "Decentralizing Foreign Trade," *China-International Business* 1 (1981): 454; and *China Business Review*, September-October, 1980, p. 11. The actual practice, however, may be somewhat different. In Tianjin we were told that the municipality retains 30 percent of the foreign exchange earned from tourism and an "as yet not finally determined" percentage of the foreign exchange earnings from exports. Guangdong and Fujian, as we shall see shortly, are also treated differently.

43. However, MFERT's approval does not necessarily guarantee that "other departments concerned" will also consent to the project (*China Business Review*, September-October, 1983, p. 29). For example, the Minister of Finance will need to approve any tax provisions written into a special trade contract. In other words , to guarantee final approval, the participants to a joint venture should consult with every government department that may have jurisdiction over any aspect of their agreement.

44. *Beijing Review*, 30 May 1983, p. 8 and *China Business Review*, September-October, 1983, p. 12. In a sense, these limits discriminate against equity joint ventures, because their limits apply to the total dollar figure, while the limits on the other forms apply to the foreign contribution only.

45. *Guoji Maoyi* [International Trade], 1982, no. 4, p. 7.

46. Larry E. Westphal, Yung W. Rhee, and Garry Pursell, *Korean Industrial Competence: Where Did It Come From?*, World Bank Staff Working Paper no. 469, July, 1981, pp. 38–45.

47. In Fujian we were told that the province can make independent investment decisions on all projects below RMB ¥5 million.

48. The *baogan* system in Guangdong and that in Fujian are similar except for a few details.

49. The amount to be remitted to the central government was to be based on the actual remittance in 1978, which was RMB ¥1.3 billion. Apparently the lower figure was agreed upon only after hard lobbying by Guangdong. Because Fujian is considered to be a "poor" province, its *baogan* involves a stable subsidy of RMB ¥150 million each year from the center, instead of a remittance in the other direction. These *baogan* arrangements contain an escape clause, however. If the central government encounters a financial emergency, Guangdong and Fujian must transfer 13.3 percent of their total revenues to the center (the percentage to be transferred from the other provinces is 20 percent except for the "have-not" provinces, which transfer only 15 percent).

50. The description we received suggests the following sharing formula:
$$FE = A_0 + \alpha(E - E_0) + \beta R,$$
where FE is the foreign exchange currently allocated to Guangdong, A_0 is the foreign exchange received by Guangdong in 1978, E_0 is the foreign exchange earned by Guangdong from exports and tourism in 1978, E is Guangdong's current foreign exchange earnings from exports and tourism, R is the remittances that Guangdong receives from Overseas Chinese, and α and β are sharing ratios. A similar system is used in Fujian, but apparently α is 0.8 in Fujian instead of Guangdong's 0.7.

51. CITIC, the Guangdong Trust and Investment Corporation, and the Fujian Investment Enterprise Corporation are the only trust and investment companies that may deal directly with foreign financial institutions, borrow directly from abroad, and hold accounts in foreign banks. All other trust and investment companies must work through the Bank of China. In 1983 the privilege of raising capital on the international market directly was extended to the Shanghai Investment and Trust Corporation (*China Business Review*, September-October, 1983, p. 12).

52. Sun Ru, "The Conception and Prospects of the Special Economic Zones in Guangdong," *Chinese Economic Studies* 14 (1980): 70. For other Chinese discussions of the SEZs, see Fang Zhoufen, "On the Nature of China's Special Economic Zones," *Jingji Yanjiu* [Economic Research], August, 1981, pp. 54–58; and Tang Huai, "China's Special Economic Zones as Seen from Conditions in Export Processing Zones in Developing Countries and Areas," *Jingji Yanjiu* [Economic Research], June, 1981, pp. 62–68.

53. The Shenzhen SEZ borders the New Territories in Hong Kong; the Zhuhai SEZ is near Macao; and

the Shantou SEZ is near the old port city of Shantou (Swatow), about two hundred miles northeast of Hong Kong. Hainan Island has also been granted many of the privileges of an SEZ, and in fact might be said to be an SEZ in all but name. See Christopher M. Clarke, "Hainan," *China Business Review*, January-February, 1983, pp. 44–47.

54. CMSNC has the authority to approve all investment projects in Shekou except for the very large ones ("certainly all projects with investment below HK$20 million"). For large projects that require supplies and labor from either Guangdong or interior China, CMSNC, through the Ministry of Communications, will need to consult with "relevant departments." Once there is agreement on a project and the contract is approved by CMSNC, the enterprise is registered and incorporated at the Shenzhen Administrative Bureau of Industry and Commerce. There is no need to involve the administration of the Shenzhen SEZ.

55. The development of two additional SEZs in Fujian, one on Longqi Island near Fuzhou and the other in Xinglin (twenty-five kilometers from Xiamen), much discussed in 1980, has been put aside. At one time there were also reports that Shanghai, Tianjin, and Qingdao were considering the establishment of SEZs. However, it is now fairly clear that China will not permit any more SEZs (particularly outside of Guangdong and Fujian) in the near future. In mid-1983 Shanghai announced its plan to establish an industrial estate in its Minhang district to house equity joint ventures (*China Trade Report*, September, 1983, p. 8). However this industrial estate is not a SEZ since enterprises in the estate will not operate under a separate legal framework as do those in the SEZs in Guangdong and Fujian.

56. Fujian has drafted a set of regulations concerning SEZs, but as of early 1983 they had not been approved by the central government. When we visited China in mid-1982, we were told that Fujian officials have asked the central authorities to delay approval so that they can "sum up their experience" and perhaps revise the draft regulations. In the meantime, Fujian will follow the Guangdong rules. However, Fujian may offer more generous tax holidays and lower wages in order to compete with the locational advantage of Guangdong's SEZs in terms of their proximity to Hong Kong and Macao. It should also be noted that the incentives offered to enterprises within an SEZ may also be granted to acceptable projects outside the SEZ but within the boundaries of the city that administers the SEZ.

57. "Regulations on SEZs in Guangdong Province," article 4.

58. Ibid., article 1. In addition to direct foreign investment, portfolio investment is also possible. In July 1983, four state enterprises in Shenzhen (the Shenzhen Special Economic Zone Development Corporation, Shenzhen Cereals, Oils and Foodstuffs Import and Export Corporation, Shenzhen Foodstuffs and Beverages Corporation, and the Shenzhen branch of the China Aviation Technology Import and Export Corporation) joined together to establish a new corporation called San He Holdings, which will offer shares to overseas investors. San He hopes to raise RMB¥50 million (about US$25 million) by selling 5,000 shares valued at RMB¥10,000 each (*Far Eastern Economic Review*, 7 July 1983, p. 7). In August 1983, the Yinhu Tourist Centre, a Sino-foreign joint venture, announced its plan to offer 10,000 shares valued at RMB¥10 each to foreign and overseas Chinese investors (*China Trade Report*, October 1983, p. 6).

59. Ibid., article 9.

60. Ibid., article 14. See Chapter 4 for a more complete discussion of China's joint venture income tax law and Chapter 5 for a discussion of the foreign enterprise income tax law. When the Shekou Special Industrial Zone was first created, it was announced that enterprises in the zone would pay a corporate income tax rate of 10 percent. However, this was subsequently changed to 15 percent to make it consistent with the "Regulations on SEZs in Guangdong Province."

61. Ibid., article 13.

62. Ibid., article 17.

63. Ibid., article 10.

64. The Shekou Special Industrial Zone does specify, however, that "the average monthly wages for ordinary workers of an enterprise shall be higher than those for workers working in the same kind of enterprise in China and lower than those for workers working in the same kind of enterprise in Hong Kong." This is so general that it is not very restrictive. However, Shenzhen has sometimes insisted that wages be only 10 to 15 percent below Hong Kong rates for similar work. Economic reality intruded, and in 1982 Shenzhen accepted wage rates that are "50 percent lower than those in Hong Kong under similar working conditions." See *China Business Review*, November-December, 1982, p. 4.

65. We were told that in 1981 the average worker in the Shenzhen SEZ took home about RMB ¥120 per month (including bonuses), which was about 60 to 70 percent of what workers in Hong Kong made in similar lines of work and was significantly higher than what the average worker made in other parts of China. However, prices in Shenzhen were also considerably higher than elsewhere in China.

66. When we visited Shenzhen in mid-1982, the floating wage system was just beginning to be introduced, and several of the enterprises we visited were discussing ways to implement the system. For a description of the system in two enterprises in the service sector, see "The Form of Wages in Shenzhen's Friendship Restaurant and Bamboo Garden Hotel," *Gang-Ao Jingji* [The Economies of Hong Kong and Macao], 1982, no. 5, pp. 43–44.

67. The review and appeal procedures for dismissal are the same as those stated in the joint venture regulations, discussed in Chapter 4.

68. The power is not unlimited, although we were told that Shenzhen may approve any project that does not require the province to rebalance supplies, transportation, capital funds, and so forth.

69. Hong Kong's corporate income tax rate at the time China was formulating its tax regulations for the SEZs was 17 percent. In 1981 it was reduced to 16.5 percent, retroactive to 1 April 1980.

70. For the Chinese view, see Xu Dixin, "China's Special Economic Zones," *Beijing Review*, 14 December 1981, pp. 14–17.

71. Hong Kong is composed of Hong Kong Island, Kowloon (Jiulong), and the New Territories. Hong Kong Island was ceded to Great Britain in 1842 by the Treaty of Nanjing, Kowloon was ceded in 1860 by the Treaty of Beijing, and the New Territories (which contains over 90 percent of the 409 square miles that constitute Hong Kong) was leased by the Convention of Beijing to Great Britain in 1898 for 99 years. China takes the view that these are unequal treaties, imposed unilaterally by an imperialist power. Therefore, it claims that it is not bound by these treaties and that it will recover the whole Hong Kong area "when the conditions are ripe." Increasingly, it looks like the conditions will be ripe when the lease on the New Territories ends in 1997. See *Beijing Review*, 23 August 1982, pp. 16–18, and 11 October 1982, pp. 10–11, and the discussion in Chapter 7.

72. For a discussion of this point, see Ian H. Macdonald, "The Role of Hong Kong in China's Modernization," *China — International Business* 1 (1981): 431–44; Y. C. Jao, "Dependence Is a Two-Way Street," *Far Eastern Economic Review*, 20 January 1983; pp. 38–42; and Christopher Howe, "Growth, Public Policy and Hong Kong's Economic Relationship with China," *China Quarterly* 95, September, 1983, pp. 512–33.

73. *China Trade Report*, August, 1982, p. 5.

74. It may be presumed that as the other SEZs become more developed they too will allow central ministries and other provinces to utilize them as contact points with foreign companies.

75. Chen Qiaozhi, "The Economic Integration of the SEZs and the Interior Regions," *Gang-Ao Jingji* [The Economies of Hong Kong and Macao], 1982, no. 2, pp. 11–15. By early 1983, Shenzhen (the most developed of the four SEZs) had established over four hundred joint ventures with cities and provinces from other parts of China.

76. *China Reconstructs*, July, 1983, p. 15.

77. Of course, the interior provinces have always done this. Indeed, over the past thirty years, substantial resources have been transferred from the old industrial centers on the coast to help industrialize the interior.

78. *Beijing Review*, 4 January 1982, p. 23.

79. *Beijing Review*, 16 August 1982, p. 25.

NOTES TO CHAPTER 3

1. Detailed discussion of Chinese statistics and the Chinese statistical system can be found in Choh-Ming Li, *The Statistical System of Communist China* (Berkeley and Los Angeles: University of California Press, 1962); Nai-Ruenn Chen, "An Assessment of Chinese Economic Data: Availability, Reliability, and Usability," in U.S. Congress, Joint Economic Committee, *China: A Reassessment of the Economy* (Washington, DC: Government Printing Office, 1975), pp. 52–68; and Alexander Eckstein, ed., *Quantitative Measures of China's Economic Output* (Ann Arbor:

University of Michigan Press, 1980). For those not interested in the detailed analysis of China's data, a useful short article that discusses some of the problems with Chinese statistics is Ian H. MacFarlane, "Understanding and Using Chinese Statistics: The Cement Industry as an Example," *Journal of International Law and Economics* 13 (1979): 619–31.

2. As revealed in a speech by the First Secretary of the Communist Party in Guangdong in April 1982, reported in James B. Stepanek, "Direct Investment in China," *China Business Review*, September-October, 1982, p. 24. Our findings also confirm this. We were told that, as of June 1982, "foreign investment" pledged in special trade arrangements in Guangdong was about US$2,600 million, while the amount actually in place at the end of 1981 was about US$515 million (interview notes with Guangdong Provincial Commission on Foreign Economic Work, 25 June 1982). This implies a ratio of arrivals to amount pledged of about 0.2. The Guangdong figures were defined somewhat differently (for processing agreements, they include the amount of the fees, not the value of the equipment supplied), but this makes little difference to the overall conclusion.

3. The $4.1 billion figure is from *China Market*, May, 1983, p. 24; the $1.7 billion figure is from *Beijing Review*, 6 June 1983, p. 4.

4. See Table 3.1, note j.

5. For the definition of total investment, see note c, Table 3.2.

6. For details of the problems encountered in building the Great Wall Hotel, see Robert Boorstin, "The Great Wall Story," *China Business Review*, September-October, 1982, pp. 6–9.

7. *China Business Review*, September-October, 1983, p. 28.

8. Ibid.

9. In 1983, several large industrial joint venture agreements were signed. In May, China and the American Motors Corporation announced a US$51 million project to produce Jeeps and Jeep engines in China. The Chinese partner is the Beijing Auto Works. Under the agreement, AMC will contribute US$8 million in cash and another US$8 million in technology to update the Beijing Plant. (See *Newsweek*, 16 May 1983, pp. 75–76.) In June, the agreement creating the Shanghai Yaohua General Glass Plant (total investment: US$119 million) was approved. The foreign participants are a British firm and a Hong Kong firm, and the Chinese parties are the Ministry of Building Materials Industry and the Bank of China. In July, the agreement creating the Shanghai Bell Telephone Equipment Manufacturing Co. (initial total investment: US$20–25 million) was signed. (See *China Business Review*, September-October, 1983, pp. 21–25.)

10. For a more detailed discussion of these developments in the energy sector, see Chapter 6.

11. Interview notes of 25 June 1982: Guangdong Provincial Commission on Foreign Economic Work. By the end of 1982, Guangdong is reported to have attracted 20,653 special trade projects involving US$4.1 billion in foreign capital (*China Business Review*, September-October, 1983, p. 12).

12. *Shijie Jingji Daobao* [World Economic Herald], 17 May 1982, p. 1.

13. Interview notes of 25 June 1982: Guangdong Provincial Commission on Foreign Economic Work.

14. See Table 3.1, note k.

15. Interview notes of 25 June 1982: Guangdong Provincial Commission on Foreign Economic Work.

16. *Shijie Jingji Daobao* [World Economic Herald], 10 May 1982, p. 4.

17. Ibid. The foreign investment figures for equity joint ventures in Shanghai is overstated because one of the two agreements is the China-Schindler contract, which also involves facilities in Beijing. By the end of 1982, Shanghai had five joint ventures with a total foreign investment of US$14.88 million. It is also reported that, by the end of 1982, foreigners had invested US$380 million in joint venture, compensation trade, and co-operative venture deals in Shanghai (see *China Business Review*, September-October, 1983, pp. 12 and 20–25.)

18. *China Trade Report*, August, 1983, p. 12 and *China Business Review*, September-October 1983, pp. 21–25. Foreign investment is overstated since one of the nine joint ventures is the China-Schindler contract which also involves facilities in Shanghai.

19. Interview notes of 7 June 1982: Tianjin Import-Export Commission.

20. *Shijie Jingji Daobao* [World Economic Herald], 17 May 1982, p. 1.

21. Interview notes of 7 June 1982: Tianjin Import-Export Commission. In 1982, Tianjin signed more than 130 compensation trade and processing contracts (*China Trade Report*, September, 1983, p. 10), and by the end of 1982 it had eight joint ventures with a total foreign investment of US$5.69 million (*China Business Review*, September-October, 1983, pp. 21–25).

22. *China Trade Report*, June, 1982, p. 10.
23. Interview notes of 21 June 1982: Fujian Import-Export Commission and *China Business Review*, September-October, 1983, pp. 21–25.
24. Calculated from data in *Shijie Jingji Daobao* [World Economic Herald], 17 May 1982, p. 1.
25. At the end of 1981, foreign parties had pledged US$1.73 billion to projects in the SEZs. See *China Business Review*, September-October, 1982, p. 21.
26. Ibid. Of the total foreign funds pledged to Shenzhen by year-end 1981, 78 percent was committed during 1981, much of it in the last half of the year. See *Beijing Review*, 12 April 1982, p. 5.
27. *Asian Wall Street Journal*, 5 February 1982. The reported figure was US$1,570.5 million which was converted to HK$ at US$1 = HK$5.64.
28. *China Reconstructs*, July, 1983, p. 10.
29. *Wen Hui Bao*, 8 September 1983.
30. *Far Eastern Economic Review*, 11 August 1983, p. 66.
31. Interview notes of 30 June 1982: Shekou Special Industrial Zone.
32. Lu Ji, "The Development of Industry in the Shenzhen SEZ," *Gang-Ao Jingji* [The Economies of Hong Kong and Macao], 1982, no. 4, pp. 54–55. To put these statistics in perspective, it should be noted that in 1981 Shenzhen accounted for only about 1 percent of Guangdong's GVIO.
33. 800,000, if the rural areas administered by Xiamen City are included.
34. In 1981 Xiamen's GVIO amounted to RMB ¥1 billion, of which handicrafts and light industry accounted for 60 percent. Products produced by its heavy industry include items such as shoe soles and bicycle tires as well as forklifts, electric motors, ball bearings, and switches. Xiamen had 700-plus industrial enterprises in 1981 — 120 were state-owned and the rest were collectives. Total industrial employment was about 100,000 in 1981. The 120 state-owned enterprises produced about 80 percent of the city's GVIO and employed 50 percent of its industrial workers. Only 5 percent of the city's industrial output was exported in 1981. This information is drawn from interview notes of 18 June 1982: Xiamen Municipal Economic Commission.
35. The problem is less serious in Xiamen. But even in Xiamen workers cannot easily travel from their homes to the SEZ because the city lacks a good public transport system. Thus, the Xiamen SEZ is also planning to build a new urban community adjacent to its industrial estate at Huli.
36. It is not clear what financial commitments the central government has made towards the development of the SEZs. In 1980, CMSNC announced that it was investing US$20 million (about HK$110–120 million or RMB ¥35 million) for site preparation at Shekou. See *China Trade Report*, March, 1980, p. 5. In mid-1982, when we visited Shekou, we were told that CMSNC had invested between HK$250–300 million in land preparation and infrastructure development (roads, water, power, transport, and telecommunications). In Guangzhou we were told that the central government has provided seed money of RMB ¥30 million in the form of a loan for the development of the Shenzhen SEZ. In Shenzhen, however, we were told that the SEZ administration is expecting the state to contribute RMB ¥900 million toward the development, though we were not told whether this amount covers all levels of government, nor whether it includes the amount that CMSNC has invested in Shekou. Despite this confusion about the numbers, however, there was general agreement among all those we interviewed that most of the resources needed to develop Guangdong and Fujian's SEZs will have to be generated either within the two provinces or abroad. In fact a recent article in *China Reconstructs* (July, 1983, p. 10) states explicitly that "China has not, as other countries have in similar situations, made large initial investments of state money in developing the infrastructure for her special zones."
37. The Guangdong regulations specifically permit the use of foreign funds, when necessary, to finance infrastructure. See "Regulations on Special Economic Zones in Guangdong Province," article 5.
38. One agreement, valued at HK$2 billion, was for the development of a new town in Shenzhen, and another, valued at HK$2.4 billion, was for the construction of a 6 km^2 scientific, cultural, and education area. These two projects alone account for 57 percent of the total foreign funds pledged to projects in Shenzhen by the end of 1981. See *Beijing Review*, 12 April 1982, p. 5. Several large projects involving infrastructure development were also signed in 1982. See *Business Standard* (Hong Kong), 31 July 1982, and *China Trade Report*, August, 1982, p. 10.
39. Anita Li, "Foreign Investors Are Encouraged Despite the Labor Problem," *China Business Review*, September-October, 1981, p. 44; and *China Trade Report*, May, 1980, p. 6.

40. *China Trade Report*, July, 1981, p. 5.
41. The hope is that eventually the SEZ Administration will have authority over all matters within the zone. Whether this will be achieved is an open question. Indeed, the difficulty of starting a business in Shenzhen is such that recently a "buffer" company (owned 60 percent by the Chinese and 40 percent by a Hong Kong group) was formed in Hong Kong to develop and operate an industrial estate at Buji in Shenzhen (seven kilometers from the Hong Kong border, immediately adjacent to the SEZ, but with all SEZ privileges). Foreign companies interested in operating in Buji need only deal with the "buffer" firm. Indeed, all contracts are with the "buffer" firm and in accordance with Hong Kong laws. In effect, the "buffer" company, for a fee, takes the responsibility for dealing with the Chinese bureaucracy on behalf of its clients. See *China Trade Report*, February, 1982, pp. 8–9; and *Asian Business*, February, 1982, pp. 25–27.
42. Very few projects were in operation in the other SEZs in 1982. Contracts signed since August 1981 have not altered the basic situation as described in the text.
43. Derived from data reported in *Wen Hui Bao*, 8 September 1983.
44. For the complete list, see *Wen Hui Bao*, 8 September 1983.
45. For a description of the current Chinese plans for Shenzhen, see K. Y. Wong, ed., *Shenzhen Special Economic Zone: China's Experiment in Modernization* (Hong Kong: Hong Kong Geographical Association, 1982). In 1983, the Shenzhen municipal government reported that as of year-end 1982 it had invested RMB ¥630 million in infrastructure development in the SEZ (*China Trade Report*, October, 1983, p. 7.).

NOTES TO CHAPTER 4

1. Strictly speaking, the Beijing Air Catering Company is not the first joint venture permitted to operate in the People's Republic of China. Numerous joint ventures between China and the Soviet Union operated in the 1950s, but they were terminated in 1960 as a consequence of the Sino-Soviet split.
2. *Shijie Jingji Daobao* [World Economic Herald], 3 May 1982, p. 2.
3. Article 6 of the "Constitution of the People's Republic of China," adopted on 4 December 1982, by the Fifth National People's Congress.
4. Apparently the joint venture law that was eventually promulgated is more hazy and less explicit than the initial draft. See *China Trade Report*, September, 1979, pp. 9–10.
5. In addition, there are special regulations for the SEZs, which are discussed in Chapter 2. China's economic contract law was issued in December 1981 and came into force on 1 July 1982.
6. Joint Venture Law, article 1.
7. Article 3 of the joint venture law requires that a decision either to approve or reject the agreement be made within three months. The body originally designated to review joint venture agreements was the Foreign Investment Administration Commission. In March 1982 China reorganized some of its government structure, and the Ministry of Foreign Economic Relations, the Ministry of Foreign Trade, the Foreign Investment Administration Commission, and the State Import-Export Administration Commission were combined into the Ministry of Foreign Economic Relations and Trade. Under the new ministry is a Foreign Investment Administration Bureau, which now has the primary responsibility for reviewing joint venture agreements. However, MFERT has entrusted provinces, municipalities, autonomous regions, and central agencies directly under the State Council the authority to review and approve those joint venture projects that 1) "require no additional state allocations of raw and other materials, do not affect the national balance on matters of fuel, power and transportation, and produce no products that take up the state export quotas," and 2) involve foreign investment below a certain specified limit (US$10 million for Shanghai, US$5 million for Liaoning, Beijing, and Tianjin, US$3 million for other provinces and agencies under the State Council, and no limit for Guangdong and Fujian). See *China Economic News*, Supplement no. 3, 12 May 1982, p. 3, and the discussion in Chapter 2.
8. "Regulations for the Implementation of the Law of the People's Republic of China on Joint Ventures Using Chinese and Foreign Investment" (hereafter, "Regulations for the Implementation of the Joint Venture Law"), article 14.
9. For a detailed description of the investment process, from initial contact to final agreement, see

Guide to Investment in China (Hong Kong: Economic Information and Agency, 1982), chapter 12. Also see "Regulations for the Implementation of the Joint Venture Law," articles 9 and 10.

10. "Regulations on the Registration of Joint Ventures Using Chinese and Foreign Investment," articles 2 and 5.

11. Joint Venture Law, article 4.

12. Joint Venture Law, article 5, and "Regulations for the Implementation of the Joint Venture Law," article 25.

13. Joint Venture Law, article 12. In general, the duration of joint ventures in heavy industry is twenty to thirty years; in light industry, ten to fifteen years; and in tourism and services, five to ten years. However the duration for large projects with long construction periods and low rates of return may be longer than thirty years.

14. Joint Venture Law, article 13.

15. Joint Venture Law, article 6.

16. Ibid.

17. Ministry of Foreign Economic Relations and Trade, "Questions and Answers Concerning Foreign Investment in China," *China Economic News*, Supplement no. 3, 12 May 1982, p. 4. (Hereafter, this document is referred to as MFERT, "Questions and Answers.") It now appears that "Questions and Answers" was based on an earlier draft of the just promulgated "Regulations for the Implementation of the Joint Venture Law." Indeed, in many instances, the two documents use nearly identical language. The power of the chairman is not defined beyond the fact that he is empowered to call and preside over meetings of the board.

18. Detailed discussions of these rules can be found in Timothy Haosen Wan, "A Comparative Study of Foreign Investment Laws in Taiwan and China," *California Western International Law Journal* 11 (1981); William P. Alford and David E. Birenbaum, "Ventures in the China Trade: An Analysis of China's Emerging Legal Framework for the Regulation of Foreign Investment," *Northwestern Journal of International Law and Business* 3 (1981); and Joseph E. Pattison, "China's Developing Legal Framework for Foreign Investment: Experiences and Expectations," *Law and Policy in International Business* 13 (1981).

19. *China Business Reivew*, September-October, 1983, p. 20. The Chinese call these ventures *duzi jingying* — that is, sole ownership and management.

20. For example, see MFERT, "Questions and Answers," p. 5. It is reported one such application may soon be approved (*China Business Review*, September-October, 1983, p. 20).

21. In 1979, shortly after the joint venture law was promulgated, Rong Yiren, the Chairman and President of CITIC, suggested that "special regulations will be adopted" to govern 100 percent foreign-owned enterprises in China. See *China Business Review*, September-October, 1979, p. 6.

22. MFERT, "Questions and Answers," p. 7, and "Regulations for the Implementation of the Joint Venture Law," article 48.

23. Interview notes of 27 May 1982: Foreign Investment Administration Bureau.

24. Jerome A. Cohen and Owen D. Nee, Jr., "Joint Ventures: Behind the Headlines, Part I," *Asian Wall Street Journal*, 20 July 1979.

25. Pattison, "Experiences and Expectations," pp. 109–10. The recently promulgated "Regulations for the Implementation of the Joint Venture Law" states that "site use fee shall be set . . . according the purpose of use, geographic and environmental conditions, expenses for requisition, demolishing and resettlement and the joint venture's requirements with regard to infrastructure" (article 49).

26. Speaking about China's approach to joint ventures in 1980, Xu Dixin, vice-president of the Chinese Academy of Social Sciences, said, "We can't have clear-cut directives yet. Depending on circumstances, there is bound to be contradiction and some degree of confusion. But the different approaches will be used for comparison. We will draw lessons from them and then formulate a unified approach." See *Far Eastern Economic Review*, 30 May 1980, p. 80.

27. These guidelines can be found in MFERT, "Questions and Answers," p. 2. They were also mentioned in nearly every interview we had in China where foreign investment was discussed. The recently promulgated "Regulations for the Implementation of the Joint Venture Law" gives an almost identical list except that coal is replaced by energy development and that the manufacture of off-shore oil exploitation equipment is mentioned explicitly.

28. Article 18 of the "Constitution of the People's Republic of China," adopted 4 December 1982.

29. Joint Venture Law, articles 2, 10, and 11. However, only 50 percent of the after-tax income earned by foreign personnel may be remitted abroad.' See "Provisional Regulations for Exchange Control of the People's Republic of China," article 25.

30. MFERT, "Questions and Answers," pp. 2–3.

31. Trademarks can be registered and receive a degree of protection in China. China also has an invention law, which provides rewards to those inventors who turn their inventions over to the state but does not offer protection to intellectual property rights.

32. *China Business Review*, November-December, 1980, p. 42.

33. "The Income Tax Law Concerning Joint Ventures with Chinese and Foreign Investment," articles 2 and 3.

34. Ibid., article 4.

35. "Detailed Rules and Regulations for the Implementation of the Income Tax Law Concerning Joint Ventures with Chinese and Foreign Investment," article 13.

36. Ibid., article 16.

37. Joint Venture Income Tax Law, articles 7 and 16.

38. "Regulations on Special Economic Zones in Guangdong Province," articles 14 and 15. Fujian has not as yet issued its regulations on SEZs, but has advised potential investors to use the Guangdong regulations as a guideline. The Guangdong regulations do not mention a tax on remittances, and officials at the Shenzhen SEZ Development Company confirmed during our visit that joint ventures in the zone are subject only to the 15 percent profit tax.

39. Joint Venture Income Tax Law, article 5.

40. Ibid., article 6.

41. Joint Venture Law, article 7.

42. China is currently considering a reform of the CICT to eliminate some of its cascading features. Among the alternatives under consideration is a value-added tax.

43. In 1982 China had at least eleven taxes. Industrial joint ventures, however, would not in general encounter such Chinese taxes as the agricultural tax and the slaughter tax. For discussions of Chinese taxes, see Audrey Donnithorne, *China's Economic System* (New York: Praeger, 1967), chapter 14; George N. Ecklund, *Financing the Chinese Government Budget: Mainland China, 1950–1959* (Chicago: Aldine, 1966); and Richard D. Pomp, Timothy A. Gelatt, and Stanley S. Surrey, "The Evolving Tax System of the People's Republic of China," *Texas International Law Journal* 16 (1981): 11–78.

44. MFERT, "Questions and Answers," pp. 6–7.

45. For discussions of China's individual income tax law, see Pomp, Gelatt, and Surrey, "The Evolving Tax System," pp. 40–51; and Timothy A. Gelatt, "Doing Business with China: The Developing Legal Framework," *China Business Review*, November-December, 1981, pp. 52–56.

46. Interview notes of 27 May 1982: Foreign Investment Administration Bureau.

47. Joint Venture Law, article 19.

48. However, article 24 of the "Provisional Regulations for Exchange Control" state that foreign participants in joint ventures are to remit profits and capital abroad by "debiting the foreign exchange deposit accounts of the enterprise concerned." The interesting question is: what if the account does not have sufficient funds to cover the remittance?

49. MFERT, "Questions and Answers," p. 5. Nearly all the industrial joint ventures that we are familiar with are committed to exporting some of their output to cover their foreign exchange needs (imports of supplies and remittance of foreign partner's profits). The recently announced joint venture between AMC and the Beijing Auto Works (one of the largest industrial joint ventures to date) plans to export a fourth or more of the Jeeps it makes — potentially, about ten thousand vehicles a year — to Southeast Asia. There are a few exceptions to this pattern. For example, the joint venture agreement between Foxboro and Shanghai (to produce process-control instruments) does not commit Foxboro to buy back products for export, although Foxboro may in the future use the joint venture as a source of supply for its East European markets. In addition, two recently signed agreements in the pharmaceutical industry commit the foreign partner only to "purchase sufficient amounts of the product from the joint venture [for export] to offset Chinese foreign exchange purchases of equipment and materials." In other words, the foreign partner's profit remittances need not be covered by the venture's export earnings. See *China Business Review*, November-December, 1982, pp. 4–5.

50. Ibid.
51. Certainly this is the impression we gained from our discussions with Chinese officials, Chinese managers, and foreign investors.
52. The Chinese recognize that they will need to negotiate the re-purchase price (interview notes of 27 May 1982: Foreign Investment Administration Bureau). Presumably, any disputes that arise over the re-purchase price are subject to the usual mechanisms for dispute resolution set out in the joint venture law.
53. "Regulations for the Implementation of the Joint Venture Law," article 106.
54. "Regulations for the Implentation of the Joint Venture Law," articles 57 and 63.
55. MFERT, "Questions and Answers," p. 6.
56. Ibid., pp. 4–5.
57. Ibid., p. 6.
58. The MFERT guidelines mention only that the joint venture needs to report its prices "to the department in charge and the local authorities for the record" (MFERT, "Questions and Answers," p. 6). But our discussions with joint ventures in China indicate that, when prices are set, the local price bureau is always consulted in advance. The precise handling of prices depends on whether the commodities fall into categories 1, 2 or 3 (interview notes of 27 May 1982: Foreign Investment Administration Bureau).
59. Joint Venture Law, article 9.
60. *Guide to Investment in China*, p. 220. Indeed, article 56 of the "Regulations for the Implementation of the Joint Venture Law" states explicitly that "departments in charge of the joint ventures and planning and administration departments at all levels shall not issue directives [regarding production and operation] to joint ventures."
61. This discussion is based on MFERT, "Questions and Answers," p. 6, and on our interview with the Foreign Investment Administration Bureau.
62. "Regulations for the Implementation of the Joint Venture Law," article 63.
63. "Regulations on Labour Management in Joint Ventures Using Chinese and Foreign Investment," article 3.
64. This includes the use of a probationary period (interview notes of 26 May 1981: MFERT, Department of Treaties and Law).
65. Regulations on Labour Management, article 4.
66. Ibid., article 12.
67. Ibid., aricle 5.
68. Ibid., articles 6 and 14.
69. Interview notes of 26 May 1982: MFERT, Department of Treaties and Law.
70. Regulations on Labour Management, articles 8 and 9.
71. Ibid., article 2.
72. More detailed regulations on labor management are being drafted, and in the future the approval procedure will be used to check whether the labor contract is executed according to these detailed regulations (interview notes of 26 May 1982: MFERT, Department of Treaties and Law).
73. Joint Venture Law, article 8, and Provisional Regulations for Exchange Control, article 22.
74. See the "Provisional Regulations for Providing Loans to Joint Ventures of Chinese and Foreign Ownership by the Bank of China."
75. MFERT, "Questions and Answers," p. 9. The highest total percentage reported so far is 20 percent. See Jerome A. Cohen, "Equity Joint Ventures," *China Business Review*, November-December, 1982, p. 30.
76. Ibid.
77. Provisional Regulations for Exchange Control, article 24.
78. MFERT, "Questions and Answers," p. 8.
79. Joint Venture Law, article 6.
80. MFERT, "Questions and Answers," p. 4. Also see "Regulations for the Implementation of the Joint Venture Law," article 36.
81. Ibid.
82. For example, see the U.S.-China Trade Agreement.
83. MFERT, "Questions and Answers," p. 10.
84. Ibid., p. 9.
85. "Economic Contract Law of the People's Republic of China," articles 48, 49, and 50.

86. If the two parties to a dispute belong to the same ministry, then the organ that governs the contract is that ministry. However, when the two parties belong to different units (as would be the case in a dispute involving a joint venture and a Chinese enterprise), then the organ that will do the mediation and arbitration is the General Administration Bureau of Industry and Commerce (GABIC). GABIC also oversees the management of economic contracts in China. See Robin M. Elliot, "The Economic Contract Law of the People's Republic of China: A Window on China's Legal and Economic Worlds," presented at the International Trade Conference sponsored by the Institute of International Relations and the Institute for Research on Public Policy, Vancouver, BC, 5 June 1983.

87. The first economic tribunal was established in Chongqing in 1979, and by the end of 1981 similar tribunals had been established within the Supreme People's Court, the higher People's Courts of various provinces, provincial-level municipalities, and autonomous regions, and 293 intermediate People's Courts.

88. Jerome A. Cohen and Owen D. Nee, Jr., "Joint Ventures: Behind the Headlines, Part II," *Asian Wall Street Journal*, 23 July 1979.

89. Unless otherwise noted, the information used in the following discussion is drawn from our interviews with Jardine-Schindler in Hong Kong, China-Schindler's head office in Beijing, and China-Schindler's plant in Shanghai.

90. Jardine-Schindler, a joint venture between Jardine and Schindler, is Schindler's marketing arm in Asia. Hereafter, for convenience, we will refer to Schindler and Jardine-Schindler jointly as Schindler.

91. Apparently, about the same time contact was also made in Hong Kong between Schindler and a delegation from Tianjin. See *Far Eastern Economic Review*, 30 May 1980, p. 80.

92. Of the other four, one was only interested in selling technology and the remaining three have plants in Asia and therefore did not want to invest in an enterprise in China that would compete against their existing operations.

93. The agreement and the articles of association were first published by the *China Economic News* in Hong Kong, which suggests that the leaked texts were provided by the Chinese.

94. The first agreement between China and Schindler read in part:
    It is agreed that a further objective is to incorporate the Tianjin operation with the JVC at a later stage when circumstances permit to do so. The parties shall work together with a view to making Tianjin a manufacturer and supplier to the JVC under sub-license from the JVC as soon as possible. . . . If Tianjin agrees to become a sub-licensee of . . . the JVC, the JVC shall grant the necessary sub-license to Tianjin and Tianjin engineers will have the opportunity of taking part in JVC training courses and programmes.

95. The Chinese first offered to lease the sites and building at Hong Kong rates. This was not accepted. According to the March 1980 agreement, the fees to be paid are RMB ¥15 per square metre per year for the sites and 10 percent of the construction cost per year for the new building in Beijing. However, the joint venture has the right to purchase the new building at a price to be negotiated.

96. It is interesting to note that the word "premium" replaces a clause in the first agreement that referred to "a percentage to be negotiated and to reflect the future profitability of the joint venture." If the premium is not to reflect future profitability, then what will it be based on?

97. The precise percentage is not known. In other license agreements that China has signed recently, royalties as low as 2 to 4 percent of turnover have been reported. See *China Business Review*, March-April, 1981, p. 24. It is interesting to note that article 46 of the recently promulgated "Regulations for the Implementation of the Joint Venture Law" states that "payments for technology are generally made in royalties, and the royalty rate shall not be higher than the standard international rate, which shall be calculated on the basis of net sales of the products turned out with the relevant technology or other reasonable means agreed upon by both parties."

98. The manager of a Chinese enterprise that had invented a small automatic processing machine told Peter V. Kwok during his visit to the plant that if he were a representative of a competing Chinese enterprise, rather than a foreign guest, he would not have been taken to the room housing the equipment. See Peter V. Kwok, "Bureaucracy and the Ailing Chinese Management System," n.d., mimeo.

99. Before the revision, the agreement implied that the joint venture would be subject only to the income tax.

100. The first agreement called for arbitration in London under the rules of the International Chamber of Commerce. This was apparently changed because Taiwan is a member of the ICC. For discussions of other minor differences between the original and final agreements, see *Far Eastern Economic Review*, 11 July 1980, pp. 67–69; and *China Trade Report*, August, 1980, pp. 8–9.

101. The Beijing plant was originally a spring factory. Until the construction of the new building in Beijing is completed, China-Schindler's main production facility is its Shanghai plant. Opened in 1954 as an elevator repair shop, it gradually expanded and by 1980, when it became part of the joint venture, it produced not only elevators but also escalators and passenger conveyors. The Shanghai plant moved to its present site in 1972 and now has some 24,000 square metres of factory floor space.

102. The Beijing head office told us that input-output norms are in the process of formulation and that once production becomes more settled, these norms — which will remain unchanged for a period of time — will be used by the plants to determine material needs.

103. For the Shanghai plant this procedure represents a slight change. Before it became part of the joint venture, it received its supply allocations through the local government, presumably one of Shanghai's industrial departments.

104. Before the enterprise became a joint venture, suppliers were designated from above.

105. In Shanghai the basic wage paid to new high school graduates in 1982 was RMB ¥42 per month.

106. The Chinese even approached Schindler to see if they would agree to a different royalty formula but continue to receive the same amount of royalty.

107. On one occasion, Schindler pressed China-Schindler to deliver sixteen crates of parts that were already late by setting an absolute deadline. Sixteen crates arrived in Hong Kong before the deadline, but when workers opened the crates they discovered that they contained the wrong parts.

108. Schindler quickly learned that not only is the Chinese government not monolithic, but that intense rivalries exist among its various departments. The rivalry between CCMC (and its higher authority at the central level) and the municipal government of Tianjin is clearly apparent in the dispute between China-Schindler and Tianjin. Since the formation of China-Schindler adversely affected a number of Chinese enterprises not directly associated with CCMC, the new joint venture caused considerable ill-feelings in some quarters.

109. *China Business Review*, September-October, 1982, p. 57, and September-October, 1983, p. 21. It is also reported that Fujitec Company and the city of Shenyang have reached a basic accord to establish a joint elevator manufacturing plant in Liaoning. See *China Business Review*, January-February, 1983, p. 52.

110. We pursued this matter with MFERT and were told that "the detailed rules will require equal pay for equal work, but it is clear that a foreign technician is more productive than his Chinese counterpart." In other words, the spirit of the rule will not be "equal pay for equal rank."

111. Article 93 of the "Regulations for the Implementation of the Joint Venture Law" (promulgated on 20 September 1983) states that "the salary and bonus systems of joint ventures shall be in accordance with the principle of distribution to each according to his work, and more pay for more work." Thus, it would appear that the rule is not "equal pay for equal rank." But it remains to be seen how the Chinese will interpret the rule.

112. Unless otherwise noted, the information in the following discussion is based on our interviews at the Fujian-Hitachi Television Company, Ltd. in Fuzhou.

113. The Chinese estimate that by importing the components and assembling the television sets themselves they could save about one-fifth of the foreign exchange that they would otherwise spend to import the same number of fully assembled sets. In addition, of course, some of the assembled sets can be exported to earn additional foreign exchange. See *Jingji Daobao* [Economic Reporter], no. 1747, 25 November 1981, p. 19.

114. In mid-1981 the State Council, on the recommendation of the Ministry of Commerce, temporarily suspended all imports of television sets. See JETRO *China Newsletter* 34 (September-October, 1981), pp. 2–3, and no. 36 (January-February, 1982), p. 22.

115. Ibid., p. 24.

16. Ibid., p. 19. This is also what China-Schindler pays for its sites in Beijing and Shanghai, which is

somewhat surprising, since one would think that sites in Beijing or Shanghai would be more valuable than those in Fuzhou.

117. Ibid., p. 24. It was made clear during our discussions with Fujian-Hitachi that the agreement can be extended by mutual consent.

118. We were given the impression that some negotiation is expected if the book value diverges significantly from reality.

119. JETRO *China Newsletter*, no. 36 (January-February, 1982), p. 20.

120. Fujian-Hitachi is one of two television manufacturers in Fujian; the other is a Chinese enterprise. Both are under the Fujian Television Industry Bureau. However, in the case of Fujian-Hitachi, the Bureau plays no management role.

121. Fujian hopes to produce television components in the future and is currently discussing its plans with foreign businessmen (see *Jingji Daobao* [Economic Reporter], 25 November 1981, p. 19). Hitachi is already helping China to build a color tube plant in Shaanxi (see *China Market*, February, 1983, pp. 38–40). Other Japanese firms are also involved in China's electronics industry (see JETRO *China Newsletter* 39 (July-August, 1982), p. 21).

122. Fujian-Hitachi told us that their calculations show that, for every RMB¥100 of take-home pay, the government provides RMB¥104 in direct and indirect subsidies and RMB¥46 in rent subsidies. The State Planning Commission estimates that the average urban resident receives RMB¥164 in subsidies (*Beijing Review*, 25 October 1982, p. 7). In his speech to the China Investment Promotion Meeting in June 1982, the vice-minister of MFERT reported that the payment made by joint ventures and co-operative ventures to the government to cover labor insurance, medical care, and other subsidies provided by the state was about 1.3 times the workers' average take-home pay (*Beijing Review*, 26 July 1982, p. 22).

123. We were told that the average basic wage increased 46 percent after Fujian-Hitachi became a joint venture. This represents an increase of RMB¥25.76 (0.46 × RMB¥56), which means that the average basic take-home wage in 1982 was about RMB¥82.

124. JETRO *China Newsletter*, 36 (January-February, 1982), p. 20.

125. Ibid.

126. The first person to arrive late to work after the rule was announced was the Chinese assistant manager, who was duly fined!

127. These figures are from *Jingji Daobao* [Economic Reporter], 25 November 1981, p. 19. When we visited Fujian-Hitachi in June 1982, we were told that the managerial staff had been reduced from about 150 to 90. "About 150" probably means the same thing as "over 140," but the discrepancy between 70 and 90 seems large. Perhaps 70 was the number of managerial staff in 1981 and 90 the number in 1982.

128. In 1982 the domestic retail prices for Fujian-Hitachi's products were: 12″ black-and-white TV, RMB¥410 (about US$228 at the exchange rate then ruling); basic 14″ color TV, RMB¥1080 (about US$600); and basic 20″ color TV, RMB¥1900 (about US$1055). These very high prices reflect the sheltered nature of the domestic Chinese market and Fujian-Hitachi's position as the sole producer of color television sets in Fujian.

NOTES TO CHAPTER 5

1. Zhao Ziyang, "Report on the Work of the Government," *Beijing Review*, 4 July 1983, pp. vii-xvi; Robert Delfs, "Return to the Centre," *Far Eastern Economic Review*, 23 June 1983, pp. 56–58.

2. Xiao Weixiang, "On the Question of Upgrading the Technology of Light Industry," *Jingji Guanli* [Economic Management], June, 1982, p. 20.

3. Chu Baotai, "What Are Cooperative Ventures?", *China Market*, December, 1982, pp. 53–55.

4. Ibid.

5. JETRO *China Newsletter* 39 (July-August, 1982), pp. 3–5.

6. Chu Baotai, pp. 53–55.

7. Phil Kurata, "Lower Costs Lure China Traders," *Far Eastern Economic Review*, 27 February 1981, pp. 68–72.

8. E. Sabina Brady, "Getting a Shoe in the Door," *China Business Review*, May-June, 1982, p. 41.

9. The executive who provided this information requested that his identity not be revealed.
10. Robert C. Goodwin, Jr., "The Evolving Legal Framework," *China Business Review*, May-June, 1983, p. 46.
11. Certain co-operative ventures are exceptions and are treated like equity joint ventures. See *Guide to Investment in China*, pp. 52–53.
12. Interview notes of 26 May 1982: MFERT, Department of Treaties and Law.
13. Ibid.
14. In mid-1983, the Chinese announced revised rules reducing the withholding tax on non-operating income. See *China Trade Report*, April, 1983, p. 7, and *China Business Review*, July-August, 1983, p. 4.
15. Rules for the Implementation of the Individual Income Tax Law of the People's Republic of China," article 5.
16. Joan Marie Richards, "Protectionism and the ITC," *China Business Review*, September-October, 1982, pp. 28–31.
17. Ibid. As of late summer, 1983, the ITC had ruled that a "margin of dumping" exists in the case of Chinese mushroom exports to the U.S. but had not yet made a determination on the question of injury.
18. Ibid.
19. Alternatively, about 20 percent of total foreign exchange earnings.
20. The discussion in this paragraph is based on Malcolm Subhan, "A Peking-Brussels Hit," *Far Eastern Economic Review*, 9 April 1982, p. 66.
21. Patrick Orr, "Quantitative Restrictions," *University of Toronto Faculty of Law Review* 38 (1980): 52–82.
22. Martin Weil, "The Textiles Deadlock," *China Business Review*, November-December, 1982, pp. 31–35.
23. Ibid., and Vember K. Ranganathan, "China's Textile Exports to the United States," *China-International Business* 1 (1981): 585–603.
24. Ranganathan, pp. 588–93.
25. Ibid., p. 589.
26. Weil, p. 32.
27. Xinhua reported that the American offer was for annual growth of less than 1 percent. See *China Trade Report*, September, 1982, p. 1. Other sources have suggested that the offer was in the 1.5 to 2 percent range. See *Far Eastern Economic Review*, 27 January 1983, p. 62.
28. Interview with Huang Wenjun, *China Trade Report*, November, 1982, pp. 4–5.
29. Ibid., and also Weil, p. 31.
30. *China Trade Report*, September, 1983, p. 1.
31. *Far Eastern Economic Review*, 11 August 1983, pp. 72–73, and 29 September 1983, pp. 118–20.
32. *Far Eastern Economic Review*, 29 September 1983, p. 120.
33. Interview notes of 27 May 1982, Beijing Radio Factory.
34. Peng Shulian, "China's Electronic Industry Readjusts Its Product Structure," *China Market*, August, 1982, pp. 11–13.
35. *China Business Review*, January-February, 1982, p. 20.
36. For an interesting discussion of running royalties vs. lump-sum royalties in the China context, see Karen Berney, "Technology Transfer via Licensing: The Options," *China Business Review*, March-April, 1980, p. 56.
37. Unless otherwise indicated, our discussion of the NIKE case is drawn from interviews with NIKE executives held in August 1982 and March 1983.
38. Scott D. Seligman, "Nike's Running Start," *China Business Review*, January-February, 1982, pp. 42–44.
39. Ibid., p. 42.
40. Interview notes of 17 June 1982: Xiamen Cigarette Factory.
41. State Statistical Bureau, *Statistical Yearbook of China 1981* (Hong Kong: Economic Information and Agency, 1982), p. 234.
42. Ibid. The relevant data are:
    Output of cured tobacco: 1.279 million metric tons (p. 147), Retail sales of cigarettes: 17.50

million cases (p. 341), Value of retail sales: RMB ¥13.559 billion (p. 341), and Purchases of cured tobacco: 1.259 million metric tons, worth RMB ¥2.078 billion (p. 349).
It should be noted that the implied retail price (RMB ¥1.55 per pack) seems implausibly high; our inquiries suggest a retail price of between RMB ¥0.2 and 1.4, depending on quality. However, even if the average retail price is only RMB ¥0.7 or 0.8, the revenue per case is still about RMB ¥350–400, and the general conclusion remains: the state's mark-up accounts for the major part of the retail price.

43. A preliminary agreement to form a joint venture was signed in June 1983, with equity share split between Reynolds Tobacco International (50 percent) and Xiamen Cigarette Factory and Xiamen Construction and Development Co. (50 percent). See *Chinese Business Review*, September-October, 1983, p. 25.

44. Our field notes say that the split was 2,000 cases to Hong Kong and 12,000 cases to domestic outlets, but *China Market*, September, 1982, p. 41, implies the reverse.

45. *China Business Review*, March-April, 1981, p. 28.

46. Edith Terry, "Fujian Province: Decentralizing Foreign Trade," *China Business Review*, September-October, 1980, p. 17.

47. This was the price at the Beijing Friendship Store in early March, 1983. *China Market*, September, 1982, p. 41, implies a price of RMB ¥4, but this must be an error.

48. Interview notes of 17 June 1982: Xiamen Boatyard.

49. *China Trade Report*, June, 1982, p. 12.

50. This information is drawn from correspondence with a major American yacht dealer in February 1983.

51. *Economic Reporter*, August, 1980, p. 11; Steven Hendryx, "How to Build a Yacht in China," *China Business Review*, July-August, 1983, pp 32–35.

52. Interview notes of 30 June 1982: Shenzhen Printing Company.

53. "Provisional Labour and Wage Regulations for Enterprises in the SEZs of Guangdong Province," article 2.

54. *Far Eastern Economic Review*, 24 February 1983, p. 72.

55. Interview notes of 1 July 1982: Happiness Soft Drinks Factory.

56. Interview notes of 1 July 1982: Happy Home Furniture Factory.

57. A short study of this agreement has been published in "Two Aspects of the Experience of Shenzhen's Happy Home Furniture Factory," *Gang-Ao Jingji* [The Economies of Hong Kong and Macao], May, 1982, p. 45. This short article offers a good example of the imprecision with which special trade ventures are categorized. The agreement is referred to both as a processing agreement and as an equity joint venture, and yet it is neither one of these.

58. Ibid.

59. This is not just an abstract possibility. Recently, a Chinese magazine carried an article that criticized Coca-Cola, which is also produced in China, as unhealthy and overpriced. The article went on to say that Chinese Coke drinkers "lose their national pride, succumb to capitalist decadence, and harm China's basic national interests to satisfy the profit motive of foreign financial groups. . . . They willingly fulfill the role of slaves for the foreign sellers. . . This is not only shameful, but criminal." See the Vancouver *Sun*, 17 June 1983, p. 1.

NOTES TO CHAPTER 6

1. A. Doak Barnett, *China's Economy in Global Perspective* (Washington, DC: The Brookings Institution, 1981), p. 459.

2. In 1971, China imported about 353 thousand metric tons of crude oil and petroleum products and exported about 263 thousand. In 1972, the imports were about 382 thousand tons and the exports were about 1,834 thousand. For the import data, see A. Doak Barnett, p. 459. For the exports, see Table 5.3.

3. Norman A. White, et al., *Financing the International Petroleum Industry* (London: Graham and Trotman, Ltd., 1978), p. 20.

4. Selig S. Harrison, *China, Oil, and Asia: Conflict Ahead?* (New York: Columbia University Press, 1977), p. 268.
5. Harrison, *China, Oil, and Asia*, p. 19.
6. Ibid., pp. 20 and 30.
7. Chang Qian, "What Lies Behind the So-Called 'Energy Crisis,' " *Hong Qi* [Red Flag], 1974, no. 2, pp. 83–86.
8. Li Guangan and Wei Liqun, "Energy Is the Key Point in Economic Development Strategy," *Jingji Yanjiu* [Economic Research], November, 1982, p. 10.
9. State Statistical Bureau, *Statistical Yearbook of China 1981* (Hong Kong: Economic Information and Agency, 1982), p. 17.
10. For detailed descriptions of these developments, see Vaclav Smil, "China's Energetics: A System Analysis," in U.S. Congress, Joint Economic Committee, *Chinese Economy Post-Mao* (Washington, DC: Government Printing Office, 1978), pp. 333–38.
11. *Beijing Review*, 20 December 1982, p. 12.
12. *Beijing Review*, 24 January 1983, p. 6. Standard coal is coal of 7,000 kilocalories per kilogram.
13. Li Guangan and Wei Liqun, p. 14.
14. Huang Yuqing and Xiao Zhe, "The Communications and Transportation Sector Must Be Energetically Developed," *Jingji Guanli* [Economic Management], December, 1982, p. 13.
15. Ibid. For a detailed technical discussion of what such a locomotive might look like, see California Institute of Technology, Jet Propulsion Laboratory, *Future Fuels and Engines for Railroad Locomotives*, JPL Publication 81-101, 1 November 1981.
16. *Beijing Review*, 20 December 1982, pp. 11–12. Zhao Ziyang's report does not explicitly state a target growth rate for industry, but it calls for 4 percent for industry and agriculture together, and 4 to 5 percent for agriculture alone, so the target for industry must be slightly less than 4 percent per year. Interestingly, this implied growth rate for industry is almost identical to that projected by Robert Michael Field and Judith A. Flynn on the basis of an energy-constrained simulation model of the Chinese economy. See Robert Michael Field and Judith A. Flynn, "China: An Energy-Constrained Model of Industrial Performance through 1985," in U.S. Congress, Joint Economic Committee, *China under the Four Modernizations* (Washington, DC: Government Printing Office, 1982), part 1, p. 351.
17. *Beijing Review*, 20 December 1982, p. 12.
18. For the relative shares of agriculture and industry in total output value, see *Statistical Yearbook of China 1981*, p. 17. If the growth targets to 1985 are achieved, then a continued growth of agriculture of 4 percent will mean that industry must grow at 9.4 percent per annum after 1985 if the output target for 2000 A.D. is to be achieved. If agriculture grows at 5 percent, the required growth rate for industry drops slightly, to about 9.2 percent a year.
19. *Beijing Review*, 28 February 1983, p. 12.
20. Li Guangan and Wei Liqun, p. 12.
21. *Beijing Review* 20 December 1982, pp. 13–14.
22. Seiichi Nakajima, "The Prospects for Achievement of China's Long-Term Economic Target: An Investment Perspective," JETRO *China Newsletter* 42 (January-February, 1983), p. 19.
23. Ibid.
24. *Beijing Review*, 6 April 1981, p. 7.
25. *Economic Reporter*, August, 1980, p. 16.
26. *Beijing Review*, 19 July 1982, p. 5.
27. Ibid., and *Beijing Review*, 6 December 1982, p. 7.
28. Our discussion of the Gezhouba project is based on the following sources: *Beijing Review*, 31 August 1981, pp. 20–27; *Economic Reporter*, August, 1980, pp. 14–18; Nicholas H. Ludlow, "Gezhouba on the Yangzi," *China Business Review*, May-June, 1980, pp. 11–15; and Martin Weil, "Hydropower," *China Business Review*, July-August, 1982, pp. 9–23.
29. Li Guangan and Wei Liqun, p. 13.
30. Ibid., and Seiichi Nakajima, p. 19.
31. The percentages for Gezhouba and Longyangxia were calculated from data in *Economic Reporter*, August, 1980, p. 15. The percentage for Liujiaxia was calculated from data in Li Guangan and Luo Yuanzheng, "The Energy Constraint and the Open Economic Strategy in China's Moderni-

zation," paper presented at the 12th Pacific Trade and Development Conference, Vancouver, BC, 6–11 September 1981, p. 9.

32. *Beijing Review*, 31 August 1981, p. 25. See also William Clarke, "China's Electric Power Industry," in U.S. Congress, Joint Economic Committee, *Chinese Economy Post-Mao*, vol. 1, p. 417.

33. Nicholas H. Ludlow, "Harnessing the Yangzi," *China Business Review*, May-June, 1980, p. 16.

34. JETRO *China Newsletter* 35 (November-December, 1981): 17.

35. Information on the "728" project is taken from Martin Weil, "The First Nuclear Power Projects," *China Business Review*, September-October, 1982, pp. 40–44. See also *Beijing Review*, 20 December 1982, p. 14.

36. For further background on the Guangdong nuclear project, see *Far Eastern Economic Review*, 10 October 1980, pp. 48–52, 27 August 1982, pp. 41–42, 26 November 1982, pp. 19–20, 20 January 1983, p. 8, and 24 March 1983, p. 8; *Beijing Review*, 4 April 1983, p. 9; *China Trade Report*, January, 1981, p. 6, October, 1982, p. 7, and November, 1982, pp. 1 and 9; JETRO *China Newsletter* 35 (November-December, 1981): 17–18; Dori Jones, "Nuclear Power: Back on the Agenda," *China Business Review*, January-February, 1981, pp. 32–40; and Martin Weil, "The First Nuclear Power Projects," pp. 40–47.

37. The U.S. is reluctant to grant export licenses for nuclear equipment until China permits inspection of its nuclear facilities. In mid-July, 1983, a Chinese delegation arrived in Washington to discuss a nuclear co-operation agreement that will try to resolve this issue so that U.S. companies can sell nuclear technology to China. See *Far Eastern Economic Review*, 19 May 1983, pp. 80–81, and 23 June 1983, p. 11; Vancouver *Sun*, 11 July 1983, p. 1.

38. *Far Eastern Economic Review*, 19 May 1983, p. 80.

39. See, for example, *China Business Review*, May-June, 1980, pp. 21–22, and March-April, 1981, pp. 9–13.

40. *Economic Reporter*, March, 1981, p. 24.

41. Dori Jones, "The Dawning of Coal's 'Second Golden Age,' " *China Business Review*, May-June, 1980, p. 38.

42. *Economic Reporter*, March, 1981, p. 24; and Martin Weil, "Technology Transfers," *China Business Review*, March-April 1981, p. 24.

43. *Beijing Review*, 19 April 1982, p. 5, and 20 October 1982, p. 17.

44. Cao Yalin and Wang Yungyin, "Increasing the Economic Effectiveness of Railway Construction in Our Country," *Jingji Yanjiu* [Economic Research], December, 1982, p. 49.

45. Li Guangan and Wei Liqun, p. 11; and Huang Yuqing and Xiao Zhe, p. 11.

46. Martin Weil, "China's Troubled Coal Sector," *China Business Review*, March-April, 1982, p. 27; and *Beijing Review*, 20 December 1982, p. 13.

47. *Beijing Review*, 11 October 1982, p. 6, and 20 December 1982, p. 13.

48. Li Guangan and Wei Liqun, p. 13.

49. See *China Trade Report*, August, 1976, p. 4.

50. See Dori Jones, "The Dawning of Coal's 'Second Golden Age,' " and Martin Weil, "China's Troubled Coal Sector."

51. Kosaku Matsumoto, "External Elements of China's Economic Policy and Japan's Financial Assistance to China," JETRO *China Newsletter* 42 (January-February, 1983): p. 10.

52. John L. Davie and Dean W. Carver, "China's International Trade and Finance," U.S. Congress, Joint Economic Committee, *China under the Four Modernizations*, part 2, p. 27.

53. On the Long-Term Trade Agreement, see Tadao Iguchi and Hironao Kobayashi, "The Japan-China Long Term Trade Agreement," JETRO *China Newsletter* 16 (January, 1978): 1–18; and Yasuhiro Yamada, "The Long-Term Trade Agreement and the Future of Japan-China Trade," JETRO *China Newsletter* 18 (June, 1978): 1–24.

54. Kosaku Matsumoto, p. 10.

55. Kenji Hattori, "Sino-Japanese Coal Cooperation," JETRO *China Newsletter* 36 (January-February, 1982): 5.

56. Kosaku Matsumoto, p. 11; and *Beijing Review*, 21 January 1980, p. 8.

57. JETRO *China Newsletter* 35 (November-December, 1981): p. 5, and Kosaku Matsumoto, pp. 10–12.

58. Kosaku Matsumoto, p. 13.

59. Martin Weil, "China's Troubled Coal Sector," p. 30.
60. Kenji Hattori, p. 15.
61. John M. Pisani, "The Big Seven," *China Business Review*, January-February, 1983, p. 18.
62. Our discussion of Pingshuo is based on the following sources: Dori Jones, "The Dawning of Coal's 'Second Golden Age,' " p. 40; Martin Weil, "China's Troubled Coal Sector," pp. 31–32; *Beijing Review*, 5 April 1982, p. 10; "Occidental Signs Big Coal Mining Pact with China," *The Asian Wall Street Journal Weekly*, 14 March 1983, p. 23; "Occidental's Giant China Mine Project Hits Snag as World Coal Price Plummets," *Wall Street Journal*, 10 August 1983, p. 29; and interviews with Ministry of Coal personnel in Beijing (May, 1982) and in Vancouver (November, 1983).
63. "Occidental's Giant China Mine Project Hits Snag as World Coal Price Plummets," p. 29.
64. Ibid.
65. Information on the Zhangji project is drawn from *China Trade Report*, December, 1982, p. 14; *Coal Asia* (23 June 1982): 1; and our interviews at the Minister of Coal, 29 May 1982. The data provided in *China Trade Report* must be treated with caution: they have apparently all been adjusted by a factor of 0.9, in the mistaken belief that the Chinese data are in standard tons, when in fact they are already expressed in metric tons.
66. *Economic Reporter*, March, 1981, pp. 22–26, June, 1981, pp. 23–26, October, 1981, pp. 10–13; *China Market*, July, 1982, p. 55; *China Market*, May 1983, pp. 75–76.
67. Martin Weil, "China's Troubled Coal Sector," p. 32.
68. Kenji Hattori, p. 11.
69. Various reports indicate that there may be Romanian involvement in a mine in Shanxi, British involvement in Shandong, and American involvement in Inner Mongolia. See *China Trade Report*, April, 1983, p. 1, and October, 1983, pp. 3 and 12; *Beijing Review*, 12 September 1983, pp. 14–16; *China Reconstructs*, August, 1983, p. 35.
70. *Statistical Yearbook of China 1981*, p. 383.
71. For outside estimates of China's coal markets, especially in Japan, see Masahiko Ebashi, "The Future of China's Foreign Trade," JETRO *China Newsletter* 22 (July, 1979): 23–24; *China Trade Report*, April, 1982, p. 5; and *Coal Asia* 2 (23 June 1982): 1–3.
72. John M. Pisani, pp. 16–22.
73. *Beijing Review*, 27 December 1982, pp. 4–5.
74. *Coal Asia* 2 (23 June 1982): 3.
75. *China Business Review*, May-June, 1980, p. 45; and Henri Hymans and Michael McAbee, "Energy Diplomacy Threatens Japan's Bid for US Coal," *Petroleum News*, March, 1982, p. 10.
76. Ibid., p. 11.
77. See the discussion in Kenji Hattori, pp. 11–14.
78. Interview notes of 29 May 1982: Ministry of Coal.
79. Vancouver *Province*, 13 March 1983, p. E1; Vancouver *Sun*, 19 March 1983, p. C1.
80. *Statistical Yearbook of China 1981*, p. 427.
81. For the history of these negotiations, see Tadao Iguchi and Hironao Kobayashi, and also Yasuhiro Yamada.
82. Tadao Iguchi and Hironao Kobayashi, p. 7.
83. *China Trade Report*, May, 1980, p. 3; and *China Business Review*, November-December, 1980, p. 24.
84. *Far Eastern Economic Review*, 7 April 1983, p. 62.
85. *Beijing Review*, 20 December 1982, p. 13, and 23 May 1983, p. xiii.
86. According to the Ministry of Petroleum Industry, the pattern of production in 1980 was:
    Daqing — 51.5 million metric tons (48.6 percent)
    Shengli — 17.6 million metric tons (16.6 percent)
    Renqiu — 16.0 million metric tons (15.1 percent).
    See Kim Woodard, "China and Offshore Energy," *Problems of Communism*, November-December, 1981, p. 37. The pattern in 1981 was reported to be:
    Daqing — 51.75 million metric tons
    Shengli — about 20 million metric tons
    Renqiu — 11.1 million metric tons
    See Adi Ignatius, "Renqiu — Output Down but Stable," *Petroleum News*, May, 1982, p. 17.

87. Woodard, "China and Offshore Energy," p. 36; *Far Eastern Economic Review*, 10 October 1980, p. 64.
88. *Beijing Review*, 23 May 1983, pp. xiii–xiv.
89. *China Market*, March, 1983, p. 52, and May, 1983, p. 60.
90. "Onshore Cooperation with the Chinese," *Petroleum News*, May, 1982, p. 18; Dori Jones, "Enticing Foreigners Inland," *China Business Review*, September-October, 1980, p. 51.
91. "Onshore Cooperation with the Chinese," p. 18; Dori Jones, "Enticing Foreigners Inland," p. 51; and *Far Eastern Economic Review*, 28 May 1982, p. 8. For an unvarnished description of the serious problems encountered in the Qaidam basin, see *China Trade Report*, February 1983, pp. 1 and 6.
92. *China Business Review*, November-December, 1981, p. 25.
93. *Beijing Review*, 11 April 1983, pp. 6–7.
94. Kim Woodard, *The International Energy Relations of China* (Stanford: Stanford University Press, 1980), p. 153; and *Far Eastern Economic Review*, 7 August 1981, p. 26.
95. Harrison, *China, Oil and Asia*, p. 46.
96. Kim Woodard, *The International Energy Relations of China*, p. 153.
97. Ibid., pp. 156–66.
98. Ibid., pp. 167 and 195–97.
99. Ibid., pp. 149 and 169.
100. Tatsu Kambara, "Foreign Participation in the Bohai," *Petroleum News*, December, 1981, p. 16.
101. Kim Woodard, *The International Energy Relations of China*, p. 204. For the suggestion that the "Bohai I" may not have been completed until *after* the "Bohai II" was imported, see Harrison, *China, Oil and Asia*, pp. 64–67.
102. Richard Breeze, "Safety First in Industry," *Far Eastern Economic Review*, 10 October 1980, p. 61.
103. Kim Woodard, *The International Energy Relations of China*, p. 200.
104. Ibid., p. 203.
105. Vaclav Smil, "China's Energetics: A System Analysis," in U.S. Congress, Joint Economic Committee, *Chinese Economy Post-Mao*, vol. 1, p. 346; *China Trade Report*, June, 1978, p. 3.
106. The Institute of Petroleum, *A Guide to North Sea Oil and Gas Technology* (London: Heyden and Son, Ltd., 1978), pp. 49–50.
107. Tatsu Kambara, "Foreign Participation in the Bohai," pp. 16–17.
108. Kim Woodard, *The International Energy Relations of China*, p. 218.
109. Kim Woodard, "China and Offshore Energy," p. 38.
110. Ibid.; Tatsu Kambara, "Foreign Participation in the Bohai," p. 16; and *Far Eastern Economic Review* 6 March 1981, p. 41.
111. *China Trade Report*, October, 1980, p. 5.
112. Dori Jones, "China's Offshore Oil Development," *China Business Review*, July-August, 1980, p. 52; Kim Woodard, "The Drilling Begins," *China Business Review*, May-June, 1983, pp. 18–19; *Petroleum News*, January, 1982, p. 14; *Ta Kung Pao*, 24 July 1980, pp. 4–6.
113. Dori Jones, "China's Expanding Offshore Oil Fleet," *China Business Review*, November-December, 1980, p. 51.
114. For discussion of the Bohai contract terms, see Tatsu Kambara, "Foreign Participation in the Bohai," pp. 16–17; "Background on Recent Sino-Japanese Oil Strike," JETRO *China Newsletter* 32 (May-June, 1981), pp. 26–27; Dori Jones, "China's Offshore Oil Development," pp. 52–53; and *Petroleum News*, January, 1982, pp. 12–14.
115. *Far Eastern Economic Review*, 22 October 1982, pp. 70–72.
116. JETRO *China Newsletter* 32 (May-June, 1981); 27.
117. Kim Woodard, "The Drilling Begins," p. 18; *Far Eastern Economic Review*, 22 October 1982, p. 70; and *Beijing Review*, 7 March 1983, pp. 8–9.
118. *China Market*, April, 1983, p. 71.
119. For detailed discussions, see Harrison, *China, Oil, and Asia*; Kim Woodard and Alice A. Davenport, "The Security Dimensions of China's Offshore Oil Development," *Journal of Northeast Asian Studies* 1 (September, 1982): 3–26; and Choon-Ho Park, "Joint Development of Mineral Resources in Disputed Waters: The Case of Japan and South Korea in the East China Sea," and Masahiro Miyoshi, "Some Comments on Legal Aspects of Precedents for Joint

Development," both in Mark J. Valencia, ed., *The South China Sea: Hydrocarbon Potential and Possibilities of Joint Development* (Oxford, New York, Toronto, Sydney, Paris, Frankfurt: Pergamon Press, 1981).

120. Woodard, "China and Offshore Energy," p. 44.
121. Harrison, *China, Oil, and Asia*, pp. 67–68; and Woodard and Davenport, "The Security Dimensions of China's Offshore Oil Development," p. 12.
122. *Petroleum News*, January, 1982, p. 14; and Woodard and Davenport, "The Security Dimensions of China's Offshore Oil Development," p. 12.
123. Selig S. Harrison, "Conflicting Offshore Boundary Claims," *China Business Review*, May-June, 1983, p. 51.
124. Woodard and Davenport, "The Security Dimensions of China's Offshore Oil Development," pp. 6–7.
125. For further discussions, see Harrison, *China, Oil and Asia*; Woodard and Davenport, "The Security Dimensions of China's Offshore Oil Development;" Sheila Ocampo-Kalfors, "Easing Towards Conflict," *Far Eastern Economic Review*, 28 April 1983, pp. 38–39; K. Das, "Perched on a Claim," *Far Eastern Economic Review*, 29 September 1983, p. 40.
126. *Petroleum News*, January, 1982, pp. 20–22.
127. Harrison, *China, Oil, and Asia*, pp. 208–12.
128. Woodard, *The International Energy Relations of China*, pp. 160–61.
129. *China Trade Report*, November, 1977, p. 4.
130. *China Trade Report*, June, 1978, p. 3.
131. Woodard, *The International Energy Relations of China*, pp. 201–2.
132. *China Trade Report*, January, 1980, p. 2.
133. Woodard, "The Drilling Begins," p. 19.
134. Woodard, "China and Offshore Energy," p. 40.
135. *Petroleum News*, March, 1982, p. 1.
136. Stephanie Green, "Offshore Business," *China Business Review*, May-June, 1982, p. 17.
137. Woodard, "The Drilling Begins," p. 18.
138. *Far Eastern Economic Review*, 11 June 1982, p. 26.
139. *Vancouver Sun*, 10 May 1983, p. C5.
140. For details, see *Wall Street Journal*, 8 August 1983, p. 2; *Globe and Mail*, 24 August 1983, p. B3; *Beijing Review*, 15 August 1983, p. 9, and 5 September 1983, p. 9; *China Daily*, 7 September 1983, p. 1; and *Far Eastern Economic Review*, 1 September 1983, p. 8, and 6 October 1983, p. 68.
141. Woodard, "China and Offshore Energy," p. 42; Woodard, "The Drilling Begins," p. 19; and *China Trade Report*, October, 1982, p. 3.
142. *China Business Review*, November-December, 1981, p. 24.
143. *China Market*, August, 1982, p. 7.
144. Kevin Fountain, "The Development of China's Offshore Oil," *China Business Review*, January-February, 1980, pp. 23–35; and Kim Woodard and Robert C. Goodwin, Jr., "Supplying Offshore Services," *China Business Review*, March-April, 1982, pp. 8–19.
145. JETRO *China Newsletter* 42 (January-February, 1983): p. 18.
146. Reported by Michel Halbouty after discussions with Tang Ke, *Business Standard* (Hong Kong), 22 May 1982, p. 1.
147. Woodard and Goodwin, "Supplying Offshore Services," p. 11; and *Petroleum News*, March, 1982, p. 22.
148. Woodard, "China and Offshore Energy," p. 32, suggests that an investment of about $20 billion is required for each 100 million tons of output per year, plus an equal amount for infrastructure. Fountain, "The Development of China's Offshore Oil," p. 34, suggests a total figure of $45 to 60 billion for a capacity of 100 million tons a year.
149. Chris Brown, "Tough Terms for Offshore Oil," *China Business Review*, July-August, 1982, p. 35.
150. For discussions of "dual-use" technology, see Harrison, *China, Oil, and Asia*, pp. 74–82; and John W. DePauw, "Overcoming Hindrances and Impediments in United States-Chinese Commercial Negotiations: The Experience of the Control Data Corporation," U.S. Congress, Joint Economic Committee, *China under the Four Modernizations*, part 2, pp. 345–67.

151. One Chinese trade official is quoted as saying, "We've heard all the good news, but we don't see any changes" (*China Trade Report*, August, 1982, p. 11).
152. *Newsweek*, 5 September 1983, p. 13.
153. For further details of the model contract, see Stephanie R. Green, "Offshore Business," pp. 17–19; Chris Brown, "Tough Terms for Offshore Oil," pp. 34–37; and the series of articles in *China Business Review*, May-June, 1983, pp. 18–53. See also the texts of the relevant laws and regulations. Our discussion is also based on confidential conversations with some of the participating oil companies.
154. Woodard, "The Drilling Begins," pp. 22–25.
155. The West Scotland Branch of the Institute of Petroleum and the Norwegian Petroleum Society, *North Sea Development: Experiences and Challenges* (London: Heyden and Son, 1979), p. xliii.
156. *Beijing Review*, 28 February 1983, p. 12.
157. Sun Shangqing, "The Structure of Energy," in Ma Hong and Sun Shangqing, eds., *Zhongguo Jingji Jiegou Wenti Yanjiu* [Research on Questions Concerning China's Economic Structure] (Beijing: People's Publishing House, 1980), vol. 1, p. 274.
158. Ibid.
159. These conversion factors are taken from *Statistical Yearbook of China 1981*, p. 232.
160. *Beijing Review*, 11 April 1983, p. 7.
161. *Beijing Review*, 7 February 1983, p. 15.

NOTES TO CHAPTER 7

1. For a more detailed discussion, see Yasuhiro Yamada, "China's Foreign Financial Position," JETRO *China Newsletter* 35 (November-December, 1981): 2–12.
2. However, about $6 billion of this amount was in short-term (six-month) loans, which should perhaps be removed from the total.
3. *China Trade Report*, April, 1982, p. 3.
4. *Beijing Review*, 6 June 1983, p. 4.
5. *Newsweek*, 6 June 1983, p. 81.
6. Ibid.
7. "The National Council Meets with Vice Premier Deng Xiaoping," *China Business Review*, July-August, 1979, p. 14.
8. Political risk is used here in the usual manner, meaning "the probability of occurrence of some political event(s) that will change the prospects for the profitability of a given investment." See Stefan H. Robock, "Political Risk: Identification and Assessment," *Columbia Journal of World Business* 6 (July-August, 1971): 7.
9. When one equity joint venture claimed a tax holiday for its first-year profits under the Joint Venture Income Tax Law, its claim was disallowed. The local tax authorities argued that tax exemption is permissible only when the profit is the result of technology transferred from the foreign partner to the joint venture, and since the technology in question had not yet been transferred, the joint venture did not qualify for the tax holiday. The foreign investor challenged this interpretation and received a favorable ruling from the central authorities. See Jerome A. Cohen, "Equity Joint Ventures," *China Business Review*, November-December, 1982, p. 30.
10. Another serious systemic problem is low labor productivity and poor management that derives from lack of motivation.
11. For example, when Schindler was considering its investment in China, it had only a very vague idea of the size of China's elevator industry.
12. For an illuminating discussion of the negotiating practices used by the Chinese, see Lucian Pye, *Chinese Commercial Negotiating Style* (Santa Monica: Rand Corporation, 1982).
13. In Shanghai we were told of one case in which the foreign businessman had to visit the city thirteen times before an agreement was reached. Needless to say, the Chinese appreciated his patience. In general, equity joint ventures (the most complicated form of special trade) have usually involved about two years of negotiations.
14. Interview notes of 25 June 1982: Guangdong Committee for Foreign Economic Work.
15. Quoted in the *China Business Review*, July-August, 1983, p. 4.

16. *Beijing Review*, 9 May 1983, p. 7, and 3 October 1983, pp. 4–5.
17. The changes include: 1) All machinery, equipment, parts, and construction materials (instead of only "advanced" and "when the product cannot be purchased in China") imported as part of the foreign participants' investment or with funds from the total initial investment (the registered capital of the joint venture) are exempted from import duties and the CICT. 2) Previously joint ventures may apply to the Ministry of Finance for the exemption of import duties and the CICT on imported capital goods and on imported materials, components and parts used in the production of export goods. Now these exemptions are no longer at the discretion of the Ministry of Finance but are automatic. (See "Regulations for the Implementation of the Joint Venture Law," article 71 and MFERT, "Questions and Answers," pp. 6–7.) Even though the new rules do not provide a great deal of new incentives, they do eliminate the need for joint ventures to negotiate the exemptions, and thus they reduce the transaction costs of doing business in China.
18. "Regulations for the Implementation of the Joint Venture Law" article 72.
19. Ibid., article 65.
20. Ibid., article 79. Also see "Rules for the Implementation of Exchange Control Regulations," article 15.
21. *Beijing Review*, 3 October, 1983, p. 4.
22. "Regulations for the Implementation of the Joint Venture Law," article 75.
23. Thirty-one joint venture agreements were either signed or approved during the first nine months of 1983 (see Table 3.2). However, much of this activity was not in response to the announced changes in the rules governing joint ventures in China. Rather, it was in response to the signing of offshore oil exploration contracts in 1982–83 (fourteen of the thirty-one joint venture contracts signed in 1983 involved activities related to offshore oil exploration).
24. C.I.A., *China: International Trade, Fourth Quarter, 1982*, June, 1983, Table 5.
25. Damian T. Gullo, "China's Hard Currency Export Potential and Import Capacity Through 1985," in U.S. Joint Economic Committee, *China under The Four Modernizations*, part 2 (Washington, DC: U.S. Government Printing Office, 1982), pp. 89–90.
26. Indeed, in part because of rising protectionism, the growth of Chinese exports (in US$) to the United States declined from more than 30 percent in 1980 to 14 percent in 1981 and less than 4 percent in 1982. The US$ value of Chinese exports to Western Europe, where protectionism is particularly strong, declined absolutely in 1981 and again in 1982.
27. *China Business Review*, January-February, 1983, p. 49.
28. Ibid. There are U.S. government estimates, but they agree with what the Chinese have said. Based on preliminary statistics released by MFERT, China's foreign exchange reserves in September 1982 amounted to about US$9.23 billion. See *Beijing Review*, 6 June 1983, p. 4.
29. See, for example, *China Trade Report*, October, 1983, p. 4.
30. Interview with Wei Yuming, *Far Eastern Economic Review*, 25 December 1981, p. 47.
31. *Beijing Review*, 7 February 1983, p. 14.
32. Ji Chongwei, "China's Utilization of Foreign Funds and Relevant Policies," *Beijing Review*, 20 April 1981, p. 15.
33. "The 6th Five-Year Plan (1981-85) of the People's Republic of China for Economic and Social Development (Excerpts)," *Beijing Review*, 23 May and 30 May 1983.
34. China estimates that its exports (presumably in constant prices) will reach RMB ¥40.2 billion in 1985, with an average annual growth rate of 8.1 percent. This implies that total export earnings in constant prices between 1981 and 1985 will amount to RMB ¥183.1 billion. Total foreign exchange earnings, including invisibles, will be about 15 percent more, or about RMB ¥210 billion. Over the same period, China expects its repayments of foreign loans, principal and interest together, to be about RMB ¥24.3 billion, suggesting a debt-service ratio of about 11 or 12 percent.
35. *Beijing Review*, 20 December 1982, and 23 May and 30 May 1983.
36. Ibid.
37. In his report on the Sixth Five-Year Plan, Zhao Ziyang also gave special emphasis to these three areas.
38. *Beijing Review*, 23 May and 30 May 1983.
39. The State Economic Commission reported that, in the first half of 1982, "foreign investments" pledged amounted to only US$100 million, or about 6.5 percent of the value of foreign funds pledged in 1981. See *China Business Review*, November-December, 1982, p. 4.

40. For the background to the current controversy over the legal status of Hong Kong, see Anthony Dicks, "Treaty, Grant, Usage or Sufferance? Some Legal Aspects of the Status of Hong Kong," *China Quarterly* 95, September, 1983, pp. 427–55.
41. Reportedly, MacLehose asked the Chinese whether it would be possible to renegotiate the lease on the New Territories but was rebuffed (*Far Eastern Economic Review*, 20 January 1983, p. 27).
42. *Far Eastern Economic Review*, 1 October 1982, p. 10.
43. As expressed in 1972 by Huang Hua, then China's permanent representative to the United Nations, and quoted in *Beijing Review*, 23 August 1982, p. 18.
44. Derek Davies and Mary Lee, "The Future Starts Here," *Far Eastern Economic Review*, 7 July 1983, p. 10; Derek Davies, "Traveller's Tales," *Far Eastern Economic Review*, 14 July 1983, p. 31, and Mary Lee, "1997 and All That," *Far Eastern Economic Review*, 6 October 1983, p. 73.
45. *Beijing Review*, 11 July 1983, p. 9.
46. *Far Eastern Economic Review*, 20 January 1983, pp. 30–31.
47. This is strongly suggested by comments Chinese leaders have made. For example, Deng Xiaoping is reported to have told Hong Kong's delegates to the Chinese People's Political Consultative Conference in June 1983 that "it is possible that the negotiations will not begin with 'regaining sovereignty' but with the second question, that is, what shall we do after 1997?" (*Far Eastern Economic Review*, 18 August 1983, p. 12.) In his interview with a group of Japanese reporters on 15 August 1983, Hu Yaobang also stated that "the talks we are having with the British side are concerned with the question of how to maintain Hong Kong's prosperity after 1997 as well as the problem of how to proceed during the transitional period from now until 1997" (*Far Eastern Economic Review*, 25 August 1983, p. 14).
48. *Far Eastern Economic Review*, 18 August 1983, p. 12, and 6 October 1983, p. 73.
49. For example, see Jin Fu, "China's Recovery of Xianggang (Hong Kong) Area Fully Accords with International Law," *Beijing Review*, 26 September 1983, pp. 16–18.
50. *Far Eastern Economic Review*, 25 August 1983, p. 14.
51. The students were representatives of the Hong Kong Federation of Students in Beijing to discuss the Hong Kong issue with Chinese officials. The ten-point guideline was subsequently published in Hong Kong on 2 August 1983 as a part of the statement issued by the Hong Kong Federation of Students. The ten points, as reported in the *Far Eastern Economic Review* (19 August 1983, p. 14), are:
    1. Apart from defence and diplomatic issues, China will not interfere in Hong Kong's internal affairs, which are the responsibility of the local administration.
    2. Beijing will not send representatives to Hong Kong. Under certain conditions, it would be best if Hong Kong residents elected the future mayor or chief administrator, who would be approved by the central government. The approval is subject only to one condition — that the person is a patriot (that is, a supporter of China's reunification) who has prestige and public support but who does not have to be pro-Beijing. . . .
    3. Hong Kong's legal system can be retained and the territory will have its own legislative powers. The territory's legislative structure can be negotiated, and as long as its highest court of appeal is within Hong Kong, it can have its own independent legal system. China's legal system cannot be applied to Hong Kong and vice versa.
    4. Hong Kong's way of life will not change.
    5. The people of Hong Kong can keep their freedoms — of the press, speech, assembly, movement and others.
    6. Activities of Kuomintang followers, Trotskyites and others will not be restricted unless they engage in sabotage.
    7. Internal security will be the responsibility of the local administration and the existing Hong Kong police.
    8. Hong Kong's capitalist system, free port and financial-centre status will be maintained. . . .
    9. While diplomatic issues will be handled by Beijing, Hong Kong will have a great deal of power to deal with its own foreign affairs in economic and cultural matters and other international activities. The local authority can also issue its own travel documents.
    10. Social reforms will not be imposed by Beijing but will be carried out when there is general consensus among local residents from all walks of life.

According to the press, the above outline is based on draft regulations for the Hong Kong SAR.

52. The statement by Liao Zhengzhi that "unhealthy speculation [in property] will be stopped" and articles in Chinese newspapers, including *Renmin Ribao* [People's Daily], about the need for class struggle against the bourgeoisie in Hong Kong (subsequently retracted) have not added credibility to China's reassurances that the status quo in Hong Kong will be maintained.

53. According to the *Far Eastern Economic Review*, 17 March 1983, p. 43, applications to leave Hong Kong in January and February of 1983 were running at three times normal levels.

54. *Far Eastern Economic Review*, 6 October 1983, p. 114. This came only ten days after the prime rate was raised by 1.5 points in an earlier attempt to strengthen the HK dollar. It is unclear at this time how much of the currency weakness is owing to capital outflow and how much to the switching of deposits in HK dollar to that in foreign currency.

55. *New York Times*, 16 October 1983, p. 17.

56. A joint statement described the fifth round of talks as being "useful and constructive," a phrase that was not used in the communiqué after the third or the fourth round of talks.

57. *Beijing Review*, 20 December, 1982, pp. 24–26.

58. The most recent warnings reported in the Western press are those voiced by Zhao Ziyang and Yao Yilin in their speeches to the Sixth NPC in June 1983.

59. Appropriate technology is usually discussed, as it is here, in terms of factor proportions and the technological and economic environment of the recipient country. However, Francis Stewart, among others, has stressed that

> the question of whether or not an "efficient" alternative technology exists is closely tied up with the whole strategy of development, and can only be assessed within the context of a particular strategy.

See Francis Stewart, *Technology and Underdevelopment* (Boulder, CO: Westview Press, 1977), p. 109. In other words, what is appropriate for a country committed to an export-oriented strategy may be inappropriate for one that has adopted a basic-needs approach to development. Thus the issue is more complex than suggested in the text. As one Western economist has written:

> Since the use of any particular technology is not an end in itself, the criteria of appropriateness for the choice of technology must be found in the goals of development. These goals are concerned not only with the volumes of output and income generated by an economy but also with the way they are produced and distributed among the population; they include, as well, particular patterns of national political change and national independence.

See Richard S. Eckaus, *Appropriate Technologies for Developing Countries* (Washington, DC.: National Academy of Sciences, 1977), p. 10.

60. David Morawetz, "Employment Implications of Industrialization in Developing Countries," *Economic Journal* 84 (September, 1974): 491–542; Howard Pack, "Technology and Employment: Constraints on Optimal Performance," in Samuel M. Rosenblatt, ed., *Technology and Economic Development: A Realistic Perspective* (Boulder, CO.: Westview Press, 1979), pp. 59–86; David J. C. Forsyth, Norman S. McBain, and Robert F. Solomon, "Technical Rigidity and Appropriate Technology in Less Developed Countries," *World Development* 8 (1980): 371–98; and Lawrence J. White, "The Evidence on Appropriate Factor Proportions in Manufacturing in Less Developed Countries: A Survey," *Economic Development and Cultural Change* 17 (October, 1978): 27–59.

61. Chen Huiqin, "The Orientation of Technology Transfer Must Be Changed," *Jingji Guanli* [Economic Management], April, 1981, p. 25.

62. Of course, not all of these pressures come from the Chinese side. The quest for higher profits may push the foreign suppliers to offer technology in a "big and complete" package. The reason for preferring a big sale to a small one is too obvious to require elaboration — so obvious, in fact, that the Chinese are presumably fully alert to the danger. But the foreigner's reasons for preferring a complete package to a partial one are more complex. In the purest (least packaged) case, technology is sold in disembodied form, simply as engineering information. But in other cases the seller may offer only a package deal, including hardware, engineering consultation, marketing services, financial assistance, supply of intermediate inputs, or a variety of other features. In the extreme case, the technology may be offered only in fully packaged form — that is, as a wholly owned subsidiary of the foreign firm. If packaging allows the seller to perform tasks or supply goods that could be obtained at lower cost from alternative sources, either domestic or foreign, then packaging raises the cost and increases the foreign exchange burden of technology transfer. On the

other hand, de-packaging, even when it is technically feasible, may cause delays, undermine product quality, limit access to favorable financing, hamper the training of local personnel, or create other problems, and thus it may represent utterly false economy. Each case must be judged on its own merits.

63. Gustav Ranis, "Appropriate Technology: Obstacles and Opportunities," p. 31.
64. *Beijing Review*, 27 April 1979, p. 16.
65. A simple numerical example may help to clarify this point. Imagine a project that costs $1,000,000 to build and then produces an output worth $600,000 annually. Suppose further that the annual payments for wages, fuel, raw materials, and similar non-capital costs are $350,000, so the net earnings each year are $250,000. Such a project is said to have a payback period of four years, because the net earnings in four years will just equal the original investment. If such a project can be built instantaneously and if it lasts forever, then the true rate of return to the investment is 25 percent. Because of these numerical relationships, it is quite common to see the inverse of the payback period used as a proxy for the rate of return. That is, a project with a payback period of four years is treated as if its rate of return were 25 percent, a project with a payback period of ten years is treated as if its rate of return were 10 percent, and so on. In the real world, however, projects have substantial gestation periods and finite lifespans, and these two factors can affect the rate of return significantly. Suppose, for example, that the hypothetical million-dollar project takes five years to build. Although its payback period is still four years, its actual rate of return drops to about 13.4 percent. Or alternatively, suppose that the project can be built instantly, as previously assumed, but that its useful lifespan is only eight years. Again, its payback period remains unchanged at four years, but its true rate of return is only about 18.6 percent. If the two adverse factors (a five-year construction period and an eight-year production period) are combined, the rate of return plummets to about 7.7 percent. Yet the payback period is still four years.

The arithmetic lying behind these results is just the arithmetic of compound interest and is certainly not unknown in China. For example, an article by Hua Menglin entitled "The Time Factor in the Appraisal of Economic Effectiveness," which appeared in *Jingji Guanli* in April, 1981, spells out the mathematics of compound interest quite clearly. However, the payback period continues to be widely used in China as a proxy for the rate of return, even by sophisticated technical personnel, so it is evident that the practical implications of the mathematics have not yet been fully absorbed.

66. For example, the fact that the steel mill at Wuhan had to limp along far below its planned capacity because the planners failed to anticipate the need for electricity correctly is certainly a legitimate grounds for criticism. But this was a failing of the planning apparatus, not of the steel mill project. To show that the mill itself was an unwise investment, the critics would have to demonstrate that the project's rate of return would be unsatisfactory even under more favorable conditions.

67. Sun Yefang's experience is a case in point. See "Socialist Construction and Class Struggle in the Field of Economics: Critique of Sun Yeh-fang's Revisionist Economic Theory," *Beijing Review*, 17 April 1970, pp. 6–12; He Jianzhang, "Sun Yefang, Indomitable Economist," *China Reconstructs*, June, 1980, pp. 13–15; and Cyril Chihren Lin, "The Reinstatement of Economics in China Today," *China Quarterly* 85 (March, 1981): 1–48.

68. An interesting and seemingly intractable example of this difficulty, which was mentioned to us several times during our discussions in China, is the problem of deciding how much to invest in cigarette factories. By comparison to most other commodities, cigarettes have been priced well above the cost of production, because Chinese tax authorities — like their Western counterparts — are well aware of the fiscal implications of an inelastic demand curve. Because of this wide gap between revenues and costs, the apparent rate of return to investment in a cigarette factory is very high. But the factory's revenue picture does not reflect the health costs imposed on the economy as a whole. Therefore, emphasizing the apparent rate of return will lead to overinvestment in this industry. However, the health costs are hard to measure, the state's fiscal appetite is never likely to be satiated, and the decision-makers themselves may well be chain-smokers. Under the circumstances it seems safe to predict that cigarette production in China will continue to expand, regardless of the true rate of return.

69. Liu Guoguang and Zhao Renwei, "On the Relationship between Planning and the Market in a Socialist Economy," *Jingji Yanjiu* [Economic Research], May, 1979, p. 46.

70. See, for example, Xue Muqiao, *China's Socialist Economy* (Beijing: Foreign Languages Press, 1981), pp. 135 and 140.

71. The topic of shadow prices is by no means a new one in the context of a planned, socialist economy. The Russian mathematician L. V. Kantorovich did his seminal work on this subject in the 1930s, although a full exposition of his ideas (the book *Economic Calculation of the Optimal Utilization of Resources*) was not published by the Soviet Academy of Sciences until after Stalin's death.

72. For example, in the petrochemical sector input prices are so low and product prices so high that any proposed petrochemical project displays an artificially attractive rate of return when the calculations are done in domestic prices. Consequently, project evaluations for this sector are now done using the world market price as a shadow price for oil. Of course, calculations of this sort require that the world oil price (a dollar price) be converted to RMB ¥, which brings us to a second example of the use of shadow prices. Although the official exchange rate has recently ranged between RMB ¥1.7 and RMB ¥2.0 per U.S. dollar, the petrochemical project evaluations are done at a shadow exchange rate of RMB ¥2.8 per dollar (the internal settlement rate used by the Bank of China in converting the foreign exchange earnings of exporting enterprises). It is difficult to judge how familiar Chinese planners and economists are with the concept of a shadow price. Certainly, at least a few economists in China were aware of Soviet work in this area as early as the 1950s. The change of atmosphere since the Third Plenum has meant that the interchange of methodological ideas with international agencies such as the World Bank has been quite vigorous since about 1978. We suspect, however, that Chinese economists at the local level may still find the concept of a shadow price relatively new and unfamiliar. An elementary article on the subject appeared in *Jingji Yanjiu* only in 1982. See Zhang Shouyi and Liu Shucheng, "The Essence of Shadow Prices," *Jingji Yanjiu* [Economic Research], September, 1982, pp. 40–47.

73. The insistence of some joint ventures to interpret the rule of "equal pay for equal work (result)" to mean that Chinese technicians and staff must be paid the same wage as foreign technicians and staff of equal rank also discourages the participation of foreign technicians and managers on a regular basis in joint ventures.

74. Until recently, Chinese enterprises did not retain any of their depreciation funds.

75. For an illuminating further discussion, see Bruce L. Reynolds, "Reform in Chinese Industrial Management: An Empirical Report," in U.S. Congress, Joint Economic Committee, *China under the Four Modernizations*, Part 1, pp. 119–37.

76. Oskar Lange, *On the Economic Theory of Socialism*, edited and with an Introduction by Benjamin E. Lippincott (Minneapolis: University of Minnesota Press, 1938; reprinted New York, Toronto, and London: McGraw-Hill, 1964).

77. *Far Eastern Economic Review*, 28 April 1983, p. 41.

78. Xue Muqiao, *China's Socialist Economy*, pp. 69 and 100.

79. *Far Eastern Economic Review*, 28 April 1983, p. 44.

80. This dilemma is not unique to China, of course. The Soviet Union and the countries of Eastern Europe have faced the same basic dilemma and have responded to it with many different institutional arrangements. For discussions of the Soviet and the Eastern European reforms, see Michael Ellman, *Planning Problems in the USSR: The Contribution of Mathematical Economics to their Solution, 1960–1971* (Cambridge: Cambridge University Press, 1973); L. A. D. Dellin and Hermann Gross, eds., *Reforms in the Soviet and Eastern European Economies* (Lexington, M.A.: Lexington Books, 1972); Ota Šik, *Czechoslovakia: The Bureaucratic Economy* (White Plains, NY: International Arts and Sciences Press, Inc., 1972); and Myron E. Sharpe, ed., *Planning, Profits, and Incentives in the USSR*, vol. I: *The Liberman Discussion* and vol. II; *Reform of Soviet Economic Management* (White Plains, NY: International Arts and Sciences Press, Inc. 1966).

Bibliography

This is not an extensive bibliography. It is limited primarily to the references cited in the text. In the Chinese language section, titles of articles are given in English translation, instead of romanization. However, books and journals are given in both romanization and English translation.

Chinese Language Publications

Periodicals and Newspapers

Gang-Ao Jingji (The Economies of Hong Kong and Macao, Guangzhou).
Guoji Maoyi (International Trade, Beijing).
Jingji Daobao (Economic Reporter, Hong Kong).
Renmin Ribao (People's Daily, Beijing).
Shijie Jingji Daobao (World Economic Herald, Shanghai).
Wen Hui Bao (Hong Kong).

Articles and Books

(Articles in the periodicals listed above are not included in this section.)

Cao Linzhang, Wu Shaozhong, Xu Ying, and Gu Guangqing. *Yinjin Jishu he Liyong Waizi* (Importing technology and using foreign capital). Shanghai: People's Press, 1980.
Cao Yalin and Wang Yungyin. "Increasing the Economic Effectiveness of Railway Construction in Our Country." *Jingji Yanjiu* (Economic Research), December, 1982, pp. 46–51.
Chang Qian. "What Lies Behind the So-Called 'Energy Crisis,'" *Hong Qi* (Red Flag), no. 2 (1974): 83–86.
Chen Huiqin. "The Orientation of Technology Transfer Must be Changed." *Jingji Guanli* (Economic Management), April, 1981, pp. 22–25.
Fang Zhoufen. "On the Nature of China's Special Economic Zones." *Jingji Yanjiu* (Economic Research), August, 1981, pp. 54–58.
Gao Lu and Chang Ge. "A Critique of Deng Xiaoping's Comprador-Bourgeois Economic Thought." *Hong Qi* (Red Flag), 1 July 1976, pp. 25–36.
Hua Menglin. "The Time Factor in the Appraisal of Economic Effectiveness." *Jingji Guanli* (Economic Management), April, 1981, pp. 66–68.
Huang Yuqing and Xiao Zhe. "The Communications and Transportation Sector Must Be Energetically Developed." *Jingji Guanli* (Economic Management), December, 1982, pp. 10–13.
Li Guangan and Wei Liqun. "Energy Is the Key Point in Economic Development Strategy." *Jingji Yanjiu* (Economic Research), November, 1982, pp. 10–16.

Lin Senmu. "The Lessons of the 22 Imported Complete Plant Projects." *Jingji Guanli* (Economic Management), June, 1981, pp. 12–14.

Liu Guoguang ed. *Guomin Jingji Guanli Tizhi* (National economy management system). Beijing: China Social Sciences Publishing House, 1980.

Liu Guoguang and Zhao Renwei. "On the Relationship between Planning and the Market in a Socialist Economy." *Jingji Yanjiu* (Economic Research), May, 1979, pp. 46–55.

Ma Hong. *Jingji Jiegou yu Jingji Guanli* (Economic structure and economic management). Beijing: People's Publishing House, 1982.

_____, and Sun Shangqing, eds. *Zhongguo Jingji Jiegou Wenti Yanjiu* (Research on questions concerning China's economic structure). Beijing: People's Publishing House, 1980.

Shen Yue. "Vigorously Increase Economic Results, Bring about Genuine Speed." *Jingji Guanli* (Economic Management), July, 1982, pp. 10–13.

Su Xing. "The Responsibility System and the Development of the Collective Economy in Rural Areas." *Jingji Yanjiu* (Economic Research), November, 1982, pp. 3–9.

Sun Shangqing. *Qianjinzhong di Zhongguo Jingji* (China's economy in progress). Shijiazhuang: Hebei People's Publishing House, 1983.

Sun Yefang. *Shehuizhuyi Jingji di Ruogan Lilun Wenti* (On some theoretical problems of a socialist economy). Beijing: People's Publishing House, 1979.

Tang Hui. "China's Special Economic Zones As Seen from Conditions in Export Processing Zones in Developing Countries and Areas." *Jingji Yanjiu* (Economic Research), June, 1981, pp. 62–68.

Xiao Weixiang. "On the Question of Upgrading the Technology of Light Industry." *Jingji Guanli* (Economic Management), June, 1982, pp. 20–23.

Xue Muqiao. *Dangqian Woguo Jingji Ruogan Wenti* (Certain questions concerning our national economy at present). Beijing: People's Publishing House, 1980.

_____. *Woguo Guomin Jingji di Tiaozheng he Gaige* (The Adjustment and Reform of Our National Economy). Beijing: People's Publishing House, 1980.

Yao Jianyou. "An Enquiry into the Expanding of Enterprises' Retained Profits." *Jingji Guanli* (Economic Management), August, 1981, pp. 69–71.

Wang Zhengxian. "Special Economic Zones and Our Country's Employment Problem," in *Jingji Tequ Dili Wenji* (Collected essays on the geography of special economic zones). Zhongshan University, Department of Geography, October, 1981, pp. 31–36.

Zhang Shouyi and Liu Shucheng. "The Essence of Shadow Prices." *Jingji Yanjiu* (Economic Research), September, 1982, pp. 40–47.

Zhongguo Baike Nianjian 1980 (Chinese encyclopaedia yearbook, 1980). Beijing and Shanghai: 1980.

Zhongguo Jingji Nianjian 1981 (Chinese economic yearbook, 1981). n.p.: 1981.

English Language Publications

Periodicals and Newspapers

Asian Business (Hong Kong)
Asian Wall Street Journal (Hong Kong).
Beijing Review (Beijing).
Business Standard (Hong Kong).
The China Business Review (Washington, D.C.).
China Economic News (Hong Kong).
China Market (Beijing).
China Newsletter (Tokyo).
China Reconstructs (Beijing).
China Trade Report (Hong Kong).
China's Foreign Trade (Beijing).
Coal Asia (Hong Kong).
Coal Outlook (Arlington, Virginia).
The New York Times (New York).

Petroleum News (Hong Kong).
The Province (Vancouver).
The Sun (Vancouver).
Ta Kung Pao (English ed., Hong Kong).
Wall Street Journal (New York).

Articles and Books

(Articles in the periodicals listed above are not included in this section.)

Alford, William P., and Birenbaum, David E. "Ventures in the China Trade: An Analysis of China's Emerging Legal Framework for the Regulation of Foreign Investment." *Northwestern Journal of International Law and Business* 3 (1981): 56–102.

BA Asia Limited, The Consulting Group. *China: Provincial Briefing Series*, 1982.

Balasubramanyam, V. N. *International Transfer of Technology to India*. New York: Praeger, 1973.

Barnett, A. Doak. *China's Economy in Global Perspective*. Washington, DC: Brookings Institution, 1981.

Baum, Richard, ed. *China's Four Modernizations: The New Technological Revolution*. Boulder, CO: Westview Press, 1980.

Brodsgaard, Kjeld Erik. "Paradigmatic Change: Readjustment and Reform in the Chinese Economy, 1953–1981." *Modern China* 9 (January, 1983): 37–83 and 9 (April, 1983): 253–72.

California Institute of Technology, Jet Propulsion Laboratory. *Future Fuels and Engines for Railroad Locomotives*, JPL Publication 81–101, 1 November 1981.

China Council for the Promotion of International Trade. *China's Foreign Trade Corporations and Organization*. Beijing: n.p., 1982.

Dellin, L. A. D., and Gross, Hermann, eds. *Reforms in the Soviet and Eastern European Economies*. Lexington, MA: Lexington Books, 1972.

Denison, Edward F. *Accounting for United States Economic Growth*. Washington, DC: Brookings Institution, 1974.

_____, and Chung, William K. "Economic Growth and its Sources," in Hugh Patrick and Henry Rosovsky, eds. *Asia's New Giant* (Washington, DC: Brookings Institution, 1976).

Dernberger, Robert F. "Economic Development and Modernization in Contemporary China: The Attempt to Limit Dependence on the Transfer of Modern Industrial Technology from Abroad and to Control Its Corruption of the Maoist Social Revolution." In U.S. Congress, Joint Economic Committee, *Issues in East-West Commercial Relations*, 95th Congress, 2d sess., 12 January 1979.

Dicks, Anthony. "Treaty, Grant, Usage or Sufferance? Some Legal Aspects of the Status of Hong Kong," *China Quarterly* 95 (September, 1983): 427–55.

Donnithorne, Audrey. *China's Economic System*. New York: Praeger, 1967.

Eckaus, Richard. *Appropriate Technologies for Developing Countries*. Washington, DC: National Academy of Sciences, 1977.

Ecklund, George N. *Financing the Chinese Government Budget: Mainland China, 1950–1959*. Chicago: Aldine, 1966.

Eckstein, Alexander. *Communist China's Economic Growth and Foreign Trade*. New York, Toronto, London: McGraw-Hill, 1966.

_____. *China's Economic Revolution*. London, New York, and Melbourne: Cambridge University Press, 1977.

Eckstein, Alexander, ed. *China Trade Prospects and U.S. Policy*. New York, Washington, London: Praeger, 1971.

_____. *Quantitative Measures of China's Economic Output*. Ann Arbor: University of Michigan Press, 1980.

Elliot, Robin M. "The Economic Contract Law of the People's Republic of China: A Window on China's Legal and Economic Worlds," presented at the International Trade Conference sponsored by the Institute of International Relations and the Institute for Research on Public Policy, Vancouver, Canada, 5 June 1983.

Ellis, Sally Lord. "Decentralization of China's Foreign Trade Structure." *Georgia Journal of International and Comparative Law* 11 (1981): 283–304.

Ellman, Michael. *Planning Problems in the USSR: The Contribution of Mathematical Economics to Their Solution, 1960–1971*. Cambridge: Cambridge University Press, 1973.

Feuchtwang, Stephan, and Hussain, Athar, eds. *The Chinese Economic Reform*. London & Canberra: Croom Helm, and New York: St. Martin's Press, 1983.

Forsyth, David J. C., McBain, Norman S., and Solomon, Robert F. "Technical Rigidity and Appropriate Technology in Less Developed Countries." *World Development* 8 (1980): 371–98.

Goldman, Josef, and Kouba, Karel. *Economic Growth in Czechoslovakia*. White Plains, NY: International Arts and Sciences Press, 1967.

Gu, Nianliang. "China's Current Effort to Import Technology and Its Prospects." *Chinese Economic Studies*, 14 (Fall, 1980): 54–67.

Harrison, Selig S. *China, Oil, and Asia: Conflict Ahead?* New York: Columbia University Press, 1977.

Hayden, Eric W. *Technology Transfer to East Europe U.S. Corporate Experience*. New York: Praeger, 1976.

Ho, Samuel P. S., and Huenemann, Ralph W. *Canada's Trade with China: Patterns and Prospects*. Montreal: Canadian Economic Policy Committee, Private Planning Association of Canada, 1972.

Holliday, George D. *Technology Transfer to the USSR, 1928–1937 and 1966–1975: The Role of Western Technology in Soviet Economic Development*. Boulder, CO: Westview Press, 1979.

Howe, Christopher. "Growth, Public Policy and Hong Kong's Economic Relationship with China." *China Quarterly* 95 (September, 1983): 512–33.

Institute of Petroleum. *A Guide to North Sea Oil and Gas Technology*. London: Heyden and Son, 1978.

Janossy, Ferenc. *The End of the Economic Miracle*. White Plains, NY: International Arts and Sciences Press, 1971.

JETRO. *China A Business Guide: The Japanese Perspective on China's Opening Economy*. Tokyo: JETRO and Press International, 1979.

Lange, Oskar. *On the Economic Theory of Socialism* (edited and with an introduction by Benjamin E. Lippincott). Minneapolis: University of Minnesota Press, 1938: reprinted New York, Toronto, and London: McGraw-Hill, 1964.

Lardy, Nicholas R., and Lieberthal, Kenneth, eds. *Chen Yun's Strategy for China's Development* (translated by Mao Jong and Du Anxia). Armonk, NY: and London: M. E. Sharpe, Inc., 1983.

Li, Choh-Ming. *The Statistical System of Communist China*. Berkeley and Los Angeles: University of California Press, 1962.

Lin, Cyril Chihren. "The Reinstatement of Economics in China Today." *China Quarterly* 85 (March, 1981): 1–48.

Li, Guangan, and Luo Yuanzheng. "The Energy Constraint and The Open Economic Strategy in China's Modernization." Paper presented at the 12th Pacific Trade and Development Conference, Vancouver, Canada, September 6–11, 1981.

Macdonald, Ian H. "The Role of Hong Kong in China's Modernization." *China-International Business* 1 (1981): 431–44.

MacFarlane, Ian H. "Understanding and Using Chinese Statistics: The Cement Industry as an Example." *Journal of International Law and Economics* 13 (1979): 619–31.

Mah, Feng-Hwa. *The Foreign Trade of Mainland China*. Chicago & New York: Aldine-Atherton, 1971.

Morawetz, David. "Employment Implications of Industrialization in Developing Countries." *Economic Journal* 84 (September, 1974): 491–542.

Oksenberg, Michel. "Economic Policy-Making in China: Summer 1981." *China Quarterly* 90 (June, 1982): 165–94.

Orr, Patrick. "Quantitative Restrictions." *University of Toronto Faculty of Law Review* 38 (1980): 52–82.

Pack, Howard. "The Substitution of Labour for Capital in Kenyan Manufacturing." *Economic Journal* 86 (March, 1976): 45–58.

Pattison, Joseph E. "China's Developing Legal Framework for Foreign Investment: Experiences and Expectations." *Law and Policy in International Business* 13 (1981): 89–175.

People's Republic of China, Ministry of Foreign Economic Relations and Trade. *Guide to Investment in China*. Hong Kong: Economic Information & Agency, 1982.

People's Republic of China, State Statistical Bureau. *Statistical Yearbook of China 1981*. Hong Kong: Economic Information & Agency, 1981.

Pomp, Richard D., Gelatt, Timothy A., and Surrey, Stanley S. "The Evolving Tax System of the People's Republic of China." *Texas International Law Journal* 16 (1981): 11–78.
Pye, Lucian. *Chinese Commercial Negotiating Style*. Santa Monica, CA: Rand Corporation, 1982.
Ranganathan, Vember K. "China's Textile Exports to The United States," *China-International Business* 1 (1981): 585–603.
Robock, Stefan H. "Political Risk: Identification and Assessment." *Columbia Journal of World Business* 6 (July-August, 1971): 6–20.
Rosenblatt, Samuel M., ed. *Technology and Economic Development: A Realistic Perspective*. Boulder, CO: Westview Press, 1979.
Sharpe, Myron E., ed. *Planning, Profit, and Incentives in the USSR* Vol. 1: *The Liberman Discussion* and Vol. 2: *Reform of Soviet Economic Management*. White Plains, NY: International Arts and Sciences Press, 1966.
Sĭk, Ota. *Czechoslovakia: The Bureaucratic Economy*. White Plains, NY: International Arts and Sciences Press, 1972.
Stewart, Francis. *Technology and Underdevelopment*. Boulder, CO: Westview Press, 1977.
Sun, Ru. "The Conception and Prospects of the Special Economic Zones in Guangdong." *Chinese Economic Studies* 14 (Fall, 1980): 68–78.
Terry, Edith. "Decentralizing Foreign Trade." *China-International Business*, 1 (1981): 445–60.
U.N., Economic and Social Council, Commission on Transnational Corporations. *Transnational Corporations in World Development: A Re-Examination*. 20 March 1978.
U.N., Economic Commission for Europe, *East-West Industrial Cooperation*. New York, 1979.
U.S., Central Intelligence Agency. *Electric Power for China's Modernization: The Hydroelectric Option*. May, 1980.
_____. *China: International Trade, 1977–78*. December, 1978.
_____. *China: International Trade*. Issued quarterly, 1979–1982.
_____. *China: The Continuing Search for a Modernization Strategy*. April, 1980.
_____. *China: International Trade Annual Statistical Supplement*. March, 1983.
U.S. Congress. Committee on Science and Technology. *Technology Transfer to China*. 96th Congress, 2d sess., July 1980.
U.S. Congress. Joint Economic Committee. *An Economic Profile of Mainland China*, 2 vols. 90th Congress, 1st sess., February, 1967.
_____. *People's Republic of China: An Economic Assessment*. 92d Congress, 2d sess., 18 May 1972.
_____. *China: A Reassessment of the Economy*. 94th Congress, 1st sess., 10 July 1975.
_____. *Chinese Economy Post-Mao*. 95th Congress, 2d sess., 9 November 1978.
_____. *China under the Four Modernizations*. 2 vols. 97th Congress, 2d sess., 1982.
U.S. Department of Commerce. Industry and Trade Administration. *China's Economy and Foreign Trade, 1978–79*. September, 1979.
U.S. Department of Commerce. International Trade Administration. *Countertrade Practices in East Europe, the Soviet Union and China: An Introductory Guide to Business*. April, 1980.
_____. "Prospect for PRC Hard Currency Trade Through 1985: An Update." East-West Trade Policy Staff Paper, July, 1980.
_____. *Doing Business with China* (revised and expanded). November, 1980.
Valencia,Mark J., ed. *The South China Sea: Hydrocarbon Potential and Possibilities of Joint Development*. Oxford, New York, Toronto, Sydney, Paris, Frankfurt: Pergamon, 1981.
Wan, Timothy Haosen. "A Comparative Study of Foreign Investment Laws in Taiwan and China." *California Western International Law Journal* 11 (1981): 236–301.
Wang, George C., ed. and transl. *Economic Reform in the PRC*. Boulder CO: Westview Press, 1982.
Wang, N. T., ed. *Business with China An International Reassessment*. New York, Oxford, Toronto, Sydney, Paris, Frankfurt: Pergamon, 1980.
Watson, Andrew, ed. and transl. *Mao Zedong and the Political Economy of the Border Region*. New York: Cambridge University Press, 1980.
The West Scotland Branch of the Institute of Petroleum and the Norwegian Petroleum Society. *North Sea Development: Experiences and Challenges*. London: Heyden and Son, 1979.
Westphal, Larry E., Rhee, Yung W., and Pursell, Garry. *Korean Industrial Competence: Where Did It Come From?* World Bank Staff Paper No. 469. Washington, DC: World Bank, 1981.

White, Lawrence J. "The Evidence on Appropriate Factor Proportions in Manufacturing in Less Developed Countries: A Survey." *Economic Development and Cultural Change* 17 (October, 1978): 27–59.

White, Norman A., et al. *Financing the International Petroleum Industry.* London: Graham and Trotman, 1978.

Woodard, Kim. *The International Energy Relations of China.* Stanford: Stanford University Press, 1980.

———. "China and Offshore Energy." *Problems of Communism,* November-December, 1981, pp. 32–45.

———, and Davenport, Alice A. "The Security Dimensions of China's Offshore Oil Development." *Journal of Northeast Asian Studies* 1 (September, 1982) 3–26.

Wong, K. Y., ed. *Shenzhen Special Economic Zone: China's Experiment in Modernization.* Hong Kong Geographical Association, 1982.

World Bank. *China: Socialist Economic Development.* Washington, DC: World Bank, June 1, 1981.

Xue, Muqiao. *China's Socialist Economy.* Beijing: Foreign Languages Press, 1981.

Abbreviations and Acronyms

AMC	American Motors Corporation
ARCO	Atlantic Richfield Company
BOC	Bank of China
CASS	Chinese Academy of Social Sciences
CCMC	Chinese Construction and Machinery Corporation
CCP	Chinese Communist Party
CHINATUHSU	China Native Produce and Animal By-Products Import and Export Corporation
CICT	Consolidated Industrial and Commercial Tax
CITIC	China International Trust and Investment Corporation
CMSNC	China Merchants Steam Navigation Company
CNOOC	China National Offshore Oil Corporation
COCOM	Co-ordinating Committee for the Control of Strategic Trade with Communist Countries
CTI	Container Transport International
ECAFE	Economic Commission for Asia and the Far East

EEC	European Economic Community
Elf	Societe Nationale Elf Aquitaine (also SNEA)
Ex-Im Bank	Export-Import Bank
FIAB	Foreign Investment Administration Bureau
FIAC	Foreign Investment Administration Commission
FIC	Foreign Investment Commission
FICC	Foreign Investment Control Commission
FTAB	Foreign Trade Administration Bureau
FTB	Foreign Trade Bureau
FTC	Foreign Trade Corporation
GABIC	General Administration Bureau of Industry and Commerce
GATT	General Agreement on Tariffs and Trade
GNP	Gross National Product
GVIO	Gross Value of Industrial Output
Huafu	Fujian Electronic Import and Export Corporation
ICC	International Chamber of Commerce
IEAC	Import-Export Administrative Commission
IEB	Import-Export Bureau
IEC	Integrated Export Corporation
IMF	International Monetary Fund
INDUSTRY	China National Light Industrial Import and Export Corporation
ITC	International Trade Commission
ITT	International Telephone and Telegraph
JCODC	Japan China Oil Development Corporation
LDC	Less Developed Countries
LIBOR	London Inter-Bank Offered Rate
MFERT	Ministry of Foreign Economic Relations and Trade
MFT	Ministry of Foreign Trade
MFTC	Ministerial Foreign Trade Corporation
NFTC	National Foreign Trade Commission
NPC	National People's Congress
OECF	Overseas Economic Cooperation Fund
OPEC	Organization of Petroleum Exporting Countries
OPIC	Overseas Private Investment Corporation
PEC	Provincial Economic Commission
PFTC	Provincial Foreign Trade Corporation
PIEC	Provincial Import and Export Commission
PPC	Provincial Planning Commission
PRC	People's Republic of China
PTIC	Provincial Trade and Investment Corporation
SAR	Special Administrative Regions
SEC	State Economic Commission
SEZ	Special Economic Zones
SGAEC	State General Administration of Exchange Control
SNEA	Societe Nationale Elf Aquitaine (also Elf)
SPC	State Planning Commission
SSIZ	Shekou Special Industrial Zone
TECHIMPORT	China National Technical Import Corporation
TIED	Technical Import and Export Department
Total	Total Chine
U.N.	United Nations
U.S.	United States

Subject Index

Name Index

American. *See* United States
American Motors Corporation (AMC), 228n.9, 232n.49
Anqing, 16
Anhui, 26
Arab-Israeli War, 118
Atlantic Richfield Company (ARCO), 167
Australia, 62, 157, 187

Bank of China, 36, 151, 175, 225n.51, 249n.72
  and joint ventures, 87, 96, 205
  partnerships of, 228n.9
  and PIECs, 41, 44
  and remittances abroad, 88, 206
  as state enterprise, 37, 223n.20
Baoshan General Iron and Steel Works, 143, 199
  contracts of, 151, 160
  difficulties of, 18-20, 151-52, 194, 198
Beibu Gulf. *See* Tonkin, Gulf of
Beijing, 1, 20, 52, 152. *See also* Beijing Radio Factory; China-Schindler Elevator Company, Limited; *names of individual administrative bodies, trade laws, and special trade arrangements.*
  foreign relations of, 165, 166
  FTCs in, 34, 37
  and Hong Kong, 189, 246n.51
  special status of, 52-54, 224n.38
  special trade arrangements in, 45, 55, 65, 223n.21
    and China Schindler, 91, 97
Beijing Air Catering Company, 73, 230n.1
Beijing Auto Works, 228n.9
Beijing Chemical Factory, 16
Beijing, Convention of, 227n.71
Beijing Foreign Trade Corporation, 39
Beijing Radio Factory, 122-26
  agreement of with Philips, 125-26
  compared with Fujian Hitachi, 125
  and labor, 123, 124
  output of, 123
  and quality control, 124
  supplies, 124-25
  wages, subsidies, and bonuses at, 123-25

Beijing Review, 175, 203
Beijing, Treaty of, 227n.71
Beijing Yanshan Petrochemical Corporation, 16, 39
Beilun, 19
Belgium, 62, 156
Bern, 90
Bohai Gulf, 160, 161
  offshore oil projects of, 163-64
  expected start-up dates of, 167
Bohai I, 161
Bohai II, 162, 163
Bohai X, 163
Borneo, 161
Bo Yibo, 120
Brazil, 175
Britain. *See* Great Britain
British Petroleum Company, 167
Broz, Josef (Tito), 1
Brunei, 165
Building Materials Industry, Ministry of, 228n.9
Burmah Oil Company, 170

Camel cigarettes, 131, 132
Canada, 120, 157
Canada China Trade Council, viii
Canton. *See* Guangzhou
Capital Steel Company, 11
Carter, James Earl, 120, 162
Celestial Yachts, 133, 134. *See also* Xiamen boatyard; Xiamen Boatyard-Celestial Agreement
Changshou, 15
Chen Huiqin, 15-16
Chen Muhua, 173
Chengbei, 163
China Business Review, 203
China Construction Machinery Corporation (CCMC), 90. *See also* China-Schindler Elevator Company, Limited
  and China-Schindler; financial arrangements with, 92, 100
  policies, 93, 96, 102
  representation on board, 94-95